THE SUN
IN MY EYES

THE SUN IN MY EYES

Two-Wheeling East

JOSIE DEW

Maps and drawings by Peter Wilson

LITTLE, BROWN AND COMPANY

A *Little, Brown* Book

First published in Great Britain in 2001 by Little, Brown and Company

Text © 2001 by Josie Dew
Maps and drawings © 2001 by Peter Wilson
Photographs © 2001 by Josie Dew
All photographs taken by the author,
many with the aid of a self-timer and mini-tripod.

The moral right of the author has been asserted.

The author gratefully acknowledges permission to quote from the
following:

The Land of the Rising Yen by George Mikes, © George Mikes 1970, by
kind permission of Mrs Judith Evans and by permission of Penguin
Books Ltd. *Discovery Road* © Andy Brown by kind permission of Dan
Hiscocks at Travellerseye. The Extracts on pp 139–140 are drawn from
Stuff: The Secret Lives of Everyday Things by John C. Ryan and Alan Thein
Durning, © 1997 Northwest Environment Watch, Seattle, WA, USA. All
rights reserved. *The Road to Sata* by Alan Booth (Viking, 1986) © Alan
Booth, 1986, by kind permission of Penguin Books Ltd.

Every effort has been made to contact copyright holders for material
reproduced in this book. If notified the publisher will be happy to
rectify any omission in future editions.

A CIP catalogue record for this book
is available from the British Library.

ISBN 0 316 85362 3

Typeset in Baskerville by M Rules
Printed and bound in Great Britain by
Clays Ltd, St Ives plc

Little, Brown and Company (UK)
Brettenham House
Lancaster Place
London WC2E 7EN

www.littlebrown.co.uk
www.josiedew.co.uk

For my builder

Only those who take leisurely what the people of the world are busy about can be busy about what the people of the world take leisurely.

Chang Ch'ao
from *The Importance of Living*
by Lin Yutang

Contents

Acknowledgements

Special thanks must go to: my parents, to whom I've caused unmitigated worry-ings; Barbara Boote, for multiple extended deadlines; Val Porter, for once again extricating some sort of meaning and sense from a large pile of two-fingered (and one thumb) typings; Hilary Foakes, for leaving me in Barbara's remarkably tolerant hands; Peter Wilson, for all his drawings and mapping out of my maps; Hiroshi Nagai, for all his help and kindness; Andy Brown and Derek Pritchard, for squeezing me and my cumbersome baggage on board the Outward Bound *Ji Fung*; Dan Hiscocks at Travellerseye for permission to quote from *Discovery Road* by Tim Garratt and Andy Brown; Dave Pegler at Pegler's Expedition Advisers and Suppliers for so expertly advising and supplying; The North Face (UK) for my rip-stop nylon home and feathered bedding; Ortlieb for my totally waterproof panniers; Andrew Porteus, Mary Wilders and Mick and Olive; Toshi Marks, for her enthusiasm and hard work; Etsuko Kenyon, for putting me straight; James Shaw, for tracking down backward bicycle bits; Owens Cycles for fast, efficient service; Charles at The Sensible Bicycle Company for more than sensible bits; the CTC (Cyclists' Touring Club) for endless information; and Chas Roberts, for a small, strong bicycle that makes all this cycling-round-the-world lark so enjoyable and so much fun.

THE SUN
IN MY EYES

CHAPTER 1

Where There's a Wheel There's a Wave

Fragrant Harbour. It was an unlikely name for Hong Kong, one of the most densely populated areas on earth, in which resided more Rolls Royces per capita than anywhere else in the world – perhaps not the sort of place in which you want to find yourself on a bicycle.

For someone who has a strong affinity for wild empty places and a keen aversion to cars, I'm not quite sure just what I was doing immersing myself in this territory of only 1000 square kilometres with a population of 6.8 million people, most of whom were crammed into a feverishly paced forest of concrete, steel and glass. A spur-of-the-moment idea might have had something to do with it, but then so did an unerring urge to see a far-flung and compact last morsel of a British Crown Colony that a couple of years later would become a Special Administrative Region of the People's Republic of China. Above all, it seemed like a good place from which to return to Japan by boat.

I got a fairly good idea of the frenzied mayhem I was heading for when the plane I'd boarded in Dubai approached Kai Tak airport. The density of buildings and implausible lack of space were such that surely a crash landing was inevitable. As an aerial chicane of the city's cloud-soaring high-rises raced past my window, the Emirate's wings miraculously avoided lopping off their tops by a mere dragon's breath.

On the surface, Hong Kong looked like Manhattan; it was the sort of place that would be in the West if it wasn't in the East. But beneath and between the razzle-dazzle of big time, big money and big buildings lay the inimitable clamour and glamour of the glorious Chinese Orient – junks and flat-bottomed sampans, soups of shark's fin and bird's nest, black pyjamas and coolie hats, chopsticks and joss-sticks, and everywhere the unfathomable face.

As I teetered uncertainly along Nathan Road in downtown Kowloon (Nine Dragons), the pulsating heart of Hong Kong that teemed with 54,000 people per square kilometre, the heavy tropical air felt sticky and enervating. Though it was an arm and a leg past midnight, the city was far from asleep. Lights blazed from every window. Endless tiers of neon signs, flickering and flashing and rippling in a kaleidoscopic continuum of multifarious colour, clung to everything, from skeletal frames of entwined bamboo scaffolding to sheer glass-walled edifices that soared into an improbable fluorescent-reflecting night sky.

Such overwhelming busy-ness, such all-enveloping noise, shattered its way through anything that lay in its path – my head included. In hypnotic state, my eyes dazzled, disbelieving, ablaze with the harlequin flashes of neon reflection, I fought through a tide of eddying swirls of people as they flowed erratically towards me, occasionally weaving around emaciated forms in grimy vests sprawled on worn-torn cardboard beds beneath window displays bedecked with Cartier watches and ruby rings.

Evidently rush hour in Hong Kong lasted not only all day but all night. Buses heaving with passengers snarled past in clouds of throat-clogging fumes, bumper-to-bumper with energetically hooting trucks and taxis, delivery vans and preposterous stretch limousines as big as ships. Motorbikes, mopeds, heavy-duty bicycles, wheelbarrows and the odd rickshaw roared or clattered or collided indefatigably through this fantastic, fazing nocturnal mêlée.

Further along in this area of bedless bedlam, I looked up to see an army of construction workers swarming across floodlit frameworks of bamboo scaffolding as they raced to finish yet another futuristic edifice of steel and mirrored glass. Nearby, a dilapidated warren of comparatively low-lying apartment blocks, strung together with furlongs of laundry and bursting to the brim with a prolific web of Hong Kong Chinese, clung to its shallow and uncertain roots knowing that, sooner than later, a history-flattening bulldozer would come knocking on its doors. Families would be upturned and uprooted to make room for yet another dollar-spinning enterprise. It was hardly surprising that the 97 per cent Chinese population felt so alienated from the high-earning, high-spending *gwailo*, or 'ghost people/foreign devils' (Cantonese slang for white people).

I spent a few days doing what most tourists do when they go to Hong Kong: immersing myself in the giddy glitz of this temple of wealth and conspicuous consumption; tramming it along Des Voeux Road and up to the heights of the Peak; skimming back and forth across Victoria Harbour on the Star Ferry, through a rip-tide of tugs and junks and sampans and yachts, hydrofoils, tankers, freighters and ferries, all watched over by architect I.M. Pei's triangular masterpiece – the seventy-two-storey Bank of China, which stares like a dagger over one and all. I escalated along the world's longest moving staircase and peered at typhoon shelters and bird markets – not to mention bird sanctuaries, where I came face-to-face with the likes of fire-tufted barbets, scaly-breasted bulbuls, Wompoo fruit doves and Bartlette's bleeding-heart pigeons.

Unlike most tourists, however, I didn't go shopping. I had neither the stomach for it, nor the space to stash frivolous booty. Anyway, I had to save my dollars to make my yen stretch further. So instead, suffering from a claustrophobic dose of city overload, I spent a couple of weeks camping and walking over a handful of Hong Kong's virtually car-free 234 outlying islands – Peng Chau and Cheung Chau; Po Toi and Tung Lung Chau; Lamma and Lantau. By then, feeling orientally acclimatised and much refreshed, it was time to get down to the business of finding a boat to Japan.

My original plan had been to board the *Macmosa*, a weekly ferry that ran from Macau to Taiwan. Having almost ended up in Taiwan six months before, when cycling around the islands of southernmost Japan, I fancied heading slowly and sedately by sea back up to mainland Japan through this natural succession of islands. But it was not to be. The *Macmosa* had unfortunately been scrapped the previous year after losing business to airborne travel.

Allergic to flying, I was determined to fulfil the heady and romantic notion of returning to Japan by sea. I spent a fruitless few days making enquiries around the harbour, port and sailing clubs, trying to find a friendly skipper to take me along for the seafaring ride in return for a spot of deck-scrubbing and galley work. But no one was sailing – or, if they were, the complications of unions and insurance and suchlike were too convoluted and expensive to make it worth their while. Wishing I'd been born in the happy hop-on-board era of the no-fuss banana boat, I put my wave-riding whim on momentary hold and went to ring Andy Brown.

I'd first met Andy in Nomad bookshop in London's Fulham Road on his return from a year's cycling adventure across Australia, Africa and South America in the company of Tim Garratt, a teacher of English and physical education. Andy had dived headfirst into the trip, leaving behind his stylish stripped-pine cottage, Monet prints, girlfriend and successful corporate job (in the petroleum retail industry).

I am always curious about what suddenly prompts someone to go gallivanting off like that on some big adventure when they have never done anything like it before. If someone asks what made me cycle to Africa or Iceland or across America, I don't really know what to say because cycling is just something I do and have always done since I was eleven. My life revolves around my bike, so gadding about on my wheels in distant lands is not uncharacteristic behaviour. There's no out-of-the-blue, turn-your-world-upside-down, life-changing conscious decision. Without wanting to sound too dramatic about it, no cycling for me is like no bones for a dog, no fish for a fisherman or no mountains for a mountaholic, except that (when I'm feeling particularly self-obsessed) I'm sure it's ten times worse. Cycling is normal and not to cycle is most abnormal. In fact, if I don't cycle every day, I not only feel ill, I *am* ill.

I know this, because for a while at home in England my knee went wonky – no, not from an overdose of cycling but when my foot disappeared down a most inopportunely placed rabbit-hole. (When, I wonder, will rabbits learn not to bury their burrows? And anyway, what's wrong with trees? Birds and squirrels seem to make do with them.)

With knee wonked, my body and mind collapsed inwards on themselves. I failed to function like a normal human being. It didn't help that for 815 days no one knew what was wrong with my woeful knee. I tried this and I tried that, leaving a flotilla of baffled doctors and surgeons and physiotherapists and aromatherapists and sports injury specialists and acupuncturists and orthopaedists and chiropractors and osteopaths and homeopaths and psychopaths and lead-me-up-the-garden-paths in my wake.

Until that knee-malfunctioning moment, if someone had taken me by my crucial cruciate ligaments and squarely declared, 'Ah, nothing more than a spot of prepatella bursitis!', I would have looked at them as though they had handlebars growing out of their ears and said, 'Come again?', or perhaps, 'Don't you prepatella me, matey!' But if they were to say the same thing to me today, I would look them knowingly in the eye and reply with a cocky, know-all tone: 'Ah-ha! Housemaid's knee, eh?'

Not that my injury was housemaid's knee, mind – though I believe that in my hazy lazy schooldaying past I did once find my port-side patella turning decidedly housemaidish. But the local doctor soon put an end to that by thrusting, with undue gusto, a foot-long syringe needle into my hugely swollen-out-of-all-proportion knee and siphoning off enough liquid to fill a bath. Disgusting! But at least after that most memorable of manoeuvres things turned out just swell (not swollen) on the knee front.

And they stayed that way for over two decades of perpetual pedal-pushing until, a few years back, I found myself with a rabbit-holed starboard patella playing up. To kneecap it all, my creaky knee was not so much playing up as sailing straight on off up the creek. Forced to dismount, I found myself floating or, rather, limping around utterly lost without my wheels.

Suddenly, life had turned complicated. For my new form of transport, I had to rely on crutches and, although crutches are a bit like bicycles in that they are unpollutingly simple and effective, they're . . . well, not quite the same as cycling. But they were something and so twice a day I ponderously swung myself along aboard my pegleggy crutches over a hilly, deeply wooded, fallen-tree, four-mile circuit as fast as I could in order to vent an excess of pent-up frustration and energy. Arms turned into tree trunks. Legs turned to twigs.

The longer I was unable to cycle, the more my impatience grew. I proved to be a hopelessly ants-in-the-pants and furiously fidgety impatient patient. And all I had was a wobbly knee. How, I wondered, did people manage who really did have reason to complain? A leg blown off. A terminal, or even minimal, illness. A life of war. A life on the street. A life without sight. A life without limbs. A life in a wheelchair. A life without love. How did they cope?

Months rolled by as the wheels stayed still. Nothing happened. Nothing mended. Without cycling, my world caved in. I had to get back on board, come what may.

I tried pedalling my geared bike with one leg. Not easy. I then adapted my old junkyard cruiser into a fixed-wheel. Bit easier, especially when I mastered the art of hooking my inoperative leg up and over the handlebars to get it out of the way. Strange glances from passing motorists. Quick quips from schoolboys. Stopped by a Plod and warned for riding without due care and attention.

I carried on. Hills were impossible, both up and down: up, because I didn't have a hope in hell's teeth of ascending with one leg; down, because being a fixed-wheel meant no free-wheeling, and as my good leg couldn't keep up with the manically spinning pedal, I had to hitch it up over my rear rack to avoid being bashed in the shin. Thus, with the dead leg jutting forwards over my handlebars and the good one rammed up my rear (so to speak), I felt as if I was attempting some dare-devil contortionist feat while simultaneously performing life-threatening saddle-perched splits.

I needed something else. I made multiple enquiries. Finally I was given a name: Paul Butterworth, maker of the Unicam. Maker of the what? I rang Paul at his Somerset home and he explained all – all about the mechanical adaptations he made for people with disabilities. Did he have a device for people with skew-whiff knees who could only ride with one leg? Yes, he did. I went to see him.

Paul was the sort of big-hearted man of whom you wish the world had more, with an equally wonderful wife and equally wonderful sons. I turned up on their doorstep with my mother, who had been roped into driving me to Somerset in . . . aargh . . . a dreaded car (but I suppose cars do have their uses, ditto mothers). We were both swept off our feet-cum-crutches by the family's kindness. Multi-course supper, multi-course laughs. Fine chats, fine new innovative adaptation for my mount – an adaptation that answered to the name of Unicam Retroflex.

Suddenly I was away. A bit gingerly at first. Not very far. Mustn't overdo things (so said my latest knee man). Got to take things gently. Mustn't give the unexercised knee a heart attack by too much too soon. But I couldn't hold back. Up hill, down hill, over hill 'n' dale, and one-leggedly negotiating dog-legged hairpins in Wales. It was mindblowingly stupendous to be back in the saddle. Never mind the dead leg: I was cycling, moving.

Unfortunately a lot of car drivers didn't seem to like cyclists at the best of times and, judging from the degree of their unprecedented revving impatience, they unequivocally despised one-legged ones. I put my (good) foot down. One leg was better than none, and it was definitely a whole lot better than the bus.

For travelling at a whim over distances more than was possible by crutch or one-legged bike, I needed to take some sort of motorised means and, appalled at the prospect of sitting in a car, my means had to have two wheels. Traffic jams and bottlenecks and gridlock were not my cup of tea.

My careering career as a motorcyclist graduated gradually. At first I was a mopedist, learning my noisy skills upon some cheap, smoky buzzbomb of a contraption that sounded like a hairdryer. I bought it off an old man up the road. With no need for left-foot motorcycle-style gear-changing, I simply lassoed my crutches to the pillion, plonked a tin-pot of an open-faced crash helmet on my head together with a toss-pot pair of Biggles goggles, kicked the start and I was off, buzzing along on a cacophonous two-stroke engine that caused an ear-shattering curse in the neighbourhood. I soon learnt that riding a moped is one way of not winning friends and influencing people.

I have to admit that my first few minutes of scooting along on board my potato-coloured Yamaha QT50 were a hoot. I had never realised that the upness in hills could be so much fun! Whereas on my bicycle I was used to slowing down to a leg-wobbling crawl, I was now nipping up the inclines very nicely. Downhills were altogether different. Whereas my maximum speed on a bike has been an invigorating 54 mph (87 kph), my highest speed on my scooter was a paltry 32 mph (51.5 kph) – and that was with the help of a frisky tailwind.

Needless to say, the novelty of travelling without expending a nanojoule of energy soon wore off. Added to that, it didn't take me long to realise that mopeds are a lot more dangerous than bicycles. Actually, it's not so much the bicycles or mopeds themselves that are dangerous as the worrisomely large proportion of motorists who like to see straight through their riders.

On a bicycle (an object which, as we smug, self-righteous cycling souls all know, is a benign and silent, happy-go-lucky invention of freewheeling joy), most motorists see you as someone either to love or to loathe, depending on how much you encroach upon 'their' sacrosanct road space. On a moped, the matter is not so clear cut: you are not so much loathed as hated with frightening ferocity, especially when travelling out of urban areas. This is because, by being attached to a piddling, pint-sized engine, you buzz along like a demented bumble-bee at an infuriatingly not-able-to-keep-up-with-the-traffic speed right in front of their biff-you-up-the-bum bonnets. On winding country lanes, this obviously inhibits a motorist's ability to overtake – a situation that naturally does not make for a happy travelling companionship. Having said that, I have encountered far too many brain-dead drivers (haven't we all?) who prefer to put several lives at risk – their own and their passengers' included – by overtaking on blind corners, hidden dips and humpback hills as well as into oncoming traffic.

So I ditched the time-bomb scooter and progressed up a few cc's to a Yamaha SR125. This was more like it! I got the full-face lid, got the leathers, got the test, got the stare-death-in-the-face full-monty throttle-blasting speed. But although hurtling along the highway like a bad Mad Max was (dare I say it?) terrifying fun, I'm no motorcycling convert. Sitting astride a throbbing engine was a huge improvement on driving a car, but it came nowhere close to the blood-pumping, cheek-rosying and endorphin-exploding carefree exuberance of riding a bicycle. A motorbike means noise, danger and climbing into too much clobber – too much non-contact with the local yokels as you blast on past. On a bicycle you're open, free, quiet and approachable and I love it to death.

Trouble was, knee got worse. Finally I couldn't even one-leg cycle, couldn't even limp-walk. Men in white coats poked and pinched and prodded and declared it was my iliotibial, while others prodded and pinched and poked and declared it was my medial meniscus. Some said it was all my own fault – my knee had had excessive wear and tear. Others announced that it was flappy cartilage or a 'loose body'. Loose screw, maybe, but surely no loose body – not while I was still in it, at least. Then there were the ones who, with razor-sharp sabre in hand, said, 'Come, let us carve you wide open.' Others of a more alternative nature emphatically declared, 'Let them in and you won't come out!' – at least, not with the requisite rotations that the immensely pleasurable pastime of cycling employs.

After trying more of this and more of that and with nothing getting better, I found myself reduced to groaning pitifully, 'Oh Lord of the Chainrings, where the devil are you? Let me twist your arm or even, pray, your long white beard, and give me my bike back. At least give me a kneecap that functions.'

When a long-awaited MRI scan revealed a cartilage tear, I tried a few more months of experimenting with all sorts of pills and potions and sports injury people, until I begrudgingly relented and allowed a surgeon in to sort me out. But no sorting did he do. No tears or wears or loose bodies did he find. Instead, with holes stitched up in my elephantine swollen limb, he declared, 'Tis a lovely knee!' Lovely knee? My foot!

With knee worse off than it had been before, I wasn't happy at all. All exercise ordered on to back burner. Endorphin-starved. An unheard-of sedentary lifestyle was forced to prevail. Transmuted into a blob of a slob. Hated everything. Constantly exhausted, from doing nothing. Pined for the pedals, the wind, the rush, the freedom. Instead heavy, cold, dark dismal days. Winter within. Winter without. No pounding heart, flushing face. No, not happy.

But now, many a pitiable blue-moon whingeings later, it's back to feeling the Bee of all Knees (well, almost) and I count my blessings that the wind's in my wheels again.

And so, having diverted on to the long, winding, hypochondriacal road to nowhere, let me backpedal back to Andy and his motivations for leaving his house, girlfriend and job to take off for a year and cycle 15,000 kilometres across some of the most demanding terrain on earth – and raising in the process over £35,000 for Intermediate Technology, a British-based charity and international development organisation whose aim is to build the technical skills of poor people in developing countries.

Andy knew his life had to change when, one dark and drizzly Friday evening, he found himself stuck in yet another stationary traffic jam on the M25, caused by rubberneckers looking at a crane. As he explained in *Discovery Road*, the book he and Tim wrote about their journey, he looked about him at the type of cars that were hemming him in:

People driving expensive company cars; they had power and position. They were off to warm, comfortable homes in the suburbs. All this talent, education, ingenuity, drive and skill being wasted on trivia; making and selling things that we do not need, while the world is crumbling about our ears. Their lives so dull that a crane was interesting. People LIKE ME!!

I realised I had always wanted to be in their gang and bit by bit, over the last years, I had joined. I was one of them, self-absorbed, inward-looking, unproductive and I despised myself for it.

That was when it hit him – he didn't want to be one of those people any more, 'or more accurately I did not want to be me any more'. He remembered that, only two or three years ago, there had been something else he had wanted to do, something involving travel and adventure and perhaps being able to 'do someone a little good at the same time'. So he did.

With plenty in common, Andy and I got on well and had kept in touch. He was now working at the Hong Kong Outward Bound School based over on Sai Kung Peninsula. One feverishly sticky Kowloon night we met up over a multi-dished dinner of tasty Chinese fodder to catch up on news and views. In mid-egg-drop soup, I mentioned my unsuccessful attempts to re-enter Japan by ship. He looked at me with a look that told me all was not lost before saying that, funnily enough, in a few weeks' time it just so happened that there was an International Outward Bound course sailing for Japan on the school's 132-foot brigantine, *Ji Fung*.

Knowing precious little about Outward Bound courses, I asked Andy if he thought there might be any room on board for an extra deck-scrubber – oh, and a small bicycle? As Andy wasn't going to be an instructor on this particular course and because this was the school's first ever voyage to Japan (past courses aboard the mighty square-rigged *Ji Fung* had been to Vietnam and the Philippines), he didn't know what the position was regarding space and the possibility of working my passage – not to mention storing superfluous equipment (such as a bicycle and a tent and a Dog Dazer) which was of absolutely no benefit to anyone else on

9

board. He did know that Outward Bound were pretty strict on banana-boat wannabes cadging lifts but, after giving me the name of the school's Executive Director, Derek Pritchard, he promised to make some enquiries.

I left it for a day and then, feeling this was too good a chance to let slip through my fingers, I dialled Derek Pritchard's number without really knowing what I was going to say (making sense on telephones is not my favourite pastime). Mumbling away, I tried to explain my situation and what I was after as best I could. Things didn't sound promising when Mr Pritchard told me he was inundated with requests such as mine and that, anyway, the ship already had its well-established quota of crew. 'I see,' I said, and that was that.

Meanwhile, back at the Outward Bounding ranch, Andy was doing his bit to put in a word or two for me. Over the next few days I pestered Derek Pritchard several more times, until happily he agreed to take me on board to help out as the *Ji Fung*'s general deckhand and dogsbody, which is exactly what I'd been hoping to be. What's more, he thought there should be room to squeeze my bike on board. Things were looking up.

With just under a month to go before the *Ji Fung* set sail for Japan, I felt myself being drawn inexorably in the opposite direction from the Rising Sun. The great dragon of China, so big and so close, was a tantalising prospect.

Despite rumours of problems with taking in bicycles, not to mention talk of expensive and hard-to-get visas, I took myself off to Harbour Road where, on the fifth floor of the Ministry of Foreign Affairs of the People's Republic of China, I paid HK$100 (£14), filled in the requisite forms and simply returned the following day to collect my stamped passport. It was as easy as that.

Boarding one of the numerous ferries, I slid sideways sixty-five kilometres or so in a south-westerly direction across the mouth of the prodigious grey-green Pearl River Delta, to the tiny peninsula that hangs off the coast of China's Guangdong Province – Macau, the 'City of God'.

But God wasn't much in evidence as far as I could see. More apparent were storming battalions of earth-movers, stone-breakers, pile-drivers and sky-scraping cranes working flat out in an ongoing cacophony of noise and hazy-grey, fume-humid heat. If the music of the local anthem was the sound of the pneumatic drill, the national bird should have been the crane. Macau's once-famous image as a tranquil refuge from neighbouring Hong Kong had obviously fallen by the wayside.

With a shoulder-rubbing 410,000 people living in Macau's 19½ square kilo-metres, the average population density was 26,775 people per square kilometre – which made the human pressure cooker of Hong Kong, with a mere 5962 people per square kilometre, appear positively underpopulated. (For the sake of comparison, there were only 240 people per square kilometre in the UK, 52 in Ireland and an echoey 1.6 in Mongolia.) Macau was the most crowded patch of land in the world.

The first European settlement in the East and the smallest of Beijing's lost lands, Macau (which also included the two small neighbouring islands of Taipa and Coloâne) was where southern Europe met China. It had been governed by Portugal since the middle of the sixteenth century and, as a trading centre, Macau had dealt in a delicious mixture of spices, pepper, cloves, sandalwood, ginger, nutmeg, tea, silk, silver and plates. The Portuguese settlers also pros-pered by taking silks and porcelain to Japan and returning with silver, which they sold to China at highly advantageous rates.

Even when a foreign king ruled in Lisbon, Macau continued to fly the Portuguese flag. When a handful of revolutionary Portuguese leaders tried to hand their oriental territory back to China in 1974, China didn't want it. More recently, realising that Macau had one of the fastest-growing economies in the world, Beijing changed its mind and Portugal signed a treaty that Macau would follow the example of Hong Kong and revert to its 600,000-times bigger Big Brother at the end of 1999.

Macau's territory was spreading rapidly over land reclaimed from the sea. It was a curious blend of Latin and Oriental, of peeling pastel-coloured colonial buildings and grandiose wrought-iron balconies and verandas festooned with flapping canopies of Chinese laundry. Baroque churches sat alongside Buddhist monasteries and steamy noodle houses, whose windows displayed various delicacies such as dismembered wind-dried duck and awe-inspiring sabres of shark's fin. Scraggy and mangy xenophobic mutts limped and snarled along narrow cobblestone streets (which had names like Rua de San Domingos and Travessa Chan Loc) as swarthy, suave-suited businessmen from the Iberian Peninsula sauntered beside their compact Oriental colleagues, conversing in an improbable mix of Portuguese, Cantonese and English.

Cycling round the car-crammed city in search of a place to stay, I crossed teeming Leal Senado (Loyal Senate) Square with its illustrious European archways and wedding-cake façades before heading down a narrow alley overlooked by breezy verandas and Chinese apothecaries. Here I came across the covered St Dominic's Marketplace, full of stalls piled with pyramids of mangoes, loquats and lychees and fierce-looking fish being filleted alive, their gory viscera being nonchalantly tossed out to pulsate and twitch on the side. Buckets and cages full of tortoises with pinched eyes were stacked compressed, one on top of the other, dutifully awaiting the knife alongside blood-smeared and bubbling aquariums jammed with stomach-churning forms of squirming reptilia.

Leaving the fish and chelonians to their fate, I opted for a hefty bunch of red bananas and a bagful of strange grenade-shaped fruit, into which I started making inroads while taking a breather from the heat and the fumes and the crush on a shady bench in a littered and tiny courtyard behind a church. Hot and headachy, I sat and listened to the hum of conversation in the relative calm of a Chinese-Iberian afternoon, but my appetite was rapidly quelled when, whiffing a dubious smell, I discovered a dead ginger cat in the bench-side bin.

The first pension I tried was not pleasant. Cheap and uncheerful and crawling with fat cockroaches, my room (shown to me grudgingly by a frail, grim-faced old woman with matted hair and bare, blistered feet) was a dive, a windowless cell with a cold, filthy stone floor. A forty-watt light bulb dangling on the end of a frayed and wire-exposed lead lit up a sagging, fetid mattress adorned with a myriad of stains, some of which were obviously blood. There were no sheets but a dirty grey blanket lay roughly folded on the end of the bed. Outside the room I had to watch where I walked as the corridor was alive with a good-for-nothing posse of whining, scraggy, ribby cats – eating, scrapping, crapping and vomiting wherever they chose.

Past the earthquake-proof Floating Casino (gambling was Macau's main local industry, its economic lifeblood; there were more casinos here than in any other city in Asia), the second pension I tried was situated on the third floor of a ramshackle apartment block and was owned by a genial old Chinese mother and daughter who let out a small cluster of rooms. Unable to communicate in a common tongue, I just grinned and grunted and gesticulated – and got more than I bargained for when, after storing my bike in their bedroom, this cheery flat-faced duo insisted I join them for their sardine and noodle supper, through which they were adroitly chopsticking their way in a corridor that apparently doubled up as an impromptu kitchen.

My room, though not much bigger than the body-sunken bed that filled it and overlooking a twenty-four-hour head-shattering, dust-billowing building site, was a distinct improvement on the cockroach-and-cat hell-hole I'd tried earlier. All I had to contend with here were an off-putting gossamer of coarse black body hair covering the floor, a crumpled and far-from-clean sheet (no blankets, but that was good – they are a haven for livestock anyway) and the insanely shrill talkative squawkings of a myna bird lodged outside my window.

After cleaning up the room as best I could and unpacking my panniers, I turned on the small, dusty pink and static-crackling television (which needed the handle of a toothbrush wedged into the switch to keep it on) and watched a documentary in English that revealed how twenty-six Hong Kong Chinese families were living in a single apartment of an old and dilapidated tenement in downtown Kowloon. Dark and windowless, and divided by rickety partitions, it was not only a horror of a fire hazard but a health hazard as well. One wiry old man cooped up in his dingy humid hole explained how one night he had caught seven rats in the communal kitchen, with his bare hands. The tenants' 'rooms' were more like shelves (a primitive form of Japan's capsule hotels) piled on top of each other and each containing all of their occupier's minimalistic belongings. A minute, twig-thin old woman was filmed clambering un-certainly up a ladder to her coffin-like dwelling, whose 'ceiling' was so low she couldn't even sit up straight. On the other hand, a young father was so rotund that he could only move through the cordoned-off corridor by breathing in and shuffling sideways. With such a scrum of people crammed into death-trap warrens like these (Hong Kong was riddled with 6000 illegal structures), it was no surprise that fires all too frequently anihilated property and lives.

As I wandered around the city over the next few days, it was not difficult to see that Macau's small but ever-expanding land surface had been turned into one big multi-billion-pound building site. Everywhere there was clamour and clatter and digging and bone-shaking drilling and billowing clouds of throat-clawing dust. The building projects were neither small nor hard to miss and included the £445 million airport, a ferry terminal, a ring road linking Macau to Guangzhou in China's Special Economic Zone, a second bridge linking once-sleepy Taipa with the mainland, plus a mass of furiously mushrooming industrial and housing estates. Even the famous waterfront Praia Grande, home to some of Macau's best restaurants and most gracious old hotels, was closed to strollers because of road-widening upon yet more reclaimed land.

The highlight of my days in Macau was walking across the 2.6-kilometre bridge that connected the peninsula to the nearest island, tiny Taipa (less than 4 square kilometres), and on across the almost equally long causeway to charming Coloâne, less than twice the size of Taipa. Here I went to view a piece of the right arm-bone of St Francis Xavier, enshrined in a silver reliquary which was housed in a small sixty-seven-year-old chapel that sits between the Nga Tim Cafe and Kun Lam Temple.

St Francis, whose vocation to the East had taken him from Rome to Madrid, Lisbon, Goa, Cochin, Macau and Kyushu, found himself on the China coast after his successful mission in Japan and died on nearby Shang Chan Island in 1552 while waiting to enter China. Later, the remnants of his arm were shipped to Japan but, despite this being quite a harmless arm, Japan didn't fancy some scraggy bit of foreign limb and denied it entry. The Macanese, taking the matter in hand, appeared suitably impressed when it arrived on their shores

and, after holding on to the arm for the odd century or two, even went to all the trouble of housing it in a chapel built in the saint's honour. Had I fancied piecing together a few more osseous bits of this missionary man, I would have had to take myself off to southern India, where a selection of his bones was on display. That, I decided, could wait for another day.

Just when I was thinking I might as well stay in Macau and 'save' China for when I had more time, I found myself on impulse boarding the night ferry up the Pearl River to enter the 'Motherland' at Guangzhou, the city formerly known as Canton or, as some people have it, 'that place with the snake restaurant'.

The ferry, more rusty bathtub than boat, carried only passengers (no cars), including the odd goat, chicken and pig scurrying around free-range on the litter-ridden deck. Any ideas I might have had for sleeping outside were hastily sunk, as the short stretch of deck open to passengers lay cluttered with perforated styrofoam crates crammed with panicking chickens travelling to the pot, battered and leaking oil drums, a rank of stinking bins overflowing with kitchen waste, a heap of broken beer bottles and a wide assortment of sharp, jagged objects perfectly positioned for either amputating your foot or sending you rocketing headfirst over the side into the unpearly murk of the mighty Pearl River.

Instead, I entered a passageway lined with moth-eaten maroon carpeting and squeezed with my loaded bike through the throng of male onlookers, all straining to get a touch of either my pink Western wheels or my white Western anatomy. Or both.

Suddenly the ship's cook burst on the scene, wearing a fierce expression and sporting a stain-splattered butcher's apron and a cleaver so bloodied that it looked as if he had just decapitated half the crew for a lark. Wielding his unappetising instrument, he carved a path through the jostling crowd towards me. Then, thrusting out his fat bull-like neck, he fired a wholly unintelligible tirade of words into my face.

By the manner in which they were delivered, I interpreted them as: 'Oi! You foreign oik! Leave your bike in my gory hands or else I'll have your head!' Feeling in no position to argue, I dutifully abandoned my steed – after whipping off as many panniers as I could lest I never see them again. But all he did was to wheel it a few yards down the corridor and leave it there. As soon as he was out of sight, I locked it safely to the railings.

Unable to find my cabin, I lugged my weighty bags around the ship in search of a steward who might be able to shed some light on the multiple numbers on my ticket, which appeared to bear no resemblance whatsoever to the numbers on the cabin doors. But I just kept coming across the cleavered cook, who looked increasingly like a raving loony serial killer rather than a ship-shape chef.

Finally, among the smoking and hawking hordes milling around the shabby labyrinthian passages of the lower deck, I stumbled upon a surly aproned woman with a severe black helmet of hair. She was brandishing a toilet brush and, taking this tool of trade as an auspicious sign, I asked her if she would be so good as to point me in the right direction for my elusive cabin. This seemingly simple and innocuous request prompted the woman to bark a highly ill-tempered and indecipherable reply before lunging forwards as if to give my oral cavity a most uncalled-for toilet-brushing if I didn't swiftly step out of her way.

Although this cantankerous dragon apparently spoke no English, I audaciously gave my cabin-search request one last shot, which spurred her into snapping, 'What species room you?'

'The cheapest,' I said.

This initiated a frenzied waving of the toilet brush in a dispiritingly vague direction that seemed simultaneously to encompass both below and above my head.

A chance encounter with a student who spoke a little English led me at last to the correct cabin. My relief was dashed when, on opening the door, I found a small dormitory of bunks choking with smoke and semi-prostrate men all preoccupied with either de-phlegming their throats or cracking monkey nuts and slurping endless bottles of beer, the empties rolling around among the nutshells on the gobbed-upon floor.

The moment I stepped into the cabin, I wanted to step swiftly back out. But did I fancy the alternatives of spending the night in the packed and vomit-reeking corridors or on the windy and wet deck (it was thundering down with rain outside) with the oil and the filth and the free-range fowl and at least two headless rats, while risking the possibility that the cleaver-wielding cook might mistake me for something that blended well with cat paws, monkey brain and noodles? I decided I had better stay put.

But where should I sleep? All the bunks were full. Through a momentary break in the smoke haze I discovered that one of the men was actually a woman, who noticed my predicament and shuffled to her feet. She roughly ejected a sallow youth from his upper bunk, propelling him forcefully out of the door. Recognising the mouth of a horizontal gift horse when I saw one, I launched myself into the vacated spot without further ado.

The night proved a memorable one, totally devoid of sleep and to the tune of an overly close, horrendous and violently vomiting soundtrack. One man was so continuously sick out of the porthole (situated little more than a foot from my face) that every time he retched, half his body disappeared clean out of the window. Occasionally his somnolent companion would slap a weary hand on his belt to haul him back again before delivering a hefty thwack between the shoulder blades in a manner which I felt certain would only induce another bout of heaving sickness. And so the night passed. China never came so slowly.

It was 4 a.m. and I thought the ordeal was over when the sick-tub docked at Guangzhou's Zhoutouzui Wharf. But, oh no – just because we had arrived in China didn't mean we could feel its terra firma: Customs didn't wake up until 7.30 a.m. and so we were all kept locked on board. I spent this fretsome and fidgety three-and-a-half hours squashed among the malodorous and malcontent crowd as I tried to shield my bike and bags from any nimble-fingered pilferings, because at least half a dozen people in Macau had told me that my possessions wouldn't last two seconds in Guangzhou which, in terms of theft, is known as the most dangerous city in China. Feeling at that point of a particularly paranoid and vulnerable disposition, I didn't fancy taking any chances.

At one point I found myself pressed up against a friendly couple from Macau who spoke English. Jimmy, who owned a camera shop in Hong Kong, was spending the day in Guangzhou with his petite wife, Ling (a Macanese policewoman) – not to sightsee or shop but to visit a Chinese back doctor who would work on Ling's painful spine.

'What method does he use to treat you?' I asked, visualising a snap-cracking procedure with perhaps a hefty dose of snake venom or dried tiger semen for good measure.

'Ah, it is simple but painful process,' said Ling, 'which involve using bamboo knife.'

Before I'd had a chance to digest this rather startling piece of information, Jimmy had pulled down the collar of Ling's tracksuit top to reveal the results of her previous treatments: a filigree of scars criss-crossing the base of her neck.

'Urgh!' I said, a trifle tactlessly. 'Does it work?'

'I am very hoping so,' said Ling.

I told her I hoped it would too, while inwardly thinking: ow!

Seven thirty came and went. So too did eight o'clock, eight thirty and nine. Still stuck on board and with a bladder fit to burst, I asked Jimmy and Ling to keep an eye on my bike while I squeezed my way through the crowd to the stinking, overflowing toilet housed in a cubicle so small that I couldn't shut the door without decapitating my knees. There was only one light-hearted part of my lavatorial mission: when tearing up a bit of makeshift toilet paper from a sheet of newspaper, I discovered a piece good enough to stick in my diary:

HORNS OF DILEMMA

Lagos, Nigeria – A bus driver is to be charged with killing a road-safety official, after running him down in his van. The *Nigeria Tribune* reported that the driver's explanation of the incident was that 'I saw the man standing by the side of the road, but I mistook him for an antelope and decided to run it over'.

More than five hours after docking, Jimmy, Ling and I finally found ourselves through Customs ready to do battle with the chaotic madhouse of Guangzhou. After inviting me to meet them for supper that evening at the Seamen's Hotel, Jimmy and Ling headed off for the knife-carving back doctor, leaving me with some good advice.

'Please go specially careful and watch always your bicycle,' they said. 'Guangzhou is very bad crime city with very many bad men all stealing and pickpocket. Remember, if you have needing for help don't ask police – they just take your money too.'

My first port of call was the port. As my Chinese days were limited if I wanted to return to Hong Kong in time to sail to Japan (which I did), I had decided that, rather than plunge headlong willy-nilly into the immensity of China and have no time to cycle or see much before I had to do a U-turn, I would tackle something that I could comfortably accomplish in a couple of weeks. Thus, as islands rate high on my cycling agenda, my plan was to ride around Hainan Island – a tilted teardrop of land sandwiched between the Gulf of Tongking and the South China Sea.

I joined the feverish scramble surrounding the ticket booth, which contained an incredibly irascible woman. In no mood to waste any more time crushed in a crowd, I dived among a sea of legs before surfacing at the window. Here I embarked upon some lengthy and patience-exhausting linguistic difficulties with the irate woman which, needless to say, did little to improve her spectacularly sour mood. Eventually, after establishing that the ferry to Hainan only ran on alternate days (the even days of the month), I bought my ticket and hoped for the best (while fearing the worst) before launching into the mad-hatted anarchy of the city.

CHAPTER 2

A Taste of the Dragon

Noise. Dirt. Pollution. Crowds. Gridlock that stayed locked – engines snarling. Hell on wheels. Hell on foot. Hell inside and outside head. So this was China, the land with an unfathomable population where dogs and dissidents shared the same fate?

But Guangzhou wasn't really China. It was Hong Kong without the meddlesome veneer of British order, capitalism out on a limb, out of control. Around every corner there was a scene of ceaseless tearing down and building up, with no visible organising principle, just decrepit neighbourhoods vanishing into gaping construction holes. More noise. More money. More rush. Less sleep.

This for sure was not Macau – a mind-shatteringly frenetic enough city in itself, but where at least the lunch hour was still two hours long (down from three not so many land-reclamation projects ago). Guangzhou: sleep? Never. Here dollars took the place of dreams. Dress shops were open at midnight, nocturnal construction workers drilling at 3 a.m., vendors hawking way before dawn. Guangzhou – a crazed city living around the clock. Around the block. Around the bend.

Guangzhou had been infected by capitalism's mercantile excesses ever since the West forced open its doors as a treaty port in 1842. A century later, Guangzhou was the first city in China to open for business after its presiding 'genius', Deng Xiaoping, launched his economic reforms in 1979. No wonder he was seen every day by millions, smiling contentedly down from the face of a giant mural.

There was nothing to smile about in Qinping Market – a choose-it, kill-it, cook-it, take-away zoo. Once past the lotions and potions and aphrodisiacs, selection of medicinal herbs and spices, dried starfish and seahorses, snakes and lizards, deer antlers, dried scorpions, leopard and tiger skins, bear paws, semi-toxic mushrooms, tree bark and all manner of weird herbs and plants, there were on offer creatures of a mainly furry nature waiting to be slaughtered. Mangy monkeys were crammed into cages with no room to move, and it was the same sorry story for owls, pigeons, badgers, rabbits, rats, ant-eaters, racoons, bears, boars, foxes, deer, dogs, cats, weasels, tortoises, frogs and a selection of unidentifiable rodents. The air stank of feral fear and certain death.

Some of the vendors slept on boards beside the bloody remains of gutted dogs or cats being held in skull-crushing tongs and plunged whole into giant boiling vats to skin them, while the sleepers remained oblivious (or perhaps innately immune) to the nauseous stench around them. This for sure was no '*Yum Sing*' (the Chinese equivalent to the toast, 'Bottoms up!'). It is said that the Chinese will eat anything with four legs except tables and chairs, and after witnessing the scene at Qinping Market I was willing to believe it.

I watched a scab-ridden beggar with no legs shuffling the stump of his ragged-clothed body along on his arms through the muck and viscera-splattered filth of the market's central aisle. All the way he was derisively mocked and spat at by the cleaver-swinging, bloodstained butchers for his efforts and I felt sickened and hopeless at heart. With a brain-grating headache and a lacklustre air, I spent the rest of the day lost in my own low-ebbed world while half-walking, half-wheeling through the bilious pollution and heavy humidity of a bizarre and frantic city.

Not long before my six o'clock rendezvous with Jimmy and Ling, I jostled with the crowds back across the sludgy brown Pearl River through the everyday, every-minute turmoil of Renmin Bridge, heaving with a constant swathe of converging traffic: cars, buses, trucks, motorbikes, scooters, rickshaws and unpredictable throngs of identical bell-clanging bicycles laden with an improbably chaotic assortment of beds, fridges, three-piece suites, gas cylinders, crates, televisions, pig corpses, cement-heavy sacks of rice or an acrobatic medley of family or friends, either balanced on or lassooed to any available space on the bike.

As we sat down to supper in the Seamen's Hotel, Jimmy told me that the Chinese have a saying that to get the best from life one has to 'be born in Suzhou, live in Hangzhou, eat in Guangzhou and die in Liuzhou'. This, he explained, was because Suzhou was renowned for the most beautiful women, Hangzhou for stupendous scenery, Liuzhou for the finest wood for coffin-making. 'But,' he stressed, 'for food, Guangzhou is Number One.'

There was a particular fish, famous to the region, that Jimmy was eager for me to try and he was hell-bent on having it cooked to his instructions and delivered to the table, whether the restaurant provided it or not. From the bewilderingly fast and exotically indecipherable conversation that Jimmy conducted in Cantonese with the befuddled waitress, I surmised that the fish in question was worth causing a song and dance about. The only problem was that the waitress appeared to have no idea what type of fish Jimmy was demanding.

After a lot of pointing by the waitress to the piscatorial dishes of the surrounding customers and a lot of shakings of head from Jimmy, there followed a lengthy lull in service when our waitress vanished through the steamy swing door of the kitchen for over forty-five minutes. Having given her up for lost, I was extremely surprised when she reappeared and strode defiantly up to our table, holding a big cellophane bag containing a tail-flapping and fiercesome-snouted fish which, amazingly, was precisely the species that Jimmy had requested. I have no idea whether the waitress had won the fish in a funfair or found it in a fish market or the murky depths of the odorous Pearl River, but from wherever it had been hooked I ate my portion gladly.

I had planned to spend the night at the Guangzhou Youth Hostel on Shamian ('Sand Surface') Island but, unbeknown to me, Jimmy and Ling had booked me in 'gratuit' to a room seven floors above our heads and they helped me up there with my panniers after supper. On turning on the light in my room, Jimmy exclaimed, 'Ah, you have a visitor!' I just caught sight of a cockroach the size of a mouse, scuttling beneath the bedside table.

I then joined Jimmy and Ling for a mad dash through the dark backstreets in a sudden storm to Zhoutouzui Wharf, where they leapt on to the night-boat back to Macau with only seconds to spare.

Early next morning I too was afloat, heading for distant Hainan Island on what turned into an unpleasant twenty-nine-and-a-half-hour journey surrounded by people being horrendously seasick. Oh please God, not again, I thought. But God wasn't listening. Everywhere I looked I was greeted by the sight or smell of vomit. The worst person I saw being violently ill was a small, round woman, entwined amongst a string of rosary beads and the wires of a battered Walkman held together with sellotape, who lay beneath me on the lower bunk of my stiflingly hot, sweaty, noisy and smoky six-berth cabin. Unfortunately the woman was so unwell that she was totally incapable of directing her vomit into any sort of receptacle, disposable or otherwise. Instead she jettisoned her stomach's offerings directly on to the floor, which was already awash with orange peel, sweet wrappers, nutshells, cigarette butts, phlegm and empty pot-noodle containers.

The first time the woman was sick, I braced myself and set about clearing it up – as it looked as though the other four occupants of the cabin (all men, one of whom was her son) were quite content to step over and even occasionally through it, as if it was no more than a simple and inoffensive puddle of spilt milk. But twenty-four hours of the woman's intermittent bouts of vomiting completely defeated any sick-cleansing ability I may have momentarily possessed, making me realise that I would make neither a nurse nor a good mother.

To add to the fun, there was scarcely a spot on the ship that appeared to be entirely sick-free. Despite a relatively calm sea, it seemed as if everyone I came across was in a serious stomach-retching way. The corridors, the toilets and the 'restaurant' all proved to be severe danger zones stinking from high heaven to the lowest of decks of sick. Even the 'fresh air' of the outer decks was a no-go area, as the risk of being hit by a projectile of airborne vomit was too great to take. I was reduced to flaking out in despondent mood on my upper bunk (thankful for small mercies that at least I had elevation away from the sick-swilling floor) and lay on my side with my face to the wall, plugs in my lugs, trying to dream that I was lying in a bracingly clean, clear people-less land. Like Iceland.

Such dreams were certainly not the stuff of Haikou, the capital of Hainan. A head-whirring scene of shouting and chaos and dust-choking dirt, congestion, pollution and insufferable heat greeted me as I rode through the gates of the port. Horn-blaring traffic, in every shape and form, came at me from every direction.

Still reeling from the effects of the stomach-churning crossing, I rode in an exhausted daze through insane weaving swarms of dusty and dented hand-on-horn vehicles joined by ingeniously practical three-wheeled bikes attached to sidecar-cum-platform contraptions used for hauling improbable loads. At one point I looked up above these whirring heads and saw a banner strung across the street, bearing the proclamation:

ENSURING CAREFUL DRIVING HELPS PRESERVING YOU AND OTHERS LIVES

– words that I felt were lost long to the wind. Up the road more slogans stood out above the spluttering of another honking mad jam. A big billboard bore the incongruous message:

PALM TREES AND SURF HELPS INTOXICATING TOURISTS

All for being intoxicated by the seventh-heaven thought of swaying palms and thundering surf, I forced my leaden limbs into action and accelerated south-wards on the fastest route I could find to ferry me out of the cloyingly sticky, heaving scrum of the city. This turned out to be the Eastern Expressway, which just so happened to be a spanking new strip of very dapper-looking motorway – not quite the thing I had in mind for whisking me south but, unless some self-important official ordered me off, it looked as if it should do the job nicely.

No one did order me off. They just waved to me or tried to sell me coconuts or lured me into playing a game of traffic-dodging football. Not that there was much traffic, mind, because this Expressway was more like a Slow-way. Once outside the motoring pandemonium of the city limits, the fat, smooth ribbon of blacktop seemed to be used more by pedestrians than by cars. Boys on bikes used it for perfecting their wheelies (v. impressive ones at that) while others utilised the central reservation for a spot of high-jump practice. Old women, fearless of the odd thundering bus or truck, used it as a short-cut for walking home a cow or a squabble of ribby goats. Occasionally the sight of a bloated corpse (animal, not human) rotting at the side of the road was evidence that not all made it home in one piece, but the majority seemed to trot along and get by just fine.

Finer than me, that was for sure, as I suddenly became ill. Well, actually, not so suddenly, as I'd been feeling a bit dicky for days. Once past Wancheng (a curious town whose dusty, pot-holed street was crowded with the bizarre spectacle of snooker-playing men and boys leaning over an incongruous green sea of pot-black tables that lined the fronts of the town's ramshackle roadside shops), some alien ailment took a hold and I came down with a fever. I needed to collapse on a bed. Unable to find anything that was either clean or vacant or that fitted the bill, I forced myself onwards to the southern city of Sanya.

Although the city was full of hotels, I spent hours traipsing around the traffic-choked and cacophonous streets trying to find one that had a vacancy. Finally I discovered a small, seedy place where I lay sucked to smithereens by endless supplies of mosquitoes in a palpitatingly hot, dark windowless cell of a room with a broken air-conditioner and surrounded by the whamming, beeping, banging, blaring, shrieking, ringing, yelling, shouting, tooting and hawking world that only China (and possibly India) could produce.

And there I stayed for days – I'm not sure how many – soaking my sheet in sweat while eating nothing, drinking little and thinking sinking thoughts. Occasionally, when I had the energy, I thought of the newspaper cutting that I'd picked up in Hong Kong and which now lay Pritt-stuck to a page in my diary, confirming that I'd fallen prey to the law of the following statistics:

Along with India, China is the destination where tourists are most likely to become ill, the Consumers' Association *Holiday Which?* magazine found. In a survey of 20,000 readers, more than one in three who visited China and India became unwell.

For those who take a keen interest in the Delhi-Belly, Katmandu-Quickstep, Turkish-Trotting malfunctions of infected intestines when cavorting away from home, the next most dicy destinations after the afore-mentioned countries were Egypt, Morocco and Turkey, where 32 per cent of visitors fell ill. Following hot on their tail in the sickness stakes were Indonesia, Kenya and Mexico (Montezuma's Revenge). The countries where tourists were least likely to spend a sizable proportion of their holiday running with clenched urgency to the toilet were Denmark, Britain and, curiously, Corsica.

Eventually I resurfaced from my deafening hovel, feeling almost worse for wear than when I had checked in. When I caught sight of myself in the mirror behind the reception desk, I looked as if I had chickenpox, my face pock-marked with the countless, madly scratched-raw welts of a myriad mosquito bites.

Although I rode over a thousand kilometres around the coast of Hainan Island, I remember little about it, my air of lethargy being so great that to see and to note and to notice was too much of an effort. However, certain memories stuck in my mind, like the heat and the dust and the spitting and the staring and the shoving – and the crack-windscreened buses that rolled silently past me on the descents, their engines switched off to save on fuel. Nor was it hard to notice that few motorists drove with their lights on at night; they preferred to veer blindly towards each other at suicidal speeds.

Through the daze of my malaise, I was vaguely aware that the west coast of Hainan would have been really most enjoyable if only I had been bouncing along with more energy. Compared with the east coast, it was wilder and emptier and more behind the times. Had I been able to muster even the slightest inkling of rip-zipping zeal, I would have veered off into the interior, up to the dense tropical forests covering the Limu Lingshan mountains that stretch down the centre of Hainan, so that I could see the markets of the Li and Miao minority peoples – the island's original inhabitants, who had been there for 3000 years after migrating from the southern provinces of the mainland. But with a pounding head, knotted stomach and legs behaving like a pair of hopelessly uncoordinated chopsticks, all I could channel my pitiful dregs of energy into was heading back to Hong Kong to feed up and get fit before sailing the seas to Japan.

Back in Haikou and in desperate need of a decent night's sleep for the first time in weeks, I booked into the cheaper of the two Overseas Chinese Hotels. In my extravagant £12-a-night fourth-floor room, a dog-eared notice hanging off the back of the door alerted me to the fact that:

in order to protect the safety of the hotel and guests, inflammable goods, explosive, poisonous, radioactive materials are forbidden in the hotel as well as poultry and animal, motors and bycicles. Any guests who behaves in a disorderly manner eg excessive drinking, tussling, fight with weapons, soliciting, gaming, drug taking and trading, illegal specalating activities and threating safety of others shall be guilty of an offence. Our hotel will deal with in a serious way. Fireworks and firecracker are forbidden to let off, either.

Feeling I would pose the hotel no danger whatsoever, I collapsed on the flimsy bed (almost breaking it in the process) and fell into a sweaty and exhausted sleep.

Early the next morning, a toothless man on a platform bicycle latched on to me, insisting on showing me the way to the port even though I knew (for once) where I was going. We bounced through the narrow streets of the market along with a chaotic tidal wave of other cyclists on their black Flying Pigeons, everyone cutting each other up but somehow always managing to avoid a cataclysmic pile-up and staying afloat. Fruit-sellers in conical hats – some woven, some paper, some plastic – walked and hawked their wares: mini melons, minute mangoes and green bananas, apples, oranges and fat, black grapes that they carried in a couple of big laundry-sized baskets attached to a yoke balanced across their bony shoulders. A bevy of women perched on some steps in pairs, each holding a pineapple with one thick, black-rubber-gloved hand while using the other dexterously to peel and de-eye the fruit with a super-sharp dagger-type knife. The finished product, resembling a juicy helter-skelter of golden flesh, was stabbed on a stick and consigned to a large, sticky-sided, clear plastic jar of the sort once found in British corner-shops filled with gob-stoppers and wine-gums.

When we arrived at the docks for the dreaded sick-boat, the platform-bicycle man spat, then smiled, before giving me a Chinese-style Custard Cream (which tasted of cat-litter) and a pair of pop-socks (which for some reason he just happened to be carrying in his pocket) so that I could now look like half the population of China, whose womenfolk evidently considered the unflattering pop-sock to be the heady height of fashion.

The boat journey back to Guangzhou was just as spectacularly unpleasant as the outward crossing, surrounded as I was again by the sight and smell of passengers being violently ill. My cabin, another deck-level dormitory, was used as a thoroughfare by all and sundry who kicked open the broken, handleless door, sending it crashing against my metal bunk with infuriating and relentless repetition. What with this and the incessant insanity of the distorted marching music blaring out loud enough to wake the deadest of deads, from a speaker embedded in the wall beside my head, sleep was a luxury that was only the stuff of daydreams.

In between vomiting, gawping, hawking, giggling, ogling, slurping, staring, copying, spitting, chewing, laughing and shouting, my fellow bunk-mates (all men) spent their time playing cards and smoking. Had I been sailing this way a couple of years later, maybe then I would have been able to see from one side of the cabin to the other without my eyes smarting from a choking haze of cheap cigarette smoke: in March 1997 China astonishingly announced a ban on smoking on all public transport. For a country of 1.2 billion people, a quarter of whom smoked, I imagine such a ban would not be easy to maintain.

Back in Guangzhou I spent another couple of days cycling around the city's sights and non-sights, feeling as if my legs were living on separate planets from the rest of my body, before catching the night-ferry back to Hong Kong. On board I met a German toy salesman, a Spanish shoe salesman and an American sports-clothing salesman – the latter wearing a T-shirt emblazoned with the command to 'GO CLIMB A ROCK'. For the past few days this international threesome had been in Guangzhou for something called the 'Overseas Sales and Business Fair'.

'Vair ver all you people?' the German asked me in a faintly accusatorial tone. 'In my opinion you Brits are all-vays too lazy to come to make business in China. It's my experience that if the Chinese don't speak English, then the Brits are not interested.'

In no mood to become embroiled in an Anglo-Teutonic argument, I found a small nook beneath the staircase where I laid out my mat and went to sleep for a surprisingly sick-free night.

Back in Honkers (as the high-flying expats apparently call it), I had only a handful of days to regroup my intestines and senses before clocking on at the

Outward Bound basecamp. As I didn't feel my delicate state was up to the maelstrom of the overpopulated scramble of the city, I whipped myself off to Lantau Island for a bit of camping and hill-walking peace.

Arriving in the main town of Mui Wo (Five-Petal Flower), I stocked up on food supplies at the Wellcome and Park-'n'-Shop supermarkets before taking myself off to a hostel (situated down the track from a Christian drug rehab centre) which, without some small seaworthy craft, could only be reached by an enjoyable forty-five-minute walk following a narrow path that wound its way alongside scenic Mong Tung Wan Bay.

For HK$13 (£1) a night, I chose to camp in the shade beneath trees filled with weird bird-whooping sounds rather than spend the night in the coming-and-going girls' dormitory in which everyone, despite the humidity, chose to sleep with all the windows shut. And much the better I felt for it. In fact, I find that camping (at those hostels that allow it) is by far the best option. For a fraction of the price you can use all the facilities – toilets, showers, washing machines, telephones, kitchen, common-room, reading material, games and so forth – and yet have the freedom to retreat to your own familiar domain of quiet privacy and thought whenever you so fancy. What's more, you don't have to tolerate other people's preference for stuffy rooms, or their grating of teeth, clipping of nails, cheesy feet, putrid 'pits, breaking of wind, hyperactive school-party chatter and crisp-packet-rustling midnight feasts or endless hours of seismic snoring.

The hostel was run by Anthony, a sunny, bleach-haired Brit with a tattooed, nut-brown torso, who told me he had been working at the hostel for ten months.

'Well, not so much working as relaxing,' he said.

The first night, while I was in the middle of putting up my tent, Anthony wandered over to me, followed close at heel by a frisky and muscular alsatian that I kept a wary eye on, and said, 'Just thought I'd better tell you there's a lot of snakes around here.'

'Snakes?' I said, poised with pole in hand. 'Are they big ones or small ones?'

'Oh, only a couple of metres,' replied Anthony nonchalantly.

Gulp. 'Ah, mere tiddlers then.'

As with most hostels, there was an interesting mix of people coming and going. Kim, a bronzed policeman from New Zealand with a triangular torso terminating in slinky red shorts, was waiting for a visa for Vietnam. Talking about some of the places he'd been to, he said, 'Tell you what: Las Vegas is the place for a family holiday. It's cheap and entertaining and, if you're lucky, you can arrive home with more money than when you set out.'

Then there was Patsy, now living in Hawaii, who complained to me in the cockroach-and-beetle-crawling toilets about a long-haired sari-clad woman from Oklahoma who, Patsy claimed, had stolen her shoes. 'She's just a typical Christian!' declared Patsy, a little illogically. She then dropped her lighter down the squat toilet and when I helped her to hoick it out with the aid of my head-torch and a specially fashioned stick she declared, perhaps a trifle theatrically, 'Gee thanks – you've just saved my life!'

One evening I found the hostel's kitchen invaded by a brigade of eight backpacking Brits feasting off a tower of tins of chicken soup and Spam and Spicy Pork. Having just arrived in Hong Kong at the beginning of their gap year, they were all fresh of face and clothes and rearing to go. All clutched Lonely Planet guides and all were heading for Thailand, Malaysia and Indonesia with the ultimate intention of working in Oz.

Then along came more fellow countrymen – two English lads in their twenties living in Cardiff, one lean and lusty with long blond locks who had been working for British Telecom, the other big and brawny with convict-cropped hair who had been a car-cleaner. They too had just arrived in Honkers and were on their way to Oz, but not sounding quite as accommodating of each other as the energetic eightsome. Their original plan had been to head together first into China before sliding southwards through South-East Asia but, although they had only been away from home for two days, I became aware of a serious altercation taking place. I surreptitiously scribbled down their powwow (rather than my everyday happenings) in my diary.

CONVICT-CROP: What d'ya say to giving China a miss? Can't say I'm too smitten by the Chinks from what I've seen so far.

BLONDY:	Oh, well, that's fuckin' great, eh? We've only been here two fuckin' days and now you want to fuckin' chicken out.
CONVICT-CROP:	I don't want to fuckin' chicken out, I just don't fancy doing China – all right?
BLONDY:	Well, why the fuck not?
CONVICT-CROP:	I've just fuckin' said – I don't fancy the Chinks. They get up my fuckin' nose.
BLONDY:	So where d'ya want to go, then?
CONVICT-CROP:	Well, how about heading straight for Oz and then go from there?
BLONDY:	Fuck me! What about the rest of fuckin' Asia?
CONVICT-CROP:	What about it? It's not exactly going to fuckin' disappear overnight, is it, eh?
BLONDY:	Fuck you – fuckin' chicken. [*Pause for perfunctory swig of beer*] Well, I'm still going to China for sure.
CONVICT-CROP:	[*Looking very sweaty and turning towards the door*]: Well, that's fuckin' fine by me. Have a great fuckin' time!

And so they went their separate fuckin' ways.

That night, after scaring a snake (not to mention myself) which was loitering with intent beneath my groundsheet, I crawled into my tent and turned on the radio in the middle of a World Service programme that recounted three people's experience of rowing across the Atlantic. Unfortunately I'd missed the first two (too busy sniggering into my diary), but the third person's account provided riveting listening. A woman, whose name I missed, had rowed the Atlantic with a male companion during the 1970s. Asked what had made her embark upon such an arduous journey, she replied that she'd reached a stage where she felt life was passing her by and was in need of a little excitement to pep her up.

'It was either row the Atlantic or fight in Israel's Seven-Day War,' she said, quite matter-of-factly.

She went on to recall how one day, when the two rowers were feeling hungry as usual, a small shark 'came up to say hello'. Personally, I would rather have said 'goodbye', but her friend, spotting a good stomach-filler when he saw one, slipped over the side of the boat with a knife, telling her he was off to prepare dinner. An aquatic tussle ensued, after which the man hauled himself back into the boat clutching a severe arm wound.

'I was awfully worried,' said the woman. 'He looked ever so pale.'

But before he allowed her to run to his aid and dress his injuries, he insisted that she first stick his pipe in his mouth and grab the camera.

'We still have a giggle over the picture,' said the woman. 'There he is, blood everywhere, clutching his shark-bitten arm while casually smoking his pipe and looking as cool as a cucumber.'

The last thing I heard on the radio before falling asleep was a small but remarkable snippet on the news about how a British doctor, Professor Angus Wallace, carried out a life-saving operation on Paula Dixon, a passenger who suffered from pneumothorax, or collapsed lung, during a flight from Hong Kong to England. He used a coat-hanger, an empty British Airways mineral-water bottle, sellotape, brandy, and tubing from an oxygen mask. This most celebrated in-flight incident became known as 'Operation Coat-hanger'.

One morning I went for a walk over a jungle-like mountain, fighting my way through a tangle of cobwebs as springy and thick as elastic, and ended up at a wall of barbed wire, on the other side of which a lot of people walking around in a uniform of brown shirts and shorts or trousers seemed to be living. Momentarily perplexed, I suddenly realised that I had stumbled upon a prison, or 'detention centre', for the Vietnamese boat people.

During the 1970s more than 200,000 Vietnamese refugees had arrived in Hong Kong and 20,000 of them remained in prisons scattered about the colony. The authorities no longer referred to these people as vagrants but as 'economic migrants' who must go home. While many thousands had been forced screaming and kicking on to aeroplanes back to the land they so feared, others had been encouraged to leave by cash incentives and by stories of how Vietnam was developing economically. These hapless people, destined for inevitable repatriation, were not stupid and they were understandably fearful about returning 'home' to possible persecution.

A short distance from the prison lay a jetty. I ambled on to it, thinking about how I'd like to get out my Swiss Army knife to saw a hole through the barbed-wire cage that formed the walls of their incarceration. The shore was knee-deep in rubbish. After staring at it for a while in a semi-daze, I sauntered past a fisherman to the far end of the jetty.

The West Lamma Channel was littered with the usual flurry of craft that, depending on their size, either busily buzzed or sedately slid between Victoria Harbour and the South China Sea. I watched a small wooden sampan containing a couple of people as it bounced through the waves, coming gradually closer and closer, until they drew up and moored at the foot of the jetty's steps beneath me. Amidships, steering the boat, sat an elderly Chinaman in a pointed wicker hat; in the bow perched a tanned, blonde 'foreign devil' – an attractive female one, whose age I guessed to be somewhere around fifty.

'Hi!' she said, in a well-to-do English accent. 'Are you going to Cheung Chau?'

'Cheung Chau?' I repeated. 'Where's that?'

'It's that island over there,' she said, pointing to a small hazy blob.

'Errr . . . well . . . why not?' I said and jumped aboard.

As she rolled a cigarette, the woman told me that the boat we were on was a sampan that she had hired privately to take her from Lantau (where she was living) to Cheung Chau in order to pick up the ferry over to Central, as she had a 4 p.m. flight to catch to England to visit her ageing mother at home in Dorset. I asked her if she had lived in Hong Kong for long.

'Since 1980,' she said, 'apart from the time I spent in England when my children were at school.'

Her home on Lantau was in Yi Long Wan, a small community that just happened to be a few spider-webs away from where I was camping on Chi Ma Wan Peninsula. I was surprised to hear that she was totally unaware of the existence of either the hostel or the drug rehab centre. When I asked her what she found so great about Hong Kong to have lived there for so long, she tossed back her head and exhaled a lungful of smoke before contentedly sighing, 'Ahh . . . the weather . . . the people . . . the lifestyle . . .' – which sounded good enough to me.

Despite Cheung Chau ('Long Island') being no bigger than 2.5 square kilometres, it was home to over 40,000 people, about 10 per cent of whom lived upon a chaotically colourful smorgasbord of sampans lashed together in the typhoon shelter of Cheung Chau Wan. In topsy-turvy contrast to this, the occasional fat-cat's wave-skimming speedboat was tethered to the quayside. At one point I watched a wiry and flimsy-looking grandmother as she transported her little clutch of neatly uniformed grandchildren back from the shore to their sampan in a very rocky 'rowing' boat in which she stood up, propelling it by way of a single oar in the stern. On her return journey she adroitly navigated her way through a constant flurry of flittering boats until, after cutting an unfaltering course across the bows of the Hong Kong ferry, she moored up alongside a twin-engined, super-sleek powerboat called *Happy Hour*.

After a wander around the island that included watching a group of nimble-footed men festooning a lorry-load of buns (for the imminent 'Bun Festival') from a curious sixty-foot tower of bamboo scaffolding that dominated the courtyard of the Pak Tai Temple, and after looking on in amazement while two women as round as Chinese dumplings raked an endless profusion of plastic bags out of the sea on Nam Tam Wan ('Morning Beach'), I boarded the early-evening inter-island ferry back to Lantau.

Standing in the open in the aft, I met Werner and Miriam, a Swiss couple (he a goldsmith, she a nurse), who had just spent seven months cycling from Switzerland to Hong Kong. Their route had taken them through Italy, Turkey, Iran, Pakistan, India, Burma, Laos, Vietnam and China. Their only accident had been in Turkey, when one of the metal stays of Mirian's mudguards had sliced into her leg, leading to a serious infection.

Amazingly, Miriam had never cycled any great distance before this trip – a trip which she said, without the slightest hesitation, was something she would never do again.

Werner agreed. 'We think a trip like this is too hard, too long for always to be travelling by bicycle. We think for us it would be preferable to choose a particular location for exploring by foot only or on bicycle. That way we could avoid the long and difficult and ugly areas.'

'Ahh, but Werner is many times more sufferable of the problem areas than I,' said Miriam. 'Specially for me, I would never go back to China – because really it was a feeling of always being cheated.'

Back at the hostel there were two new arrivals. One was an Austrian investor-cum-patisserie-maker who told me he was feeling miserable because he had come all this way to Hong Kong only to discover he was allergic to it.

'The pollution is very terrible,' he said, 'and my breathing is having difficulty.'

The other newcomer was a hip, pie-in-the-sky dreadlocked girl from California. I asked her where she was from.

'Man, everywhere,' she replied.

The following morning, when she saw me packing up my tent before catching the ferry back to Central, she said, 'Cool – so you're gettin' ready to motivate, huh?'

'Motivate?' I said. 'Err . . . oh, well . . . yes . . . that sort of thing. Actually, I'm off for a bit of a sail.'

CHAPTER 3

Unpredictable Teaspoons

Gulp.

My time had come to be Outward Bound so, with fluttering waves of apprehension, I cycled through the traffic anarchy of Kowloon before sweating over Razor Hill and plummeting down to Sai Kung along Hiram's Highway.

Moored on Minn's Pier, the 132-foot multi-sailed, multi-sparred ship that was to be my home for the next little while looked truly magnificent – just the sort of craft from which you'd imagine Captain Cook and his merry men to be poking their galleon-hatted heads with a bellowing great cry of 'Land ahoy!' or even 'Thar she blows!'

But there was no time for fanciful dreaming: the Outward Bound school was indeed a-bound and a-buzz with activity. Troops of youngsters and troops of not-so-youngsters were bouncing here and there with alarming enthusiasm while being herded by worryingly fit-looking instructors. Everywhere there were teams of people charging in and out of buildings, in and out of the sea, in and out of dinghies or up and down the climbing wall. Others were marching past with vast crates of weighty and serious equipment in their arms. Everyone was going somewhere with a purpose.

Feeling tired and hot from my morning's exertions of cycling through Hong Kong, I'd arrived at the O.B. school hoping for a quiet snooze in the shade, but this whirlwind of activity taking place around me didn't seem to be quite the right ambience for a sedate siesta. It all looked a bit busy, a bit too much like collective hard work for my liking. 'OUTWARD BOUND – TO SERVE, TO STRIVE AND NOT TO YIELD' was the troubling slogan displayed on the T-shirts of several over-keen and enthusiastic forms striding past with purpose. Oh dear, I thought. Clearly I was in for no Jolly Roger holiday. And, after all, aren't holidays what life is all about?

Feeling lost and decidedly uneasy (like a first day at school) I thought, not before time, that it might be an idea to enlighten myself about just what the Jolly Dickens the Outward Bound was all about – or, more like, what the devil I was letting myself in for. My excuse for having done virtually no research was that, up until now, I'd been a bit occupied, either being ill in China or having an exhausting rest on Lantau.

In the Administrative Building, I found a table displaying a pile of information about the school. I swept up a leaflet.

'OUTWARD BOUND: 25 YEARS OF SERVICE IN HUMAN DEVELOPMENT,' it told me on the cover. In even bigger print it declared: 'STRENGTHEN YOUR CHARACTER, CONFIDENCE AND RESOLVE.' With a nauseous feeling of trepidation, I turned the page and read on about METHODOLOGY OF OUTWARD BOUND:

> In the Outward Bound tradition, life is rugged. . . . [We] put you through exciting challenges at sea and in the mountains as a teaching medium . . . [and] present you with a series of increasingly difficult physical and mental problems. Outward Bound is about adventure, dealing with challenges and working together in close-knit teams. All the courses focus on the development of what we call 'Life Skills'. These are skills of initiative, leadership, communication, decision-making, co-operation, risk-taking and trust. [We] use challenging outdoor activities to help you learn more about yourself. [Uh oh!] The emphasis is on 'learning by doing'. You'll be encouraged to reach for your limits. What you'll find, oddly enough, is that most limits are self-imposed.
>
> Outward Bound is an adventure with a purpose to discover, understand and improve yourself. You must persevere at what you're doing. If you fail at something, try, try, try again.

On a page with a photograph showing six fit trainee Hong Kong Chinese brandishing completion certificates, peace signs and dazzling smiles, I read the bold quote:

37

AT FIRST I THOUGHT
I'D NEVER MAKE IT. NOW
I KNOW I'LL NEVER QUIT.

Gulp again, and double gulp. Clearly there was no backing out now.

Feeling more than a droplet dubious about the forthcoming sea voyage, I sauntered back outside. Amid another rush of excitable activity, I found myself sucked into the flow before being siphoned off at the pier where the tall, lengthy vessel *Ji Fung* swayed gently under the blistering midday sun.

A line of new recruits, which had formed along one of the ship's narrow outer decks, slowly diminished as each trainee stepped one at a time into the 'mess room', where the captain and chief officer were signing them in and retaining passports. Immediately, I felt (as the Japanese would say) like a sticking-out nail – not so much because, as far as I could see, I was almost the only Western 'trainee' (a fact that relieved me greatly) but because, unlike everyone else who carried their minimal belongings in a neat rucksack on their backs, I had arrived with a very unseaworthy bicycle loaded to the gunwales with enough luggage to sink a ship. Hopefully not this one.

Feeling all at sea on land, I lurched down the jetty with my ungainly mount – trying my utmost not to lose balance and cause a spectacle by falling into the harbour – before tethering my steed against the movable block of steps and clambering unsteadily aboard to join the queue. Happily I fell in line behind Ming T. ('call me M.T.') Liu, a vivacious and vigorous forty-year-old Hong Kong Chinese architect, bureaucrat, creative-workshop lecturer and Tai Chi master, who was to become one of my firm favourites on board.

Finally, forms filled and paperwork complete, I was allotted my cabin, S12 (code for 'twelve-bunk dorm on starboard'), which I shared with eleven young women of various nationalities: two Japanese girls called Yuki and Yumi, a Filipino called Grace, an American called Renée and the rest all Hong Kong Chinese whose confusing names escaped me then as they do now, apart from one called Loo Sau-Ting (otherwise known as Brenda).

The bunks, all stacked in multiples of three, came with a plastic mattress, a folded sheet, a pillow (which I used for plugging the porthole over my upper bunk) and a life-jacket. There were two small portholes, which let in no air and little light and, as I later discovered, which leaked. There were three tiers of bunks, diminishing in size the higher they went, like a wedding cake. Thus those on the lower bunk had the most room to manoeuvre, but what they gained in space they lost in privacy, because as the cabin had no room for awkward trip-over or fall-off-and-break-your-leg ladders, the bunks acted as steps for those abiding above.

Not fancying the thought of my bed-space doubling up as a thoroughfare for potent foot traffic, I was pleased to discover that my allocated berth was way up top. But set against the lack of sleep-disturbing comings and goings was the lack of comfort. Okay, I realised that this multi-bodied cabin was not pretending to be a sumptuous five-star hotel, but as I entered the twilight of my twenties I did find that my progressively pernickety old-maidish bones increasingly favoured a little creature comfort. So, perhaps understandably, the wind was taken from my sails on finding that I was supposed to sleep (ha!) with my head crushed against a preposterously noisy and antiquated air-conditioning unit that sounded like a mixture between a dinosaur in labour and the geriatric growlings of some prehistoric tractor.

To add to the fun, the air-conditioned air was spewed out a rate of knots directly over my shivering prostate form, its Herculean wind as biting as an arctic gale. When I finally managed to get the ship's engineer, Chang Han (known as Alan), to comprehend my request and desire for him to temper the air-conditioner's clamorous and icy assault, he indicated that there was nothing he could do because it was broken and only 'worked' at its present setting. In that case, I asked him, hugging myself for warmth, was it not possible simply to turn it off? No, no, he gesticulated; the rules were that each cabin must have an air-conditioner on at all times, even if it was broken. So that was that.

The rest of Sign-on Sunday was spent working much too hard for a supposed day of rest. All sweaty afternoon a small platoon of us staggered up and down the ship's main but very narrow staircase with back-breaking boxes and crates of tins and jars and cans and bottles and bags and hefty sacks of rice, flour, beans and noodles – enough food to sustain a colony of gluttons for a year on a desert island, never mind for a couple of weeks adrift on the East China Sea.

By now I had been recruited as ostensibly one of the trainees, instead of my initial wish to be a teach-me-new-tricks dogsbody deckhand. We thirty-three trainees were divided into three colour-differentiated groups – Redwatch, Greenwatch and Bluewatch – and I found myself answering to my new title of Blue Six (short for Bluewatch 6). Each watch was commanded by one of the Outward Bounding and preposterously energetic Action Man instructors. Redwatch was watched over by Mike, a blond pony-tailed English Chippendale from deepest, darkest Devon; Greenwatch was in the hands of Ming, an unflappable multi-tongued and multi-muscled Hong Kong Chinese; while us Bluewatchers were the charges of twenty-six-year-old Simon-Smiling-Beames, a cheerful, guitar-strumming, songful Canadian from Quebec whom M.T. and I dubbed Tintin, on account of his cropped blond quiff.

We were rounded up and herded into the galley for a prompt 5.30 tea of spare ribs, fried chicken and beancurd all whipped together by the dexterously fast and furious hands of Paul Wong, the ship's comical and manic cook. Then each colour-coded watch was summoned to heel by its respective leader and trotted obediently after him, disembarking to be led to a relatively quiet spot not far from the ship for what I can only describe as a spot of 'bonding'.

All Blue twelve of us were told to sit in a circle ('I like circles!' beamed a chirpy Tintin) before embarking upon a roll-call that involved taking turns to announce our allotted numbers followed by our names and motherland. It went something like this: 'Blue One. Chow Wai Ming – Erwin. Hong Kong'; 'Blue Two. Lai Yin Ling – Pierce. Hong Kong'; 'Blue Three. Mohd Y. Abdullah – Elleys. Brunei'; 'Blue Four. Haji Ramli Haji Kurus – Haji. Brunei'; 'Blue Five. Ming T. Liu – M.T. Hong Kong'; 'Blue Six . . .' and so on and so on.

Returning to Blue One, Tintin instructed us to call out not only our Bluewatch number, shortened name and homeland but also everyone else's, in turn, until we had learnt them by heart. Then to everyone's number and name and country we had to add our favourite food, favourite colour and favourite animal – a lengthy rigmarole that was all a bit too reminiscent of a six-year-old's birthday party. I certainly couldn't see how knowing Yumi's or Erwin's favourite animal would help with teaching me how to hoist a sail, climb a pitching spar or knot a round turn and two half hitches.

Things deteriorated even further when Tintin announced that one of the objectives of our group was to 'learn a circle of communication'. In order to 'identify a group problem', he set us a 'little exercise' which unfortunately necessitated jumping on to each other's backs in order to form some sort of 'big blue monster'. The taxing part of this 'exercise of communication and co-operation' was that, out of our twenty-four combined legs of various nationalities, our 'monster' was only permitted to have eleven feet in contact with the ground. A physically acrobatic conundrum was the order of the day.

Oh dear, I thought, is this really happening? Just as I was wondering if I could untangle my legs from the multiple limbs and slip away unseen to do something more useful – like, ummm . . . well, have a nice non-communicating and co-operative bonding with a big banana sandwich – Tintin shouted from the sidelines: 'You'll be able to apply these learning points to your next problem.' Hating to imagine just what the next problem might be, I thought: we will?

Perhaps I was suffering from a particularly hefty bout of cynicism or a serious dose of premature cycling-and-being-on-my-own withdrawal symptoms, but my claustrophobic feelings of unease at being thrown into such a falsely close-knit circle of strangers, with whom I couldn't quite seem to tune my ocean-going wavelengths, made me feel as if I was flailing around wildly, well out of my depth. I tried to tell myself not to fret, to give it a whirl, that things would improve and, if they didn't, then surely it could only do me good to experience a bit of mass mutual 'communication and cooperation' and participatory give-and-take rather than forever riding along as a lone ranger in my own little easy-come, easy-go, two-wheeling world.

Try as I might, though, I just couldn't seem to get into the swing of making multi-legged monsters from the limbs of foreign strangers. Why couldn't I? Everyone else seemed to be having a hoot and cooperating incredibly well. Obviously I had a problem – the sort of problem that many people would probably tell me could only be sorted out with the help of several wallet-emptying sessions of mind-unravelling 'therapy'.

Finally, monster mission accomplished, Tintin delivered the *coup de grâce*. He instructed us to compose a rallying team chant that could be used to buoy up our spirits and bond our watch for the forthcoming voyage ahoy. Inwardly cringing and dying a death, I found myself being chivvied into a circle ('I like circles') to have my reluctant arm hoisted by enthusiastic Blue Nine (Yau Man Kong, known as Frankie) to join forces with a raised palm-clasping bond of everyone's sweaty monster mitts as the new team motto was cried with lusty lung: 'Gambolé! Gambolé! Gambolé!' – which I always thought was Italian for lobster (but I could be wrong).

It would seem that God had not cut me out for cooperative and communicative teamwork and chanting. I had been built for being alone. Built for a life on a bike. And I was more than happy with that.

After a sleepless night of being blasted both aurally and icily by the malfunctioning air-conditioner, I was loudly 'awoken' at 5.30 a.m. for a compulsory team-bonding jump off the jetty into the lurking jellyfish murk of the harbour. Another spot of monster-making activity took place after breakfast before we were allocated various tasks to get the ship into shape for our high-noon departure. The sky was blue, the sun was burning down, the wind was . . . well . . . windy.

Suddenly midday was upon us. A flutter of apprehension swept through my stomach, bringing with it a feeling of mild nausea. Not a good start – feeling sick and we hadn't even set sail yet. Various girlfriends and wives of the crew came to wave us off. Andy, bless him, was also there to give me a hearty hug. Giving him a little playful squeeze on his port-side buttock, I thanked him for getting me into this mess. (It's always nice to have someone else to blame, is it not?)

Before I knew it, the hazy shape of Hong Kong had drifted out of sight as the multi-sailed (about twelve of them) *Ji Fung* slid rather majestically across the north of the South China Sea towards Japan.

After we'd been under way under sail for a while, and after having had a 'character-building' pep talk from Tintin, all three watches were summoned to the aft deck behind the wheelhouse, where we were to have a few facts and figures drilled into our ocean-bobbing heads by Greg, the boisterous Aussie captain (brought up in Sydney and the Philippines, and now living in Perth), and Gerhard, the hirsute German chief officer.

Greg, clad in sneakers, blue shorts, blue baseball hat and red Fred Perry shirt, finished introducing himself and then asked if anybody wanted to go home yet. No one said anything, not even me.

'Good,' said Greg. 'So you've all decided you want to see Japan. But why didn't you fly? Flying is much easier, much faster, much more convenient than sailing. Instead you've chosen a far harder way to reach Japan and now that you've all decided to stay on board, in three or four days I really want to see your efforts. Up until that time the purpose of the drill is communication – to work together and effectively in groups – and for all of you to see and get the feel of the ship and sails in full working order. We want to see if you get progression or depression.

'We don't, of course, expect you to be perfect sailors by the end of this course, but we do expect you to put your best effort into it and only you will be able to judge whether it has been a success for you or not. The course involves hard work and little sleep, but at the end of the day we want you to be able to say, "I put my best effort into solving those problems and for me the course – or that particular day – was a personal success."'

Greg ran a challenging eye over his motley crew, and continued: 'This is not a course of survival, but of brain-training. We create problems for you. Gerhard and I will find as many problems for you as possible, which we'll help you with for the first part of the sea voyage. For the second part, you'll take over while we slip into the shadows to watch how well you can navigate and run the ship. Then, when we think you're too familiar with the ship, we'll send you off on a land expedition in Japan for you to face fresh problems.

'We hope that when we reach Kagoshima at the end of the course in a fortnight's time, you'll not only be stressed out from the endless hard work but you'll have learnt a lot too. In return for the hard work and little sleep, we will provide you with six meals a day – three that go down and three that come up!'

Here Greg emitted a congratulatory chortle of laughter at his own wit, raising a few feeble and uncertain chuckles from the gathered group of trainees.

'But remember,' he added, adopting a more serious tone, 'it's important that for every litre you vomit, you drink a litre of water. Okay, now I think I've said all I need to for the moment so I'll pass you over to Gerhard, who will fill you in with the safety brief.'

Deutschlander Gerhard, who, on account of his surplus of facial hair, I involuntarily nicknamed Herr Hirsute, made it clear from the start of his 'safety brief' that he was neither predisposed to acts of compassion nor one to mince his words.

'Okay!' he bellowed, with a fiercesome Teutonic glare, 'sor vee are on a sheep – yah? – and vot material eeze ziss sheep made?'

Silence.

'Ah! Sor vee have a promising start – yah? Vot do all you people have in your heads – air? Ziss sheep eeze made of vood. And vot have you if you mix vood and var-ter?'

Silence.

'You have fun-guy – yah? Of course var-ter on zee outside of ziss sheep eeze no problem. But var-ter on zee inside . . . ? Just get zee bloody var-ter out fast! Vot ever happens, you must keep zee inside of zee sheep dry. Okay, ziss eeze zee first part of zee sermon.

'Now, as for accidents on zee sheep, telephoning nein nein nein eeze not so much help. Sor, I am zee doctor on board – yah? I have had very good doctor's training in a butcher's shop! Remember, all-vays votch your feet on zee deck. I see many of you are only vare-ing zee sandals. I too am vare-ing zee sandals, but for me ziss eeze okay because I am zee doctor. But for you, vare-ing zee sandals eeze not okay. Look around . . . zee sheep has many toe-breakers attached to zee deck and if you break your toes I have only two spare toes on board. No more. Keep your toes in safety – yah?'

Feeling sheepish, we kept our eyes fixed firmly on his sandalled toes.

'Now for fire. Ziss sheep eeze a non-smoking, drug-free flight. But if you hear zee fire alarm you move immediately to zee muster station. Also, if you are still sitting on zee toilet or being sick or eating breakfast at zat moment you hear zee fire alarm, you move immediately up here. Fire eeze zee most dangerous of all zee sheep problems. Sor, if you find some fire, vot do you do?'

Silence.

'You blow it out, of course! But if zee fire eeze larger than anysing you can manage, zen vot do you do?'

Silence.

'YOU BLOODY SHOUT! Zat's vot you do – SHOUT! You vake up your guys and shout FIRE! FIRE! VAKE UP! You get everyone out of zee cabins fast and zen close zee door. Maybe zee fire vill go out if zair eeze a lacking of oxygen. Twenty-four hours a day someone should all-vays be on zee bridge. Okay, you bright people – so vot eeze zee opposite of zee fire problem?'

Silence.

'FLOODING! Maybe vee have a hole in zee sheep. And how do vee get a hole in zee sheep?'

Silence. I was just about to call out, 'From colliding with an iceberg,' but then I realised I was getting my oceans a bit muddled up – a 'tropical iceberg' is perhaps a bit of an oxymoron.

'Maybe vee have a collision with a rock or a sheep in zee var-ter – yah? And vot do you do if you find a small hole in zee side of zee sheep?'

Here I could hold back no more. 'Stick your thumb in it!' I called helpfully. Herr Hirsute turned to glare at me.

'Ah! Sor vee have a sheep jester – yah? Sor vot zen,' he asked me accusingly through a faceful of fur, 'do you suggest vee do if zee hole eeze bigger zan our sumb?'

I felt like replying, 'If not your thumb, then try your bum,' but fortunately didn't. Instead, feeling decidedly flush of face, I mumbled something about maybe trying a spot of pumping or Maydaying.

'Yah, yah. Remember, you must all-vays let zee votch people know you have found a fire and zey vill press a button. If zee sheep eeze no longer safe, zen vee make some other sheeps – lifeboats – yah? Vee have four of zeeze little sheeps and each little sheep can carry twenty-five persons. Ziss means vee have space for one hundred persons. As zair are forty-sree persons on board – sirty-sree trainees and ten staff – zen ziss should be no problem.

'Each lifeboat has var-ter stored in plastic bags, some fishing lines and many kilos of emergency food. Zee purpose of zee lifeboat eeze not to give you an enjoyable life, but to save it.'

Well, that was nice to know.

'Okay, sor now for anozer problem,' he continued, hardly drawing breath between one problem and another. 'If a man can no longer stand zee seasickness any more and decides to jump overboard, zen please consider ziss a serious problem, because vee vont to get zee man back. Ziss operation is called MAN OVERBOARD. Zair eeze no such sing as "Vooman Overboard", so if you female people have a problem vizz zat, zen don't fall overboard – yah?

45

'Okay, sor if you see a man fall into zee sea, you must all-vays keep votching him. Don't turn to your mate and say, "Gee, did you see zat? Zat guy just fell overboard." Because zat man vill disappear very, very easy. Srow zee man a life-ring. Each life-ring can send a smoke signal and flare to help people to find him. Also send some people up zee mast for a better visibility of zee overboard man. If you are sitting on zee toilet and you hear people shout "MAN OVER-BOARD!" – don't vait to finish your mess – you can finish zat later. Get up fast to zee muster station to see who has gone. And all-vays remember to vare your life-jacket. A life-jacket is your best friend . . . and maybe your last.'

Gulp.

'Now for zee cleaning. Vizz David, who eeze here to take over from me as chief officer ven I leave zee sheep in Japan, vee vill together be vonting all-vays for zee sheep to be sweet-smelling – yah? Vee have a small drying room but ziss can cause problems as zair eeze not space enough to have everyone's clozing drying at zee same time. So if zee sun eeze shining, vee sometimes permit maybe some trousers and shirts for hanging outside. But not too many at any one time because, remember, ziss eeze still a sheep and not a Chinese laundry!

'As zee sheep carries only two sousand gallons of var-ter, each trainee eeze strictly rationed to four gallons – about vun bucketful for each person each day. Ziss var-ter includes everysing for drinking, personal cleaning, cooking, vashing up and maybe a little laundry. For everysing else you use zee sea-water – yah? – because, as you see, ziss eeze somesing of vich vee have no shortage. You vill be allowed a shower vunce every two days. Ziss takes place on deck and your votch leader vill direct zee fire-hose on you for precisely ten seconds only.'

Power shower, I thought to myself.

'Ah, now, Greenvotch,' barked Herr Hirsute, 'you vill probably have noticed that you have a problem wizz your toilet: no var-ter! So, unless you find a friendly Red or Bluevotch man to let you use zairs, zen I have a simple remedy to ziss problem. Stop eating and drinking – yah? Hah!'

Green glances all round.

'Lastly, for zee seasick people – vich usually ends up being for most persons – being seasick can be dangerous. It makes zee deck slippery and can block up drains and basins and toilets.'

Greener glances all round.

'I see you are not looking too happy at sinking of zee seasickness, but if you never experience *real* seasickness, zen you vill miss out on one of life's greatest experiences. At first you vill feel like dess, but by zee sird day you vill start to come back to life and feel no longer zee seasickness. Sor, as for being sick, you must all-vays come up on deck before you srow up and you must also all-vays check zee direction of zee vind *before* you hang over zee side of zee sheep. Only zen are you allowed to srow up, but all-vays make sure before you are sick to clip your harness on to zee rails, because to be seasick is not very convenient but to go overboard is slightly verse.

'If you cannot keep to zeeze rules, zen you must all-vays clean up your own mess vizzout any delays – yah? And remember to keep drinking, but not more zan your allowed ration! Var-ter is very important in seasickness. Your body needs var-ter and if you do not drink, your body vill take it from zee easiest source, which eeze zee brain. Ziss causes headaches. Sor, if you are seasick and have a headache, zen ziss eeze zee clear sign zat you are dehydrated. Also, even if you are feeling sick you should all-vays try to eat or else you vill start to srow up your stomach bile and ziss eeze not so fun.'

Well, that certainly made me feel better . . .

'All of ziss may not be sounding so easy for you but remember you are not here for an easy time. Like Greg said, if you vonted an easy time you vood have taken a JAL flight – yah? Okay, sor now zee sermon eeze over and it's time for you to go to verk.'

Over the next few days we Bluewatchers soon got into the seasicking swing of things while simultaneously trying to hone our monster-building tactics into a cheerily chanting cooperating team. Apart from the sickness, of which (at least for the first few days) I was happily free, our lives rotated around twenty-four-hour days divided into seven watches (Middle, Morning, Forenoon, Afternoon, First Dog, Last Dog, First) which consisted of utter sleeplessness and almost constant activity. My bodily functions didn't know whether they were coming or going. Whatever hour of day or night or whatever state of stomach or bowel, we all had to spring merrily to attention to arrive at our appointed Bluewatch Muster on time and shout with forced gusto our respective Blue numbers to prove that we were all 'well' and present.

Each team member had to take turns to be Leader of the Pack, whereby they assigned a rota of tasks to each Bluewatcher in turn – tasks that centred on 'wheel', 'navigation', 'journal', 'port-side lookout', 'flood and fire', 'messenger' and 'kitchen'. For the 'flood and fire' watch, two of us would check that there were no signs of either a flood or a fire in the front store cupboards, the drying room, the cold cupboard, the crew and trainee cabins, the galley and mess room, the deck store or the 'lazarette' – the capacious, clamber-down-into hatched locker in the stern that housed the massive and multitudinous sails. To this roller-coasting roster we also had to snap our brain-weary minds into gear enough to remember to check the bilges (not sinking?), the moorings (not in a tangle?), the anchor (still there?), the ship's position (hadn't sailed clean off-course into . . . an ocean of icebergs, perhaps?) and the lifeboats (ready to go in case we . . . hit said iceberg or other unwanted flotsam?).

Day and night we put up sails, took down sails, tripped over toe-breakers and pulled to high heaven on ropes – whoops, I mean sheets. We scrubbed decks, plates and toilets (I should have said 'heads') or were mustered to attention for summit meetings with Captain Greg or Big Chief Herr Hirsute.

Despite my initial monster-making misgivings, all of this was actually not too bad. Even with the lack of sleep, I enjoyed the doing and the learning and all the 'getting on' bits. But I did find myself shying away in a big way when Tintin rallied us around for what he called 'Bluewatch Self-Analysis'.

'Okay, babes!' he said jauntily, referring to both male and female trainees, 'let's focus here for a moment.'

And he sat us on the deck in a circle ('I like circles') before instructing us to 'take each other apart'. At this point I shrank into myself, thinking: take each other apart? But I want to stay intact!

'I want you to find two strong points,' Tintin continued, 'and two weak points in not only yourself but other team members, and we'll discuss these openly before I give each of you, one at a time, a moment to go away and analyse yourself while the rest of the team stays here to analyse *you*! Sound good?'

Good? Sounded to me like a bloody nightmare! Surely learning to get my digits around a spot of rope 'whipping' or a nice sturdy 'rolling hitch', not to mention studying the finer art of securing any wayward cockpit tackle (just so long as it wasn't backwinding at the time), would be a lot more useful than trying to tear trainees apart? But seemingly not. With amazement, I watched the ever-bonding Blues enthusiastically clapping and cheering the super-quiffed ring-leader before gripping each other's raised fist and chanting for the umpteenth time that day the morale-boosting team chant: 'Gambolé! Gambolé! Gambolé!' Lobster! Lobster! Lobster!

'Okay, babes!' said Tintin. 'A couple more things. I want you all to make a combined journal of your Bluewatch experience – entering things such as your personal goals, your learning points that emerge from day to day, your open assessment of other team members, your observances, your faults, your impressions, your highlights, your low points – that kind of thing. Oh, and I also want a team song. Okay? Right, babes, let's move it. Let's swing it!'

Oh dear. This was definitely getting more than a little too analytically claustrophobic for comfort. I certainly hadn't joined the ship to chant team songs and rallying cries or to punch the air in 'We arrre the cham-pions' style. Nor had I joined the ship to get to grips with the ropes of self-analysis, or to trumpet and publicise my 'challenges' and inner (or even outer) thoughts, or for that matter to criticise others. Unlike the ship's trainees, I wasn't looking to learn 'team skills' in order to apply them to my 'workplace'. (The fact that I didn't have, nor had ever had, anything as formal as a 'workplace' was perhaps a moot point not worthy of discussion.) I had joined *Ji Fung* simply because I hated air travel and loved the ocean wave and for years had fancied 'working' as a ship's odd-jobber and arriving in a land that manifests itself slowly up from the horizon, rather than just being plonked upon it in a plane.

But now, despite being afloat on the wild and watery immensity that covers 70 per cent of the earth, life had turned paradoxically suffocating. So, desperate to escape from the all-enveloping clutches of the stuck-together Bluewatch Brigade, I made my wishes known first to Tintin (who, thanks to M.T., was now also known as 'Young-Looking Sunshine Boy') – wishes that he took in his jaunty, sandal-footed (toe-breaking) stride before passing me over for a summit meeting with Captain Greg and Oh Hirsute One.

Greg took the news in his matey and laid-back Antipodean way while Herr Hairiness ordered me to join him on the roof of the mess room to grill me a lot further about my wayward seafaring desires. Despite his ferocious appearance – arms as strong as hawsers, face like a Viking's battleaxe – Herr Hirsute was really quite a tame sauerkraut at heart. On hearing my wishes to be more hands-on ship-hand rather than a learn-and-act-all-as-one trainee, he assigned me the position of Bosun's Mate Assistant. I was to report to him daily, he said, although I was to take most of my work instructions directly from the Bosun's Mate, Ken Morris.

This news cheered me enormously. Not only did I suddenly feel as if I had a shipworthy role to play on board (no matter how minor) but also I was to work with bonny young Ken – an eighteen-year-old fine-featured, good-natured and grand-humoured jocular jock from Glasgow to whom I had immediately warmed from the start of this *Ji Fung* jaunt on account of the tender loving care that he had administered for the welfare of my unwieldy steed. On Day One, when I had felt immensely awkward about arriving on the ship with a very unstowable heavy mount, Ken had received this jutting and cumbersome lump of two-wheeled ballast in a cheery, north-of-the-border 'och aye' fashion, assuring me that it was no trouble to leave my bike in his hands. Requiring no assistance, he deftly dissected my bike into several parts and carefully stowed it in a shallow locker beneath the wheelhouse.

Although I was still to keep in close contact with the remaining eleven Bluewatchers by way of following and recording their progress, my position as Bosun's Mate Assistant suddenly opened up a way into the everyday life of the workings of the ship, which included the crew. As well as Ken, I worked with Berman-the-Bosun, a Hong Kong Chinese who was a sort of Jim'll Fix It with practically anything and everything to do with the ship. Then there was Chang Han ('Alan'), the engineer – the one who didn't fix broken air-conditioners; he wore a white boiler suit and a pair of shiny black loafers that looked more appropriate for wearing to the office than for clambering around in the bowels of a yawing ship's engine room. And there was frisky Sam, the Hong Kong Chinese cook's assistant, who kept trying to kiss me over his cleaver.

Ken was a card. Blessed with a pair of fine vocals, he had an endearing habit of breaking out into pitch-perfect renditions of nostalgic heart-stirring ballads and hearty Scottish songs as we polished and scrubbed and heaved and reefed and gybed. No longer obliged to participate in the team analysis and the get-to-know-yourself workshops of the Bluewatch Brigade, I now had free rein to clamber up the dizzying rigging to the giddy heights of the 'Land ahoy!' crow's-nest mast-top, learn a cluster of knots, tinker with Alan around the engine room, stitch and mend acres of sails and colossal sail bags, take the wheel, screw open and close every bulleye cover (the heavy porthole shutters), clean the Captain's 'head', and scrub and peel and chop and cook under the chaotic instructions of tiger-tattooed Paul Wong in the saucepan-clanging galley.

For some bizarre reason I decided to set up a ship's newspaper, entitled the *Daily Ji Fung Express*, the object of which was to record the everyday happenings and non-happenings of our short-lived life on the ocean wave. If anyone on board had hoped for an enlightening and informative read, then they were to be bitterly disappointed. Instead, they found a four-page offering that rapidly deteriorated into a two-page disappointment of Blue-Petered Pritt-stuck nonsense containing such riveting items as a cack-handed attempt at a collaged 'Weather Window', a nonsensical limerick, a child's-play crossword, a cartoon and a Joke Department, for which I'd cajole various trainees and crew to donate what they considered to be a snigger-worthy few words.

For example, donated by Boston-based Renée: 'Did you hear the one about the Polish couple who froze to death in their car at a drive-in movie? They went to see "Closed For Winter".'

Or from Ken: 'How do you sink an Irish submarine? Knock on the door.'

And from Herr Hirsute: 'Why do you bury cyclists face down? So you can use their bottoms as a bicycle stand.'

All of these were bad enough to be good enough to fill a few gaps in the *Ji Fung Express*.

For those on board who fancied something a little deeper in a shallow news-paper, something to stretch a horizon or two perhaps, I offered 'The Philosophising Philosopher's Corner of Philosophy', which contained useful nuggets such as 'The Meaning of Life is to Live' which, as the size of the waves increased, became 'The Meaning of Life is to Stay Afloat' or 'The Meaning of Life is Not to Drown'. Hmmm. It's perhaps just as well that, once I left the ship, the *Ji Fung Express* sank without trace.

One of the most memorably enjoyable moments of the whole voyage was when Captain Greg allowed us all to leap overboard for a joyous frolic of high-spirited hilarity in the Pacific just south of Taiwan. But while we were queuing up on deck for our ten-second fresh-water shower to wash off the salt of the swim, word came from Greg to hurry up and to get back to our positions because it looked as if a storm was closing in fast from the east. Informing us that the East China Sea should be much like a millpond at this time of year, he did little to quell the rising apprehension of the seasick-prone trainees as to what stomach-churning horrors lay ahead.

While the majority of the trainees had been suffering from severe bouts of 'motion sickness' already, I had been feeling quite pleased with my internal workings because, so far, I had still managed to keep seasick-free. But it was not to last and my stomach was in for a shock.

As I sat on deck with Ken, doing a spot of last-minute sail-mending, I overheard a couple of instructors giving their charges a quick spurt of morale-boosting pep talk.

'Difficult circumstances,' said the Bluewatch's Young-Looking Sunshine Boy, 'are a good opportunity to analyse people's leadership capabilities – so look for-ward to a discussion in which we will openly criticise and commend!'

Ming said something unintelligible to his Cantonese-speaking Greenwatch.

Mike, the leader of Redwatch (who now called themselves the Dream Team), addressed his troops with 'a thought':

'There is only one thing more uncomfortable than learning from experiences, and that is not to learn from them.'

At this point Ken leant across to me and murmured his own offering of thought by asking, 'How many Irishmen does it take to milk a cow?'

'I hate to think, Ken.'

'Four to hold the udder and twenty to lift it up and down!'

Meanwhile, another pep talker was piping up: 'No one wants to be a pessimist. Everyone wants to be an optimist and this is my experience after more than ten years at sea. Optimists make poor people as they lack imaginative power – they can't imagine all the things that can go wrong. What's important is how to deal with the problem. See it as an opportunity to do something new without arriving purposefully into danger, as this tends to be a generally much more productive angle to view a particular problem rather than to just say, "Fine, I see it as such," and run the other way. By doing that you will have missed the opportunity to stretch your mind.'

Phew. How glad I was to be mending sails – no matter how many people it might take to milk a cow. Next, Dr Darrell Ho-Yen's philosophy was brought up for air:

'A pessimist is someone who sees disaster in every opportunity. An optimist is someone who sees opportunity in every disaster.'

Then, just as I was thinking that surely the pep-talking must be over, Young-Looking Sunshine Boy chipped in with a quote from Martin Luther King:

'The ultimate measure of a person is not where they stand in moments of conflict and convenience, but where they stand during challenge and controversy.'

There then followed a party political broadcast from Redwatch, who unfortunately felt the need to give us all a rendition of their Dream Team ditty, sung imaginatively to the tune of Rod Stewart's 'I am sailing . . .':

> We – sail – the sea-hee
> We – sail – the sea-hee
> We – are – the – Red – Watch
> On – *Ji Fung*
> We serve, we stri-hive
> We don't yi-ield
> We are the Red – Watch
> On *Ji Fung*. Yeahhh.

Yes, well, each to their own, as they say.

When the storm came, it came big. And it came bigger. At first I found it hilariously exciting – a feeling akin to clinging on for dear life while plummeting at ridiculous speeds strapped to the seat on a death-ride at some monstrous out-of-town amusement park, submerged as I was in a whipped-up frenzy of shrieking wind, scary waves and lashing rain.

Once the novelty had worn off and the pain and exhaustion set in, I realised it was perhaps not quite so much fun after all. In fact, it seemed a bit serious. The ship and its crew were hounded for hours by the sea. Never for a second did we allow a hand to lose contact with a sturdy hold as we reeled like drunks about the ship, repeatedly tossed and roughly thrown into sharp corners and objects. I watched the bruises as they mushroomed in front of my eyes. Cuts opened, gashes bled. No hope of healing, at least for some days. Everything saturated inside and out. Skin shrivelled like a prune. Wounds and eyes stinging with salt.

Hours went by. The storm worsened. Gigantic swells. Waves as big as buildings slamming into the ship, crashing with detonating force before bursting over the deck, drenching us all. The sea was raging, smothering, callously charging towards us from every direction with impervious malevolence. You could tell it was enjoying itself – it had us in the palm of its mighty hand, the wind pouncing, the waves tossing us all over the place like mouse-teasing cats. Enormous walls of water smashed over the prow, sending a miniature tidal wave foaming and spuming down decks that flooded and drained, flooded and drained. Gallons of sea water entered my mouth, my ears, my boots, and coursed down my back. I was heavy with water, drowning on deck, sinking in the undrinkable drink . . .

At one point I found myself hurled into Greg on the wheel and he informed me that the hurricane winds were blowing a frenzied forty-eight knots. I'm not too hot on my knots so looked blank.

'Thirty-five to forty is gale force,' shouted Greg above the din.

All I managed to say was, 'Oh,' before we were separated by a shuddering wave that shattered into the side of the ship, hurling me on to the rails. Had I not been harnessed, I would have been a man overboard for sure.

Although I was feeling a drop green around the gills, my internal workings stayed in place until I went below deck. Suddenly, stomach rose, contents threw. Once started, couldn't stop. Joined the limp line of the mother of all sea-sicking troops, heaving over the side. Nothing stayed down, not even water. Sleep impossible. My cabin, located in the starboard bow, was in the worst possible position, taking the full force of the warring waves exploding like shells into the side.

Clambering up to the top of my multi-storey bunk was a feat in itself. As the ship violently pitched and yawed, I had to judge each move with precision and extreme caution to prevent being hurled across the cabin like a lump of boneless meat. Limbs flailed wildly out of control as I clumsily scaled the giddying heights, clinging and grappling for hand-holds and foot-holds. As the ship rolled back, I made full use of the rough oscillation and with a final burst of effort hurled myself on to my sodden bunk before the bow was jarred by another watery explosion and tipped the other way.

Quickly I fumbled to tie up the lee-cloth – the flimsy makeshift partition that we all used to avoid being jettisoned to the floor as the ship seesawed and slammed and creaked and moaned and violently lurched this way and that. The bulleye-covered porthole seemed to be leaking so I plugged it with my pillow – might not have done much to prevent us from sinking but for now that didn't matter, as just the act of concealing the dripping porthole made me feel better.

Everything was wet: sheet, sleeping-bag, shoes, socks, clothes, hair. Never mind – my stomach was in such turmoil that I was almost beyond caring. I flopped horizontal and closed my eyes, my body a wreck. Felt as if I'd just crawled off a battlefield: scarred and scoured, battered and bruised, mangled mind, nerves shredded to pieces. I'd always thought I loved the sea, but now I hated it. I hated the things it was doing. It wouldn't stop. It wouldn't still. It had lost its marbles, its senses, its temper. It could drown us all if it wanted.

The very real prospect of drowning reminded me that I'd better get praying. So I did. I prayed to be anywhere else but here. And then I started to count the waves, recalling Tim Severin, who sailed a medieval boat, made of leather, across the Atlantic. He began his book *The Brendan Voyage* with the words: 'The seventh wave is said to be the worst, the one that does the damage in the turmoil of an ocean gale.' One . . . two . . . three . . . but I gave up, I didn't want to know.

The ship was riding an unpredictable switchback of waves. It climbed monstrous walls of water, balanced momentarily and uncertainly on the crest as if wobbling on a tightrope and not quite sure which way to fall, before rapidly plunging down into a deep and enormous trough. Every so often a rogue wave slammed with sickening force into the side of the ship inches from my head, sending an explosive cracking noise ricocheting along the bow. I lay in the screaming darkness, wincing, waiting any moment for the whole side of the ship to be ripped open by the colossal impact of the steely waves. I was being tossed roughly about my bunk, bashing limbs and bones into the angular metal walls. More cuts. More bruises. More sickness. No sleep.

Then a shout from above – I was needed on deck. The inner jib stay had snapped. I climbed into my soaking oilskins, tied on the life-jacket, fastened the harness, staggered up the steps and fought my way across a battlefield on the wave-soused deck up to the bow to join Ken and Berman-the-Bosun and Herr Hirsute, who were trying to fix the stay in impossible conditions. Towering waves broke clean over us as the bow-spit speared a black wall of water, crests torn into foam. The noise of the howling wind, the roaring ocean and the whining and ripping rigging was horrendous. We spoke in shouts and still couldn't hear each other.

I crawled along the deck, clinging on tight with everything I had, praying a wave wouldn't catch me out when I was moving between harness points, while simultaneously trying to pass the Fix-it Boys the equipment they needed for the emergency repairs. My stomach was churning and turning. I felt like death. My energy sapped. But I had to hold on – had to hold out.

Hours inched by. I was freezing, my salt-shrivelled hands gripping on to metal so tightly that the blood had all gone. A rope was hurled my way. I wrapped it round a winch.

'HEAVE!' screamed a voice.

I heaved and heaved, but it was no good – my muscles had long since been swept overboard. Ken clambered back to me on all fours, looking like a hermit crab, a drunk one at that.

'How many cows does it take to milk . . .?'

I laughed. But only just, before I turned my head to vomit again over the side, the sea racing up to crash into my face like a concrete slab. The ship groaned. I groaned. What was I doing here? Was this really happening? When would it end? Today? Tomorrow? Next week? Where was the East China Sea millpond now, eh, Greg? I couldn't imagine ever being still again, listening to the sound of silence. I couldn't imagine what it felt like to have a stomach that was not constantly stuck in my mouth.

I wondered whether I should start doing some proper praying, but then God probably couldn't hear me over the banshee moan of the storm. I couldn't even hear myself. But that was okay, as I had to hear Herr Hirsute, who was bellowing again like a Teutonic warrior from hell.

'HEAVE! Get zat bloody line and HEAVE!'

Hell's teeth on earth, on ocean, in mind. Oh, for a nice gentle cycle, pootling along a quiet leafy lane. I heaved, this time on the snapped and frayed stay.

'HEAVE! Bloody HEAVE!'

I heaved and heaved. My hand slipped. A jagged wire, razor sharp, ripped through the leather cycling mitts that I was wearing for grip, and sliced open my starboard palm. Blood sprang to the surface. Ha! So I still had some blood in my hands after all! I stared at the gash. Best wound to date. I'd be proud of it later, I was sure. But not now. I needed hands that worked.

Another yell: 'HEAVE! Get zee bloody line and bloody HEAVE!'

I heaved and the gash opened up further. But this was no time to play nurses, as the storm was too intoxicatingly terrifying to fuss or to linger for long over a mere slip of a slit.

Finally the combined bulldozing strength and nautical expertise of Herr Hirsute, Berman-the-Bosun and Ken managed to replace the snapped inner jib stay with a 'jury rig' that they said would be strong enough to hold ten tons. Sounded good to me – but would it prevent us from sinking?

The storm and its turbulent aftermath raged for days. Everything and everyone continuously crashed and slammed and slid from one side of the ship to the other. The galley was a scene of pantomimic farce, resounding with a constant and clamorous uproar of crashing pots and pans and tins and baking sheets as they were pitched back and forth on the huge steel shelves. The super-chunky industrial stoves swung like bats out of hell to keep equilibrium. Cupboards of seasick-green plastic crockery shunted violently from one end of the shelf to the other, occasionally spilling like nine-pins all over the floor when somebody forgot to shut the cabinets. Vast arsenals of cutlery clashed and clattered, escaped pieces becoming dangerously airborne. Once, when a couple of trainees lost their balance on account of the recklessly pitching ship and collided mid-mess room, I narrowly missed being impaled against the wall by a wayward knife that was sent flying by the impact. I envisaged some unsavoury headlines: 'SEABORNE CYCLIST DIES FROM FLYING FORK'; 'INNOCENT

DECKHAND TEASPOONED TO DEATH'. The possibilities seemed inexhaustible.

With the seas still furiously raging, mad cook Paul Wong one night decided to rustle up perhaps the most inappropriate dessert for forty-three sea-churned stomachs: vast trays of a chocolate and banana cake, stupendously gooey enough to send the strongest of digestions into sickly auto-kill at the best of times, never mind at the height of an East China Sea tempest. A trainee picked up a trayful of the gloopy cake from the galley counter to transport it to a mess room table but never made it, thanks to his hilarious ill-judgement of the ship's violent oscillations. The chocolate and creamy banana slop became airborne and splattered and splayed itself over a sea of stunned faces. Paul Wong was not amused.

Finally, after what felt like a lifetime, the whirling-dervish wind slowly diminished down to twenty knots – a soothing breeze in comparison. But the rain still sheeted, drumming our heads and stinging our skin. The waves continued to charge at us as monumentally mountainous as ever; the ocean resembled a lunar landscape, cratered and gouged and deformed by the wind. Glimpses of the bleak horizon (the one thing in our whole world that wasn't moving) could only be snatched at as we tipped over head after thunderous head of fearsome faces of water before diving back down into a dark valley of landsliding sea.

For days the conditions remained wild and tempestuous. Save for the iron-stomached Deutschlander, and perhaps Captain Greg, everyone on board fell victim to seasickness. Exhaustion ruled. Japan felt about as out of reach as Outer Space. I can safely say, from the bottom of my heart to the heart of my bottom, that I have never felt or been so catastrophically ill in all my life.

Despite the seasicking advice that Herr Hirsute had delivered upon us fresh-of-face and settled-of-stomach souls at the outset of the turbulent voyage, I couldn't eat for five long days – even sips of water made me sick. With no food left to rise to the surface, my stomach was left with little choice other than to bring up that bile, which looked like orange-juice. Not a pretty sight. All I wanted to do was to collapse and remain collapsed. Everything, even sitting, even blinking, felt like hard work. But no one, however poorly they might be (apart from a small clutch of seriously ill trainees), could be spared the time to tend to their own woeful states.

So, putting mind over stomach, I continued trying to pull my weight (which, incidentally, was dropping away alarmingly fast) by trying to help here and there, sliding and colliding with Paul Wong around the galley as well as clambering life over limb up the rigging to help Ken at the top of the mast, from where the world tipped and swayed across the sky in great stomach-lurching arcs – we were clinging to a giant pendulum as the sea raced up to meet us. Not good for a dicky stomach.

To add to my sick-making tasks around the ship, I was determined to keep my half-hearted *(Sometimes) Daily Ji Fung Express* rocking and rolling off the press. To fill the pages and to make my pitiful innards feel a tad perkier, I decided to ask every trainee on board to sum up in two or three words their reactions and feelings for the voyage to date. In my very lovely charitable way, I secretly hoped that they all felt as monumentally ill as I did and I captioned the piece, 'SO WHAT DO YOU THINK OF THE SEASICK TRIP SO FAR?' The answers were as follows.

1. Learning some more.
2. Think to the future.
3. Seasick time.
4. New experience.
5. Very exciting.
6. Very difficult.
7. Homesick.
8. Seasick.
9. Tough.

10. No sleep.
11. So far so good. [So far so good? This was way too positive for my liking.]
12. Fun. [Liar!]
13. Pure Hell! [That's more like it!]
14. Frightened of the waves. [Ditto.]
15. Good team spirit. [Yuk!]
16. An adventure.
17. Exhausting.
18. New thoughts. [??]
19. Thinking it over.
20. Seasick.
21. Terrific! [Deserves to be shot.]
22. Sleepless . . .

And so on and so on.

In desperate need to know when I would be able to send a hopeful word down to the sorry remains of my stomach, I accosted Captain Greg to find out just what this forever agitated weather was playing at. Sounding like a combination of an Aussie Michael Fish and the Shipping Forecast, Greg said:

'An area of low pressure off the coast of Okinawa has mixed with an area of high pressure, which increases winds from the east. Another gale is moving south towards us but we should be out of the way before it hits. With strong easterlies like this, we're going to have to keep constantly tacking. Without the engine we'd have to sail sixty degrees to the wind, but with the engine we can push it to forty-five degrees. Any more than that and the ship'll bang too much if we sail too close to the wind – something that would risk damaging all the rigging. As you can see, learning about the weather is essential for the management of the ship.'

'How much further have we got?' I asked, feeling like a whining child in the back seat of a never-ending parental car journey.

'I'm afraid we've still got a long way,' replied Greg (and I could see he was thinking: no ship-shape soul is she). 'Yup, it's going to be an uphill battle to get there in time.'

'And what delights does today hold in store for us?'

'Today's going to be another hard-working tacking day. You know, the chance of getting this wind at this time of year is about seven per cent – which I guess is probably not something you want to hear just now!'

'Oh well – they do say sailors have to weather the weather, whatever the weather, whether they like it or not. It's just a little unfortunate on the stomach, that's all.'

After a bit more bile came up for air, I tried to console my wishy-washy-wasn't-here insides with the thought that at least I wasn't having to contend with the savage seas of the Southern Ocean. According to the Met Office, the so-called Roaring Forties (the latitudes between 40° and 55° south in the Atlantic and Indian Oceans, and between 50° and 60° south in the Pacific) have an average wave height of more than four metres in winter and are the roughest waters in the world.

One evening I was sitting in the rocking mess room where I was struggling to compile another page for the *(Sometimes) Daily Ji Fung Express*. Young Ken sashayed up to my table and, noticing that I was having trouble trying to think of something to write or stick or Pritt, said, 'Here's one for the Joke Page. What do you call a boomerang that won't come back?'

I raised an uncertain eyebrow or two.

'A stick!'

'Ken, me bonny Bosun's Mate,' I said in my best Scottish accent, which sounded more akin to Japanese, 'you've been reading too many Christmas cracker jokes.'

Then, spotting a member of Greenwatch being violently sick over the side, I was struck by a usefully useless idea with which to pep up a few peptic spots in my paper. Picking up my pen, I wrote:

SEASICKNESS TIPS OF THE TRADE

1. Don't get seasick.
2. If you do, pretend to yourself you're not.
3. But if stomach wins over mind, remember to be sick over leeward side of ship.
4. Drink lots.
5. Don't forget to eat something, lest stomach-lining rears its ugly head.
6. Don't go below deck longer than you have to.
7. Eat dry biscuits rather than Paul Wong's spectacular creamy constructions.
8. Eat ginger or drink ginger tea (which, following further investigation, you can't, as there's none on board).
9. When going to bed, turn horizontal fast, as it's kinder on stomach.

10. When off-duty, head to where there is least movement, e.g. centre of ship.

11. If still feeling seasick while on deck, fix gaze on horizon (if you can find it over waves) – it's the only thing not moving. (Queasiness is often prompted by conflict between what eyes see and what other senses report is happening. Simply matching the two – by going on deck and staring at fixed point, e.g. horizon – helps relieve nausea. At least, that's the nice idea.)

12. Perform DIY Acupressure Point Remedy. Apply pressure with right thumb to wrist's Nei-Kuan point. Find Nei-Kuan point by placing middle three fingers of right hand on inside of left wrist, with edge of third finger on first wrist crease. The Nei-Kuan point is located just under edge of index finger and between the two central tendons. Apply pressure with thumb for five to ten minutes every hour.

13. Still feeling ill? Then resort to old (fishermen's) wives' tale: sit on a piece of newspaper. Broadsheets are said to work best, presumably being more versatile for doubling up as impromptu sick-bag.

14. If all else fails – try time-honoured guaranteed cure: lie under a tree.

Life continued to revolve and sway around days of sleeplessness, seasickness, hard work, high seas and relentlessly strong easterlies that produced a great roaring sound – the evocative sound of big winds in the rigging of a big ship. Slowly I started to eat again, but in nowhere near the dramatic volumes that I had been throwing down the hatch prior to stepping on board. My daily diet now consisted of a bowl of watery soup and a bowl of watery porridge, the latter made with a couple of thimblefuls of oats. This Voyage to the Sun was proving to be one easy way to shed a stone.

One morning I spent a few moments chatting to Young-Looking Sunshine Boy, who told me how seasick he used to be when he first joined the ship.

'The worst was when I had to climb the rigging and ended up chundering all over the sails. When I made it back to deck, Gerhard made me go straight up again and of course the same thing happened. He wasn't impressed! Now I rely on suppositories . . .'

Later, while perusing the ship's noticeboard, I saw that the Greenwatch now appeared to have a team song. Its lyrics were pinned to the wall:

> I'd like to lead our members
> think the world give harmony.
> If we collapse for the wind, then
> we will lose a lot.

Hmm. Greenwatch had also listed their 'Team Goal':

1. To bring up the adaptability of our members among whom most are not tough enough to face the environmental challenge.
2. Through the course, to make everyone knows how to be a good leader and a good member as well.

Meanwhile, having free access to Bluewatch's fast-filling journal, I was able to keep abreast of their thoughts and feelings. In the section entitled 'BLUE WATCH PERSONAL GOALS', I read:

M.T. LIU
* Learn navigation without GPS
* Know more about marine engine
* Solve some important philosophical questions.

PIERCE [Lai Yin Ling]
* To take the challenges those we would never have in our community
* See the world by the way other than by air
* I know there will be tons of troubles and try if it will be fun.

KENNETH [Kwok Ka Chuen]
* To strengthen myself in both physically and psychologically.

GRACE [Chow Chua]
* Fully participate and grow.

YUMI
* Speak up and not be shy.

BRENDA [Loo Sau-Ting]
* Hand an experience in sailing
* Initiation to ask and practise (admit one's ignorance)
* Assurance of my endurance in failing challenge.

FRANKIE [Yau Man Kong]
* Release my fear in group meeting
* Be able to work as a team from multi-educational background which hopefully it will leave me educated this kind of background people do arrived later on of my life.

ERWIN [Chow Wai Ming]
* To understand my degree of endurance in outbound challenge
* To find out a better way to live in a situation of uncertainty.

A few pages later, Alfred (real name Wong Sek Keung) had written:

Impression on Those I hate so far:
* Not enough sleep
* Others doing so well.
Those I love so far:
* Got to know 12 good friends
* Jumping into the water.

Further on, Yumi had drawn a picture of two gaily smiling dolphins and had written in big, page-filling script:

> I saw Dolphins!! I achieved my 1st Goal!!
> I saw shooting stars!! and sparking jelly fish!!
> I achieved all my goals!!

Meanwhile Brunei-bred Elleys had written something a little more probing:

> Don't walk behind
> me I may not lead
> Don't walk in front
> of me I may not
> follow
> BUT WALK BY MY
> SIDE.

Beneath this, Alfred had felt prompted to scribble:

> pleased to learn from U . . .
> That's great!

Over the page, Alfred featured again – this time in thoughtful mood of his own:

> Life is a short journey . . . trying to
> get most out of it meaningfully . . .

Meanwhile, Erwin proved to be more down to earth:

> 2-HR HAND ON EXPERIENCE IS MUCH BETTER
> THAN 1-MONTH LESSON IN CLASSROOM
> YOU IMMEDIATELY FIND YR FAULT.

As both the weather and the state of my stomach slowly began to improve and the chances of sinking both literally and metaphorically became ever slimmer, I felt it was high time to find something else to start fretting about. So, apart from falling off the top of the eyrie-mast to certain death, or getting entangled and throttled by the obdurate tackle of such a big ship, I decided to concern myself with the hairy prospect of the ship being attacked by a good-for-nothing bunch of swashbuckling, cutlass-wielding pirates.

This might sound like I'd gone a bit overboard, or at least slipped off my rocker, but piracy, the scourge of shipping in the seventeenth and eighteenth centuries, was once again very much alive and kicking in the waters ranging from around South America and West and East Africa to the Far East. Of all the world's waters, the most dangerous were the island-studded seas off Indonesia and the Philippines (which, I might add, were a mere parrot-squawk away from the seas I was sailing), where hooded men, armed not with the throat-cutting cutlasses and shoulder-perched parrots of yore but with a vast arsenal of automatic rifles, rocket-propelled grenade launchers or anti-tank missiles, took ships by surprise. It was in these capriciously tempestuous South China Seas that entire cargoes, ranging from costly alloys to sugar, could disappear along with the ship that carried them. These vessels then reappeared as 'phantom' ships with forged documents and new names, taking aboard fresh cargo from unsuspecting shippers before vanishing over the horizon.

I had recently read a piece on piracy in *Time*, which described how armed men had stormed the 4594-tonne tanker *Suci* only six hours after it had left Singapore, bound for Borneo, with a cargo of diesel oil. In one swift move the pirates overpowered the bridge, tied up the crew, daubed out the ship's name and painted the funnel in new colours. The next morning, the crew was forced into a lifeboat and could only watch as the tanker, renamed *Glory II*, steamed off into the blue. The crew survived but the ship disappeared.

Other crew members have not been so lucky. In 1997, fifty seafarers were killed and thirty injured in piracy attacks worldwide. More than 400 crew members were held hostage that year. In all, there were 229 reported cases of piracy. According to the International Maritime Bureau, attacks by armed pirates rose 122 per cent during 1997/98. More than half happened in or around the South China Seas and fewer than 5 per cent of all the attacks resulted in arrest. Marauders completed most of their raids in less than thirty minutes. Alarmed by a fivefold increase in piracy over the past four years, Japan's shipping industry had been testing a device that could detect when a grappling-iron was thrown on deck: if a taut wire along the deck rail was stretched or cut, an alarm was triggered and floodlights illuminated the area.

I tried to think what *Ji Fung* was carrying that might be of some interest to warrant a surprise attacked from a band of not-so-Jolly-Rogering, machine-gun-wielding, modern-day cut-throat mutineers, but I couldn't think of anything – apart from my 1981 super-smooth Campagnolo leotard pedals and headset. Anyway, one whiff of forty-three mildew-rank pairs of feet was surely enough to keep any hint of piracy at bay.

And so it was that, without further incident, *Ji Fung* – the 'Spirit of Resolution, donated by the Royal Hong Kong Jockey Club to the Outward Bound trust of Hong Kong to enable them to carry the Outward Bound Challenge onto the China Seas' (so said the bronze-plaque inscription fixed to a carved ship's wheel on the mess room wall) – made it intact to Japan.

I felt in high and buoyant spirits when the familiar land of Okinawa materialised out of the brilliant, shimmering heat. Naha was the port where we were to moor overnight before heading for the northern island of Yakushima, still another three days' sail away.

As we approached Naha, Captain Greg told us that, before docking, we must 'dress' the ship with a bonanza of colourful flags from top to bottom, prow to aft. Along with this fiesta of streamers flapped the 'courtesy' flag on the foremast, the Outward Bound one on the main, the British ensign on the stern pole and the yellow-flag. The latter signalled our need to be cleared for a clean bill of health: we could not step ashore until we had permission to lower our yellow duster. It took from noon to 5 p.m. before Japanese quarantine, Customs and immigration officials finally gave us the go-ahead to reacquaint ourselves with our wobbly, sea-lubbing land-legs on what was not the firmest of all the earth's terra firmas (Japan has eighty-six active volcanoes packed into an archipelago smaller than California).

Captain Greg had issued us with five hours of 'shore leave', which gave us little time to find our feet and explore the hubbubbing streets of Naha before having to clock on board again at 10 p.m. Having been constantly sandwiched together in a confined space for days and days, I had presumed that everybody would be only too eager to 'do their own thing' and relish a breather from the voyage's almost suffocating companionship. I was wrong: the trainees filtered off through the gates of the port still glued together in their respective colour-coded teams.

Although I had been at sea for only a mere drop in the ocean compared with the true sea dogs of this water world, it was most definitely my all-time record and touching land again was a shaky experience. For the first few hours my world oscillated among solid waves of concrete and neon – those favourite old building blocks of earthquake-prone Japan. But being under the influence of a reeling gait didn't stop me from realising that, for the first time since leaving Hong Kong, I actually felt like eating. On setting foot and mouth back into a world of solidity, my appetite had returned in a flash. So, after paying a visit to a small supermarket, I sat in a park and munched my way through two carrier bagfuls of fattening fodder. After that, having regained at least half a stone in a matter of minutes, I felt ready and rearing to go. But to go where? I know, I thought, I'll go and visit Mrs Ota – the bed-and-TV-loving owner of a *minshuku* (guesthouse) in which I had stayed once or twice during my earlier cycle around Japan.

Despite being in an ugly city of cars and chaos and noise and throngs of people, it was so good to be on my own again and I trotted through the streets feeling free and happy of heart. Added to that was my elation at being back in Japan – very different to my emotions when I had first encountered this far-flung eastern land the previous year. Then, everything had been so odd, so alien, so inexplicable, so incomprehensible, so utterly weird. Now, despite still being all of these things, it was at the same time strangely and comfortingly familiar. The currency, the language, the food, the smells, the quirky mannerisms and endearing idiosyncrasies of the people – they were all something I recognised and was glad to be among.

During the previous winter back at home, I'd spent hours devouring as much information as I could about Japan. I scoured libraries and bookshops and book fairs and carboot sales for any reading material I could find. Half an hour's cycle away from home I had found Hideko Martin, a typically generous and warm-hearted Japanese woman, married to an English schoolteacher, and we had spent several afternoons together while she fired me with Japanese. Slowly the sounds, a lot of which were already familiar to me, had seeped through my system, spurring me on to say more and more. Now, back in Japan exactly a year after I had first stepped foot in this curious and complex land with not a word of the lingo to boot, it was reassuring to be able to string together ill-grammared sentences and hold ding-dong conversations with a people with whom I had been so enchanted.

Close to Mrs Ota's *minshuku*, I bought a bunch of flowers before scampering up the steps of her 'Marien House' to pay her a momentary visit. She was just where I'd left her all those months before: lying beneath her poster of Snoopy, surrounded by a medley of whirring fans and watching a raucous Japanese game show on the blaring TV set fixed to the foot of her hole-in-the-wall hospital-style bed.

She seemed surprised and then happy to see me and together we drank a pot of green tea while she told me about the typhoons, her hatred of life and her continuously injured ankle. Then, with only half an hour of shore leave left, I nodded and bowed and said goodbye and ran back through the blipping and buzzing streets, thinking that I would most likely never see Mrs Ota again in my life. But there again, maybe I would, because although she already looked like a wizened centenarian, who was to say that she wouldn't live for another few decades? Okinawa's weather and easy-going lifestyle supported what was believed to be the longest-lived population on earth: the Japanese were statistically the longest-lived people in the world, and Okinawans were the longest-lived people in Japan.

After three more days of choppy sailing up in the Okinawan archipelago we arrived at the isle of Yakushima, where the trainees were to embark on a land expedition and I was to find my wheels again. Thanks to Ken's tender care in stowing it beneath the wheelhouse among a padded bed of tarpaulins, my bike had sustained no damage during the storm apart from a hefty dose of salt corrosion on the chainset.

I packed up my panniers with tent and sleeping-bag and books and maps and tools and radio, and clothes still wet from the storm, and all the rest of my paraphernalia of 'essential' cycling and camping clobber. How different I was from William Empson, the poet, critic and teacher from Yorkshire who, on landing in Japan at the beginning of the 1930s, puzzled his hosts by arriving from England on the Trans-Siberian Railway with only a lemon and a pair of shoes in his luggage. He then puzzled them further by developing a tendency to fall out of rickshaws.

Finally, following an extended session of hearty hugs and farewells, I was away, bowling along the coast with the wind in my wheels again. Rediscovering the unique and spectacular sensation of self-propulsion was fantastic. Wind, humming spokes, spinning speed. Moving home, moving days, moving life on in one easy move. Freedom. Free to move where I wanted, when I wanted, if I wanted. No noise, no mess, no fuss. No itinerary. Just itinerancy. Anonymity. Simplicity. Heaven!

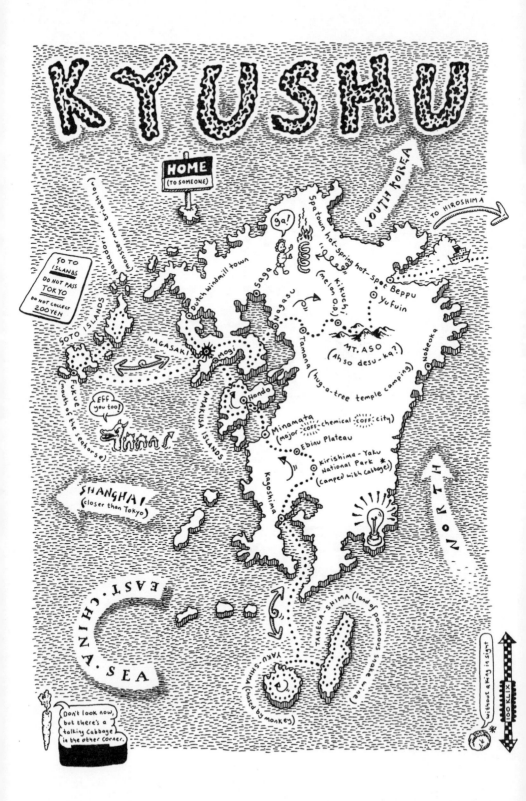

CHAPTER 4

Divine Mountains Embrace You Gently

After I'd spent a few days cycling and hiking in and around Yaku-shima, an island (*shima* means island) twenty-five kilometres across that rises like a cone from the sea, and after standing dwarfed by the giant thousand-year-old *yaku-sugi* cedar trees whose ancient and deeply grooved girths were as wide as windmills, I slipped sideways for a fleeting visit to the long, thin, low-lying island of Tanega-shima. Despite fading into pale topographical insignificance compared with the mountainous 2000-metre marvels of ragged, rough-hewn, rain-forested Yaku-shima, Tanega-shima features high in Japanese history as it was here that Japan first came into contact with Western technology.

In the summer of 1543, three Portuguese sailors were washed ashore in a Chinese junk after their ship had been destroyed in a storm. They became the first Europeans to set foot in Japan. The local bigwig, the *daimyo*, soon learned that they could bring down ducks out of the sky simply by pointing noisy metal tubes at the birds. The metal tube was an arquebus, a kind of musket, and its impact was sensational. The *daimyo* asked the Portuguese for lessons in shooting and bought a couple of 'arqs' for an exorbitant price. He then ordered a swordsmith to make reproductions and by 1560 firearms were being used in battle.

Today Tanega-shima is the location for another sort of explosive technology: an earth-tremoring, rocket-launching space research centre.

These two most northern of the Satsusan islands remain most memorable to

71

me not so much for their ancient trees or detonating history but because I was chased up a mountain by a boisterous male monkey on Yaku-shima, given a bunch of bananas and a box of *sushi* by a petrol-station attendant in Tanega-shima's main town of Nishinoomote, and offered a glass of *habuzake urume* – a sort of snake wine made in the normal *sake* fashion but with the addition of a coiled, deadly poisonous *habu* (snake) left whole within it which, over a period of ten years, slowly disintegrates into bones. The man in the noodle shop who offered it to me said that the wine was believed to enhance both stamina and sexual prowess. Even so, it was not a particularly hard decision to leave the poisonous *habu* stewing in its own unappetising juices in the glass.

And then it was back to sea, albeit briefly. A stormy four-and-a-half-hour ferry journey across the Osumi Straits to Kyushu delivered me back across Kinko Bay and into the volcano-dominated semi-tropical city of Kagoshima (the 'Naples of the Orient'), where I raced through the ash-laden rain along the seafront, past a garage offering a 'TUNE UP LUBE NOW' service, until I came to rest outside the familiar sight of the Honda family's *minshuku* – another of my earlier temporary homes, where I had offloaded my excess clobber the previous year. Here a futon awaited me, along with a pile of letters and books from home. After my first hot shower for weeks, I weighed myself and discovered that I'd shed one-and-a-half stone over the course of the turbulent voyage from Hong Kong.

Back in my room, despite being early summer, Mrs Honda had switched on a strange electrically heated grey square of carpet that lay sandwiched between the futon and *tatami* matting. Good for pressing shirts, I thought, had I had any. Instead, I pressed my socks – which, incidentally, dried a treat.

Among my letters was an Easter card from Yancho, a Bulgarian friend. I'd only met him once, as a result of a close shave I'd had with a dubiously drunken madman in Bourgas five years before. Yancho, who wrote to me on a remarkably regular basis, had an excellent grasp of English peppered with an enchanting turn of phrase. Beneath the card's Easter message (printed in Bulgarian), Yancho had written in careful hand:

> Health, Happiness, Hope,
> Hilarious disposition!

Once Mrs Honda had finished loading me down with riceballs wrapped in *nori* (seaweed) and giant too-rosy-red-to-be-real Fuji apples (at around £4 apiece), I took off out of Kagoshima, heading north along the horrendous traffic-pounding National Route 10, all the time being watched over by the brooding silhouette of Sakurajima, the city's very own Vesuvius, which has erupted at least thirty times.

My first obstacle was a tunnel too dark and fast and full of stampeding vehicles for me to ride on the road, forcing me on to a dangerously open ridge of kerb that ran alongside a blackened, fume-stained inner wall. The kerb was not only too narrow to ride along with a heavily pregnant-bagged bicycle but also too narrow to push along in any position other than from behind – an awkward technique that necessitated lying across my saddle in order to steer with out-stretched arms as my legs paddled along from the rear.

Unbearable heat and humidity, choking pollution, head-splitting noise and inconveniently sharp signal boxes planted at regular intervals that required me to heave my bike over them without tumbling into the path of a thunderous *torakku* (truck) didn't make for a pleasant start to the day's ride. But in Japan, every strugglesome moment seems to be outshone by one of heart-warming generosity. As I emerged into the brilliance of day at the other end of the tunnel, a bottled-water salesman pulled over and, with a spontaneous bow, gave me eight litres of chilled mountain water from the back of his van.

I noticed that the water had been bottled from the underground sources at Mount Kirishima, part of the Kirishima-Yaku National Park (consisting of twenty-three volcanic peaks, fifteen intact craters and ten crater lakes) – the very park I was heading for that night. It proved to be a pleasant taster of things to come.

The ride, though hot and hard and upward, improved dramatically when I veered off Route 10 at the first opportunity. Prolific birdsong and an abundance of wildflowers with their bountiful aromas made the unpleasantness of the tunnel seem a world away. At last, greenness prevailed over concrete. I arrived on the fringes of Kirishima in the late afternoon; the sun had already slid behind the mountains, sending the plunging valleys into deep shadows of exquisite cool compared with the panting, broiling sauna of the day.

On the look-out for a suitable place to camp in an area of either rocky or vertical or cultivated or inhabited unsuitability, I spotted a small tent-sized space sitting beside someone's vegetable plot. I rang the doorbell of the nearest house to the plot. The sliding front door was opened, after a long pause and an even longer slipper-footed shuffle, by an old man in a white vest and baggy white pantaloons. Behind him I caught sight of his wife, kneeling on the *tatami* at a table laden with food. Understandably, they both looked most surprised to find a dusty *gaijin* (foreigner) at their door. Scraping around for the best of my shaky Japanese, I explained that I'd just cycled up from Kagoshima and asked if it would be possible to camp by the vegetable plot, as I was feeling a bit weary.

After a lot of sucking in of air through teeth (a habit in Japan that usually signifies difficulty) and throaty exhalations of amazement, the man told me in his inimitable way to, please, help myself. No sooner had I erected my home and crawled inside (with that immensely contented sensation that sends a happy tingle surging through your system when you have secured a good, safe camp-spot after a tiring day's ride) than the man's slipper-footed wife came calling at my door, loaded with a tray of food.

'*Dozo, dozo*,' she said.

Knowing that she meant 'please, take it', I did not need much persuasion. The woman said something else about me being all alone, and on a bicycle, and all the mountains and the strength of my legs, before disappearing with a little bow.

Just as I was swallowing my last mouthful of rice and tentacle of some deep-fried unidentifiable sea creature, the woman reappeared and invited me in to use her shower and *furo* (bath). Half an hour later, having scrubbed and washed away the last of my sweaty, tunnel-stuck grime down the drain, I emerged from the *furo* rejuvenated and shiny-skinned, only to find that Mr and Mrs Slipperfoot were now urging me to sleep inside their house. I tried my best to assure them that they had been more than helpful enough already and that I would be fine in my tent. After a lot of '*dozo, dozo*' on their part and several insistent responses of 'no, no, really, really, I'll be okay' on mine, they finally relented and allowed me to sleep beside their copious spring cabbages and other brassicas – but not before Mr Slipperfoot had placed his mobile phone in my hands.

'For safety during the night,' he said.

'Safety?' I said, with a raised eyebrow. With the aid of a rapid flick through my mini Japanese dictionary, I asked whether he thought I was putting myself in danger by sleeping with his vegetables.

'*Hai, hai!*' he confirmed, looking genuinely concerned. 'Maybe there is danger.'

Giving me his number, he showed me how to ring him up in the night if I needed help. In such an unlikely event, I thought, would it not be easier simply to walk (or run, depending on the state of urgency) the ten strides from tent to house to bang on his door? And anyway, in the very unlikely chance that I should find myself peering down the wrong end of a barrel (according to the latest statistics, the numbers of annual gun-related deaths per 10 million people were: United States, 1424; Scotland, 54; England and Wales, 41; Japan, 5), what was I supposed to do? Would my would-be assailant be patient if I said, 'Hold on, matey – before you proceed any further, be so good as to bear with me while I quickly get on the mobile to let my elderly cabbage-growing neighbour know that I'm on the point of being shot'?

More to the point, how many people would entrust to a stranger who had come knocking on their door a piece of flashy and not cheap technological equipment and let them take it away with them for the night? I found such spontaneous trust astounding. I mean, either I looked as innocently benign as a sheep in stripy cycling shorts, or else I was just a lot more cynically suspicious and sour about the goodwill of mankind than they were.

To keep the solicitous Mr and Mrs Slipperfoot content about my nocturnal welfare, I gratefully accepted their offering and agreed to ring them during the night should anything untoward happen to me. Of course, nothing did happen to me (apart from nearly measuring my length when tripping over a wayward cabbage on my way to an unearthly-hour pee) but I did coincidentally hear on the Far East Network (FEN) that at least two Japanese telecom firms were thinking of developing a mobile phone for pets. They believed there was a potentially huge market for such a phone among owners who felt guilty about leaving their dogs or cats at home alone. The telecom companies were said to be working on prototypes of pet mobiles to be fitted to animals' collars. The mobiles would be activated without the need to press any buttons, so that the owners could make reassuring calls to their animals from the office and be comforted in return by familiar barks, or miaows, in response. Oh dear. And to think that there are people starving in this world.

The following morning I left at dawn (minus the mobile) in order to pay a visit to Kirishima Jinja before the peace-posing, *chiizu*-grinning, photographing masses arrived. The site of the giant *sugi*-pine-shadowed *jinja* (shrine) dated back to the sixth century and the present structure was a surprisingly old (by Japanese standards) 1715 rendition. A rock that sat near the steps leading up to the main part of the shrine was mentioned in Japan's national anthem: it was clearly not just any rock and it symbolised, in its solidly rock-like way, how the Japanese people could form a stronger nation by sticking together as a group, rather than acting as individuals like those of us in the self-centred West.

From the shrine, I embarked on cycling up a virtually vertical road festooned with blazing bushes of magnificent flushed-pink azaleas, leading me to the foot of dome-shaped Mount Takachiho. I was now, according to a tourist brochure I'd picked up, in the 'heart of the park of birthplace of myth'. Apparently this was where the first Emperor of Japan had been born. According to legend, Ninigi-No-Mikito, grandson of the sun-goddess Amaterasu (to whom the Kirishima *jinja* is dedicated), threw his sword from

76

the home of the gods and it landed on the peak of Mount Takachiho. Ninigi-No-Mikito then descended to earth with eight other gods to rule over the land that was later to become Japan.

My glossy Kirishima tourist brochure was written with a lyrically gushy turn of phrase, the like of which I had never come across before. 'DIVINE MOUNTAINS EMBRACE YOU GENTLY' were the words emblazoned on the gleaming front cover. And inside I found:

kaleidoscopic, magnificent nature pictures four seasons . . . The story of Historic Daybreak Described . . . The hot springs in Kirishima are embraced by mountains, just like being hugged by mother . . . Pleasure spreads out on the map and the knapsack is full of joy.

Loading my micro-knapsack (foldable and stowable) not so much with 'joy' as with water bottles, waterproofs, fleece, camera, mini tripod, bananas and sweet rice cakes, I set out to scale the red-grey, shaly, volcanic stoned slopes of Mount Takachiho, whose mighty conical head loomed high above its lower-slope skirtings of brilliant fuschia-fired azaleas.

I had imagined that the route of the climb would resemble an unbroken chain of marching sightseers stampeding up and down this venerable mount, as seen on Fuji. But as I slipped and slid my way up the steep scarp, the only people I saw were what appeared to be half the Japanese army descending together with impressive speed and with cheerful cries of '*Konnichiwa! Konnichiwa!*' (Hello! Hello!), '*Ganbatte!*' (Have strength!) and 'Harrow America!' (which needs no interpretation). Among them was a bowing man clad in a sugar-candy cardigan, wrapping-paper tie and slippery-soled, spit-clean black office shoes. This bespectacled man gawped at me for a moment before suddenly bursting out triumphantly, 'Please you my country. Thankyouvellymuch!'

I had no idea why this man decided to thank me, as all I had done was to appear in front of him up a spectacularly slithery mountain. But sometimes, and in some places in life, that is apparently enough.

Once past the candy-cardigan man, I was out on a limb on my own. An hour or so of steady climbing (and slipping), past the striking blood-red and black delineations of the lunar crevasses that carved into the bullet-straight volcanic scarp like a mountainous fusion of giant Liquorice Allsorts, took me up the sharp slopes to the windy raw edge of the caldera rim. After wandering around the edge of the volcanic basin, I decided to forge ahead to tackle Takachiho's

1574-metre peak, which I know is but a molehill compared with real mountaineering matter but I still felt as if I was on my way to conquering some
distant Himalayan peak.

To reach Takachiho's peak entailed scaling a much steeper and much more
shaly red-rocky incline than the one I'd just struggled up. It was definitely a
hands-and-feet job: for every step forward I slipped back four. Wearing a pair
of tatty trainers didn't help. I had to keep stopping to tip out the quarry-loads
of loose chippings that insisted on spilling in over the sides and under my soles.
A pair of robust walking boots would have been nice, but then so would have
a turbo-boost and a cup of tea. Anyway, this was pretty elementary stuff –
simple safe fun. (How many mountain rescuers, I wonder, have heard that
one before?)

Soon I was standing abrim with euphoria on Takachiho's top, admiring a
melodramatic view that encompassed volcanic lakes and valleys and forests and
foothills and plains and sea – and, in the distance, the grand smoking volcanic
cone of Kagoshima's ash-pluming Sakurajima. Beside me flapped the Rising Sun
ensign of this tremulous land, while on the other side, rearing up out of a small
monumental pile of rocks, rose the Amano Sakahoko – the 'inverted halberd'
which, as one of Japan's legends has it, was brought from heaven.

The object of most interest that stood upon this peak was a hefty wooden
hut. As I approached it the heavy door suddenly opened and out stepped a
diminutive old man, as thin as a chicken's neck, wearing a pair of slip-on sandals. On an intricate metal frame attached to his back he carried a strange
contraption that looked like a cross between a microwave and an anti-tank mis-
sile. Appearing unsurprised by the unexpected sight of a 'foreign devil' (as we
gaijin are known), he bid me a cheery '*Konnichiwa!*' before scuttling off down
the slippery scree with remarkable speed and agility for a man of such age bearing a load so cumbersome.

I had a brief scout around the hut, peering at walls and floors of paraphernalia and memorabilia that bore a connection with the reverence accorded to
this spot, over which the mighty shrine of Kirishima once used to preside,
before taking off in slip-sliding fashion back down the mountain, sustaining
several spills along the way but no major injuries.

Half an hour before sunset, I arrived back at my bike. The car park was
quiet; the gift shops were all closed for the night. After doing my ablutions in
the gents (the ladies was locked), I ventured into the nearby woods to lay
myself to rest beneath the simple pleasures of a canvas home (rip-stop nylon,
in fact) around which strange birds chattled and whooped and inquisitive deer

sniffed and tripped. By 9 p.m. I was lost in a dream that saw me trying to teach a classroom of old men in party hats how to make mashed potato.

My curious culinary dreams were rudely interrupted shortly after 1 a.m. when I awoke with a start to the menacing and eerie sounds of a car being thrown skidding and slamming and revving and screeching at joy-riding hot-rodding speed for nearly an hour around the dark and deserted car park. When the mountains were returned to their rightful reassuring solid silence, I fell into a fitful spud-free sleep.

Kirishima's 'Park of Birthplace of Myth' held me captivated for the next few days. I happily discovered that, as the tourist brochure had promised, 'the hot springs are embraced by mountains', though I wasn't so sure about the 'just like being hugged by mother' bit. Basing myself with three motorcyclists at a rocky campground in the village of Ebino high up on the Ebino-kogen Plateau, I spent many enjoyable hours wallowing in the steamy and sulphurous waters of numerous hot springs and shouldering my 'knapsack full of joy' as I hiked along the full length of the undulating ridge of Kirishima's volcanoes, whose 'pleasure spreads out on the map' as well as in the mind.

Dropping off the Ebino Plateau towards Kyushu's west coast involved a fast, thrill-laden wheeled descent of curling hairpins and free-falling, heart-stopping, vertiginous straights that at one point logged 52 mph (23 kph) on my on-board computer. That night I camped in an open-sided, corrugated lean-to adjoining a small, hill-chiselled shrine. Fronting the shrine was a dusty *gatta-ballo* pitch for Japanese croquet. A shabby playground, consisting of a squeaky set of rusty blue swings, was tucked in the corner near my tent.

Just before sunset, a young mother brought her two little daughters to play on the swings. At first none of them were quite sure what to make of the strange *gaijin* whose head was poking out of a tent in their playground, but once I had fully emerged from my dwelling with a smile, and a number of tongue-tied Japanese words and phrases, they all fell about in giggles, the girls bubbling with delight when I gave them a push on the swings. Finally the mosquitoes forced us to move – me back to my sweaty tented abode and them back to their home.

I had been asleep for about an hour when I awoke to hear a soft patter of feet trotting across the playground. Two familiar little faces peered at me through my mosquito-netted door.

'*Sumimasen,*' they piped apologetically, '*dozo, dozo.*'

A can of iced tea and four hot seaweed-wrapped riceballs covered in foil were placed on my mat.

'*Oyasumi-nasai!*' they called to bid me goodnight, before scampering off back home.

A midnight feast seemed like a good idea and so I propped myself up on an elbow to eat and tuned in for an English-speaking station on the radio. VOA (Voice of America) crackled into life along the shortwaves. As I swallowed a riceball I learnt that animal rights activists had convinced sponsors of a Californian rodeo to cancel an event that called for teams of three men to wrestle with 500-pound steers, the idea being that, once the animals had been knocked to the ground, the teams tried to slip women's underwear on them.

Next stop: Minamata, a bustling port city on Kyushu's west coast which, following the Second World War, became infamous when the booming Chisso Corporation made a bid to turn this then sleepy fishing town into a world-class producer of chemical products. In the process, the company dumped vast quantities of waste containing diabolically high levels of methyl-mercury into the bay, poisoning millions of fish and tens of thousands of people and creating an unmitigated environmental calamity.

The lethal cancer caused by exposure to the heavy metals by way of improper safeguards and handling, resulting in a high incidence of illness and birth defects, became officially recognised in the late 1960s and 1970s – symptoms that became known as Minimata disease. The Chisso Corporation's ruthless efforts to suppress the disaster resulted for a while in Minimata becoming worldwide news and the only promising thing that came out of the catastrophe was the galvanisation of the people to launch the Japanese environmental movement.

With Nagasaki calling, I didn't linger for long in Minimata but caught a series of small ferries that swept me off to Hondo-shi via an interesting medley of islands. From there I wheeled along the pleasant coastal route of the island of Amakusa – a ride that was particularly notable for meeting my first *gaijin* since stepping ashore from the stomach-heaving *Ji Fung*. Eric was a Californian from Huntington Beach. He was also on a bicycle – an unladen one.

'Jeez,' he said when he pulled broadside, 'are you loaded or what? Where're you headin'?'

'Hokkaido,' I said, 'via Nagasaki.'

'Hokkaido? With all that? You crazy?'

'I don't think so,' I said. 'Anyway, where are you off to?'

'Me? Oh, not far. I'm just rollin' on home.'

'How long have you been living here?' I asked.

'A few months now. You heard of JET – the Japanese Exchange and Teaching Programme? I'm here with that, teaching English at the local school.'

Thinking of all the surrounding sea and islands and isolated islets to explore, I remarked that Amakusa must be a great place to be posted.

'Well, actually,' he said, 'I'm not really enjoying myself. It's kind of lonely out here. I'd rather be in a city any day. I'm just looking forward to the day I head on home.'

I asked him if he spoke any Japanese.

'No,' he said, 'I can't get motivated.'

And that was that. At least I thought it was.

'Hey, you know you're real welcome to come and crash out at my place if you want. Get a dry night before rainy season strikes.'

'Rainy season?' I said, not liking what I was hearing. 'And when is it predicted to start?'

'Tomorrow.'

'Tomorrow? Oh.'

In the event, I opted to camp.

I awoke on a wave-lashed shore to the sound of steady drizzle. Visibility was down to about a foot in front of my wheel.

The 9.40 a.m. ferry from Tomioka to Mogi carved its chugging way through a dirty cotton-wool world of thick, pressing fog. When I landed on the other side, everything was murky, damp, dripping.

Nagasaki sat over the mountains – not far, if I could see where I was going. I found a road and followed it. Gingerly. The road went up. Nothing too bad. Really quite pleasant, not being able to see how high I had to go. My mind muffled by mist. Everything strangely silent for such a noisy world. I spun onwards, upwards. Feeling my way. Careful of the edge I couldn't see. Knowing it would hurt if I found it. Despite the fog, despite the damp, the sweat continued to course. Wearing nothing up a mountain. Sweating in a saturating mist.

Then, with the top popped, and a sudden drop, the world burst back into brilliant sunshine and, feeling very hot and a little stunned, I landed in the midst of the blinding colour and blasting noise of Nagasaki. A furious pace of people. Suicidal cars from all directions. Trams, too, their cavernous metal tracks a trap for my loaded wheels – especially wheels that didn't know where they were going. Simultaneously navigating the neon, the concrete, the crowds, the converging city. Not easy. But fun.

Where to sleep? Remembering a place that had been recommended to me the previous year by a man I had met at Fuji, I turned up (not without a spot of navigational difficulty) at the door of Minshuku Tanpopo – a place I'd particularly remembered on account of the translation of its name: Sunflower. Sleeping in a sunny-sounding sort of place seemed like a nice idea in a city long associated with anything but sunshine and flowers.

The *minshuku* was owned by Naome and Akihiro Maotutake, a lively young couple who lived on the ground floor along with an assortment of numerous relations. Compared with other *minshuku*, where I had slept in one of the family's hastily vacated rooms along with selections of toys, lines of washing and unappealing armies of free-range cockroaches, the Tanpopo, with its floors of door-numbered rooms, was more a family hotel than a family home.

My *tatami* room, with futon and cushion and table and tea things, was compact, clean and comfortable. A sliding glass door opened on to a sliver of sunny balcony, which I immediately utilised by stringing up all my washing. Although I discovered that the Tanpopo was listed in a tourist leaflet (which described Nagasaki as 'an exotic city with a rich foreign culture and ten million-dollars night-time panorama'), the *minshuku*, judging from the rows of heavy, dust-scuffed boots lining the entry stairs and the raucous laughter and energetic splashing emanating from the bathroom, appeared to be mostly full of workmen.

That said, I did meet three foreigners – all Dutch. One, who was travelling independently of the other two, was a young lad who had recently come to Japan as part of a university exchange. He was studying nuclear engineering – perhaps not such a rosy occupation in the A-bombed city of Nagasaki.

The other *gaijin* from The Netherlands were two matronly women on a week's rushed tour of Japan's major cities. I first met them while brushing my teeth at the third-floor corridor's communal basins. With a mouthful of tooth-paste, I asked them how they liked Japan. They replied that they found the Japanese pastime of sitting and sleeping on floors instead of in chairs and beds was quite objectionable.

'And also,' said one of the women, 'we have decided that the reason the Japanese do not bother to speak English is because they think they are a far superior race.'

This sense of superiority kept popping up all over the place. A survey had revealed that more than half of the country's teenagers believed that the Japanese were superior to other races. Among foreigners it was sometimes felt that, in the past, the Japanese had helped to create a mystique surrounding their culture and that the reason they had openly argued that they were different was to protect their domestic markets. Some of those supposed differences had been cited in the *Harvard Business Review*:

- In 1978, the Japanese government had refused to permit imports of American-made blood analysers because, it asserted, the Japanese had 'different' blood.
- In 1986, the Ministry of International Trade and Industry had attempted to prevent US and European ski manufacturers from selling their products in Japan because Japan had 'different' snow.
- In 1987, US beef imports to Japan had been limited because Japanese people's intestines were a 'different' length from those of other people.
- In 1990, the Japanese had tried to keep out US lumber exports because the wood wouldn't be able to withstand Japanese earthquakes, which were 'different' from American ones.

Nagasaki, a slightly less ugly Japanese city than most and geographically closer to Shanghai than to Tokyo, was one of the few that I could name before I ever went to Japan. Along with Hiroshima, the very word 'Nagasaki' evoked apocalyptic images of nuclear destruction – images that, until recently, had been marketed as gifts at the US National Atomic Museum in the shape of $20 silver earring replicas of 'Little Boy' and 'Fat Man', the bombs dropped on Hiroshima and Nagasaki.

Apart from the horrors of the bomb, I knew nothing else about the city. During the days I spent tramping along the meandering streets that lay at the head of the deeply indented and beautiful Nagasaki Bay, I discovered that the city possessed an intriguing and varied history.

Although the Chinese and Japanese had traded for centuries through Nagasaki, it wasn't until the Portuguese chose it as a base for commercial activity and missionary work in about 1570 that the place turned into something more than a remote fishing village. Before long, Nagasaki had developed into a bustling port for Portuguese, Spanish, English, Dutch, Korean, Chinese and, later, Russian trade. Along with this industrious, multi-cultural hotchpotch arrived hundreds of merchants and craftsmen and labourers from other parts of Japan, eager to partake in the bountiful harvests of foreign trade.

With the Iberians had come Jesuit and Franciscan missionaries, whose Christian religion was enthusiastically embraced by thousands of Nagasakian converts, including high-ranking *daimyo*. By now no doubt feeling a little complacent, the Catholic priests began to pry into the affairs of state, especially concerning the court of Kyoto. By the time Japan's first national shogun, Hideyoshi Toyotomi, had recognised the potential political power of the Jesuits as rivals to shogun rule, the Jesuits were virtually running Nagasaki, whose citizens were by then overwhelmingly *Kirishitans* (Christians). Feeling that these Jesuits were getting way too cocky for their boots, Hideyoshi clamped down, expelling them from the country. As a warning to the people of Nagasaki, Hideyoshi had twenty-six martyrs (six foreign missionaries and twenty Japanese converts, including three children) crucified on a hill above the city.

After surviving for nearly forty years in Japan, the alien creed was outlawed. Those who continued to practise their faith (known as the Hidden Christians) did so on penalty of torture and death if their practises became known. The Japanese wives and children of foreigners were deported, and the Catholic

Portuguese and Spanish traders were expelled in favour of the Protestant Dutch, who had demonstrated that their interest in Japan was trade, not religion.

In 1639, soon after a bloody rebellion, Japan decided it had had it up to its neck with all these interfering and meddlesome Johnny Foreigners and slammed its doors shut, effectively isolating the country from the rest of the world for more than two centuries. The determination of the Tokugawa government to prevent any possible dabblings with foreign barbarians was so strict that shipbuilding in Japan was limited to boats that could navigate only in its own coastal waters. Any individual attempt to escape from the country was punishable by death. All foreigners were banned and Japanese were forbidden to travel overseas – even Japanese sailors who had been blown off course and touched down in foreign parts were put to death on their return, as the government considered them to be tainted.

Throughout this self-imposed period of seclusion, there was a tiny chink of light through a very narrow window on the rest of the world. The Japanese did permit the continued operation of a small, unprofitable Dutch trading mission post – as long as it remained within the confines of Dejima, a little island on the eastern coast of Nagasaki Bay (now a reclaimed part of the mainland). A small bridge connecting the island with the mainland was guarded by sentries at either end. The Dutch were allowed to bring in only one ship a year for the exchange of goods. Dejima, 'home' to seldom more than a score of Dutchmen at any one time, was off-limits to ordinary Japanese – with the sole exception of Nagasakian courtesans, as the clog-clad, flat-landed and apparently highly undomesticated foreigners were forbidden to bring their wives with them. As one nineteenth-century inmate put it: 'How could the Dutch residents otherwise manage to procure any domestic comfort in the long nights of winter, their tea water, for instance, were it not for these women?'

The main commodities for the Dutch traders were porcelain and lacquerware. If the word 'japan' was used in eighteenth-century England, it usually referred not to the country but to lacquer. To say that something had been 'japanned' meant that it had been lacquered in the Japanese way.

During this long period of seclusion, Edo (later Tokyo) mushroomed into one of the largest cities on earth. Japanese culture flourished and evolved into one of the world's most distinctive civilisations but the country was still a formidable society of lords, ladies, sword-wielding warriors, peasants and plebeians, whose like had not been seen in the West for many generations. The isolation lasted right up to the 1850s, when the American Commodore Perry arrived with his menacing 'black warships' and delivered an ultimatum to the ageing Tokugawa Shogunate to open up Japan, or else . . .

Introspective Japan decided that maybe it was time to shake a leg and stretch its wings and at last offered itself to the outside world. The Tokugawa Shogunate fell, parliamentary government was set up in its place and the country rapidly modernised and industrialised itself. Victorious in war against China in 1895 and against Russia in 1904/5, the Japanese speedily emerged on the international scene as a formidable people – highly disciplined and educated, and hell-bent on not only catching up with but surpassing the West at its own fun and games of industrial and military hegemony. This nationalistic fervour would lead the Japanese to the disastrous debacle of the Second World War.

One morning I left my bike at the Sunflower Inn, picked up picnic supplies at the nearby Joyfull Sun supermarket and walked over the Urakami-gawa River to the Peace Park. It was teeming with crowds and whistle-blowing bus tour guides and gaggles of giggling schoolchildren asking me to join them in their *chiizu*-grinning photographs, all of which, combined with a skull-rattling collection of pneumatic drills and earth diggers, made for a far from Peaceful Park.

Apart from all the noise, the park was dominated by the Peace Statue, a huge pedestal-seated bronze monument depicting a man resembling a cross between Goliath and a policeman on traffic duty. His right hand pointed heavenwards, signalling the threat from the atomic bomb; his left hand extended to the horizon, symbolising world peace.

Thousands of garlands of rainbow-coloured paper cranes (representing the Japanese bird of peace and longevity) festooned the barriers at the foot of the statue so prolifically that they resembled bushy hedges of kaleidoscopic leaves. On the other side of the building site spouted the Peace Fountain, built to commemorate the A-bombed victims who died from horrific burns while pleading for water.

Following in the slipstream of the clamorous masses, I passed from the Peace Park to the 'Hypocentre' of the plutonium bomb blast. 'Fat Man' (three times more powerful than the uranium 'Little Boy' dropped three days earlier on Hiroshima) had landed about three kilometres off target at 11.02 a.m. on 9th August 1945. Early that morning when the B-29 bomber named the Bockscar (after its former pilot, Captain Bock) had set off with its atomic-bomb load from the Timean airbase in the Mariana Islands, its target had been Kokura – an industrial city on the north-east coast of Kyushu. Fortuitously for its inhabitants, dense cloud covered Kokura. After circling the city three times, unable to see what they were trying to destroy, the *Bockscar* headed for its second target: Nagasaki.

Arriving at 10.58 a.m. the B-29 crew, with only enough fuel for one run over the city, discovered that it was not their day. Nagasaki, like Kokura, was covered with cloud. However, flying at 30,000 feet, the bombers suddenly spotted the Mitsubishi Arms Factory through a small crack in the clouds and unloaded their deadly cargo.

In the event, their bomb missed the port's industrial base (including the vast Mitsubishi shipyards) and exploded instead way off course over the Urakami valley in Nagasaki's northern suburbs. The resulting explosion, which a witness described as 'instantly mimicking the appearance of another sun', ripped through the valley, incinerating forests, pulverising buildings and claiming tens of thousands of lives in moments. A sign at the epicentre lists the devastating facts and figures:

DEAD:	73,884
INJURED:	74,909
PEOPLE LEFT HOMELESS:	120,820
(*number of dwellers whose houses were completely destroyed or burnt within a radius of 4 km*)	
HOUSES DAMAGED:	18,409
(*number of houses within a radius of 4 km – 36 per cent of all houses in the city*)	
HOUSES ENTIRELY DESTROYED:	1,326
(*within a radius of 1 km*)	
HOUSES PARTIALLY DESTROYED:	5,509
(*within a radius of 4 km*)	
LAND COMPLETELY LEVELLED:	2.59 sq km

Of those injured, it has been estimated that another 75,000 subsequently died as a result of their injuries. The numbers of those left homeless represented half the total population of 240,000 people.

Horrific as it was, it could have been even worse. Thanks to the shielding effect of the steep, dome-like mountains that surround the city on the north, west and east, Nagasaki (unlike Hiroshima) was not completely flattened and those living just over the hills were spared. This, together with the fact that the bomb had fallen several kilometres short of its target, had saved the harbour area and most of Nagasaki's old central neighbourhoods from destruction.

Moving a few paces away from the epicentre, I came across a scorched and crumbled brick wall adorned with headless statues of saints. This was all that remained of Urakami Catholic Cathedral (once the largest church in the East), which missed a direct hit by mere metres. Close by, the spot was marked with a stark black obelisk.

Things turned even more depressing when, passing a vivid sculpture depicting anguished and tormented mothers surrounded by the dismembered bodies of their children, I entered the ugly International Culture and Peace Hall that houses the Atomic Bomb Museum. Bearing an ever-heavying mood about the insane and wholly incomprehensible follies of mankind, I wandered in a dazed state through the multiple floors of exhibits displaying explicit photographs, reports, relics, artefacts, equipment and poignant details of the blast and its 150,000 victims.

Exhibits bore sombre labels: 'Damages Caused by Fire'; 'Damages Caused by Heat Rays'; 'Damages Caused by Blast Wind'; 'Damages Caused by Radiation'. One section illustrated the growth of the fireball over Nagasaki, which reached its full radius of 787 feet (240 metres) in just one second. The temperature at the point of the explosion shot instantaneously to several million degrees centigrade, the estimated surface temperature of the ground beneath the fireball reaching between 3000 and 4000°C. Unable to imagine such heat, these estimates were inconceivable to me until I read that the surface temperature of the sun is approximately 6000°C. The bomb was not much short of a miniature sun. A man-made sun to kill man. Mad man. Crazy world.

I shuffled along in front of cabinets and displays which seemed to contain every possible recoverable remnant from the devastation: melted scraps of warped and distorted metal, fragments of scorched and deformed concrete and brick, tortuous shards of melted glass, burnt and shattered roof tiles, a priest's robe perforated like a colander by shredded showers of flying glass and shrapnel, a clock stopped at 11.02 a.m. (the precise time of the explosion), a woman's kimono with its design scorched off the back, a partially melted lunchbox, a pair of seared spectacles (the only identifiable remains of a doctor who had simply been incinerated). There was also a buckled metal girder from the Mitsubishi Iron and Steel works – the factory that made, and continues to make, armaments. Paradoxically, Nagasaki, a staunchly pacifist and vigorously anti-nuclear city, is the company town of one of Japan's major weapon manufacturers.

Beneath the photograph of the charred wreck of the ammunition plant (operated then almost entirely by women and children) there was no mention as to what went on, or continues to go on there. Nowhere did the museum provide any historical context or background, or attempt to say anything about the reasons for the war. Nor were there any comparisons made with other mass wartime killings of civilians, such as those committed by Japan in China.

But, there again, why should there have been? The Rape of Nanking, Dresden, the Blitz, the carpet-bombing of virtually all Japan's major cities, the atomic bomb – all unimaginable horrors in their own right, but the museum wasn't about disasters that had happened elsewhere. It was about Nagasaki, and the immense atrocity that befell that city. Did it really matter what had happened before? Did it really matter what heinous barbarities the Japanese army was responsible for? Maybe, maybe not. The fact remained that, for whatever reason (such as the estimated quarter of a million US servicemen whose lives might have been lost had the Americans invaded Japan instead), a bomb of indescribable horror had been dropped out of the sky over Nagasaki. And that, no matter whose side you might be on, is a monstrous thing to have happened.

On the walls of the museum hung photographs taken of the aftermath – shocking scenes of virtual annihilation: a decimated and alien environment of smouldering rubble strewn with ragged and scorched-black bodies whose grotesquely burnt and mutilated limbs had set rigid in outlandish poses, like twisted shop mannequins pulled from the ashes. Around the corpses lay people of all ages, barely alive, their bodies covered in blood and filth, clothes ripped and ragged, vast areas of skin burnt clean away revealing grotesque wounds – raw and sticky, blasted by the horrific fire of radiation.

Leaving the museum in a daze, I walked back outside into the intense humidity and on through the Peace Park. A couple of chubby schoolgirls, whispering and giggling behind their hands, trailed me for a while before picking up courage to hand me a necklace of paper cranes that they had made, and a can of energising Pocari Sweat.

After they had scampered back to the safe company of their sailor-suited chums, I mopped my brow and sat drinking my Sweat beneath the shade of a rustling palm. Mind miles away, I picked up one of the tree's fallen fronds that lay brittle like a blade on the ground beside me and thought: in the Peace Park with a piece of palm in my hand. After the bomb, it was said that nothing would grow for 500 years, but even at the epicentre the grass grew back fairly fast. Man maybe mad, but this weird wide world is made of more sensible and resilient stuff.

I spent the next few days moseying around the old neighbourhoods of Nagasaki's crowded residential blocks tied together by a tangle of cobblestone lanes and twisting alleyways paved with weathered flagstones and overlooked by immense camphor trees. A topsy-turvy audience of old wooden homes sat shouldering each other on the steep hillsides like the stepped tiers of a grand amphitheatre encircling the harbour.

Strange and not-so-strange sights came and went. First I saw Maganebashi ('Spectacles Bridge'), the double-arched stone bridge which, if the water level of the Nakashimagawa (the narrow canal that cuts through the heart of the city) is at the right height, sends a goggle-like reflection upon the river. Near the epicentre, I found the 'One-legged Torii' (shrine entrance gate) of the Sanno Shinto-gu Shrine – the only leg or, for that matter, the only part of not just the gateway but the whole of the shrine that still stood today as it had stood at the time of the blast, when the rest of the shrine had collapsed in a heap around it. The gaudy Gaudí-ish church of San Philippo, constructed from slabs of ferro-concrete, its phallic twin spires covered in a curious mosaic of colourful pottery chippings (depicting faith, hope and charity) twisting into the sky: incongruously, inside, on a model of a mountain, stood a vast silver Buddhist goddess demonstrating that, typically of Japan, two opposites (here religions) can clash together in happy oddity. Beside the Oura Catholic Church, the oldest church in Japan (built in 1864 by French missionaries), sat a spanking new church that had incorporated a shopping mall in its basement.

After clamping surprised eyes upon the Las Vegas-style shopping-mall church, I headed for Fukusai-ji Zen Temple, thinking that it might bring me a little more down to earth. The original temple, however, built in 1628, had been destroyed by fire from the bomb blast; and its 1979 reconstruction, built totally unlike the original (as the Japanese are wont to do), took me by surprise. Also known as Nagasaki Kannon Universal Temple, it was a highly curious construction moulded in the shape of a huge aluminium tortoise. Upon the tortoise's back, also in sun-dazzling aluminium, stood the figure of Kannon (Kuan Yin in China, Avalokiteshvara in India), the androgynous Buddhist Goddess of Mercy. Kannon had started off as a god in India and, gradually gravitating east, had metamorphosed into a golden (or aluminium) goddess. In Kannon's crown, there is always supposed to be a tiny statue of Amida, beckoning the 'Western Paradise' with its ambrosia pond, lotus blossom and a host of angels.

Mercy me. Within the Kannoned tortoise, what should I find but . . . not Buddhists, or shopping malls, or Jesus, but a big Foucault pendulum – a rather fetching piece of apparatus used to demonstrate the rotation of the earth on its tilted axis, and third biggest only to the pendulums of St Petersburg and Paris.

Contemplating the marvels of pendulums, tilted earths and tortoise-riding he/she goddesses, I was jolted from my reverie by the tolling of a bell. Wedding time? Funeral time? Time for church? Time for a time check? Time for tea? No. It was time for remembrance: 11.02 a.m. The time of the bomb. How grateful I felt to be standing here in this peculiar pendulum-swinging world now, rather than then.

With a few more sights I fancied seeing, I ambled onward in a rambling sort of way feeling heavy and hot in the city's deadeningly still and clammy heat. In Nagasaki, things were not all new-old or old-new: some real-life, unreconstructed, unreplicated oldness still remained – like the Hosshin-ji Temple bell. Cast in 1483, this bell was solidly old.

Then, legs and head only just withstanding this day of heavy-duty, pavement-pounding, facts-and-figures tour, I climbed up a steep flagstone street, past abundant bundles of yellow *yamabuki* flowers sprouting from the walls, until after several more disorientating axis-tilting turns I arrived at Sofuku-ji Otera – an impressive temple founded in 1629 by a Chinese monk of the Ming Dynasty. Its intricately carved Inner Gate had been designed and cut in southern China (Nangpo, I believe) before being shipped to Nagasaki, where it had been reassembled in 1696.

By now, feeling up to my eyebrows in dates and temples and flagstone steps, I felt it was high time to call it a *hi* (pronounced 'hee' and otherwise known as a day) and give my city-tramping limbs a rest. But after chomping my way through a big bowl of *champon* (a soupy local speciality made with thick Chinese noodles), I felt ready for one final burst of historical wanderings.

At Fukusaya, where a pound cake recipe had been brought to Japan by the Portuguese in the sixteenth century, I found an old *kasutera* ('Castilla') cake shop. The Portuguese and Spanish introduced many new tastes – from breads and cakes to pepper and spices, and the fry-ups that became the basis of the ubiquitous deep-fried vegetable dish known as *tempura* (derived from *temporas*, suggesting 'meatless Friday'). Similary the Spanish gave the Japanese the word *pan* for bread.

I climbed a few more flights of stepped streets, the grandest of which was Oranda-zaka ('Hollander Slope'). Its name had come not from the fact that the Dutch dominated the colonial-style houses of the European Quarter, but because, until the mass exodus of foreigners at the beginning of the Second World War, the citizens of Nagasaki had endearingly referred to all Caucasians as *Oranda-san* – Mr and Mrs Holland. This was a distinct improvement on the early days, when scare stories ran around Japan about the newcomers: they had bushy tails, no ankles (because, apparently, of their heeled shoes) and eyes like cats or monkeys; they lifted one leg to piss like dogs and were masters of sexual technique. An astonished Japanese who had visited the Dutch on board their ship reported that they were 'just like goblins or demons'.

Before I was hit by historical overload, I managed to press on for one last sight: the Glover Gardens, which take their name from Thomas Glover, a dynamic Scot, one of the first and most important of the European traders who arrived soon after Commodore Perry's black ships. Thomas Glover contributed to the furious development of the Meiji Restoration by running an aggressive arms-importing operation; he also helped the newly opened Japan to achieve a number of its 'firsts': the first railway line; the first mint; the first printing-press with movable type; and the first modern shipyard, from which Nagasaki's massive Mitsubishi shipyard is a direct descendant. So quite handy was Glover.

When I woke up in the Sunflower the next morning, I decided on the spur of the moment to get up and go to the Goto Islands. On my way, I sailed right past those monolithic Mitsubishi shipyards. I never thought a shipyard would fill me with awe but these ones did. Their vastness overwhelmed. The immense Koyagi Dock, nearly 1000 metres long and 100 metres deep, was the largest in the world. For such a small race, it was funny how the Japanese liked to do things on such a large scale. It was as if they were saying to the outside world: 'You may look down on us in body size, but in industry you may gaze up at us in wonder.'

And so it has proved. Take shipbuilding, for example. In only a few decades, from the opening up of Japan after its two centuries of isolation (during which it was only building those basic little ships that could sail little further than its inshore waters) to the 1930s, Japan rapidly became the world's third largest ship-builder – which was one of the reasons why the Mitsubishi shipyards ended up on the atomic-blasting hit-list of the Bockscar bomber.

In Britain, meanwhile, shipyards had been struggling to maintain their order books. At the end of the nineteenth century, Japanese leaders, over-brimming with admiration for British technology and world leadership, had placed orders on the Tyne for their great warships – such as the *Mikasa*, the flagship that led the Japanese navy to its celebrated victory over the Russian Baltic fleet in 1905 during the Russo–Japanese War. Quick to latch on and embrace new ideas after emerging from their isolated feudal past, the Japanese had modelled their Imperial Navy largely on Britain's Royal Navy

Immediately after the war, the West scolded Japan for its ruthless antics by banning every shipyard in the country from producing steel-hulled ships of any kind, forcing the defeated and humiliated country into turning out only wooden fishing-boats instead. But then, in 1949, obviously realising that har-bouring bitter and twisted feelings does nothing towards making the world a happier place, America lifted the ban, resolving to do whatever was necessary to foster Japan as a strong and steadfast ally.

In typical do-nothing-by-halves Japanese style, Nagasaki's Mitsubishi ship-yards made up for lost time and soon led the way in shipbuilding. Ships were being made there like off-the-peg suits, according to a range of standard models of 80,000, 140,000 or 240,000 tons. Shigeichi Koga, who once headed the yards, said that his workers

without even having to look at a blueprint would say, 'Ah yes: one of those,' and go and do their job right away. Whatever size of ship was wanted, the model for it existed already.

To the Japanese engineers, the bulk carriers and oil tankers that were in demand in the 1960s were the easiest classes of ship to build. Mr Koga is said to have described them as 'technically extremely primitive – like huge match-boxes, not really like ships at all'.

For a while, the phenomenal Japanese capacity for productivity earned them an unenviable reputation as a nation of unashamed copiers and indus-trial cheats. It was not just the British navy that the Japanese had emulated back in the late nineteenth century. Thomas Stevens, a British-born young American journalist who was cycling in Japan in 1886, saw it quite clearly, noting how the

Japanese Government had sent commissions to different Western countries to pick up tips about methods of education, police forces, armies and navies, judiciary systems, postal services and so on, so that the Japanese could select the best in the West for their own. As Stevens wrote:

> Thus the police service is modelled from the French, the judiciary from the English, the schools after the American methods, etc. Having inaugurated these improvements, the Japs seem determined to follow their models with the same minute scrupulosity they exhibit in copying material things.

Stevens, who was born in 1855 at Berkhamstead in Hertfordshire, was a true pedalling pioneer. He completed the first recorded circumnavigation of the globe by cycle – on board an 'Ordinary' (penny-farthing) bicycle. Travelling from west to east, he set out from San Francisco and took just over two-and-a-half years to make it to his final destination of Yokohama.

In his book, *Around the World on a Bicycle*, he remarked:

> The Japs are a wonderful race; they seem to be the happiest going, always smiling and good-natured, always polite and gentle, always bowing and scraping.

He also noted:

> In every town and village one is struck with the various imitations of European goods. Ludicrous mistakes are everywhere met with, where this serio–comical people have attempted to imitate name, trade-mark, and everything complete. In one portion of the eating-house where lunch is obtained to-day are a number of umbrella-makers manufacturing gingham umbrellas; on every umbrella is stamped the firm-name, 'John Douglas, Manchester'.

Early evening. Beneath a gloomy sky lined with a uniform sheet of dripping cloud, the ferry pulled into Fukue – by far the largest of the 155 or so Goto Islands.

In the modern, spick-and-span ferry terminal I caused a bit of a stir. It seemed that *gaijin* were particularly thin on the ground on these peripheral, far-flung rocks of westerly Japan. A sea of inquisitive faces gathered round. So much, I thought, for the supposed reserved race. A hundred eyes watched my every move. It was almost like being in India.

A man with a thick pate of forward-swept black hair and wide-rimmed spectacles found the courage to pipe, 'America?'

'No, England,' I told him.

'Ahh so – Hollywood star! Ha ha!'

'No, wrong country. I'm from England – England, Europe.'

'Ahh, fine president country!'

'England doesn't have a president – it has a prime minister.'

'Ahh so, *desu-ka*? Is that so?'

'Yes, that is so.'

'You are one person only?'

'Yes, I am only one person.'

'Ahh, *sugoi*! That is great!'

'Thank you.'

'Mmmm, but where are your vacation friends?'

'I don't have any friends. I'm travelling alone.'

'You are making travelling time as one person?'

'Yes, as one person.'

'With travelling bicycle vacation?'

'Yes, I am travelling alone by bicycle.'

'Ahh, *sugoi*!,' said the man, before turning to tanslate what I had just said to the crowd of bemused faces.

'Ahh, *sugoi*!' they chorused.

'America – fine country,' said the man.

'America is a very fine country,' I said, 'but I am in fact from England.'

'England?'

'Yes, England.'

'Ahh, is that so?'

'Yes, that is so.'

'You are making travelling vacation as one person bicycle?'

'Err . . . yes, that sort of thing.'

'Now, where are you going?'

'I'm going to cycle round the Goto Islands.'

'By bicycle?'

'Yes, by bicycle.'

'Ahh, is that so?'

'Yes, that is very so.'

'Where have you sleeping time?'

'Well, mostly in my tent.'

'*Tento?*'

'Yes, in a tent.'

Thoughtful pause. 'Mmmm, but it is much raining.'

'Yes, it is raining a lot.'

Longer thoughtful pause. 'But when there is much raining, where have you sleeping location?'

'In my tent.'

'Ahh, is that so?'

'Yes, that is so.'

Another thoughtful pause, accompanied by troubled expression. 'Mmmm, but this is much danger.'

'Danger? I'm sure it's fine.'

At this point a policeman surfaced from the ever-expanding circle of teeth-sucking, ahh-soing faces pressed close around me.

'*Konbanwa* – good evening,' he said, trying to look serious while wearing the standard Japanese smile.

'*Konbanwa*,' I replied.

The policeman launched into the same sort of inquisition that the bespectacled man had delivered upon me. Where was I from? What was I doing? Where was I going? Where were my friends? Then he asked to see my passport.

Apart from at immigration, this was the first time I had been asked for my passport and the request took me so much by surprise that I immediately began to feel guilty. As I foraged around in my handlebar bag, my mind raced ahead. Was my visa in order? Had it expired? Had it been correctly stamped when I arrived in Japan by sea?

But there was no need to fret. When I handed him my old-style, hard-backed blue British passport, he exclaimed, 'Ahh, very fine book indeed!' and handed it back without even opening it.

At this point Takuma Kubo, the manager of the ferry terminal, arrived on the scene to see what all the hubbub was about. A lengthy explanation ensued which involved a number of communication breakdowns. Then Mr Kubo asked me to wait a moment while he had a tête-à-tête with the policeman and the bespectacled man. With a bladder alerting me to its high-tiding presence, I took the opportunity to whip off to the *benjo*. When I returned, Mr Kubo informed me that I couldn't camp in the rain because I would get wet.

'Ahh so, *desu-ka?*'

And because it was dangerous to camp alone, continued Mr Kubo with a jovial smile of sincerity, it was his honour to have me sleeping in his terminal.

So that was that. I would sleep in the terminal. After giving me two cans of Hokkaido beer (motto: 'Let your spirit run free and enjoy nature's rich bounty. Savour the taste of Hokkaido'), three seaweed-wrapped sticky rice triangles and a bag of fried cuttlefish, Mr Kubo gave me the key to his private and extra-ordinarily confusing computerised shower, before locking me into the evacuated ferry terminal at 9 p.m. on the nose.

Upstairs, on the shiny polished floor of the departure lounge, I erected the netting inner of my free-standing tent and went to sleep unmenaced by the blood-hunting plague of mosquitoes. Outside, the rain rained on.

The following morning I was woken at 5.30 a.m. by the clatter of a cleaner clumping up the stairs with buckets and mops and other such floor-cleaning apparatus. She was more than a little taken aback at finding a *gaijin* camping beside a bicycle on the floor of the locked terminal. Mr Kubo arrived soon after six, by which time I had packed up and was ready to roll. But Mr Kubo had other ideas.

'The rain is still falling very strong indeed. I am believing today is too much wet for bicycle. Please accept my suggesting you stay inside as my terminal guest.'

'Well, thank you, but it is rainy season now, is it not?' I said.

'Ahh, yes, rainy season, ha ha!' he said, laughing inexplicably.

'The problem is that, if I wait for the rain to stop, I might be here all month.'

'*Hai, hai!* For all one month in Fukue you are my pleasure guest for sleeping in my terminal. Here every night is dry night and much safety also!'

A nice idea, I thought, but not a very practical one. Finally, after treating me to a multi-course fish breakfast, Mr Kubo allowed me to head off into the rain as long as I promised to return to his terminal if I felt very wet and unsafe.

'You are mania of bicycle!' he said as I left.

Despite the rain, I spent several wonderful days riding around and across Fukue among misty mountains, acid-green hills, grey sea and fog. Big purple-headed thistles and headily scented wild honeysuckle crowded the roadsides. Quiet fishing villages dotted the fjord-like inlets and outlets of the coast. In the mountains, my wheels slalomed between scuttling crowds of freshwater crabs. From time to time I passed old wooden farmhouses, their eaves laden with drying corn and onions and underwear.

The air smelt of seaweed, even in the hills. Everywhere people worked, bent over double – weeding, hoeing, snipping, planting, mowing, mending nets. Everyone busy. In villages, people always worked together – amassed community spirit, old and young alike; the women in floral bonnets, *mompe* (the traditional baggy work trousers worn by women in rural areas) and short, black gumboots; the men with feet enclosed in *jikatabi* (curious split-toed boots) and their heads tied in a rope of towels. It might have been rainy season, but it was still hot, still hellishly humid.

Being part of Saikai (West Sea) National Park, the Goto Islands were relatively unspoiled compared with so much of the rest of Japan, which was fast escalating into ruination. Down around Tatsunokuchi ('Mouth of the Seahorse') on Fukue's southern tip, as well as up along the west coast, the pellucid blue bays, white-sand beaches, rugged promontories of laval fingers and a profusion of rocky, verdant-topped islets looked so perfect that I felt as if the world was my oyster.

Or even my cuttlefish. According to a tourist leaflet entitled 'Wellcomb to the Goto Islands', the local delicacies were: '*Sureme* – dried cuttlefish; *Shiokara* – salted fish organs; *Sureme Kanbin* – *sake* serving bottle made from dried cuttlefish; Goto cuttle – black-haired, strong-hoofed and grow fast . . .'. Hairy hoofed fish? How very peculiar.

Feeling in no mood to tackle a cuttle in whatever shape or form it might be, I instead sallied forth to the neighbouring island of Hisaka, where I splashed down in a rainstorm at a place called 'The Small Prison'. The tourist leaflet, misprints and all, informed me that:

in April 1868 the government decided to punish the Christians in Nagasaki, and the oppression policy spread to the Goto Islands. In September the Christians in Hisaka Island were caught and subjected to terrible torrure. More than 200 people, men and women, young and old, were confined to a tiny prison covering only about 20 sq meters . . . and suffered from mental agony and starvarion. They were jammed so tightly in the prison that they could not sit or even move, and they slept sprawled upon each other. Mothers could not lift their own children who had fallen between the bodies. Their legs became swollen. During the eight months of imprisonment, 42 Christians gave up their lives for their faith.

On the ferry to Nakadori-shima, the second largest island of the Goto group, I met thirty-year-old Sophie, a JET teacher from San Francisco, who was currently living (and teaching) in a village in the south of Fukue, not far from the 'Mouth of the Seahorse'.

'It's real isolated,' Sophie told me, 'but the people are quite friendly – although saying that, last night I went to a party and the three women sitting next to me completely ignored me even though they knew I was living in the same town as them.'

I had noticed that Sophie's Japanese was pretty hot stuff and I asked her whether she had been to Japan before.

'Oh sure,' she said. 'A while back I spent some time travelling round Asia and when I finally found myself all out of money I came to Japan to get a job as a hostess in this real neat club in Tokyo, where I lived for about a year.'

'How long ago was that?' I asked.

'Well, let me see now . . . I guess the mid-eighties.'

'Boom time,' I said.

'Sure. I was earning at least $4500 a month. It was great! You can't make that sort of money these days. I took an apartment, studied Japanese in day classes and then practised speaking to all these Japanese guys while I poured them drinks. I'm a feminist inside, so it wasn't really the sort of thing I believe in, but I knew what my priorities were so I was happy!'

When Sophie discovered I was travelling by bike, she told me how she had always fancied doing something similar.

'Maybe a bike trip from Vancouver to San Francisco – now that would be great! A guy I know did it – had a ball! You know, if you're into biking, maybe you should do that route some time.'

I was about to tell her that I'd cycled from Vancouver to the bottom of Baja a couple of years before, and that I'd heartily recommend the ride, but decided to keep my mouth shut instead. Sophie opened hers.

'I guess a bike trip's something I'll never do, as I'm getting married in three months' time,' she said with a sigh.

'Oh, are you?' I said, adding as an afterthought, 'That's nice. But you could still fit in a cycling excursion some time, couldn't you?'

'Well, you know,' said Sophie, sweeping her long, wind-tussled chestnut mane back out of her face, 'our lives are real busy with work and I can't see us having the time to sit back and watch the world go by.'

Was Sophie trying to tell me something, I wondered? Anyway, I thought, immediately feeling guiltily lazy, I'm not sitting back – I'm sitting on.

Fortunately we were just coming in to dock, so I was saved from becoming embroiled in any probing 'what are you doing with your life?' talks. Sophie asked me if she could come down to the car deck with me to take a look at my loaded bike; despite the proximity of her marriage, she was still keen to 'see how to do it', as she put it.

I told her she was welcome to come and have a look but warned her that, with a couple of deadweight cabbages (which a roadside granny had insisted on planting upon me) haphazardly hanging off the back of an excessively over-loaded steed, I was definitely not of the 'how to do it' school of pannier packing.

The island of Nakadori proved memorable for its leg-quiveringly steep moun-tain roads, its hosts of banners proclaiming the forthcoming 'Monster Man Triathlon', its floating fish factories (vast warehouses on water – like five almighty metallic strips of silvery runways shimmering upon the bay) and its spotless bus shelter, in which I slept (to take a break from rainy season) and on the wall of which hung an astonishingly expensive-looking clock that in any other country would have been nicked in a tick.

Oh, and Nakadori was also memorable for being the place where I was invited to spend a night with a family who, going decidedly overboard on the gift front, gave me a pair of 'Hello Kitty' slippers (indoor wear for slopping around in my tent?); a sunhat (for rainy season?); a pot plant (for a festive spot of inner tent foliage?); a weighty homegrown cabbage (to add to the family of cabbages already playing havoc with my rear); six pairs of fancy chopsticks (for a lonesome traveller who likes a good, no-nonsense, fast-filling, mouth-shovelling spoon); and a traditional clay doll (for . . . well . . . in my case, certainly breaking).

Back in Nagasaki, I took a day trip out to Oranda Mura (Holland Village), otherwise known as Huis Ten Bosch – which sounds more soup than city to me but which is the Dutch for 'House in the Woods'. This was a bizarre but complete European fantasy world plonked brick-by-Dutch-brick into the midst of Japan.

Built as a faithful recreation of a seventeenth-century Dutch city, Huis Ten Bosch was perhaps the ultimate example of taking the best of what another country has to offer and copying it to extreme perfection. Here in this Dutch village theme park – with its neat network of cobbles and brick lanes and bridges and four miles of canals, its red rouge-cheeked wheels of Edam cheese and its armies of gaily painted handmade clogs, not to mention its gently turning, friendly-waving windmills (all a good 8000 kilometres from their flat, dyke-fortressed motherland) – was a prime piece of 'European charm' that the Japanese could visit and enjoy without all the headaches and hassles and language problems and crime statistics of the real thing. And enjoy it they did. The Japanese (especially honeymooners) flocked to this jolly, street-entertaining, tulip-town-on-water in their millions, making it one of Kyushu's newest and most technologically advanced tourist attractions.

Huis Ten Bosch had a perfect replica of Queen Beatrix's Palace (built with ten million bricks imported from The Netherlands), the port town of Hoorn, some seventeenth-century farmhouses, Willemstad church and much more but it was not just a theme park and resort town (there were four luxury hotels): it was also a place to live.

For a country of such impermanence, where Japanese towns get demolished and rebuilt every few years, Huis Ten Bosch was fast expanding and a step ahead technologically. While many places in Japan had yet to construct sewage systems in their towns, beneath Holland Village hummed a high-tech ecological powerhouse capable of recycling all of the theme-cum-residential park's water. Unlike most of Japan's towns, there were no open drains gushing down its streets. Unusually, too, all cables were concealed – something extraordinary in a country whose skies are tangled and strangled with cat's-cradle webs of wires.

The Japanese seemed to have a particular fascination with being stimulated by simulators and they were well catered for in this most Japanese of Dutch towns. Joining at least 200 visitors inside a huge computer-driven diorama (one of the park's nine interactive media shows), I instinctively reached for a non-existent brolly as I felt myself being lashed by spray from rising tides and collapsed dykes while simultaneously being pummelled by incredibly realistic fake lightning crashing and flashing and exploding around our comically cowering forms.

Drinking a can of *oolong-cha* (Chinese tea) in front of a very European chiming clock, I was approached by a corpulent man who said he was from 'Shaky', otherwise known as California. Stretched across his ample midriff was a tasteful T-shirt emblazoned with the words: 'I SURVIVED THE LOS ANGELES EARTHQUAKE'. Assuming that I was *au fait* with the whereabouts of the toilets (did I look like a weak bladder kind of person?), he asked me for directions to 'the bathroom'.

When I opened my mouth to tell him in which direction to head, his 'bathroom' mission was unfortunately put on hold because he discovered that I had a 'real cute English accent' and lingered long enough to ask me what I was doing in Japan. I told him I was in the process of cycling round the country.

'Holy mackerel!' he said. 'How long's that gonna take you?'

'Altogether about eight months,' I said.

'Eight months? Jeez! So what do you do in real life?'

'Cycle – mostly,' I replied, which, not feeling in a particularly talkative mood, seemed to produce the desired effect of hitting all further conversation on the head. Looking a little sorry at my apparent inability to possess a 'real life', the LA Shaky Survivor ambled off in search of some light relief.

As I headed east from Nagasaki along a traffic-clogged road overlooking Chijiwa Wan Bay, gaudy castle-shaped Love Hotels with preposterous names were much in evidence. As were potatoes. Fields and fields of potatoes. And people. It was potato-digging time, and in technologically advanced Japan the fields were not groaning beneath a barrage of supersonic agricultural machinery but bent-double backs. Women's backs. Old women's backs, folded in two. All dig, dig, digging potatoes. Potatoes in Japan? Odd sight. This was the first time I had seen a potato field in Japan and it was not something I had expected to see. Rice – yes. Potatoes – no.

I stopped to have my picnic lunch in a cemetery in the rain, surrounded by potato fields. Before long, an army of potato-diggers had crowded around me, all laughing and chatting and playfully patting me with earthy, hard calloused hands, slap-bang on the back. One industrious old biddy, who looked at least 110, rigged up a makeshift tent of tarp, beneath which we all crawled to get out of the rain. *Bento* (lunchboxes) appeared and were shared. Flasks were shared. Laughs were shared.

'Ha ha!' said the bent-backs. 'Only a mad *gaijin* riding a *jitensha* would stop to eat their lunch in the rain, in a cemetery with a bunch of potatoes!'

And the mad *gaijin* (who was actually very sensible) said, in her best form of bad Japanese, 'Well, as you see, *toki doki* – sometimes – these things have their advantages,' before swallowing another piece of shared *tempura*.

Leaving the bent-backs to get back to their digging, I returned to the Love Hotel-lined road. At one point, close to the Love Yes Hotel, I paused to admire a phenomenal piece of technologically advanced roadside furniture: a fridge from Mars complete with computerised digits and dials and dazzling chrome and glass-fronted doors. Displayed within this vandal-free, graffiti-free piece of Conran-like kitchen machinery were polished glass shelves, like showcases for the most precious of jewels, but full of various varieties of speckless, dirtless potatoes so perfect they would have passed as plastic. A sign, entitled 'POTET-TOE', described in *kanji* the different types of potet-toe and the corresponding prices, which were Hatton Garden high – prices that would undoubtedly hit the old wallet more like a string of semi-precious stones than a handful of down-to-earth tubers. Clearly these potet-toes were not peanuts.

Past the spuds, I was busily cycling along in the bouncing rain when a small white van, crammed with blue-hard-hatted workmen, pulled broadside.

'*Notte kudasai!*' shouted the grinning helmsman. 'Hop in!'

Quite how I was supposed to 'hop' into a people-packed van with a laden bicycle the weight of a whale, I truly don't know. Nor, despite the stinging rain, did I want to. I liked it on my bike, come what may. So I thanked the men and said I was fine. They smiled and waved and nodded before the van accelerated off down the road, leaving me with their cheerful cries of '*Ganbatte!* Have strength!' floating on the wind.

Up the hill and round a bend, I found the same van pulled up at a bank of vending machines, every one of the van's blue-lidded occupants standing lamppost-straight in a neat line at the side of the road. As I approached, their right arms extended in perfect, right-angled unison, as if about to embark on some military parade. Each hand grasped not a spit-and-polished rifle but a cold can of vending-machine drink: coffees, teas, pops, juices, energy boosters, beer, *sake* and so on.

'*Dozo, dozo,*' said the driver.

'What, all for me?'

'*Hai, hai* – all for you!'

Some I drank straight away. Others were prised into my pannier. The overflow was lassoed in a bag and slung off the rear. Over the next couple of hours, as I handed out willy-nilly a wide assortment of teas, coffees and light refreshments to anyone who even thought of smiling at me, I began to understand what it might feel like to be a vending machine. Oddly, it proved a surprisingly pleasant occupation which one day, for want of something better to do in 'real life', I might just take up full time. I'm sure Mr 'I SURVIVED THE LOS ANGELES EARTHQUAKE' would be mightily impressed.

CHAPTER 5

Unexpected Woodsbathing

Kyushu, whose name means 'Nine Provinces' (from its ancient administrative structure), is a mountainous island a little larger than Taiwan – it accounts for a tenth of Japan's land area and population. The island is divided into an increasingly wealthy, urbanised industrial north around Kitakyushu (an agglomeration of five cities) and a poorer, still mainly agricultural south.

Historically, the rest of the country tended to view Kyushu as out on a limb, a place apart – a sort of squat, volcanic and oddly exuberant (though backward) exclamation point on Japan's island tail, inhabited by a people of southern temperament who were by nature fiery and rebellious. That image grew during the Meiji era when Kyushu's greatest hero, the philosopher, educator, samurai statesman and subsequent dissident, Saigo Takamori, led the bloody and ill-fated Seinan Rebellion against the national government that he had helped to create only a decade earlier but with which he had become increasingly disillusioned.

Saigo Takamori's aim was to prevent too much of the country's power and wealth from accumulating in its new capital, Tokyo. His flamboyant failure to do so, concluding in his ritual suicide in 1877, resulted in the escalation of Kyushans leaving their home to chase their dreams of high-paying jobs and glamorous lifestyles in the great commercial centres up north.

Despite being once so poor that it was called Nippon no Chibetto (the Tibet of Japan), Kyushu has rocketed by way of electronic arteries into a world of endless loops of fibre-optic cables and mega-data superhighways to become something of a 'silicon island' and is blooming with futuristic research laboratories and factories, where beavering armies of industrial robots produce such high-tech ware as computers, cars, memory chips and disease-fighting monoclonal antibodies.

I was now upon Kyushu's geologically unstable *hanto* (peninsula) of Shimabara, a kidney-shaped pod bordered by bays and seas and ruled by the turbulent heart of Mount Unzen, a 1369-metre volcano that, together with the peninsula and the Amakusa islands, emerged from the sea only half a million years ago – a mere stripling by scientific standards.

Shimabara Hanto had been struck by instability in more ways than one. Towards the middle of the seventeenth century, it was the uprising here that brought about the suppression of Christianity in Japan which in itself led to the country's 200 years of isolation. More recently, in 1991, after lying dormant for 199 years, Mount Unzen stirred back into life in ferocious style by blowing its top, clobbering the east-coast city of Shimabara with rocks and hot ash. The eruption was classified as a pyroclastic flow: a glowing avalanche in which the earth's deathly viscera of superheated, fluid-like gas, ash and rock raced at high speed down the slopes of the mountain – far faster than the spreading tongues of a lava flow. Knowing that a big blast was imminent, the people of Shimabara were prepared for it and only about forty of them lost their lives – a lot fewer than the 15,000 who fell victim to the previous eruption in 1792, the worst in Japanese history.

Buildings fared much worse than people in the 1991 eruption when the majority of Shimabara's homes and businesses suffered from a double blow. After scores had been burned and razed to the ground, countless more were destroyed when heavy rains washed down the volcano's ash-covered slopes and swamped the city in a grey sea of thick, glutinous mud.

Mount Unzen derives its name from *onsen*, the Japanese word for a hot-spring spa. The entire area steams and boils and it proved a luxurious place to wallow after toiling up the mount's steep, dog-legged ascent. Had I been a Christian several centuries before, my experience of Unzen's waters would not have been quite so heavenly: a favoured method of execution was to drop those who continued to practise the banned religion into the earth's boiling fumaroles. No wonder those spurting, bubbling, soul-snatching natural cauldrons are called *jigoku* – hell.

106

Crossing over the north of Shimabara Bay from Taira to Nagasu, I stood on the deck of the ferry with a twitter of excitable schoolgirls dressed in matronly blue pleated skirts that reached below the knee, criss-crossed bibbed braces and white short-sleeved shirts safety-pinned with armbands for easy identification by the teacher. These girls were a far cry from their big-city sisters, the *joshi kosei* high-school girls, who considered it fashionable to be seen in their school uniforms. Every weekend and on weekday evenings, the *joshi kosei* would flock to Shibuya (central Tokyo) in their distinctive plumage. The blue-and-white sailor suits would be drastically customised: the pleated skirts would be hitched up to alarming heights, and the white socks would be worn many sizes too large (known as *ruusu* – loose – *sokkusu*, mistakenly believed to flatter plump calves), held up with specially bought glue. The school satchels would be adorned with a variety of toys, chief among them being the ubiquitous white cartoon cat known as Hello Kitty.

As the ferry neared its destination, I went down below to the car-and-one-bicycle deck and waited with engine-idling motorists for the doors to open. Two men and three women in a white Daihatsu insisted on smiling and waving to me every time I caught their eye; I didn't know them and they didn't know me, but I smiled and waved back gaily. As they drove off up the ramp in front of me, the women, all seated in the back, turned round as one to give me a final fling of happy, shiny, smiling faces and windmill waves. Later, as I emerged from a Stork service station after filling up on water, the white Daihatsu motored by and its occupants broke into another rousing show of energetic semaphoring and radiating smiles. What was going on? It was all very odd.

Giving the hefty city of Kumamoto a miss ('been there, done that' the previous year), I turned inland, eastward, passing the 'Free Time Empty Space Café' along the way, and drew up in late afternoon at the dreary-looking city of Tamana.

Stocking up on supper supplies at the Joyfull Sun supermarket, I asked the cheerful checkout girl, whose name was Megumi Ohno (oh yes?), if she knew of a nearby temple or shrine. I omitted the more complicated fact that I was in search of a small, spare space amongst the city's all-engulfing concrete and neon in which to camp.

Miss Ohno answered my Japanese in English, which prompted me to ask her where she had learnt the language. Ohno said Oz, on a family exchange programme.

'I have very much hoping for maybe one day for living in underneath Australia,' she said.

Ahh so, *desu-ka?* At this point, a woman with two small offspring and a man whose tar-black hair lay raked flat against his scalp appeared at the till with loaded trolleys. Not wanting to cause a tailback, I didn't pursue Miss Ohno for more detailed directions to the nearest temple – but she, evidently feeling that a rare, lesser-spotted, multi-freckled *gaijin* took precedence over any homogenised, standard-issue, loaded-trolley local, launched into a confusing Oz-twanged Japlish spiel about a temple that lay down several roads, round several bends and through a tangle of traffic lights before losing me good and proper in a wriggling, twisting mesh of residential *ura dori* (backstreets) and shoulder-wide alleys.

By now, several more booty-laden customers had rolled up at the till, all craning their necks to get a good look at the *gaijin*. Had this been a buffoon of a foreigner holding up your average paucity-of-patience trolley-congested queue at, say, Sainsburys in England, there would indubitably have been more than a few xenophobic glares and stares and bloody-minded 'bloody foreigner' death-wish thoughts and murmurings from the crowd. But for the shoppers of Joyfull Sun Japan? Oh no! Instead of going off their trolleys, they were full of solicitous mirth all round. Housewives, hip-hop youngsters, *obaasan* grannies and old men alike rallied round in a convivial crowd, each one eager to lend their opinion on the direction of the elusive temple.

'I know – it's near my cousin's!' declared a diminutive old codger who looked ancient enough to have been born at about the same time as Moses.

'But your cousin's dead!' said a neighbour two trolleys back. 'Remember? He died last year!'

'Ahh, is that so?' replied Moses, who took the news of his cousin's death as nonchalantly as if he had just been told that the store shuts in five minutes. Everyone else eagerly continued to offer their differing views on the whereabouts of the temple.

'It's this way!'

'It's that way!'

'It's opposite Mr Kazo's rice paddy!'

'It's behind the *pachinko* parlour!'

'No, the Bridgestone bike store!'

'I swear it's the road to the side of the cement works – or is it the liquor store?'

As the entertaining deliberations and trolley gridlock continued, Miss Ohno put her till duties on hold and set about drawing me a map, to which everyone and his aunt (and possibly dead cousin) added their own conflicting judgement on which road led where. So much for a stereotypical people of consensus and happy harmony – the Sunny Joyfull shoppers demonstrated a fine display of individual conjectures and views.

What's more, they all expressed their opinions about the *kanji* characters that Miss Ohno had chosen to write for the name of the temple. In my view, and in the view of most Westerners, all Japanese characters comprise a mind-boggling, intricate confusion of lines and curves and sweeps and strokes that look very interesting but mean precious little. In Miss Ohno's case, it was not so much that she had used the wrong characters; it was that one of the characters she had chosen (which needed at least two dozen strokes) was deemed to be maybe half a stroke incorrect. Thus, each shopper, though still Joyfull, set about offering their own interpretation of the temple's character. To my layman's eye, they all looked more or less identically complex and as confusingly tangled as each other.

By this stage I was beginning to think that if only I had kept my big mouth shut I would by now most likely have found a temple or shrine on my own, set up base, washed my face, my feet, my crucials and my undies, made and eaten supper, washed up, had an evening stroll, brushed my teeth, read a book, scribbled in my diary, written a letter, listened to the World Service, clipped my toenails, locked my steed, drunk several gallons of canned vending-machine chilled tea, and been asleep for a couple of hours. Missing out on the supermarket's jolly audience participation may have been substantially simpler, but my life would have been a lot less Joyfull for sure.

Finally, clutching my nonsensical map and an overflowing bagful of edible fodder that my new-found friends had insisted I accept as goodwill gifts from their trolleys, I made it to a temple which, as I had become thoroughly lost and disorientated and redirected while winding my way through the diverting *ura dori*, was probably a far cry from the temple of intention. Nevertheless, it was a most impressive temple and I arrived there at the same time as a very large and gleaming car from which stepped the resident

Buddha-like Buddhist priest, clad in fine, flowing robes. Whereas I had planned on simply sneaking round the back to a secluded corner and camping undetected, as is my wont in similar circumstances, I now felt it was only right and proper to ask the priest's permission. So, in the best of my bad Japanese, I did so.

Like Miss Ohno before him, he answered my request in English – this time perfect English.

'Of course!' he said. 'But if you prefer, you are very welcome to sleep in the residential wing of the temple. We have more than enough space.'

'That's very kind,' I said, 'but really, I'll be fine camping.'

'In that case,' said the priest, handing me his 'business' card ('Rev Eisho Kawahara, SUPERINTENDENT PRIEST, RENGEIN TANJYOJI TEMPLE, Special head temple of Shingonrittshu Buddhism'), 'would you be favouring a natural or man-made environment for your tent-pitching?'

Having never been offered such a choice before in all the years of my chequered career as a camper, I wondered if this was the tent-pitching equivalent of booking into a modern Japanese hotel: 'Would madam be requiring a *tatami* or Western-style room?'

Anyway, feeling in a hug-a-tree sort of mood, I said, 'I think I'll take the natural, please.'

I followed in Rev Eisho's swishing, silken-robed slipstream to a delectable grassy spot beneath a plum tree. I imagined that would be the end of the Rev's kind show of hospitality as, being a 'Special head temple', he no doubt had to attend to pressing 'Superintendent Priest' duties. But I was wrong. Showers and excrutiatingly hot baths were at my disposal. And washing machines. Soon I was scrubbed and cleansed and bearing an octopus skin (in Japan, the expression for looking like a lobster after a hot bath is 'as red as an octopus', it seems).

When I emerged from the sizzling steam, Rev Eisho invited me into his room for chat. Crammed with books and CDs and stereos and computers and desks and tables and easy chairs and couches, it was not the sort of ascetic and uncluttered environment I would have envisaged for a Buddhist's abode. As I sat cocooned by cushions on the couch, the Rev's three daughters (aged nine, twelve and sixteen) came filtering through the door, eager to meet me. The two younger ones spoke to me shyly in standard Japanese textbook English: 'Harrow! My nem is . . . . I live in Japan. I am junior high school student.' But the older sister spoke a little more ('Christchurch is very nice city') as she had recently returned from a family exchange to New Zealand.

Next on the scene was Mrs Rev Eisho who, obviously paying heed to the widely held notion that foreigners do not like Japanese food, came gliding through the doorway bearing a large tray full of tiny triangles of white-bread egg-filled sandwiches, a ham croquette, a fishy finger, a fried egg, two ice-cream scoops of sticky rice, one slice of red apple, two plastic-perfect lettuce leaves, a side order of more Mother's Pride plain buttered bread, a glass of milk and a small cup of supremely strong, grainy black coffee. When the Kiwi-experienced daughter asked me what was one of the things I most liked about Japan, I couldn't quite find the heart to say it was Japanese food.

When the women of the family had been packed off to attend to their temple-dwelling 'duties', I spent the next hour talking alone with the Rev. He was an interesting man. After putting on a CD of some softly strumming guitar, lighting a stick of incense and settling down in his well-sunken and easy arm-chair, he told me that along with being the temple's Superintendent Priest he was also the president for ARIC (the Association for Rengein Tanjyoji International Cooperation), a privately financed organisation founded by his father back in 1980. The idea for the association had arisen after Buddhist believers asked what they could do to help Indo–Chinese refugees: he set about raising funds and collecting used clothing to send to the refugees. Rev Eisho explained that, based on the Buddhist principles of almsgiving, the association's aims were to help people and support educational projects (mainly in Thailand, Sri Lanka and Cambodia) along with broadening the international perspective of Buddhist believers.

As I was leaving, he told me how he had recently spent two weeks in Birmingham at a seminar discussing world peace.

'And do you know what the highlight of my stay was?' he asked.

'I've no idea,' I said. 'Was it something to do with getting a little closer to finding a solution for making a peaceful world?'

'No, it was eating an extremely enjoyable curry. I believe Birmingham is England's Number One curry city!'

Crawling into my plum-tree-sheltered 'natural environment' tent, I tuned in to the World Service and just heard the end of something about an IRA bomb that had exploded on a bicycle planted in Bognor town centre. The next piece of news was closer to home, or closer to tent: an earthquake had hit the Russian island of Sakhalin, which was a mere sliver of sea north from where I was heading in Hokkaido. Hundreds, maybe thousands, were said to have been killed. It was reported that President Yeltsin had refused aid from Japan because he believed Japan might use this act of charity as a 'political tool' in the ongoing fight over the Russian-controlled Kuril Islands, which lay off Hokkaido's east coast – islands that, the Japanese claimed, Russia had swiped from them towards the end of the Second World War.

So much for Rev Eisho's hopes of securing world peace, with squabbles like that still going strong. Maybe an international law should be passed whereby all intransigent world leaders head to Birmingham to let off some steam over a good, hot curry. Maybe then the world would be a more happy-go-lucky place.

The next morning I was riding along truck-rumbling Route 325 towards Kikuchi-shi in the seasonably heavy plum rain (in Japan it rains plums, rather than cats and dogs or stair-rods) when I came across an area of intensively grown melons being lovingly reared in tropical greenhouses as big as aircraft hangars. Never one to pass up an excuse for a rest, especially if there's a chance of a free taster as well, I pulled up at the tourist gift-shop foyer of one of the melon hangars. The melons had pipped the peak of priceless perfection: Ogens, Cantaloupes, Galia, Charantais – many at £50 apiece. But pieces there fortunately were, free tasters, all pronged with a cocktail stick. After consuming what would have amounted to an extortionately expensive amount of melon portionets, I returned to my bike with a stomach swilling full of super-juicy fruit.

Just as I was beginning to cycle away, an excited woman came calling and cantering after me, imploring me to stop. Thinking I was about to be nabbed for chomping through the equivalent of at least 20,000 yen-worth of melon without even opening my wallet, I was pleasantly surprised (and relieved) when she turned out to be one of the party of merrily smile-waving passengers off the Shimabara ferry. Even more surprising than seeing her again was the offering she tried to slip into my hand: a freshly folded 5000-yen (£30) note – enough to buy me several nights' stay in a nice dry *minshuku*, or at least half a hangar-grown melon.

The usual little pantomime of refusing/accepting gifts ensued ('Yes, yes', 'No, no', 'Yes, yes', 'No, no' . . .) until the smiling and highly excitable woman insisted I accept the gift as it was from her *obaasan*, who was gaily smiling and waving to me from the passenger seat of the Daihatsu some distance away. Just as I was on the point of making a move towards the car to assure granny that I couldn't possibly accept her financial offering and that I had money enough for my needs (albeit not for melons), the younger smiling woman made a mad dash back to the car which, as soon as she had shut the door, sped off down the road – the back-seat passengers all smiling and waving as vigorously as when I had first seen them on the ferry.

Despite my reprehensible indulgence in free melon, it seemed that Buddha did not feel fit to chastise me for my fruity excess. Not long after I had suddenly become 5000-yen the richer, a lorry driver pulled over to give me a couple of cans of Pocari Sweat and a laminated map (very handy for sodden rainy season) of Kyushu, printed in not-so-handy *kanji*. Then, when I stopped to use the gravity-drop toilet at a small, paint-peeling, family-operated garage, an old man sat me down in his smoky shop (cluttered with shelves of dusty cans of car oil and beer, packets of biscuits and batteries and shoelaces and seaweed and flaked fish) and brought me a cup of green tea, a saucer of pistachio nuts and a bowl of *udon* noodles.

Later, in Kikuchi-shi, a sailor-suited schoolgirl bounced along beside me on her bike and was so overcome with excitement at the sight of a rare pedalling *gaijin* that she tried to offer me her 'Hello Kitty' watch. She only came to her senses when I pointed out that she was about to collide with a wheelbarrow-pushing *obaasan* who had stopped at the traffic lights.

Still managing to avert the Hand of Retribution, I turned up that evening at a junction at the base of Kikuchi Ravine where there stood a bridge, a *ryokan* (traditional inn) and a smattering of houses. As it was still raining plums, I was overcome by a sudden act of reckless extravagance and decided to blow my newly acquired 5000-yen note all in one go for a night of *mama-san* pamperings at the plum-looking *ryokan*. However, the price of the room quoted to me by the young man behind the reception desk was so frighteningly high that I made a hasty retreat back to my bike and set about camping in the heavily pouring plums.

I found a small, rocky piece of wasteland overlooking the river a mere stone's throw from the *ryokan* and was about to put up my tent when I was intercepted by the young receptionist, accompanied by the owner, both sheltering beneath brollies. Thinking they were going to move me on for camping too close to the *ryokan*, I was grateful when instead the owner invited me to use its washing facilities for free. He would like to offer me a room as well, he said, but unfortunately they were all occupied with busloads of tourists.

Noticing the rocky ground that was to suffice as my mattress for the night, he then asked how I was going to be able to sleep on such a hard and uneven surface. It was not easy to explain in Japanese words that one of the boons of struggling by bike over several mountain passes a day meant I could sleep like a log, even with stones jammed in my back, but I think he got the gist. He still insisted on sending the receptionist scampering back to fetch several woven-reed mats and lengths of fat squidgy cardboard, which made for some luxurious foundations for the base of my tent.

So I had the best of both worlds: sleeping outside in the mountain-fresh air beside the cheery sounds of a rollicking river as well as being free to wallow for hours in the boiling, flesh-tenderising waters of the *ryokan*'s palatial lantern-lit spa, after which the manager fed and green tea-ed me to extreme. What's more, I still had a crisp 5000 yen note for another rainy-season day.

Setting off early the next morning before the string of tourist buses sparked into action, I rode through the heavy 'atmospheric drizzle' of Kikuchi Ravine, which I found described thus in the local tourist leaflet:

> KIKUCHI RAVINE – we invite you to one of 'the 100 forests recommended for woodsbathing in Japan'. Kikuchi gorge is 'People's Forest' and the river and rich virgin forest of broad-leaf trees present you a breathtaking scenery.
>
> This area is for all season.
>
> You have chilling water, murmering of the stream, and the singings of birds. You can enjoy fresh green leaves of spring, the blazing red and yellow leaves of autumn, and the glittering hoarfrosts in winter alternately decorate all over the mountains.

The traffic-free ravine was drenched in jungle-thick foliage of a thousand brilliant greens as I ascended, and the repetitive calls of copious cuckoos reverberated about the gorge's walls. Heady scents of wild blossoms drifted on the wind and I thought, well, if this is what 'woodsbathing' is all about, then I wouldn't mind a second dip.

The next few days I spent walking and cycling and hiking and biking all over the volcanic wonders of Mount Aso (Aso, *desu-ka?*), before veering off northeast into Oita Prefecture over the haymaking, cow-grazing and milking

territory of Kujusan Plateau. Cows, like 'potet-toes', struck me as a very odd sight for Japan.

The day I rode over fumarole-hissing Mount Kujusan provided rich pickings for roadside finds: a penknife (useful for slicing fruit – and fingers); a big, heavy-duty industrial tapemeasure (useful in case I fancied measuring things – except mountains – or maybe even checking to see if I'd grown or shrunk); and a frisbee (useful for . . . ummm . . . well, playing frisbee – made a good plate, too).

At one point, stopping to admire the view from the top of an impressive lunar-landscape hillock, I experienced an unusual phenomenon: it was raining hay. Straws of the stuff were free-falling from the skies, just as plums had done for days and days before. Most odd, but I suppose it was better than the fish and frogs that have been reported falling out of the sky here and there over the years.

A little further along, something else fell out of the blue (or more like grey – it was raining again): a grapefruit was lobbed to me from out of the back of a fruit van by a man shouting, '*Ganbatte!*'

That night I camped in the rain in the steamy mountain village of Yufuin, beside a shrine on the wooded shores of Kinrinko Pond. A short walk away along the waterside I found a small, thatch-roofed building enveloped in a haze of steam. It proved to be a *rotenburo*, a naturally occurring open-air bath but without the guest accommodation and other trimmings you'd find at a typical *onsen*. The unusual thing about this one was that it was communal.

By this stage in my Japanese bathing career, I no longer batted an eyelid, nor undressed in self-conscious slow motion, at the prospect of disporting in the altogether with fellow naked souls. My experience as a communal bather with other women was admittedly somewhat limited, as this sociable pastime was unfortunately on the wane, but I was quite happy to bare my birthday suit before the eyes of complete strangers.

However, the 100 yen (60p) *rotenburo* in Yufuin, in which I intended to soak away my day's travails, proved to be an eye-opener of a different nature. Undressing in the small communal changing hut, I began to realise there was a distinct lack of women's attire among the few neat piles of folded clothes. Wondering if I had misinterpreted the *kanji* sign on the outside, I pulled on my shorts again before stepping back out to check that I hadn't wandered into a 'men only' bath. Carefully scrutinising the characters, I was certain I hadn't made a mistake but asked a passing woman just in case. She reassured me that, although the bath seemed to be more popular with men, it was indeed for both sexes. Mixed communal bathing was a long-standing (or soaking) tradition in Japan, as I well knew: men, women and children had happily bathed together for centuries with not a dirty thought in any of their heads.

Being a Westerner and feeling a drop uneasy about being the only female soaking among a bathful of men, I loitered around outside the entrance for a while hoping for a woman to come along with whom I could join female forces for a bathe. None did. So, being fidgety and with curiosity getting the better of me, I decided to take the plunge. After all, isn't travelling all about taking the odd risqué risk?

Back in the hut I peeled off my clothes and padded round the reeded screen into the steamy bath's small secluded open-air area. The sight that greeted me was of four men's heads floating upon clouds of steam. On top of each head sat a white square of carefully folded flannel. The eyes of these heads all lifted to look at me with such ogling surprise that I suddenly wanted to dissolve like the soap into the cracks of the rocks.

My dilemma was that I could not distinguish whether the men's gaping, body-boring stares were as a result of my being a weird, white-skinned and freckly foreigner or because they were simply a mélange of sleazy-minded men. Ignoring my panicking instinct to scarper, I opted to play it cool and calm and, with my innards in turmoil, heard myself bid the four Flannel Heads a pleasant good evening as nonchalantly as if I had strolled past them having a smoke and a quiet gossip on a park bench. Then, getting on with my own business, I sat on my heels on the wet stones and vigorously soaped and scrubbed myself off, as is the custom in Japan – a bath is strictly for soaking, not for washing.

Throughout my energetic latherings, the Flannel Heads continued to gawp, which confirmed my suspicions that they were no more than a bunch of dirty old men. But there again, they may just have been highly impressed that a foreign buffoon knew the Japanese way of washing before bathing. Either way, when I finally plucked up courage to lower myself, inch by painful inch, into the scorching waters, I felt eight gawping eyes scanning my more sensitive areas.

As I slid beneath the body-concealing water, leaving nothing (save my face) for the prying eyes to penetrate, the Flannel Heads suddenly came to life by demonstrating that they were more than just heads: they had voices. After responding to the usual inquisition (where was I from and where was I going and where did I sleep and was I not frightened and did I like Japanese food and . . .?), I discovered that two of the men worked on the railways, another was a potter and the youngest worked in his father's liquor store. They were all friends, they said; they came here regularly – in fact most days, if they could – for a soak and a gossip. Although this was a unisex communal bath, they said they didn't see women here much any more. Said they seemed to keep to their all-women baths these days. Times were changing. It was a shame, they said. It had always been the Japanese tradition to bathe all together. But now, pah! – *shikata ga nai*, it has to be – the world changes so fast, what can you do?

They admitted, with good humour, that they had been exceptionally surprised when I had turned up. After all, it wasn't every day that a *gaijin* loomed out of the steamy mist to join them for a soak. Being a bit of a tourist town, they said, they had occasionally spotted a foreign woman peeking around the corner of the hut before swiftly turning tail.

As I wallowed with the friendly Flannel Heads in the blistering, giddy-making heat of the *rotenburo*, listening as their banter turned faster and faster and more and more raucous (most of it sailing clean over my head), I thought, where else but in Japan could I sit alone in a bath with four naked men – strangers, no less! – and feel completely and utterly safe? But here, once I had overcome my initial, Western-prejudiced unease, everything felt fine and Japan-easy. For a moment I could almost have been back in old Japan, when nakedness was not considered shameful. 'They wash twice a day,' reported a seventeenth century Portuguese missionary, 'and do not worry if their privy parts are seen.'

117

As we emerged from the *rotenburo* into the quiet, dark side-street, about to part with jests and bows, the potter foraged in his bag to give me a can of Yakult. Back at my tent, as I perched on a rock to drink it, I read the words on the side of the can:

YAKULT: well-mellowed taste and flavour make surely you feel at ease

Which struck me as an applicable ditty for the end of an appropriate day.

Riding up and over the lower slopes of Mount Yufudake took me past an interminable traffic jam in which all the vehicles were apparently heading (in the unproductive way that traffic jams head nowhere) for the Beppu Ropeway and the big-wheel, big-dipper, big-eyesore theme park that spread itself garishly across Mount Tsurumidake's otherwise wild, green hills.

Following a magnificently swift mountain descent which, for one brief hairy moment, nearly involved a front-wheel entanglement with a fat, two-metre snake, I arrived at Beppu, a sprawling, multi-spa city that lay tucked in a huge bay on Kyushu's east coast. Being one of the largest hot-spring resorts in Japan (luring more than twelve million visitors, mostly Japanese, a year to its 3795 different bubbling water holes), Beppu is pure Japanese-style glitzy hype, with its throngs of enthusiastic flag-waving tourists and gaudy, glitteringly spoilt thermal areas combined with bowling-alleys, *pachinko* parlours and abysmal concrete zoos.

Not wanting to linger with a finger against my nose in the sulphur-reeking city of Beppu for long, I scooted down towards the port, stopping off along the way to pick up some edibles at the Sun Live supermarket. As I was in the process of packing my purchases into my panniers, a slightly buck-toothed man came up to me, speaking in English.

'America?' he asked,

'No, not America.'

'Yesterday?'

'Sorry?'

'Yesterday, you know?'

Interpreting his questions as, 'Where were you yesterday?', I told him I thought I had been near Yufuin. But I had interpreted him wrongly because, before you could say 'Paul McCartney', the man had broken into an unsteady falsetto version of 'Yesterday/All my troubles seemed so far away/Now they look . . .'

After he had finished his solo, he took a carefully folded handkerchief from his pocket and dabbed his beaded brow, declaring, 'The Beatles are my very fine hero,' before bowing and walking away.

Later that day, I had a taster of death – the type of dramatic and rapid death that in Japan can come in the form of a delicacy. What's more, it was the sort of death that can cost 15,000 yen (£100) a portion for the privilege. The lethal *fugu* (pufferfish or globefish), named for its ability to inflate itself to an almost spherical shape to deter its enemies, is deadlier than cyanide, yet Oriental gourmets prize it far more highly than *foie gras*, truffles or caviar.

My near-death experience came about when, wheeling my way towards the port, I was intercepted by Seiji and Saki Kinoshita, a young and vibrant couple who excitedly stopped me in my tracks to tell me that they had passed me in their tour bus a week or so ago, up near Mount Aso. The fact that they recognised me after seeing me for only the briefest of flashes from the seats of their tour bus was obviously all that was necessary to make them feel as if they had known me for years. In a very un-Japanese display of affection (although admittedly the younger generation – who are changing so fast away from the traditions of older society that they are commonly referred to as *shinjinrui*, meaning 'strange species of human being' – are getting a lot more touchy-feely towards each other), Seiji wrapped an arm around my shoulders and insisted I join them for coffee and cakes at the Little Mermaid Bakery.

Seiji and Saki told me that their surname, Kinoshita, meant 'Under the Tree' and that 'Saki' translated as 'Blossom' – all that was needed to complete a cheery and traditionally seasonal Japanese picture in my mind was for Seiji's name to mean 'Cherry', but it didn't. They had only been married a year. Seiji was a car mechanic, while Saki was somewhat unusual in that she was fast working her way up the ladder towards a managerial post in a small publishing company. The Japanese orthodoxy that women belonged at home (the familiar word for 'wife' means 'inside the house') was no longer a reality. In fact, it hadn't been since the 1960s, when women, fed up with the deferential role of the traditional submissive child-bearing housewife, started to make a move towards improving their lowly lot in life.

These things take time and although a woman no longer had to walk ten

119

paces behind her man, Japanese society was still firmly traditional. For instance, millions of housewives across the country continued to wait, literally hand and foot, on their husband (the household patriarch) by cooking, cleaning and washing up for him before settling down to cut his toenails and clean out his ears. The standard assumption, which went back hundreds of years and was generally held by both sexes, was that the primary purpose of a woman's life was to take care of her man and rear his sons (the written ideograph for a man depicts 'power in the field'; for a woman it is simply 'womb'). Mothers tended to be far more important in a Japanese man's life than his wife and it always used to be said that, if your family were ever to be swept away in a flood, you should save your mother first – you could always find another wife.

The revered scholar, Kaibara Ekiken, wrote in the eighteenth century that:

> a woman must regard her husband as her lord and serve him with all the reverence and all the adoration of which she is capable. The chief duty of the woman, her duty throughout life, is to obey.

Even as late as the twentieth century, the great novelist, Natsume Soseki (author of the wonderful *I am a Cat* and *The Three-Cornered World*), minced no words with his prospective bride in an arranged marriage:

> I am an intellectual and have no time to trouble myself with you. Do what I say.

In similar vein, the poet Sakutaro Hagiwara wrote in 1929:

> Women are all primitive and very simple mechanisms, while men are delicate engines with a complicated system.

From an early age, Japanese women were trained to defer to men, to speak in cutesy-squeaky voices, to cover their mouths when they laughed, and to cultivate a submissive personality that would give subtle boosts to the male ego. Even at the end of the 1970s, Masahi Sada took a song to the top of the Japanese hit parade in which he commanded his wife:

> Go to bed last, be first up in the morning,
> Cook tasty food and wear pretty clothes –
> And if I have a little affair, just put up with it!

120

The old *haiku* poem put the husbandly attitude in five words:

Loved
By my wife?
Disgusting!

In the nineteenth century, women were virtually excluded from intellectual life. Politics, literature and science were closed books. As for work, until very recently Japanese women hardly ever considered a career – a job was merely a way to meet a prospective husband. After marriage, it was expected that a woman would give up working to become an obedient 'servant'. Although the number of women pursuing a career had now grown to about half the work-force, and half of all married women worked, the workplace was still a very male-dominated arena and inequality was widespread. To reach the top rungs of a company's ladder was still a long uphill climb for the *kyaria wuman* like Saki: the percentage of managerial positions occupied by women in Japan was only a fifth of the percentage in the United States, for example. In a dossier compiled by the Japanese Working Woman Institute, a dissatisfied woman reported:

Companies demand that women in regular positions think like men, act like ladies and work like dogs.

To return to the matter in hand, or, in this case, mouth – a mouthful of death: Seiji's uncle happened to be a *fugu* fish chef. So, after we had enjoyed a number of the Little Mermaid's coffees and cakes, the newly-weds invited me to visit his *fugu* shop a short bus ride away.

Although the 15,000 yen that connoisseurs paid seemed a bit steep for what could be seen as little more than a deadly side-order of raw fish, the cost, as Seiji explained, came from the preparation. After all, most people didn't want to part with a hefty sum for the sake of dying, even if it was supposed to taste quite nice in the process.

Only a handful of specially trained chefs knew how to remove the fish's venom sack, so the price came not just for the privilege of eating a potentially deadly fish but also for the expertise of the chef. Your life was literally in his fil-leting hands. Should his knife slip, should he be not quite as expert as you might have liked, death could come in the unappetising form of ataxia (inability to control voluntary movements), headaches, abdominal pain and vigorous vomiting. The first sign that death was lurking just around the corner was when your lips turned numb. Unfortunately it didn't take much to get you that way – an amount of poison barely enough to make a *petit*-sized *pois* was enough to wipe out forty adults, no trouble.

Every year there were a few deaths from pufferfish poisoning, but these were usually as a result of home-prepared fish. *Fugu* fish chefs were rigorously licensed and losing customers by way of death was not good for business. It used to be the case that the *fugu* chef who, by way of sloppy puffer preparation, had the misfortune to kill a diner was honour bound to take his own life. Some still did, which sadly added to the fact that Japan had one of the highest suicide rates in the world.

As for history, the effects of the puffer had not passed unnoticed. When Japan was invading Korea in the 1950s, it was ordered that different parts of the *fugu* be fed to Korean prisoners-of-war so that the location of the lethal poison within the fish's body could be determined. A few decades later, a neurologist, explaining to 007's boss (the long-suffering Q) in Ian Fleming's *From Russia With Love*, said, 'It comes from the sex organs of Japanese globefish.' Soon after, James Bond was duly kicked in the calf with a *fugu*-poisoned blade concealed in the boot of one of Bloefeld's unappealing agents. But, strangely, Bond survived.

Even Captain Cook had a near-death experience thanks to the perilous poison of said *poisson* when he and two shipmates unwittingly tasted a morsel during his second voyage around the world on the *Resolution*. He wrote that

we were seized with an extraordinary weakness in all our limbs, attended with a numbness . . . we each of us took a vomit and after that a sweat which gave great relief. In the morning one of the pigs which had eaten the entrails was found dead.

The fate of playing piscine roulette had also found its way into Japanese poetry:

Last night he and I ate *fugu*;
Today, I help carry his coffin.

So, tight-throated and feeling none too confident, I was persuaded to join Seiji and Saki in sampling a marble-sized ball of puffer. Apparently the whole idea of eating the highly esteemed flesh of the *fugu* was to dice with death: to taste, swallow and, as the Americans say, 'enjoy!' – oh, and preferably live to do it all over again. Sincerely hoping that they weren't on some secret lovers' suicide pact, I hesitantly popped the ball in my mouth and chewed. And chewed. My immediate urge was to eschew it instead. I was not impressed. So much for melt-in-the-mouth fish. This small portion of puffer chewed more like a piece of bicycle tyre.

Happily still finding myself alive, I rolled back down to the port, on the way passing such delights as Kentucky Fried Chicken, Italian Tomato, MacDonalds, Mos Burger, Sundelica Bakery France-kan and the steakhouse of Sunday's Sun – all of which, after my brush with the puffer, sounded positively tantalising. But I had to make haste, as I had a ship to catch – a pink-and-purple-painted ship, as it turned out – for the eight-hour journey to Hiroshima.

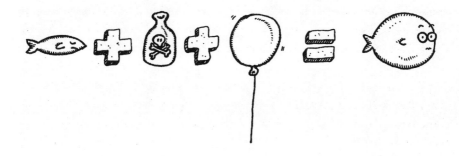

CHAPTER 6

Thrilling Man–Machine Interface

It was good to ride down the ramp of the ferry and immediately feel that Hiroshima, a city that is associated the world over with atomic death, was vibrant, dynamic and very much alive.

An eclectic mix of trams, some dating back to the 1940s, trundled noisily by, packed with people; crowds hurried across repetitive tune-blaring pedestrian crossings; multi-decibel megaphones on the outside of stores and attached to streetlamps competed with each other in a distorted and clashing cacophony. I rode down wide streets of neon and noise, concrete and glass. Everything looked and sounded wonderful for its sheer post-war ugliness.

As dusk dissolved into night, I thought about sleeping in one of the temples or shrines that I passed tucked incongruously amid the suburban sprawl, but each one I stopped at was far from free of clatter and commotion and speed-ily pattering feet. And outrageously over-amplified public announcement systems. So I saddled up again and took off in a semi-lost state until I hit the *eki* (station). Being Hiroshima, the main railway station had a big tourist desk and, as well as stacking up with maps and leaflets and pamphlets and brochures, I came away with a recommended address in hand: that of the nearby Mikawa *minshuku*.

Ten minutes later, a very nice elderly couple (who had a very nice elderly cat) said I could stable my steed in their compact, clobber-filled, subterranean garage. Then *mama-san* showed me upstairs to a dark and tiny *tatami*-matted room. At first I thought its one small window had been concreted over but, once my eyes had adjusted, I realised that what I was looking at was the 'view' – the stained-concrete wall of the next-door building, wedged up against my *minshuku*. I poked my head out of the window and looked down. At ground level, the narrow gap between the two buildings served as a landfill site, with scrunched-up cans, broken beer bottles, old comics and clothes and shoes, plastic bags, food containers, polystyrene and aerosols mounting steadily up the walls. When I craned my neck upwards, all I could see was a scanty slither of concrete sky.

As long as I didn't look out of the window, I liked Mikawa *minshuku*, even though the room was so gloomy. I liked it not least because the room came with green tea and a free energy-boosting banana. Downstairs in the hall beside the front door lay a tray full of all sorts of odds and ends that previous guests had evidently left behind but which were now destined for new owner-ship, according to a sign on the tray that invited you to 'Please Help Yourself'. Never one to pass up the offer of a free gift, I readily pocketed a map, a pen, a packet of Betty Poop handi-pack tissues, a bandanna and a bruised banana. Then, feeling guilty that I might have overstepped the pocketing mark, I refilled the tray with bits of my own that I no longer required: two maps, a book and my recent Kyushu roadside finds – the penknife and the industrial tape measure.

I discovered another English-written sign, pasted on the wall in the bath-room:

PLEAS DO NOT WASH HERE
A COIN MACHINE IS
AVAILABLE ON THE 3RD FL.

This struck me as a bit odd. What else is a bathroom for if it's not for wash-ing in? And anyway, who wants a coin machine when what you are looking for is a bath? Maybe it was a climb-in coin machine which simultaneously washed both you and your clothes? Anything seemed to be possible in Japan these days. In the town of Katsurao, about 100 kilometres north-east of Tokyo, the authori-ties tried to make life easier for its ageing population by giving some of the oldies washing machines with an eighteen-minute cycle to scrub their bodies clean, instead of their clothes.

Hiro ('broad') Shima ('island') is a city built around six delta tributaries of the Otagawa River and is the 'Oyster Capital of Japan'. Hiroshima's superlative oysters – cultivated for over 450 years in the calm Seto Naikai (the Inland Sea) – may lure a number of crustacean-loving connoisseurs to the city but of course most visitors flock to Hiroshima for only one reason: The Bomb.

Before I embarked on the sombre business of joining the heavy-duty tourist pilgrimage to Peace Parks and the like, I took off in a completely opposite direction by riding out along a sprawling shoreline fuming with factories, petrochemical refineries and steelmills until I reached the sacred island of Miyajima. Along with the sand-spit of Amanohashidate (north-west of Kyoto) and the pine-clad islands of Matsushima (lying on the fringes of Sendai), the Japanese consider Miyajima to be one of the most beautiful – and hence much photographed – vistas in all Japan.

Miyajima, also known as Itsukushima ('island of light'), is a small, reverential island liberally sprinkled with shrines and temples. Its main crowd-puller is the vermilion-painted Itsukushima Jinja, founded in the sixth century, which, because of its pier-like construction, seems to be afloat – but only at high tide. The rest of the time it looks as if it is simply sinking into the mud, which must have dampened the spirits of the commoners who, in former days, were forbidden to set foot on the island and had to approach this shrine by boat.

But today's tourists didn't mind the mud: they flocked to Miyajima in their masses to take up position on the specially constructed tiered benches where they could peace-pose with over-tame snack-snaffling sacred deer while sitting framed with the perfect 'must see' photo-album backdrop – the fine vermilion O-Torii (Grand Gate) 'floating' in the sea 200 metres in front of the main shrine. Torii gateways, a kind of wooden portico originating from India, are found all over Japan; made of wood, stone, metal or concrete, they symbolise the division between the sacred and secular worlds and it is said that they serve as a perch for the early-rising rooster crowing to the sun goddess, Amaterasu.

People lived on Miyajima, but they didn't die there – it was against the ancient religious rules, which forbade birth or death on the island, and word had it that the rules had never been broken. As I didn't appear to be pregnant, I saw no chance of my breaking the first rule; but as for the second – well, I decided to watch my step.

The small town of Miyajima, with its narrow streets and alleys and houses, would have been an appealing place had it not been overrun with armies of flag-waving, whistle-blowing tour groups and yellow-capped schoolchildren. The major attraction of the island, apart from the temple, was the cable-car ride up Mount Misen. As I fancied a stretch-of-leg rather than a car-crowded cable, I wandered out of the town to a quiet maple wood until I found a trail that led me on a five-hour trek around the island. At one point I emerged from the woods to surface on the summit of Mount Misen and was surprised to find myself with not another soul around. The riders of the cable-car (or ropeway, as it seemed to be known) all appeared to be quite content with spilling out on the viewing deck of the ropeway terminal – just a short clamber from the top of the mountain – to *chiizu*-grin and snap each other before cabling straight back down again.

And that suited me fine. The view was mine, and a spectacular one too. I could see for miles across the multiple islands and islets of the Inland Sea (which extended for more than 450 kilometres from Hiroshima to Kobe) stretching into the distance, their shorelines riddled with oyster rafts, the coruscating green-wooded mountains and outrageously vast petrochemical complexes of the mainland, and, tucked into the distant crook of the bay, the hazy flat phoenix of Hiroshima itself.

During my mountain perambulations, I kept stumbling upon an impressive array of candle-blackened temples and pagodas and shrines – all a legacy to the island's 1500-year history. One shrine, amidst its wealth of time-worn glory, offered an unusual feature in the form of an AIWA cassette player with a sign on the 'start' button saying 'PUSH'. I dutifully pushed and the AIWA burst into life, producing a series of distorted, tired-tape chanting and inner-shrine sounds. Ancient environment, modern equipment, sitting hand in hand, combining the electric and the archaic, the asinine and the sacred. Odd, but really rather practical. A twenty-four-hour Push-a-Priest. How handy! How apt! How very Japanese!

As I ventured onwards, troops of impetuously chattering and potentially aggressive monkeys gave me the evil eye. Don't even *think* about it, I thought, and kept a wary distance.

Having seen no one for a couple of hours, I was surprised when I caught sight of an old, wizard-like man with wild white hair who darted across my path before climbing a tree. I stopped in my tracks and watched him, unobserved. After a few moments, he broke into a primeval cry. Before long, a cackling monkey loped into view, swung bounding through the trees and landed on the wizard's back. They sat in the branches together for a while, conducting what appeared to be a lively and convivial conversation, before they both swung back down to the ground and lolloped off into the woods. Intrigued, I followed them at a cautious distance until they disappeared into a mountain-top temple that the monkey-man appeared to have made his home. Apart from the sounds of half-man, half-monkey chatterings, there was nothing else to hear or see and so I continued on my way.

As I walked, I thought how the monkey-man reminded me of Shoichi Yokoi, the octogenarian loyal Japanese soldier and folk hero who had hidden in the steamy jungles of Guam for twenty-seven years without realising that the Second World War was over. During his years in the Pacific, the resourceful Imperial Army sergeant had crafted clothing from tree bark and used the cycles of the moon as a calendar. He returned to Japan in 1972, with an army-issue rifle and apology in hand, saying, 'Shamefully, I've come back home alive.'

Before long I arrived at the top of a long, winding series of vast stone steps that looked as if they would lead me back down to the town. Feeling in fit and fine form from my enlivening trek, I took the steps at speed, focusing hard on each stone. Leap, leap, leap. Bounce, bounce, bounce. Blur, blur, blur. Down, down, down. Then suddenly, in mid-flight, with one leg outstretched ready to land, I caught sight of a massive snake sunning itself on the step, a nano-second away from my fast-falling foot.

The sheer shock that flooded through my veins was enough to make me alter course in mid-air and miss the snake-step completely. Sailed clean over. But two steps down, my forward foot landed with painful force, buckling and then keeling my body right over. Bang, bounce, scrape, crash. Stop. Still. Sprawled on stones. Just caught sight of a rudely awoken snake – an immense creature – slithering away between the sun-baked rocks.

Turned all shaky. Took stock. Lost flesh, fresh blood. Nothing too bad. Tested mechanical apparatus: ankles, knees, elbows. Seemed okay. But felt momentarily too paralysed with fear to continue. Maybe more snakes. Maybe man-eating snakes. Who knows? Anything goes in Japan.

But I couldn't stay on the stones. Not if there were snakes. What don't snakes like? Vibrations. Warn them I'm coming. Heavy-foot stamp the ground. I stamped and I stamped, slowly, checking each step. Odd sight should anyone see – a *gaijin* on the loose doing a wardance on the warpath on the steps. Crazy creature. Keep your distance, could be dangerous. Wild eyes, wild steps, wild vibrations. But it worked. I got back down to tourist-town in one piece. No more snakes to be seen.

129

That evening, back in my *minshuku*, I met some new arrivals: a young *gaijin* couple, Margarite and Patrick Sitskoorn, from Holland. Like all Dutch people, they spoke English better than the English. Patrick, who was of Malay descent, was an engineer; Margarite was a psychotherapist. They told me they were travelling for a year through Tibet, China, Japan, Thailand and Malaysia. Margarite said she was planning on writing a book solely about the people she met on her travels and the stories they told her.

Later, while doing our ablutions over the communal basins in the hall, I asked Margarite about her work and we got on to the subject of America. When Patrick had been posted to Detroit to work for an engineering company, she had joined him there as a psychotherapist on the eighth floor of a hospital.

'Have you ever been to Detroit?' asked Margarite.

'No,' I said, 'but I went fairly close.'

I told her how, when I had been cycling out that way three years before, I'd made sure I didn't get sucked into the city after learning that it was a crazy car-jacking place with one of the highest murder rates in the country. Margarite said she could vouch for that, and that I had been very wise to steer clear. Then she told me her story.

One day, when she was working in the hospital, a woman (an ex-patient, totally off her rocker) entered the hospital with a concealed gun, intent on shooting a particular doctor who, she claimed, had messed up an operation on her. Instead of getting out of the lift on the eighth floor, on which the doctor (and Margarite) worked, she mistakenly got out on the seventh. The moment she stepped out of the lift, she went on a mad rampage in which she shot eight doctors and nurses dead. Had the woman got out of the lift on the eighth floor as she had intended, Margarite would most likely have been the first to be shot, as her office was situated through glass doors directly opposite the lift.

Somehow, such an appalling ordeal was not enough to put the wind up Margarite and send her scuttling straight back to The Netherlands and she continued to work in Detroit – even after experiencing another close shave. There she was, she said, driving along one day in stop/start traffic, when a man stepped into the road in front of her car and calmly stood, legs apart, arms rigid, in a *Miami Vice* finger-on-trigger ready stance, his gun pointing into her face. She thought she was dead meat. She survived.

After two near-death experiences, Margarite amazingly still refrained from catching the next flight home. Instead she decided to put her training to positive use by helping out on a housing development scheme in the ghetto. In a matter-of-fact manner, she told me how every child on the project had witnessed at least one rape and one murder before the age of five.

'Most of my patients,' she said, 'were either rape victims, rapists or murderers. Many of the murderers had no remorse whatsoever, their mentality being that they knew the same thing would happen to them sooner or later anyway. They admitted that life was too short to start regretting their actions. It was a sort of "maybe I'll get shot tomorrow but so what?" attitude. For sure, our year in Detroit was a real crazy time!'

Although she seemed so calm and clear-headed, Margarite recognised that the terrible violence of Detroit must have seeped secretly into her bones. She explained what she meant.

'Just after we had returned home, Patrick and I went to a friend's wedding. Everything was fine until someone dropped a plate, which smashed loudly on the floor. It gave me such a fright – I felt certain someone had been shot. I knew then that I'd cracked.'

The next day, arming myself with a banana and two *onigiri* riceballs, I visited the Peace Park to gape at the gaunt wreckage of the Genbaku Domu (A-Bomb

Dome). Formerly the Industry Promotion Hall and built (unlike everything else in old Hiroshima) of brick, concrete and steel, it was one of the few remaining vertical structures in the vicinity that was left after the bomb exploded 580 metres above it at 8.15 on the morning of 6th August 1945, three days before the bombing of Nagasaki. Ever since then, it has been the oldest structure in the city.

Designed by Jan Letzel, a Czechoslovakian architect, and completed in 1915, the now carefully maintained skeletal wreckage of the Dome – its skull jaggedly open to the bowl of sky – continues to stand in a park beside the river as a stark, sombre memorial to the catastrophic destruction of Hiroshima.

When the American plane *Enola Gay* dropped the Hiroshima bomb, almost everything within a three-kilometre radius from the epicentre was annihilated in a blinding flash – a sudden destruction of all life forms, unimaginable suffering, bodies so horrendously mutilated that it was at first scarcely possible to distinguish the living from the dead. The casualty figures were even more shocking than those for Nagasaki: in a population of 344,000, about 200,000 died either immediately or within a short time of the explosion and many more died later as a direct result of the bombing. The world's first atomic attack flattened Hiroshima – all but wiped it out: the landscape resembled a scorched planet, an inferno of death.

The A-Bomb Dome had been preserved as a permanent and defiant symbol of world peace. Outside the Peace Memorial Museum, the Cenotaph (a concrete-stained arch caked in pigeon droppings) contained a stone chest with the names of the victims of the bombing and bore the inscription:

Repose ye in peace for the error shall not be repeated.

The Children's Peace Memorial was dedicated to Sadako, a ten-year-old girl who died of leukaemia caused by atomic radiation. She believed that she would recover from her illness if she could fold a thousand origami paper cranes – the birds that symbolise peace, prosperity, longevity and happiness. She died shortly after making her 644th crane but children from her school folded another 356, with which she was buried. All over Japan schoolchildren continue the custom of weaving together long wreaths of carefully folded paper chains of brightly coloured cranes, each one a tiny exercise of perfection, and I saw them hanging motionless in the enervating humidity of summer, like a rainbow of wreaths.

Peace – *heiwa* – has become a catchword in contemporary Japan, a national obsession, repeated throughout the country like a mantra. I heard it every-where I went, up and down Japan, a hundred times a day. Peace: a magic charm, chanted by monks, sung by schoolchildren, bellowed by masked demonstrators, solemnly invoked by industrialists and politicians. Peace: two fingers frozen into a V, raised by everyone poised before a camera lens.

The Japanese have proclaimed themselves a 'peace-loving people' with a unique role to play in the campaign for world peace and nuclear disarmament. Hiroshima is the spiritual capital of Japan's peace movement, and here 'peace studies' (one of the few subjects outside the examination syllabus) are taught with the high seriousness that the British reserve for sex education. Peace – for a country that once seemed to produce people with a taste for war and a talent for it. Peace – for a country that broadcasts an endless reel of samurai dramas on television, all swords and fighting and gruesome bloody deaths. Peace – for a country that displays gratuitous violence in the *manga* comics that everyone openly reads, from kindergarten to the grave.

The irony of 'peace-loving' Japan is that, although it continues with a con-stitution forbidding it from keeping a standing army, it maintains a 'self-defence force' of 180,000 men and one of the largest military budgets in the world.

Hiroshima's Peace Memorial Museum, like that of Nagasaki, was full of sta-tistical horrors and harrowing pictures and artefacts: a schoolboy's fingernail and skin sample; a hefty tuft of a woman's hair; human forms scorched into pavements, into buildings – shadows of women, men and children who had been incinerated where they stood. And the most famous shadow of all: the sol-dier and the ladder, a photograph I had also seen at Nagasaki and which had imprinted itself on my memory. The young soldier had been climbing a ladder to reach the watchtower just as the bomb exploded. The tar was burnt off the tower except for where he stood on his ladder, leaving his form in a scorched black outline on the remains of the building.

I thought of *Hiroshima Joe*, Martin Booth's novel, which tells the story of Captain Joseph Sandringham, who was taken prisoner by the Japanese. After years in a prisoner-of-war camp, he was transferred towards the end of the war to a slave labour camp in Japan. He happened to be just outside Hiroshima on the day when the bomb was dropped. His guards abandoned the camp and Joe made his way into the city to look for a friend he had made among the Japanese workers. Booth's detailed description of the scene of carnage – the hideously disfigured bodies in grotesquely contorted positions – that met Joe's horrified eyes is almost unbearable to read.

And I thought with a shudder how even the enormity of what had happened to Hiroshima and Nagasaki would pale into insignificance compared with the inconceivable horrors of atomic weapons today – weapons with an explosive power over a thousand times greater than Fat Man and Little Boy combined.

The exhibits of the Peace Museum focused entirely on death, destruction and suffering in Hiroshima but there seemed to be no historical perspective. As the London-born writer Alan Booth, who lived in Japan for many years, wrote after visiting the museum:

> It is as though the bomb fell on Hiroshima, figuratively as well as literally, out of the blue. Nowhere is there any suggestion that it might have been triggered by past actions. Nowhere is there the least sign that any other nation or race might have suffered comparable wartime tragedies.

There was no hint of Japanese atrocities before and during the Second World War: the massacre of 150,000 Chinese in the Rape of Nanking (Emperor Hirohito's brother, posted to Nanking, reported in his memoirs that an officer and classmate had advised him that 'the best way to develop the mettle of the troops was to have them run their bayonets into living prisoners'); the Bataan Death March in the Philippines; the lethal experiments with anthrax, plague and typhus on Allied prisoners and Chinese villagers by Manchukuo Unit 731 and the liquidation of the survivors by the Kempeitai; the rape and murder of twenty-two Australian nurses and thirty wounded men on Radjik Beach on the Sumatran island of Banka in 1942; and the six million Chinese who died between 1937 and 1945, a high proportion of whom were civilian victims of rape and pillage. In 1972 Japan's prime minister Tanaka, when 'normalising' relations with the People's Republic of China, offered amends for the 'great deal of trouble' his country had caused its neighbour. Well, that's one way of putting it.

Then there was the occupation of Hong Kong, with Japanese atrocities such as the massacre of fifty-three surrendered men (many wounded) at Eucliff and the bayoneting of wounded men and doctors at St Stephen's College Hospital followed by gang-raping of the nurses. The Cantonese slang for a Japanese is 'Turnip-head' but it could have been something much harsher.

The catalogue goes on and on and on, against almost all of Japan's Asian neighbours as well as against the Allies, whether military or civilian – the brutal beating to death of the survivors of torpedoed merchant ships, the bayoneting

134

and beheading of prisoners, the killing of prisoners for sport or sword practice or in the course of demonstrations of martial arts, the ploy of holding forced-labour prisoners in camps deliberately sited next to the Americans' bombing targets, the infamous Burma railway built by the forced labour of 54,000 Allied prisoners, of whom 12,000 died along with half of the 250,000 local forced labourers.

All of this seemed so different from the friendly and generous people I had met wherever I went in Japan. And the books I read showed that this period of aggression had no precedent in earlier wars. Foreign observers of the Russo–Japanese War of 1904/5, for example, all reported that the Japanese private soldier was disciplined and well-behaved – the word 'gentleman' was often used. Japanese officers, many of whom were members of the old feudal aristocracy, impressed Europeans with their chivalrous attitude.

So what had happened to all this 'gentlemanly behaviour' in the generation that started to fight in 1937? War historians often say that the main factors were the so-called 'samuraisation' of Japanese society that began in the 1920s, and the way in which Japanese servicemen were subsequently trained. But 'samuraisation' was a misnomer – the old samurai code had been chivalrous, not nationalistic and militaristic. The war historian John Keegan, in his BBC Reith Lecture in the late 1990s, explained:

> The Samurai class which officered Japan's new Western-style army had imposed its own knightly code of honour on the peasant recruits. It was only in the 1930s, when fanatically nationalist officers took charge, that the Japanese armed forces began deliberately to brutalise recruits in training with the object of filling them with hate that would then be turned on foreigners.

Recruits were treated so badly that it is not really surprising that they unleashed all their suppressed rage and violence against their enemies. As they had also been taught that the slightest disobedience against orders from their own officers merited beating or disfigurement, they accepted that torture and death were just deserts for an enemy who had disobeyed the fundamental duty of a soldier to die rather than be taken prisoner.

Face mattered. Even after the dropping of the Nagasaki bomb, the Japanese found the prospect of surrender so unbearably humiliating that the Minister of War, General Anami, said it was 'far too early to say that we lost the war' and that his forces would continue to 'inflict severe losses on the enemy when he invades Japan'. Later the same night, his Emperor over-rode him and the General agreed to 'bear the unbearable'.

As it happened, those hot, sultry days I spent in Hiroshima were a particularly fiery time to be in the city: the 50th anniversary of VJ (Victory over Japan) Day was approaching and the voices of Japan's Second World War victims, demanding at least an apology, were growing increasingly vociferous. They looked at the German example: they saw how Germany had acknowledged its guilt for the Holocaust as well as paying a measure of reparation to the survivors, and how Presidents Kohl and Mitterand had made a memorable pilgrimage to Verdun to settle forever their countries' differences. Japan, on the other hand, gave the strong impression of being totally unaware that there was anything for which to apologise, and prime minister after prime minister had been accused of having consistently wriggled out of expressing the slightest remorse.

The headline in a copy of the *Daily Telegraph* that I found in the reception of the ANA Hotel in downtown Hiroshima (I'd nipped in to use the *benjo*) read: 'Tokyo cannot find the words to say sorry'. Nagasaki's mayor Itcho Ito, a pacifist, stirred it all up a bit more by inaugurating a peace conference in Nagasaki and criticising the American president, Bill Clinton, for saying that President Truman had been right to drop the bomb.

In Hiroshima's Peace Museum, an exhibit entitled 'WHY THE A-BOMB WAS DROPPED ON HIROSHIMA' listed three factors that 'probably led to the hurried dropping' of the bomb:

1. The US wanted to limit its own casualties by forcing the Japanese to surrender as quickly as possible.
2. The US wanted to force Japan to surrender before the Soviet Union could enter the war to secure a stronger political position after the war.
3. The US wanted to use the weapon in war to measure its effectiveness.

Since visiting Japan, I've read countless arguments about why the bombs were dropped, whether they should have been dropped and what would have happened to the rest of the war if they hadn't been dropped. Ito laid the blame on both sides: he blamed his own country for initiating hostilities, but he also blamed America for ending them too bloodily.

Eventually prime minister Tomiichi Murayama broke ranks and expressed his personal 'heartfelt apology' for Japan's past 'aggression', promising to eradicate 'self-righteous nationalism' in his country. He promptly lost his job.

Along with its 'No more Hiroshimas' slogans, its superlative oysters, its red-throated loons (the prefectural bird) and its immensely popular baseball team (The Carps), prosperous Hiroshima was also noted for its Mazda car company. Being the sort of person who enjoys riding bicycles in a clean, quiet, safe and empty-road world (like Iceland), I can't say I go too cock-a-hoop about cars. A handful here, a handful there, kept at bay and used for necessity, would be fine. So visiting such sights as car-production lines and factories has never been high on my agenda. That is, until I hit Hiroshima.

Among the stack of leaflets I picked up at the tourist office was one heralding the glories of the Mazda car plant, which was open to visitors as part of a tour group. Suddenly my appetite was whetted. I might not find cars appealing in themselves but the opportunity of visiting a factory in which a futuristic assembly line of robots is aided by an almost robotic workforce of men to produce an amazing 4000 cars a day, from start to finish, was not easy to cycle on by – especially as the tours were free.

The small print beside the telephone booking line on the Mazda leaflet said: 'Reservation required: Application accepted 6mth in advance.' I rang the number, which was answered by an obsequiously squeaky voice.

'*Moshi-moshi,*' I piped, using the usual Japanese telephone-hello. 'I'd like to book a place on a tour of the Mazda factory.'

'Certainly,' said the squeaky voice, 'but first please you must make some application by mail.'

'Oh, but I'm leaving soon. Can I not come today? I'm only one person.'

'Mmmm. This maybe not so easy. Always today is very popular tour. Always very many people.'

I sent some exaggerated sound-effects of bitter disappointment down the line, which seemed to produce the desired effect.

'*Chotto matte kudasai* – one moment please,' said the squeaky voice.

Chotto matte passed before the voice returned.

'Yes, certainly we have one o'clock vacancy for today please.'

'Thank you,' I said.

'Sor, hotel name please?'

'Hotel?' I asked.

'*Hai, hai.* Hotel name please?'

Having never booked myself on an organised tour before and rather overwhelmed by the novelty of it all, I said, 'Why do you need the name of my hotel?'

'Excuse me?'

'What is the hotel for?'

'Mmmm – Mazda company bus travels to your hotel for collection to factory.'

'Ah so, *desu-ka?*' I said. 'I'm afraid I've just checked out of my hotel, but anyway I was planning on cycling.'

'Excuse me?'

'I don't have a hotel and I will arrive at the factory by bicycle.'

'Bicycle?'

'Yes, bicycle.'

'Ah so, *desu-ka?*'

'So, *desu-ne.*'

Suddenly the thought dawned on me that maybe it was against company policy to arrive at the car factory by bicycle. Policies can be nonsensical like that. There was an awkward silence down the line.

'Hello?' I said, sensing a communication breakdown.

'Excuse me,' came the squeaky voice.

Fearing that the whole laborious conversation was about to slip into oblivion, I decided to recapture lost ground before my factory-visiting chances went sliding off the production line.

'I will arrive at the Mazda factory for the one o'clock tour,' I said and proceeded to give my name.

'*Chotto matte kudasai,*' came the response. So, like the good citizen I am, I dutifully waited a moment.

'Hello, may I help you?' said a man's voice.

'Oh, hello,' I replied, 'I was just ringing to confirm my booking for the one o'clock tour.'

'One o'clock?'

'Yes, one o'clock.'

'You are how many person?'

'I am one person.'

'Mmmm – you are not many person?'

'No, I am not many persons.'

'Excuse me?'

Oh dear – I felt I had been here before. Perhaps the time had come to say goodbye.

'Goodbye,' I said. 'Oh, and thank you.'

Hedging my bets on the chances of getting a place on the one o'clock tour, I arrived outside the Mazda reception half an hour early. There was not another bicycle in sight, which, for urban bicycle-riding Japan, was very unusual. A man in a boiler suit appeared through a side door and said, 'Ha ha! Bicycle in car company! Ha ha!'

A young, timid-looking woman trotted out of reception and said, 'Excuse me, no bicycle allow here.'

'Oh,' I said. 'Do you mean bicycles aren't allowed outside reception or aren't allowed in the company grounds?'

'Ah so, *desu-ka?*' said the woman, which, funnily enough, is just what I thought she would say.

The boiler suit boldly took the situation into his own hands.

'Please, bicycle here is very fine indeed,' he said. And without further ado he wheeled my bike into the small storeroom from whence he had originally appeared.

'Bicycle for safety keeping, ha ha!' he said.

'Ha ha!' I replied and thanked him before walking into the Mazda reception.

On first impressions, Mazda's reception area looked like that of a well-to-do hotel – apart, that is, from an assortment of extremely shiny cars posing with a come-hither look upon the equally shiny floor. There were various framed placards on display trying to woo the visitor with words like: 'Welcome to the MAZDA MUSEUM ENTRANCE HALL . . . challenging sport and innovation . . . where the RX-7 – the Sports Car of today – is waiting to welcome you.'

I shuffled over to the RX-7, curious to know how it was going to go about welcoming me, but it just sat there, parked, looking very . . . well, car-like.

Another placard said:

MAZDA:
Clean Industry
Clean recycling
Clean engineering
Clean spirit

Hmmm. How, I wondered, could Mazda, which in its Hiroshima plant alone produced some 1.5 million lung-spluttering, polluting cars a year, call itself clean? A piece I'd read in *New Internationalist*, by John C. Ryan and Alan Thein

Durning of Seattle, about the impact that the manufacture of an average car has upon the environment compared with the average bicycle went some way to proving that Mazda was perhaps not quite as spotless as it might like to think:

> CAR: When I drive alone 95 per cent of the energy goes into running the 1,450 kilo car – not me, its 64-kilo cargo.
>
> COMPOSITION: My car contains 800 kilos of steel, 180 kilos of iron, 112 kilos of plastics, 86 kilos of fluids and lubricants, 85 kilos of aluminium and 62 kilos of rubber. Nearly half the steel began as scrap, melted in an electric-arc furnace generating eight pounds of toxic dust. The rest came from a far dirtier place – an open pit mine . . . Altogether 1,590 kilos of iron ore was mined, producing 955 kilos of waste rock which was dumped. The ore was taken to a steel mill where it was blasted in a coke-burning furnace producing carbon monoxide and dioxide. Assembling the car involved 10,000 parts, welded in 4,000 spots. Nearly 150,000 litres of water were consumed – more than 100 times its weight. My car's body was then painted . . ., dipped into baths of detergent, zinc phosphate and chromic acid, before being submerged in air-polluting primer and baked. Six more coats of paint were applied, including PVC solvent. The unusable sludge from overspray was trucked to a landfill.
>
> IMPACT: My car's mainly made of steel – the biggest industrial producer of carbon monoxide and hazardous waste. In assembly, painting was the most polluting process, emitting volatile organic compounds (VOCs) which produce smog. However, most of my car's environmental impact comes when I get behind the wheel. During its nine-year lifespan it will use about eight times as much energy as it took to make and the exhaust from my car will combine with others to constitute the world's single largest source of poisonous greenhouse gas – carbon monoxide.

> BIKE: When I ride my bike to work I use less energy per distance than any other form of transport – including walking!
>
> COMPOSITION: My . . . entire bike [uses] less aluminium than just one car wheel . . .
>
> IMPACT: On my bike I cause no air pollution and make no contribution to global warming. I consume no fossil fuels and send no toxic chemicals into the air. I take a fraction of the space that cars take on

roads and a twentieth of the parking. And biking is safer per mile than driving.

CONCLUSION: If I didn't feel like a smug, self-righteous cyclist already (which I did), then I certainly felt at the height of all sanctimonious holier-than-thous now!

The reception filled with my tour companions, most of whom were Japanese, and then, once everyone had clocked on, we were scooped up by a company bus that ferried us down the road to the Mazda museum and factory. Our tour guide was an excessively courteous young woman who, with microphone in hand, reeled off an endless array of facts and figures:

'The largest Mazda plant is in Michigan, USA, which employs 240,000 people . . . There are ninety motor companies in Hiroshima . . . The Mazda plant has its own private bridge which is the world's largest bridge owned by one company . . . Mazda transports its employees around the city in its own fleet of private buses . . . The plant has its own swimming pool and supermarket and its own port – from where it exports its vehicles to 124 countries (60 per cent of the total vehicle production is exported) . . . The car plant has no windows on the residential side of the building so as not to disturb our neighbours . . .'

The museum had several sections, in which we were allotted a precise amount of browsing time before our guide politely channelled us through to the next one. In the 'Theatre', where 'you will get to know the heart of Mazda through sight and sound . . . and see how Mazda expresses concern for people and the earth', we were force-fed multiple screens of videos showing such bizarre far-from-world-destroying scenes as glorious gushing waterfalls (in slow motion), delightful fields of flowers bursting into bloom, rolling surf exploding (again in slow motion) on the shore, angelic little girls gaily skipping through lush wildflower meadows, kingly trees bursting into leaf and blowing in the wind, and a majestic pod of spouting and diving whales – all displayed before us to the soundtrack of New Age, wishy-washy, wave-breaking, pan-pipe muzak. Truly unbelievable.

'Excuse me,' I said to the guide, 'but what has all this got to do with manufacturing motor cars?'

'Mmmm – we show how Mazda care very much for all environment.'

'Cares for the environment?' I said, disbelievingly. But before I had a chance to receive a satisfactory answer, it was conveniently time to be chivvied along to the next section: 'Automobile Technologies', where we could 'see the whole process of producing an automobile'.

Bits of cars in various stages were displayed beneath dazzling spotlights. One placard informed us that 'the average car takes four years from design to production'; other samples of car came labelled with various inexplicable captions like 'Basic Concepts' or 'Thrilling Man–Machine Interface'. On one side of the room sat a very useful life-size model of a car built in clay (that's my sort of car – a car that goes nowhere) while on the other side one was able to have hands-on experience with a sample of 'Belgian Road' cobbles. 'In Belgium there are many stone roads using stones such as these, which were sent from Belgium for MIYOSHI PROVING GROUNDS.' Ahh so, *desu-ka?*

Another section demonstrated the various stages of spraying a car's body. On reading that 'the painting is not only beautiful, but highly resistant to acid rain', I wondered if the thought had ever occurred to the Mazda-makers that if they didn't churn out so many cars then there wouldn't be so much acid rain, which would mean they wouldn't have to produce a paint that was resistant to . . .

The next bit was the best bit, the bit I had come along to see: the U1 Assembly Line. Here an expressionless workforce of robotic men worked in tandem with an unearthly encounter of futuristic robots – sticking, screwing, pasting, banging, bolting and panelling car after car after car, all sliding endlessly forward on a vast conveyor belt. Each man, with his trolley of tools and bolts and boxes of weird widgets, worked like an automaton with phenomenal speed and efficiency, utilising to maximum effect the few seconds he had to fit what looked like a million parts on to each semi-complete car: windscreen rubber, front bumper, floor carpets, inner rear panelling, roof fabric, seat runners . . . before the next vehicle was upon him and he spun his trolley of tools back a few feet to start hectically all over again . . . and again . . . and again.

In the 1950s, when the founder of Nissan cars visited the Austin Longbridge plant in England, he was shocked to see that at ten in the morning the British workers stopped and the assembly line was halted while they took a ten-minute tea break. At Nissan's plants, rest periods were staggered so that the production line kept moving.

Now in the 1990s, I found the sight of all the Mazda robots hypnotic. I could have stood there for hours, staring at the mad, inanimate 'men', their pneumatic limbs performing improbably meticulous and indefatigable tasks. But time was limited and the guide was urging me to follow the rest of the pack, who had already obediently disappeared into the museum's 'History' section.

I wanted to take some photographs but the guide said, 'Sorry, no picture allow on factory floor.'

142

'Why not?' I asked.

'Sorry no picture allow,' she repeated, in such a mechanical fashion that I wondered if she, too, was really a robot disguised as a human being. Mildly exasperated, but uncomplaining, I put away my camera. As the guide shuffled off, I turned to stare one last time at the scene of supreme organised chaos spread out below me. The constant noise, the fumes, the airlessness, the repetitiveness, the mind-bashing monotony – how could these men stand it? There was I, about to swan off across the breezy green Chugoku-Sanchi mountains to Honshu's northern coast, while these men were imprisoned in here every day for nine-hour shifts, forced to work like servomechanisms within a fast, machine-minded regime making millions upon millions of motorised objects that sucked up the mind and ate up the world.

Just before I reached the end of the glass-fronted elevated passageway, eyes still glued to the mad-cap world below, I spotted an amazing Mazda spectacle. At one end of the factory floor, sandwiched between the whirling maniacal world of the car-clumping conveyor belts, sprouted a minute Japanese garden – a mind-calming and tranquil oasis of fastidiously raked gravel and impeccably clipped bonsai forests complete with lilliputian rockeries and waterfalls and precisely laid stones. A little piece of serenity stuck on the end of a frenzied scene of manic insanity. A stark juxtaposition of extremes. How utterly bizarre! How very Japanese!

I wondered if the workers had a company song to keep them fuelled with enthusiasm. In the 1960s, Matsushita Electric was emerging as a new electronics firm. Its founder, Konosuke Matsushita, summed up what the firm was about: 'Matsushita makes people: it also makes some electric goods.' The company song's refrain went like this:

> To build a new Japan
> Let us put our strength and minds together
> Endlessly and continuously
> Like Water Gushing from a fountain
> Grow, industry, grow
> Harmony and sincerity – Matsushita Electric!

It's all too easy to scoff and disparage such a cloying corporate embrace but, at the time, the sense of the 'company as family' fitted in well with Japan's old tradition of clan and class.

The rest of the Mazda museum seemed fairly uneventful – just a yawn-worthy historical section looking back over the company's past, and a futuristic section displaying new technologies in the offing, including one memorable model that went by the unfortunate name of the Mazda HRX Hydrogen Wankel Power. Never mind that it functioned by splitting hydrogen and oxygen to get electrolysis – this compact little Wankel Power sounded like a prime contender for hand-cranking.

CHAPTER 7

Through-Leg Viewing

By mid-afternoon I was back in the saddle and slowly shaking off the sprawling urban entrails of Hiroshima as I steered inland across the mountains to Miyoshi. I was crossing Chugoku, the long, thin tail of Western Honshu, a district that is divided into two, east to west, by the spine of the Chugoku Mountains. On the leeward side of these mountains lay the balmy region of San'yo ('Sunny Side of the Mountains'), through which I was currently passing – a region that encompassed the heavily industrialised and densely populated coastline of the somnolent, thousand-island-studded Inland Sea.

To the north of this natural dividing line lay the relatively inhospitable region of San'in ('Shade of the Mountains'), which, by Japanese standards, was said to be comparatively uncrowded, rural and wild. That sounded a good enough reason to go rolling that way, shade or no shade.

Once the last of the hot, flat, beast-grey concrete city, lying sprawled beneath a sepia haze of pollution, had slid out of sight, I passed through a still, latticed landscape of shimmering rice fields interspersed with tiny, thatch-roofed wattle-and-daub huts used to store wood. Everywhere I looked there were bent-backs at work.

One morning I stopped to use the *benjo* of a small, rural railway station – the sort of quiet, sedate-paced place where the locals routinely walked along and stepped over the tracks to get home or visit a neighbour. A handful of higgledy-piggledy houses sat clustered around the station and along the narrow road by

145

which I had entered the village. A group of toddlers romped together, chasing each other among the pristine roadside flower boxes. Humming housewives flung their futons out of the window to air or draped them over the fence, the railings or the family car. Old folk pottered along on creaking bicycles or pushed loaded wheelbarrows of vegetables. Others strode around with big baskets of foliage tethered to their backs.

An *obaasan* in flowery pinny and baggy *mompe* work trousers spotted me remounting my machine and shuffled over excitedly. Owing to her lack of teeth, I couldn't catch most of what she said but that didn't seem to matter. She chattered and chuckled while I smiled and nodded and pretended to understand every word. Then, reaching up to grasp my arm (she was all of three feet tall), she said, '*Kohii, kohii*,' and, before waiting for an answer, steered me towards a vending machine, from which I imagined she was going to treat me to a can of coffee.

I was wrong. Instead, we sailed straight past the vending machine and shuffled off together along the street. The *obaasan* appeared to know everyone we passed and before long we had attracted a considerable collection of chatty and guffawing old biddies tagging along around us.

Finally we all came to rest outside an old wooden house lined with tubs of exotic flowers. A patch-backed dog lay sleeping, curled in the road. Untroubled by our clatter, the dog continued to snooze as we all stepped carefully over its restful form and in through the sliding door of what was apparently the *obaasan*'s house.

With shoes kicked off and slippers slipped into, we shuffled down the long, dark, shiny worn-wood corridor to a small *tatami*-cluttered room that led to a tiny, topsy-turvy kitchen. While *obaasan* busied herself making pots of *kohii*, I sat cross-legged on the *tatami* around a low square table with her convivially chuckling chums. They were all neighbours and had lived all their lives in the village, looking after an assortment of husbands and children and mothers-in-law-from-hell.

Cups of rich, black *kohii* appeared, along with various saucers full of *bisuketto* (biscuits) and sweet fried *nori*. Every now and then we heard the front door slide open followed by a humorous, croaky-throated shout to which *obaasan* replied with an equally raucous return, and, after a few slipper-shuffling steps, we'd be joined by another wrinkled octogenarian who'd either had wind of the fact that a WI coffee morning was taking place or had heard there was a rare *gaijin* on the loose.

At one point a neighbour's nine-year-old granddaughter banged briskly on the door and stepped boldly inside without waiting for it to be answered. While taking her shoes off in the hallway, she called out, '*Ojama shimasu*!' – a standard phrase used at times like this, which translates as something like: 'I'm going to be a nuisance!' She trotted in, nodded and bowed, took a hundred-yen coin off her *obaasan* for a can of sugar-fizz juice from the vending machine, then scampered back out, turning to give a quick little bow at the door with the words, '*Ojama shimashita*!' – 'The nuisance is now over!'

Everyone was chatting and joking and ribbing each other. They all wanted to know the usual sort of things. What was a young thing like me running around on my own for? What did I eat? Where did I sleep? Wasn't I scared? Where was my boyfriend, my husband, my children? What did my parents think? And so on and so on.

I made up half of what I said – mainly because I couldn't keep up with the speed and toothless pronunciation of the women's Japanese. To some I was married, to others I wasn't. To some I had produced a couple of offspring (sons, I believe), to others I was a poor childless soul. To some I was twenty-one, to others I was twenty-six and to others I was a more accurate twelve-and-a-half (I still am, in spirit at least). Whatever I was – which by now I wasn't quite sure myself – it all made for a spot of high-spirited banter and tongue-tied confusion.

Following the *kohii*, several leaning towers of *obaasan*'s photograph albums appeared, with pages and pages of peace-posing snaps: sitting on a multi-tiered stand of steps with a busload of grinning geriatrics in front of Japan's Number One most famous sight, while over the page . . . sitting on a multi-tiered stand of steps in front of Japan's Number Two most famous sight, while . . . what do you know, there they are again, over the page, sitting on a . . . and so the tiers of seats and people and pages went on . . . and on . . . and on – which reminded me to remember not to force-feed my holidaying snaps to my friends . . .

Because Japan's older generation grow to such wizened and ancient age (often still to be found energetically pushing wheelbarrows up vertical mountains or beavering away in sprightly fashion in their vegetable patches a good century or more after they were born), they have large numbers of grandchildren, great-grandchildren, great-great-grandchildren and probably even great-great-great . . . all very much alive and kicking around them in various extended-family shapes and forms. And the *obaasan* whose albums I was now ploughing through with gay abandon was certainly no exception. She lovingly insisted on reciting to me the names of every Tom, Dick and Harry, and who was married to whom, and who had produced whom and who was currently in mid-production, so that by the end of this lengthy family-photo saga I felt qualified to write a doctorate on the Phenomenally Extensive Family of *Obaasan.*

By now coffee morning was sliding promisingly fast into lunchtime. Together with another diminutive woman of ancient age, *obaasan* rustled up a veritable mini-banquet of a thousand tiny dishes, which arrived with aplomb and a plum (pickled) for me to suck on sourly for starters. The variety of food was extensive: *anago* (eel) *sushi, sashimi, miso* soup, chilled tofu with ginger, fried octopus, prawn *tempura, daikon* (giant white radish), deep-fried pumpkin and lotus root, seaweed-encased balls of sticky rice, *zaru soba* (cold noodles), various grilled and dried fish, *seramame* beans, spinach-like *chigen-sai* and *takenoko* (bamboo shoots), all washed down with copious quantities of iced *oolong-cha.*

At noon, *obaasan*'s husband appeared at the door just in time to join our feast. Sinking on to his knot of knees, he folded himself at the table, pinned in by the all-enveloping party of chattering and clattering hens. He said not a word – just grunted while spectacularly sucking and slurping his food. Once finished, he vacuumed his cock-eyed teeth with tongue-forced spittle. Sometimes he smiled, but not often. When I next turned round, he had gone – vanished into the woodwork.

Meanwhile, us girlies were still going strong. Super-sweet watermelon and cherries appeared. And Kirin beers. An oscillating patter of chatter. Didn't understand half of it but didn't matter. Everything turning into hazy-headed and comical confusion. These were real people with huge hearts and diabolically infectious humour.

Sitting there among such elderly souls, I wondered what horrors their fathers or husbands or sons might have committed half a century before. But then I felt almost too distant from all that to let it really matter. I hadn't been there. I hadn't seen it. I hadn't felt it. I couldn't begin to understand. All I could really feel were my own experiences with the people of Japan. And with all their curious oddities and idiosyncratic vernacular and traits, I found them a totally baffling but lovable race.

On a steep hillside not far from Shobara-shi I saw a pain-grimacing racing cyclist clad in a fluorescent pink ski jumpsuit dragging a hefty truck's tyre along the ground behind the back wheel of his bike. At first I thought my eyes were playing tricks on me after overdosing on *obaasan*'s fried octopus. But no, as I stopped to stare, this really was a pink, skin-tight-suited cyclist in the middle

Crow's-nest view of *Ji Fung* under sail before the storm struck.

Japanese sex kitten.

Japanese sex dog.

Japanese carnival.

Drying squid on Honshu.

Buried bodies in Kyushu.

Sunbathing seaweed in Hokkaido.

The green, green hills of my tented home. *Goto Islands.*

Not all Japan is concrete and cars and commotion.

Eyeing up the *ema* – shrine plaques upon which personal wishes are written.

Statues in commemoration of lost children. *Kiyomizu-dera Temple, Kyoto.*

Multi-hatted tour group more intent on shrine-viewing than pocket-watching. *Itsukushima Shrine, Miyajima, Honshu.*

Advanced form of people carrier. *San'in coast, Honshu.*

Adopting obligatory through-leg viewing style of Amanohashidate – the non-floating Bridge to Heaven. *Wakasa Bay, Honshu.*

The last supper – polishing off seaweed-laced noodles with Keiko before setting sail for the rainy rainy-free land of Hokkaido. *Maizuru, Honshu.*

If in doubt, camp in a park. *Kamisuge, Chugoku Mountains, Honshu.*

Taken under the wing of local women on their way to the bath house. *Kinosaki-cho, San'in coast, Honshu.*

Welcomed to the bosom of the bath house. *Bear Hot Springs, Shiretoko Peninsula, Hokkaido.*

My motorcycling bathing companion wallowing in the scalding waters beside the freezing sea. *eseki onsen, Shiretoko Peninsula, Hokkaido.*

The fine forms of junior sumo stars limbering up. *Asahikawa, Hokkaido.*

Feeling in tip-top form after running along volcanic ridge from yonder distant peak. *Kirishime Yaku National Park, Kyushu.*

Soaking up a rare bit of sun on Rebun Island's more hike-than-bike rocky pinnacled coastline.

On collision course with the rare lesser-spotted, reflector-chested, crash-barrier-roosting owl. *Near Mount Rausu, Shiretoko Peninsula, Hokkaido.*

It's a hard life, all this bright and breezy bivouacking on beaches. *Near Nekko Iwa, Rebun Island.*

Feeling dapper and ready for action in my freshly scavenged dustbin-dwelling climbing boots. *Mount Rausu, Shiretoko Peninsula, Hokkaido.*

Hot-footing it across a scalding sulphur-reeking stream, higher up on Mount Rausu.

lly-legged but triumphant on the top of Mount Rausu.

evived enough to soak up the sea and the sky, looking back at my distant near-coastal
arting point.

Roadside reminder of the perils of motorcycling. *Hokkaido.*

Japanese Hell's Angel – spoiling the tough-nut effect by wearing flip-flops. *Okinawa.*

Spreading wings in the motorcycling mecca of Kutcharoko Lake, Hokkaido.

he mysteries of the moment.

Workman's fetching sun-brim hard-hat.

huge-hearted, hard-working, field-tilling granny.

Sucked up into a colourful carnival convoy. *Rishiri Island.*

Japan – the only country where I've ever felt tall. *Okinawa.*

of some sort of outlandish training ritual. Up and down the long steep hill he went, eyes forever fixed on the hot, tacky tarmac a foot in front of his wheel. As I rolled on down the road, I thought how strange were the extremes to which some people went in order to get fit.

Towards evening I was merrily cycling along when I passed an old woman in short black gumboots and a large flowery kerchief. She was loading a wheelbarrow at the side of the road with mounds of shrubbery.

'*Konnichiwa!*' she called.

'*Konnichiwa!*' I responded.

'Where are you going with all that?' she asked.

'Hokkaido,' I said.

'Gaa!' she exclaimed, and promptly fell into her barrow.

Up the road I stopped at a block of brand new and exceedingly swanky public toilets that adjoined a layby. In fact, they were so swanky that they were more akin to the gold-tapped kind of thing you might expect in a five-star hotel than to a roadside convenience for grimy truckers and even grimier cyclists. Not a speck or a spit or a droplet of dirt. Not a hint or a glimmer of graffiti. No clogged pans, no dubious missiles of misfired toilet paper lurking on the floor like unexploded mines waiting to be stepped on by an unsuspecting foot, no wonky old basins on their last legs hanging off the wall, no bashed-in doors dangling precariously on a single hinge two screws short of death, no surfaces or walls or handles you daren't touch for fear of contracting some severely infectious disease. No, this spanking clean Japanese *benjo* beat the pants off any bog-standard British counterpart, for sure.

Happily there were none of our thoroughly unhygienic Western-style toilets either – just the practical, get-on-down, skidoo-shaped squats. When will the West see sense, I wonder, and scrap sit-on lavatories in favour of the East's simple but effective back-to-basic squats? I feel certain that the move would go down a treat with British women, who are particularly suspicious of germs and gremlins that may be lurking on unfamiliar lavatory seats – seats that have long been suspected as a potential source of infection, especially the type that is normally transmitted through sexual contact. In a recent survey, 89 per cent of British women admitted that they squatted over rather than sat on public lavatories. Americans, as Americans are wont to do, take it a drop further. A US health magazine advised readers to lift the seat with a toe, rather than a hand, and to use an elbow to operate the flush lever. When will that spending-penny drop that us girls just don't like the toilets we have to face with our rears?

Until going to Japan, I had always rated Scandinavia as the Queen of all

Hygiene. But not any more. It was in Japan that I discovered a supreme state of mostly impeccable WCs and it was in Japan that I learnt about *kokin guzzu*. Now, although *kokin guzzu* may sound like something you migh eat with rice, it was in fact the upshot of Japan's hygiene paranoia. *Kokin guzzu* was the antibacterial substance that the Japanese were using to create germ-free goods. So great was this obsession with cleanliness that it was possible to buy *kokin guzzu*-treated tea towels, toothpaste, ice-machines, wallpaper, toys, origami paper, steering wheels, pyjamas and even underwear.

A short distance from the sparkling public conveniences was a small country store, where I bought some supper supplies from an old man behind the counter. As I was packing my purchases into my panniers, the wheelbarrow-pushing granny whom I had just passed down the road pulled up at the store.

'Gaa! You again!' she exclaimed. Then she reached for my elbow and steered me back into the store.

'This *gaijin*,' she said to the old man behind the counter, 'is travelling to Hokkaido!'

'Gaa!' said the old man and he gave me a cup of *kohii* and a creamy, icy *aisu-kuriimu*. His name was Akira Tokunaga and he turned out to be the old woman's husband. They asked where I was sleeping that night.

'Somewhere up the road in my tent,' I said.

'But you must stay with us!' they replied in unison and pointed through the window to a house on the hill.

As I wanted to get a few more kilometres under my belt before dark, I thanked them for their offer but said I would be fine camping. Maybe thinking that I didn't fancy staying the night with a couple of old dears, Mr Tokunaga said, 'I know – you must stay with my daughter in Shobara-shi. Come on, I will give you a lift in my van.'

Definitely not fancying back-tracking some twenty kilometres to an unexciting city when I could be sleeping in the mountains, I tried my best not to sound ungrateful but reiterated that I would be fine camping as time was running short for getting to Hokkaido. Not taking no for an answer, Mr Tokunaga then rang a friend of his who had worked for six months in a local government office in Oakley, California, twenty-five years ago. After a long and mostly incomprehensible conversation of throaty and speedy staccato, Mr Tokunaga unexpectedly passed the receiver to me.

'*Moshi-moshi*,' I said.

'*Moshi-moshi*,' said a man's voice. 'Why are you wishing for camping?'

'Because I'm planning on cycling up into the mountains for tonight.'

'For one person only this is dangerous activity.'

'Why?' I asked, wondering if he might be referring to the unlikely possibility that a serial-killing bear was on the loose.

'*Hai, hai*! Very much dangerous indeed.'

'But why is it dangerous?' I asked again, sensing that I was going nowhere fast.

'Hai, hai! I offer recommendation you stay with Mr Tokunaga. Very fine friend indeed.'

'Well, thank you, but I still have a long way to go and time is running out.'

'Excuse me?'

'I was planning on cycling up the mountain before putting up my . . .'

'Mountain? Which mountain today?'

'The one up the road.'

'I suggest this offer big chance of dangerous situation.'

'Why is it dangerous?'

'*Hai, hai* – you must stay in Japanese hotel.'

'But there aren't any hotels up the mountain. And anyway, hotels are very expensive.'

'Excuse me?'

'Japanese hotels are not cheap.'

'*Hai, hai*. Very cheap hotel. And Number One safety!'

Before we could sink further into the murky mires of confusion, I thanked Mr Tokunaga's friend for his help and quickly passed the receiver back to Mr Tokunaga himself to take the matter in hand. After another half an hour of procrastinating misunderstandings, I was finally about to make a move when a car drew up outside and in swept a feisty young woman.

'Harrow!' she said. 'My name is Hiroko Katou. I am thirty years old. I work in local government town office in Saijo-cho. I am your translator. May I help?' In her hand she held a pen, ready poised to take notes on the first page of an enormous art pad.

Somewhat taken aback, I said, 'Oh, hello, Hiroko. How did you know I was here?'

'Ah, okay. My boss – his colleague he telephone to me for explaining your situation.'

'Oh, well, that's very nice of him, but he really shouldn't have troubled you, as I'm fine.'

Any plans for a speedy getaway were fast flying out of the window, especially when Mrs Tokunaga brought us a tray of tea and sweet rice cakes and invited us, in her own inimitable way, to make ourselves at home on the raised *tatami*-mat floor behind the counter. No sooner had we taken our first sips of tea – Hiroko just having time to tell me in her precise facts-and-figures way how Route 9 (which I was planning on joining to ride along the San'in coast) was exactly nine times busier than Route 183, which I was currently following – than the 'Dangerous Mountain Voice' on the telephone materialised in the form of a man who stepped through the doorway. More tea appeared. More laughably brain-blurring conversation. The Tokunagas joined in. No more gallivanting up mountains tonight for me.

I ended up camping behind the store on a narrow stretch of Japan's universal battleship-grey gravel. In the pocket of my tent lay the key to the store, which Mr Tokunaga had given me for the night as both he and his wife insisted that I should use the store's kitchen and television and help myself to any food on the shelves, and that I must promise to move inside to sleep on the *tatami* should the weather turn to rain.

Although by now I was well conditioned to the extraordinary generosity of the Japanese, their spontaneous big-heartedness still never failed to overwhelm me. For instance, I just couldn't imagine a foreign stranger on a bicycle in England turning up out of the blue at a small rural post-office (that is, if there are any left after the supermarket giants have finished eating up our traditionally quaint country ways) and having the postmaster and his wife feed and water the stranger before closing the store early (as Mr Tokunaga had done, to give me some privacy) and happily handing over the keys to their business premises with the invitation to use all the amenities and to graze their way through shelves of edibles should the fancy so strike, along with sleeping beside an unemptied till.

Later that evening, just as I was nicely stretched out in my tent and turning semi-comatose, the government office man returned, crunching across the gravel to the mouth of my nylon home.

'Jodie-*san*,' he said, 'you have satisfactory safety?'

'Yes, I have fine Number One safety – thank you!' I assured him.

Adopting his favourite Californian phrase, he said, 'Take it easy!' and left a bag of oranges and two Asahi beers for me outside my tent.

When I had been planning my route on the map in Hiroshima, I'd assumed I would nip across the tail of Honshu in no time, my approximate estimations of my jaunt from the San'yo to the San'in coast being only about 300 kilometres.

In the event, it took me days and days. This was not because of all the mountains getting in the way (by Japanese standards they were relatively harmless) or because rainy season was having a second wind and had struck with an uncalled-for vengeance, but simply because of the ceaseless hospitality I received from the country folk I met along the way. Every day I was constantly being stopped by people insisting they feed me, water me, wash me, house me and, frankly, pamper me to the extreme. Then, no sooner was I just getting going again when I would have to jam on the brakes because another cup of tea or can of beer or bowl of noodles was being proferred my way.

There was the little round housewife walking her dog in the park, for example. Espying me taking a break from the rain beneath a picnic shelter, she insisted on taking me back to her riverside home to meet her young, sumo-shaped son, feed me, wash my clothes, and give me a bath and a bed. The following morning, she made me an exquisitely prepared *bento* complete with yellow-flowered garnishes, fish-shaped sachets of soy sauce and a brand new set of 'Hello Kitty' chopsticks.

Then there was the bent-backed husband and wife team (with a combined age of least 240 years) working their abundant vegetable patch. Having beckoned me over to give me some iced tea from their flask, they refused to let me go, chirpily insisting I become their adopted daughter (or more like their great, great, great . . . . granddaughter).

Next it was the moped-riding policeman. For a moment I thought he was going to arrest me for camping in a shrine but instead he invited me back to visit the local police station, where he gave me two cups of *kohii* and took peace-posing snaps of me with his pals as they all tried to look serious.

There was the mountain-river fisherman, too, who wanted me to spend all day with him so he could teach me how to fish. I survived a comically line-hurling and fishless few hours with him before I conceded defeat and threw in the sponge. Getting tangled up in a fisherman's tackle was not quite for me.

Despite the days of continuous rain, the dense green mountains were a wonder for riding. Off the main roads, traffic was minimal and I passed through villages consisting mostly of a few old wooden houses sitting among luxuriant vegetable plots. Nearby there would always be a shrine and a shop (which doubled up as the family's front room), a bus stop (although I never once saw a bus) and an incongruous huddle of super-bright modern vending machines. Sometimes there was a school.

Always there were the infernal tannoys, attached to concrete telegraph poles or hanging off school roofs, shattering the peace with the same brain-gratingly over-amplified and distorted 'music' throughout the day. Much of Japan seemed to be set to muzak: parks, beaches, temples, towns, ski slopes, harbour fronts, botanical gardens, reverential tourist sights, pelican crossings, petrol stations, public conveniences, ferries, castles, zoos, train stations, even toilet rolls, from one end of the crenellated 3800 kilometres of the archipelago to the other – schmaltzy incidental music that opened and closed on your life, warding off the pleasurable dangers of silence. And on top of all that, politicians hired vans with multi-decibel megaphones to terrorise unsuspecting neighbourhoods at 8 a.m. on Saturday mornings, loudly broadcasting their campaign promises to reduce noise pollution.

Every primary school I passed at around four o'clock in the afternoon would be blasting out music – always the second movement from Dvořák's Symphony No. 9 (*From the New World*), which I found quite a bizarre choice for Japan. I kept asking people: why? Why all this noise and why this particularly Western piece of music? But no one could offer me an explanation. It was something that was just there, just accepted, never questioned. '*Shikata ga nai*,' they said. It can't be helped, it has to be.

It wasn't until I returned home that I got a little closer to the answer about Dvořák. One afternoon, I was chopping an onion in tune to BBC Radio 4 when the engaging, enigmatic Japanese pianist, Noriko Ogawa, came on as Andrew Green's first guest in the intriguing series *Mirrored in Music* to speak about the works she had selected that, for her, best reflected the spirit and character of her homeland. There was Puccini, there was Takemitsu – but the piece she chose that best represented Japan for her was that second movement of Dvořák's 'New World' Symphony. When Andrew Green asked her why she had chosen a piece that the West tends to associate with the United States of America (where Dvořák was living when he composed it, during the long period he spent in America towards the end of the nineteenth century), Noriko replied that it was because everybody in Japan – even young children – knew the tune. She explained how, at 4 p.m. in almost every primary school in Japan, this piece – called 'Hurry Home' – was played through loudspeakers to 'encourage all the children to go home'. (This fact in itself struck me as decidedly odd. Most British schoolchildren need encouragement to go to school, not to leave it.)

Noriko said that the four o'clock blast of Dvořák was also played for security reasons. 'Because we have so many earthquake in Japan,' she explained, 'we have to test our microphone almost every single day because schoolyard can be very useful place to evacuate.'

'By why Dvořák in particular?' asked a very puzzled Andrew Green.

That, said Noriko, she could not explain.

At last, I plummeted down off the mountains and arrived at the Sea of Japan. After everything that I had read and heard, I had imagined the reputedly rural and comparatively undeveloped off-the-beaten-track San'in coast would be a weather-battered and ruggedly wild affair. Reality, at least at the part where I joined it in Tottori prefecture, was very different.

The San'in coast was all Route 9: flat, fast, traffic-laden and obliterated with rip-off seaside eateries, glaring and blaring *pachinko* parlours, amusement parks, tourist centres, car dealers and tacky hotels (mostly of the 'Love' variety). Dirty, too. Verges of litter. Scrunched-up cans scraping and rolling across the road in the frisky wind – which was against me, of course. Wind always is.

Tottori City. Bypasses, overpasses, underpasses. Impasses – bottlenecks of jammed-up traffic. Crossroads of congestion. Confusion. Turned left; then, a few kilometres down the road, turned left again. Suddenly, a very odd sight: a flock of Japanese Lawrences of Arabia riding camels on Saharan-sized sand dunes – massive wind-rippled mountains stretching about sixteen kilometres from east to west and two kilometres from north to south, and some of them nearly 100 metres high.

These dunes were the famous (in Japan) *sakyu* – the biggest crowd-pullers in the whole of the prefecture of Tottori and the favourite 'desert' location for Japanese soft-drink commercials. Tourist buses were stacked nose to tail in a small, built-up area that catered purely for tourists. Each gift shop blasted out its own mind-shattering muzak from external speakers, all vying for the loudest distortion.

It was so bad I felt I had to spare a few moments to stay and stare. Leaving my bike against some railings, I tagged along behind a continuous procession of coach parties – shepherded by the usual flag-waving, whistle-blowing, obsequiously squealy-voiced tour guides – as they marched off across the sand towards a disorderly caravan of fed-up camels. The mouth-frothing beasts, decked out in full tourist-trapping regalia of fancy saddles and rainbow rugs and glitzy headbands and belled bridles, looked faintly embarrassed by the charade and were clearly praying that their real-desert relatives wouldn't ever see them like this, tarted up like a bunch of two-humped hippies, all tinsel and flower-power.

Eager to pay their 3000 yen (nearly £20) for a mere ten-minute camel 'trek', snaking queues of inappropriately dressed 'riders' (the women in airy frocks and heels; the men squeezed into unforgiving suits and shiny black office shoes) stretched away across the sand towards Timbuktu. At the head of the queue, each ready-to-mount tourist would be issued with a pair of ankle-high red gumboots and a Lawrence-style headdress. The Arab guide would bark some orders to his tongue-lolling, surly animal and the tourists, in two-to-a-camel duos, would peace-pose against the very un-Japanese backdrop of distant dunes to grin and say *chiizu* to the camera for a rapid-firing filmful of snaps before being led off for half a dozen padding hoof-steps in a sandy southerly direction. Ten minutes later, the giggling Orientals of the Desert could be seen donning a sandy shoe again and readjusting a hem-line or a jacket and tie before piling back into the air-conditioned world of their bus tour.

After watching these curious dromedary happenings from the sidelines, I hung my trainers around my neck and headed barefoot for the unpeopled dunes – glorious waves of sand sculptured by the wind and overlooking the humid, half-sun haze of the temperamental Sea of Japan. By the time I returned to my bike it was late afternoon and . . . raining. In the 'desert'. The tour buses had gone. The shops had shut. The speakers were silent. Bliss.

Thirsty from my desert expedition, I bought two cans of chilled *nihon-cha* (Japanese tea) from a big, beefy bank of shiny vending machines which, along with offering the usual dizzy myriad of every conceivable drink under the sun, sold anything from disposable cameras and cartoon handkerchiefs to packets of rice, computer games, pot noodles and socks. There was a machine full of comics, too – mostly the increasingly popular cooking *manga* in which you could read about the exploits of Oishimo (The Gourmet), Shota the Sushi Chef or Ryosuke Kure, the Wanderer with a Kitchen Knife. The chef heroes of these epics were like samurai in white aprons. They conducted themselves according to the strictest of samurai codes but, instead of a long curved sword, they wielded a razor-sharp kitchen knife and their quest was for the ultimate cuisine – the most exquisitely carved *sashimi*, the perfect *tempura*.

Another vending machine revealed magazines of a different nature for sale: pornography, known to students of Zen Buddhism as 'the sound of one hand reading'.

That night, I camped in some sandy pinewoods a little way down the road.

Just before midnight a pick-up pulled up a short distance from my tent. Three very drunk men piled out of the doors, shrieking with laughter as they staggered over each other in the glare of the headlamps. In any other country I would have broken out in a cold sweat, feeling both fearful and a prime target for their inebriated testosterone-induced actions. But here in Japan, instead of pestering me, molesting me, raping me or murdering me, they simply offered me a Suntory beer and a box of *sushi*. Then they banged a series of hoops into the ground and invited me to join them in a game of sandy, headlamp-lit croquet. All very jolly croquet-sticks. Only when I caught sight of a streak of fiery red tentacles of cloud splintering a dawn-stretched sky did it suddenly occur to me that the night had passed me by.

'Kyoto: 200km' read the sign. Two days' cycle – in theory. In practice, it was a very different kettle of *sushi*, as heading inland across the mountains on truck-thundering Route 9 was not my kind of morning glory. The sea was for me, and the alternative long-winded route to Kyoto along the rocky, rugged, cliff-plunging and surf-crashing shore was where the mountain-shaded San'in coast came into its own.

Small storm-battered villages of old wooden homes and craggy harbours clung to a moody and inhospitable coastline. Precipitous mountains dropping clean away into gouged steep river valleys. A continuous roller-coaster ride of severe leg-quaking gradients – hauling and falling, hauling and falling.

Compared with the bright and balmy San'yo coast, where the annual rainfall was some of the lowest in Japan, the San'in hunched its jagged shoulders to take the full force of the ferocious storms that came hurling across the tempestuous Sea of Japan, giving the region the highest annual precipitation in the country. Summer could have its gentle days, but wintering with the fog and the wet, the bitter wind and bleak heavy clouds of the notorious north-west monsoon could get nasty. Snow dumped down in the mountains, making some areas the snowiest on earth.

The taste of salt stayed constantly in my mouth from the fierce surf-spray winds. The rain fell steadily, heavily – and hurtingly hard. Late one afternoon I plunged down into the narrow-alleyed harbour town of Moroyose ('Wind-Waiting Port'). The place lay half asleep. Smells of salt and fish. Sounds of creaking wood, a cat's miaow, over-the-wall housewifely gossip, a television games show. The steady drip, drip, dripping of rain. A woman sweeping away a doorstep puddle. Then, round a corner – strange sight: washing hanging by shoelaces from the branches of big bonsai-like trees (big-small trees compressed by the wind) that were sprouting out of a concrete street wall in front of a harbourside house. Washing dripping with rain. Whiffing of fish.

Near the top of the hill, overlooking the town, I came across the Hamasaka Youth Hostel. As I fancied drying my feet for the first time in days, I rolled down the drive and knocked on the door. An amiable young man answered, apologising profusely that the hostel was closed for a three-day holiday. I explained that I had a tent and asked if there might be a small space nearby where I could pitch it for the night. Of course, he said, and led me around the back to a grassy knoll overlooking the sea which I was welcome to share with an interesting assortment of exotic wildfowl. He and his wife were just going out, but they would leave the back door unlocked so that I could use the toilets and basins. Stay as long as you like, he said. Of course there was no charge.

That evening I ran down the hill in the humid rain, back to the Wind-Waiting Port, to find some supper. When I stepped through the door of a steamy noodle shop the *mama-san* looked at me, momentarily startled, before exclaiming, 'Ahh sor! Aled Jones!'

The other customers, mostly fishermen, hunched over low tables as they slurped their bowls of *soba*, *udon* and *ramen*, looked round with faces of surprise before grinning and welcoming me in for a bumper bowl of noodles on the house. I tried to ask *mama-san* why she had called me Aled Jones, but all I could get out of her was, '*Hai, hai*! Number One Star!'

Later I discovered that the angelic Welsh choirboy – who was so memorable back in the 1980s for his 'Walking in the Air' and who had, by the age of twenty-five, produced sixteen albums during a career that had taken him to concert halls all over the world – had gained cult status in Japan, where he'd had six number ones. Although I lacked Welsh blood, testosterone and honeysweet vocals, I was nonetheless a *gaijin* – and by simply being a *gaijin* I was good enough to strike an Aled Jones chord with *mama-san*.

After a stormy night, during which I dreamt there had been an earthquake in the midst of which I had become trapped in a washing machine with a bunch of drunk fishermen, I woke up to find that it was still raining. Despite the storm, it was even more humid than ever. Two wets don't make a right.

At dawn, I had the urge to run up to the top of the hump of a mountain in the rain. So I did. Apart from the steady dripping and the sound of my footsteps and chest-pounding panting, all was silent. I was soaked right through but I felt euphoric. At the top, I climbed for a while along a trail that overlooked the island-dotted bay. Way down below I could see the huddled homes of Wind-Waiting Port waiting for the fishing-boats to return from a night on the churned-up seas. With thoughts of fish filling my mind, I decided to turn tail and trot off down to the town, as I surmised that a little, out-of-the-way place like Wind-Waiting Port would probably have a good *uoiciba* – morning fish market.

I arrived at the harbour front to find a large, open-sided warehouse humming with activity, its wet floor covered in a sea of wet, weird-looking fish and unappetising denizens of the deep. Each species had been placed on the ground in perfect formation – all being stepped around and over by a flurry of feet in short white gumboots that had seen it all before. The feet were those of fishermen, fishmongers, traders and wholesalers and housewives who knew what they were looking for and what price they wanted to pay.

After a while, the boots suddenly all accumulated around a stocky man in his early forties who was topped in a red-and-white baseball hat and wore a pair of baggy beige jodhpurs. His face meant business. He moved purposefully from one aesthetic display of floored fish to another, poking the slippery piscines – some still flapping and panting – with a long length of pipe while shouting a torrent of totally unintelligible fish-bartering spiel. An entourage of men closely followed his every move, some taking notes, others firing back prices, before a small, wooden *kanji*-inscripted plaque was dropped among the price-haggled fish. The speed of the deals was so fast that all the selling was completed within twenty minutes. The pipe man's taut, vein-protruding throat relaxed and, without further ado, he climbed into a van and drove away.

More rain. More melodramatic coastline plunging up and down. Every so often, a Cornish-like cove of dazzling white sand. Sometimes I would climb down to a cove, battered by wind, and stand on the beach among a flotsam of fishing floats, bottles and canisters, polystyrene and driftwood and a tangle of nets and strong ropes and stare at the sea. Somewhere out there, over the churning waves, was the incredible hulk of China.

One particularly wet and soggy afternoon, I hauled myself over the Ouchi Pass before washing up at Amanohashidate – the 'Floating Bridge of Heaven', another of those three most classical beauty spots in Japan. I was now two down, one to go. Would I make the third (Matsushima) to stick in my Been-There-Done-That album, I wondered?

Troops of tourists were tumbling out of their buses. '*Chiizu!*' Peace-pose, shiny grin, snap. Immortalised on film. Later: develop, stick, show. Show the workmates, the neighbours, the relatives. 'That's me!' 'Been there too!' And so the world goes round.

The Floating Bridge of Heaven. In Japanese mythology the two great progenitors, the god Izanagi and the goddess Izanami, stood upon a floating bridge that descended from heaven to create the islands of Japan. The 'bridge' is in fact a sandbar, 3.6 kilometres long and about 100 metres wide, which stretches across the picturesque Bay of Miyazu – picturesque, that is, as long as you are able to ignore (not easy) an immense industrial monolith disfiguring the shore along with a scrappy, dust-billowing cement works and a rim of commercial eyesores. But none of the tourists around me seemed to mind, or for that matter even to notice the scars. They seemed to see only what they wanted to see – what they had come to see – the sight that filled their viewfinder: the

Floating Bridge of Heaven, which didn't really look too heavenly in the dull, cloud-louring, dripping rain.

In Japan, it seemed, nature was a serious and organised affair. The ability to appreciate and respect it while simultaneously disregarding and defiling it was one of the many oddities I noticed. Many were the occasions when I'd arrive at, say, the top of a mountain overlooking a famously spectacular view at the same time as a busload of sightseers and together we would exchange exclamations of wonder over the beauty spread out before us. Then they would pile back into their bus, leaving behind them a detritus of discarded cans and food wrappers to blow away and litter the very view they had travelled long distances to see.

Growing numbers of Japanese were now venturing off into the hills and mountains to camp and to hike and to bike in the Great Outdoors, appreciating the unexpected beauty that they might come across for themselves, but it still seemed that, for so many Japanese tourists, the beauty beyond what their guide books and guides directed them to admire was usually overlooked and walked straight past without so much as a glance.

Those who have spent years living with and studying the Japanese tend to agree that, for most of them, real nature – which in Japan all too often manifests itself in the violent form of earthquakes and typhoons – is better kept at a distance, or admired after it has been tamed within the confines of a garden or a vase of flowers. Nature is, as Ian Buruma says in *A Japanese Mirror*, 'worshipped, but only after it has been reshaped by human hands'. Or, perhaps, defined by a tour guide?

I had been planning on camping at Amanohashidate, but was told by a policeman that such an activity was forbidden as it was a national park. (Funny, I thought, how such delights as a litter of cement works, gravel pits, gruesome hotels and a wailing pack of tawdry gift shops were permitted but not the erection of an ethereal, shrubbery-green abode that, disturbing neither nature nor onlookers, would be gone soon after dawn.) So, instead, I cycled up an immensely steep hill at the end of an immensely mountainous day to the Amanohashidate Kanko Kaikan Yusu Hosuteru. To top it all, I was immensely wet, as it was still raining a hard and humid rain. Had been all day. All week. Heck . . . all month. But that was okay. I mean, it was rainy season and one shouldn't really expect a season of rain to spell sun, should one?

I was the only person staying at the youth hostel (I did momentarily see a boy leaving the toilet but I never saw him again) and nothing very exciting happened there, apart from getting dry . . . oh, and reading the curtains in my bunk-bedded room:

ENJOY YOUR SPORTS – we have a pleasant time playing games this evening.

I'm not sure what pleasant type of sport the curtain-makers had envisaged for this evening's games but mine turned out to be mosquito-swatting – charging around like a headless *gaijin* to squash and crush a squadron of the blood-sucking blighters against the corpse-stained wall. In the end I conceded defeat and erected my mosquito-proof tent on the *tatami*. Thus, in effect, I ended up camping in the National Park of the Heavenly Floating Bridge after all.

Morning came. Rain. Time to get my dried-off body wet again – pack everything, including feet, into plastic bags and prepare for a drenching.

The 'proper' place to view the Floating Bridge of Heaven was reputed to be from the top of Kasamatsu Koen. So I dutifully battled through flood waters to the lofty, cloud-shrouded vantage point – but not by the conventional cable-car that elevated all the brolly-clutching coach-party tourists. Instead, I walked, a very wet, misty but lovely wooded walk. Surrounded by greenness and dripping and the raspy sounds of a demented cuckoo, the walk turned out to be the most enjoyable part of being at one of Japan's 'Three Great Views', despite the fact that I was quite unable to see the Famous Floating Sight because of the trees.

And that, in essence, is always the case: travel halfway across the world to see a famously famous sight, only to be disappointed, while bang next door an unfamously unfamous sight that you stumble upon is so much better. The untouched, the unexpected, the simplest, the freshest is always best.

When I did emerge from the woods, I found myself in an elevated viewing area with only one couple; every other tourist had ventured no further than the cable-car terminal perched a little way down the hill. When the viewing-platform couple saw me pop out of the woods, they expressed amazement that I had walked all the way up the mountain (which was actually more mole-hill than mount). I tried to assure them that the walk was neither too strenuous nor too far, but they wouldn't listen and continued to effuse utter astonishment at my mountaineering prowess.

Fortunately I managed to change the subject when, peering out through the rain over the Floating Bridge, I remarked that it didn't look very Heavenly to me.

'Ahhh, this is most important sight for looking through leg,' said the viewing-platform man.

'Excuse me?' I said.

For a mirthful few moments the Heavenly Couple tried to convince me that it was the Japanese custom to bend over backwards (or should that be forwards?) and view the 'bridge' from an ungainly inverted position in order to achieve the proper perspective for seeing the bridge afloat in the skies. So over I went, narrowly missing knocking myself out on my heavily laden handlebar bag as it came swinging over my shoulder when I stuck my head betwixt my legs.

'Sor, Jodie-*san*,' the Heavenly Wife asked eagerly, 'you see very specially Number One Japanese floating sight?'

'Err, well, not really,' I confessed. 'It looks about the same, only upside-down.'

'For longer stay down! For longer stay down!' replied the Heavenly Husband with theatrical excitement, trying to persuade me that (as I understood it) the longer I stayed down, the dizzier I would become and the more the bridge would give the impression of floating off to heaven. I tried, I really did, but with my whole world having capsized, all I felt was rather seasick.

I walked back down the mountain through the riotously green dripping woods and bumped into my upside-down friends shortly after they had disembarked from the cable-car at the bottom of Oriental Everest. They were so ecstatic at seeing me again that they not only bought me lunch but also gave me two 1000-yen telephone cards (total value £12) which pictured the Heavenly Bridge that failed to Float.

'*Miyage, miyage!* – Souvenir, souvenir!' they cried in unison as their tour bus swept them away into the mist.

I rode off along a bumpy track through a tunnel of pines and ancient trees, the latter gnarled and knotted into tortuous shapes by centuries of wind, across the Great Heavenly Sight until I reached the small town of Monju on the opposite end of the sandbar.

There then followed an afternoon of near misses. Shortly after I had cycled out of the town, a much-too-close overtaking car decided to crash into a moped-riding postman directly in front of me, the effect of which sent me sliding recklessly on a skid-pan of spilt letters into the path of an oncoming dumper truck. Somehow I managed to keep control of my overladen beast and propelled myself away from potential disaster by launching myself and my bike clean over a hefty kerb – straight into the steaming mouth of a noodle shop.

Having survived this far, my immediate reaction was to abandon ship and scurry back across the road (narrowly escaping being run over by a flat-bed van loaded with a tower of freezers) to see how the Yamaha Towne Mate Deluxe-riding postie had fared. Amazingly, unlike his crumple-fronted machine, he was fine. Even more amazingly, he was grinning and bowing to the driver of the vehicle which had just biffed him up the bumper. And what's more, the car-driving bike-biffer was grinning and bowing back at him. No words, no fusillade of heavily embroidered expletives – just grins and bows. What was going on here? Surely you don't politely grin and bow at someone who, by way of some inept and dangerous driving, has just rudely jettisoned you towards a premature death?

But here, in this strange land where things are not usually as they seem, there was not a whiff of air turning blue or heads turning road-rage red. There were no apoplectic fits; there was no exchanging of addresses or insurance details. Just grins and bows. Finding all this grinning and bowing faintly infectious, I surprised myself by joining the jovial duo with a grin and, in a nodding sort of way, offered to assist the postman with rounding up his widely scattered mail.

When I returned to the noodle shop to retrieve my steed, the owner, a small fleshy man swathed in copious aprons, gave me a bowl of noodles and an iced coffee, with two riceballs for the road.

Number Two near-miss occurred a mere kilometre or two down the road in Miyazu-shi. I had just leant my bike against the window of a supermarket, aiming to scour the store's shelves for some urgently required oriental-flavoured Quaker Oats supplies. Standing with my back to the road, I suddenly noticed in the reflection of the window that a car appeared to be heading directly towards me. Swinging round, I was just in time to see a driverless white Carol Autozam Minica mount the kerb in front of me before veering sideways and embedding itself in a concrete wall.

Some pedestrians, who had miraculously missed being slammed into by the Autozam, stopped in their tracks, momentarily startled, before breaking into a grin and continuing on their way as if nothing had happened. Moments later, the salaryman owner of the Auto-piloted Zam emerged from a noodle bar on the opposite side of the road. After slowly registering the extent of this near disaster, he casually strolled across to his Minica, which, as a result of its concertina'ed bonnet, was even more Mini than Ca. On reaching his crumpled wreck of runaway vehicle, his first reaction was not to cry, curse, or headbutt the wall, but to grin. Although he had forgotten to apply the handbrake when he parked on a slight slope and thus had almost caused a major road pile-up and pedestrian pile-down, the salaryman looked as if he had just won the lottery. I was beginning to feel thoroughly confused – people weren't behaving as I expected at all.

As if two near-deaths were not enough for one day, another near-miss occurred when a Daihatsu Hijet MPV 'People Packer' turned erratically across my path before jamming on its brakes. On realising his mistake, the driver joined his passengers by first staring and then grinning at me. All this grinning, all this sunny smiling – it was all getting a bit much for someone who was used to cycling around London, a city where people simply don't smile at you, especially if you happen to be a cyclist.

The Japanese were great smilers. The only Japanese person that I had heard of who never smiled was Daisetsu Suzuki, the famous twentieth-century Zen Buddhist, who was once described by a fellow countryman as being 'quite devoid of the habit, common among many Japanese people, of smiling for no particular reason or behaving with almost uncomfortable politeness'.

They were also great laughers. It was said that their language distinguished between five kinds of laughter: *ahaha*, merry laughter; *ihihi*, vulgar laughter; *uhuhu*, derisive laughter; *ohoho*, the modest reserved laughter of a gentleman; and *ehehe*, the sycophantic outburst of a gentleman.

I often noticed people laughing or smiling or grinning in the most unlikely situations – like missing a train, for example. Whereas the average Briton, having arrived panting in a mad, heart-pounding rush at the station just as their train was sliding away off down the tracks, would either scowl, swear, shout, hurl their bag down on the platform in a show of furious disgust or thump the nearest railway official in a fit of despair, the average Japanese simply smiled the smile of the sweet. Or, in the case of nearly running over a *gaijin* on her bicycle, or sending a car careering out of control towards a crowd of shoppers, the Japanese offender would fail to exhibit any expression of gravity or apology or aggravation or anger and instead would break into a cheesy grin. Such an apparently inappropriate response could be intensely irritating and I often wanted to ask, 'Excuse me, but what's so funny?' But I never did. In truth, it wasn't so much the smile that irritated or bemused me as my inability to interpret it.

The Japanese sometimes even smiled when there had been a real tragedy, as displays of private emotion were seen as a threat to the communal sense of well-being. The ubiquitous smile was used to conceal the true anguish, or embarrassment, of the smiler – it was used to cover discomfort. When an individual was taken to task for a fault, the smile was usually an expression of embarrassment and should be interpreted as a gesture of self-deprecation.

The Japanese were surely world masters in their amazing ability to hold back all ill-bred emotions behind a sunny surface. Of course, the strain of keeping their faces (saving face was such a Japanese thing) like that needed to be relieved occasionally. There was a Japanese expression, 'wearing a mask' – the face shown to others in public – and sometimes Japanese men would drink to 'remove the mask', giving themselves an excuse to let their hair down and be absurd if they felt like it.

It took me a long time to realise that I had perhaps totally misinterpreted the smiles I had seen on the faces of those Japanese who had been momentarily shocked or shaken or taken aback when something unexpected had happened to them or around them. They were not so much smiling as appearing to smile. An early observer of this curiosity was the gifted and assiduous Western writer, translator and teacher, Lafcadio Hearn, born in 1850 on one of the Ionian islands west of Greece and educated in Normandy and Durham. He married a Japanese woman and adopted both his wife's family name and Japanese citizenship while he lived, taught and wrote in Japan from 1890 until his death in 1904. One day, when his horse-drawn carriage was struck by another and his horse was injured, Hearn angrily hit the offending other driver (who was Japanese) with the butt of his whip. 'He looked right into my face and smiled, and then bowed,' wrote Hearn. 'I can see that smile now. I felt as if I had been knocked down. The smile utterly non-plussed me – killed all my anger instantly.'

The rain continued to fall. The sweat continued to saturate. The humidity continued to swamp all energy. Hail, Rainy Season! The sky remained dark and gloomy for days on end. I had discovered, the hard, wet way, that when it rained in rainy season it rained biblically, hellishly heavy and intense, as if the bottom of the sky had collapsed under the weight of the water. Everything was drowning under torrents of Old Testament rain. Fat and furious drops hammered my hooded head in anger, rushing in fast floods that charged down the sides of streets, greedily gurgling within the deep gutters.

Occasionally the painfully violent rain would be interrupted by unexpected breaks of sharp, bright sunshine and the sodden ground would start to steam. With my jacket ripped off in an instant and sunglasses snapped into place on my face, I'd bowl along with the wind in my hair, feeling as if I was living on borrowed time. Days-old wet washing would be hurriedly hung to flap from the straps of all four panniers, before the waterlogged clouds again sealed off the sky for days.

My 'plan' had been to ride up the coast of the Sea of Japan to the tip of Tohoku – Honshu's northernmost part – before catching a ferry to Hokkaido. But when the world around you turns consistently wet, and when tent, clothes, body and mind turn increasingly mouldy, something has to be done to avoid drowning in perpetual dampness. So, consulting my soggy map one sodden awful night as the tide marks began to rise rapidly around my clammy and dripping mildewy tent, I thought: enough's enough. I'm bailing out. I'm taking the boat to Hokkaido – now!

So, with mind made up, it was full steam ahead to the nearby port of Maizuru (twinned with Portsmouth), from where I could catch the ferry to Japan's northernmost island, famous (in Japan) for being rainy-season free.

Rain-dumped at the port one preposterously wet afternoon with the plums plummeting from a flooded sky, I discovered that I was unable to swan off to Hokkaido as fast as I would have liked as there was no ferry for three days. Giving me this information, the fresh-faced young woman at the ferry terminal

167

covered her mouth with her hand and dissolved into a bundle of repressed and embarrassed squeaky laughter. Extracting the information from her had not been a simple affair – my wobbly Japanese was getting gradually less wobbly, but it still didn't have much of a leg to stand on. However, I didn't feel it was unsteady enough to elicit such a fit of behind-hand simpering giggles. The young woman kept casting beseeching SOS glances to the moon-faced workmates sitting beside her – glances that I interpreted as, 'Help, help! Rescue me from this bungling foreign barbarian.'

Instead of helping, they simply sank into their seats, giggling behind face-cupping hands. Had I inadvertently put an octopus on my head? No, all this confidence-deflating giggling was quite normal. The young woman had simply been abiding by the customary Japanese etiquette that ladies shouldn't laugh with great open-mouthed roars but should titter coyly, covering their mouths with their hands. This custom stemmed from the ancient dictate that an inferior must never pollute a superior with his or her teeth. In the past, teeth were regarded as being so unaesthetic that well-to-do women fastidiously blackened them every morning.

Even so, I didn't quite see the funny side of it. But the ferry wasn't sailing and that was that. Plans spun, plans plunged, plans sank, plans went sailing up the Swanee – though not for long, as the plans would rise (and fall) again when I eventually took to the swelling seas.

In the meantime, instead of lingering around murky Maizuru for three days waiting for the boat to scoop me off to sunny Hokkaido, I wondered whether I had time to 'do' Kyoto before nipping back to catch the ferry. When I looked at my map and discovered that Kyoto – Japan's former capital and centre of the nation's civilisation for more than ten centuries (from 794 to 1868) – was still a mountainous 100 kilometres or so away, I thought that maybe the multi-shrined city could wait until a not-so-rainy day in the autumn.

There again, maybe it couldn't. Maybe now was the time to give my legs a rest and take the train to Kyoto. So, with a new plan in place, I cycled off decisively to Higashi-Maizuru railway station for what I imagined should be a fairly straightforward journey for such a super-efficient railway system – a system that ran more than 20,000 services over 20,000 kilometres of railway track (which, although not meaning much, still sounded suitably impressive to me).

At Higashi-Maizuru *eki*, life turned a little complicated. No one spoke English. I found myself faced with lots of different times, lots of different prices and lots of different trains for lots of different service levels. The station master fired a torrent of highly confusing questions and choices at me. Did I require a *futsu* – a slow train stopping at all stations; or was I after the more expensive *kyuku* – the 'ordinary express,' which stopped at only a limited number of stations? Perhaps I would prefer the *kaisoku* – the 'rapid' service, which was simply a variation on the *kyuku* trains? Short of time? Then maybe I should consider the *tokkyu* – the 'limited express' service. This, the station master explained to me in a bombardment of Japanese while simultaneously displaying a remarkable degree of patience, was the fastest regular train that I could get, since the bullet-nosed Shinkansen (literally 'New Trunk Line') did not operate along the San'in coast, because it needed special lines.

With head a-whirr, things turned even more complicated when I said I also wanted to travel with my bike. The station master informed me that this would involve dismantling it in order to transport it in a special bicycle bag. When I asked him for such a bag, he told me his station didn't provide any – I would have to go to a specialised bag dealer. And where was the nearest specialised dealer? Probably Kyoto, he replied helpfully. For a moment, I stood in the station scratching my head in bewilderment as I absorbed the information that I couldn't get my bike to Kyoto, where I could buy a bag, without a bag for me to buy. It was the catch-22 of catching a train.

I considered leaving my bike in Left Luggage while I travelled to Kyoto unencumbered by my problematic mount, but Higashi-Maizuru railway station didn't appear to have any such useful place. So I decided that all the effort, all the expense and all the confusion were simply not worth it for a mere handful of hours in Kyoto. Instead, I opted to take the bull by the horns and my bike by the handlebars and go and do something far more important, like find somewhere to sleep, as the dark and the rain were closing in fast.

I scoured the streets for a while until I found what I was looking for: a shrine. I was just in the middle of squirrelling myself away in a secluded corner when I was intercepted by a bent-backed *obaasan* who was on her way back from clapping her hands to the gods. At the sight of a rare, multi-moled *gaijin*, she burst into an effusive, quivering patter of excitement. As she busily chatted away at great length to her tiny, doll-like blue slippers (her bent back being set at such an acute angle that she could only snatch glimpses of the rest of the world by swivelling her head ninety degrees to the side), and as I nodded and interjected the occasional appropriately placed 'Ahh so, *desu-ka?*', a white car went past, paused, reversed and pulled up alongside. Out stepped a smiling young woman who, I was surprised to recognise, was the giggly woman from the ferry terminal. She stepped through a gap in the wall and, after performing a burst of obsequiously low bows to the *obaasan*, explained to her that I was off to Hokkaido by bicycle. Then she asked me if there was anything she could do to help me. I thanked her for the offer but told her I was fine.

In English, she said, 'Tonight where do you sleeping?'

'Well, I was thinking over there,' I replied, indicating my quiet corner behind the shrine.

'Excuse me?' said the ferry girl.

'I was planning on sleeping in my tent by that wall.'

'*Tento?* But tonight has very much raining.'

'That's all right,' I said, 'I'm getting used to the rain.'

'Is that so?'

'Well, it's sort of so.'

Thoughtful pause. 'Mmmm, please you are my guest experience for sleeping my house.'

Was this really the same giggly person from the ferry terminal who was now inviting me back to her home?

'I would love to come and sleep in your house,' I said. 'Are you sure this is okay?'

'Yes very okay, really fine.'

Leaving *obaasan* to shuffle off in a state of creaky bemusement, I retrieved my bike from against the wall, packed up and wheeled everything back to the friendly ferry girl's car.

'My nem is Keiko,' she said, in a very precise textbook style as if she was about to launch into the standard 'I am junior high school student . . .'. But she didn't.

Keiko drove off slowly and I followed her trail as we wove our way through a network of narrow backstreets. Ten minutes later she was welcoming me into her home, where she had spent all of her twenty-five years. After her parents had died, the house had been divided into two apartments – one belonged to her, where she lived alone, and the other to her brother. She invited me to sleep in her brother's apartment.

'Won't your brother mind having a strange *gaijin* in his house?' I asked.

'No, really this is no troubling,' laughed Keiko. 'My brother is away for one night fishing vacation.'

'What does your brother do?'

'He is policeman.'

'Ahh, that's handy – so you have your own personal protection.'

'Excuse me?'

'You have a very safe neighbour.'

'Yes, very fine safety indeed!'

'Does he work in Maizuru?'

'Yes, he work in Maizuru on west side – half in company office and half in police box. Sometime I worry because he work in very danger area.'

'Danger? What kind of danger?'

'Mmmm, in Maizuru on west side there is very many Russian person – always very many thief-men. My brother has many different danger moment.'

I chatted with Keiko a little longer before she went next door to her apartment, leaving me alone to have a shower. Her brother's flat was fairly sizable and included an upstairs, which I somehow managed to restrain myself from snooping around. I spent the night downstairs in a large *tatami*-matted room, one corner of which was dominated by a small altar area, with a wide-framed black-and-white photograph of Keiko's fine-featured parents hanging above it. Her mother, bound up in a kimono, bore the faintest trace of a smile, while her father, clad in a suit and tie, conveyed an expression of mild surprise. I stared at the two faces for a while, wondering what had happened to them.

As well as the downstairs *tatami* room, there was a compact bathroom, a sink unit full of fishing hooks and lines and reels and jars, and a concrete-floored *genkan* or entrance hall (the correct place where shoes were removed before stepping into the rest of the house), which was overflowing with footwear. I'd have presumed that Keiko's brother, being a policeman, would have had a shoe department containing hefty steel-toe-capped shin-bashing boots but all the *genkan* had on offer was a disorderly array of namby-pamby slippers. I suppose I shouldn't have been surprised, having seen at first hand how Japan was 'big' on slippers. Even truck drivers favoured them as on-the-road footwear, and I'd also heard that dentists liked to wear them while drilling teeth.

It wasn't just slippers. I'd read in yet another of those lovable but statistically nonsensical polls that 85.5 per cent of young Japanese men with university degrees owned a pair of rubber *zoki* (sandals). Shoes, slippers, slip-ons, sandals, thongs, clogs – call them what you will, but the fact remained that the Japanese held these handy ground-level commodities in high esteem. At Emperor Hirohito's funeral, a chamberlain carried a wooden box containing the Emperor's new shoes – special footwear to convey him to the next world.

Sometimes the slipper/shoe thing can cause slight contention among an otherwise harmonious race. In 1985, there was controversy at the Japan Ministry of Post and Telecommunications when some employees wanted to wear slippers and some wanted to wear shoes. Rather than come to blows, a typical Japanese compromise was reached when the director-general asked footwear manufacturers to design slippers that looked like shoes.

Slipping into a pair of the brother's surplus slippers, I slopped next door to Keiko's and found her sitting with Yumi, a vivacious friend who also worked at the ferry terminal. They told me that next week they were off on a three-day holiday together to Hawaii. This sounded to me like a long way to go for such a short stay, but it seemed that this was the only free time Keiko had as she not only worked from 9 a.m. to 6 p.m. every day at the ferry terminal but also did part-time work at night in a bar down the road. As if that wasn't enough, she taught evening classes on how to wear the kimono properly. Yet she managed to find time to get away for short breaks: she rattled off a number of places she had visited around the world – Los Angeles, New York, San Francisco, Hong Kong, Singapore – and added that she had never spent more than a few hours in any of them. Hopefully, she said, this would all change next year as she had just received a visa to work in Australia for a year.

As we sat on the *tatami* around a low table, drinking green tea and munching seaweed-flavoured rice cakes, I described the complicated rigmarole at the station about trying to convey both myself and my *jitensha* to Kyoto. After a moment's thought, Keiko said, 'Ahh, Jodie-*san*, I am having Number One solution – please for leaving my pleasure your bicycle in my house, so easy!'

So I did. And I boarded the train to Kyoto, revelling in the luxury of travelling unencumbered by bags of bags and bags of bicycles.

CHAPTER 8

Hypo Kyoto

Kyoto. Major city. Major concrete, glass, neon, fumes. Where to start? Where to go? No idea. Not a clue. Felt lost and hot. And odd. Odd without my bike. No wheels, no wind, no go-where-you-please ease. The sky leaden and heavy, the air weighted down with energy-sapping humidity. Plodding along the pavements, sweat oozing from every pore. Shirt stuck to back. Rucksack stuck to shirt. Mind stuck to scalp. Sucked away all thought. Too hot to think. Too hot to plan. Just humping along in the smog, trying to find a place to sleep.

I spotted the tip of a pagoda peaking above a lump of concrete. It looked like a shady spot to take stock, so I wove my way towards it through a maze of backstreets and alleys. But I never made it (not that day, anyway) as on the way I came across the small Toji-An guesthouse, tucked invitingly in a quiet, residential cul-de-sac. Children romped in the street. A housewife rolled by on her bike, her basket loaded with shopping. An *obaasan* shuffled past, pushing her trolley-pram, and remarked, '*Atsui desu-ne?* – Hot, isn't it?' Yes, I said, agreeing that it was very *atsui* indeed.

Five rickety bicycles stood on their stands outside the Toji-An. Inside, all I found was a man asleep in a sprawl on the *tatami* in front of a blaring television. Samurai warriors battling on screen, swords clashing, flesh slashing, heads flying. Screams, groans, cries. Blood, copious blood, spurting everywhere.

I turned back to the sleeping man. He was wearing jam-jar spectacles and a voluminous army-green pyjama suit. His feet were bare and I noticed that his

173

toes were covered in sores. There was a strange smell about the place which hovered on the distinctly dodgy. The man shuddered with a start and suddenly woke up. Through groggy eyes he saw a *gaijin* drifting above him in a quandary.

'*Konnichiwa!*' I piped.

'*Konnichiwa!*' he replied, heaving himself up. 'Are you married?'

'Married?' I said, surprised, wondering what had suddenly prompted him to ask such a question. Maybe he was still dreaming. After a momentary pause to assess the situation, I replied unconvincingly, 'Errr, well, funnily enough, yes, I am married.' (It's always best to bank on the safe side with strange men, especially ones with sores on their toes.)

A young couple in designer clothes walked in off the street, kicked off their shoes in the *genkan* and said hello before settling down in front of the samurai drama. They helped themselves to a cup of green tea from the big flowery flask on the table. They looked like normal people, which was a good sign when faced with a potentially dubious man. I asked them if they were staying at the guesthouse. Yes, they said, for a few days.

I turned to the pyjama man, who was now looking a little more with it, and asked him if he knew who the owner was.

'Yes, certainly. I am the owner. I am Mr Ninagawa. Can I help you?'

'Do you have a room for tonight?'

'You are one person?'

'Yes, I am one person.'

'Sorry, *ippai* – all full,' said Mr Ninagawa.

'Oh well, never mind.'

'Ahh, but let me see . . . you could have the manager's room, as he is in Tokyo for the next two nights.'

'Oh, are you sure? Can I see it?'

'Of course.'

I followed Mr Ninagawa upstairs to a small *tatami* room that was not much bigger than the futon lying unrolled on the floor. A golden reed blind swung gently in the breeze across the sliding window. I pulled the blind back a little and peered out of the window on to the peaceful street. Toddlers were playing with a kitten. I asked Mr Ninagawa the cost of the room.

'Mmm, two thousand yen,' he said.

Although bartering is not considered courteous in Japan, and although I had respected this while travelling throughout this perplexing land, I now suddenly found myself asking if he could do it for a thousand.

Appearing not in the least bit affronted, Mr Ninagawa said, 'Of course!'

So that was that – a room for £6 in the heart of Kyoto. Not bad.

The Toji-An washing facilities were interesting. The only basin was downstairs and communal, which was fine, if somewhat splattered and blocked. To reach the one and only toilet necessitated shuffling along in a pair of guesthouse slippers to the end of a narrow passageway before reaching an open door that led out on to a packed and public car park. At this point, slippers were exchanged for a pair of plastic sandals or a pair of *geta* – the traditional thonged wooden sandals with an oblong 'heel' at the front as well as the back. I favoured the *geta*, because the squat toilet, situated several clog-shod clip-clops away in a precarious outhouse with a broken-latched lock, was constantly submerged beneath an inch of leaking-cistern water. Thanks to the high-rise facility of the *geta*'s strange heels, my feet remained toilet-floodwater free.

The single shower unit sat in a phonebox-sized portacabin that was virtually integrated into the car park. Inside the washbox, it was so sauna-hot that I managed to achieve the remarkable feat of sweating while simultaneously cold-showering.

On my first morning at the Toji-An, I was rudely wrenched from a sweaty slumber at 4.15 a.m. by a man bursting into my room. The sight of me lying semi-clad on top of the futon did not appear to faze this intruder as much as the fact that I happened to be sleeping in his room. As I lunged for my shirt, I presumed that the man was simply another guest having mistaken my room for his. But he was Masa, the manager, who (Mr Ninagawa had said) was away in Tokyo.

'I caught an earlier bus back,' explained Masa before excusing himself (again) and insisting I stay where I was and go back to sleep. But by now I was wide awake and so I wandered downstairs to join him for a cup of green tea.

Masa, an artist from Otaru, in Hokkaido, was a lugubrious but intriguing character and he spoke English. I asked him where he had learnt to speak it so well.

'In 1969,' he said, 'when I was a young man indeed, I left Japan to go travelling in South America. When I went to Brazil I thought: this is very fine country – and so I live there for ten year! I have spent many time in Japan since my travel, but last year I go for one year to South East Asia – half for painting time and half for travel time. I returned back to Japan in January.

'My first night back I stay in Kobe. Because I have not so much money I sleep in Marine Hotel – very cheap price, only 2000 yen. But specially bad timing – it was the night for Kobe earthquake! I was really very lucky man. I wake up outside in street. The whole building so bad destroy – many many people in hotel die. So terrible fire. Of course I lose everything. All my painting I make in South East Asia trip, my passport, my money, my clothe. I was very naked man! I only have my watch to survive earthquake. Everything else – nothing! It was January so very terrible cold. I eat nothing for ten day and only little water. Everybody say the government terrible slow to helping Kobe people. When I try to leave Kobe very difficult operation – everything destroy like road and train and bus service. Finally I walk all way to Osaka, where I get little money from government to buy food and clothe.'

He had been very lucky: more than 6000 people died in the Kobe earthquake and nearly 35,000 were injured by the effects of a tremor that measured 7.2 on the Richter Scale. The government was roundly criticised by the media for the failure of its scientists to predict the earthquake, though billions of dollars had been ploughed into forecasting such tremors. Much less seriously, traditionalists were shocked when Empress Michiko, the first 'commoner' empress in Japan, adopted the Princess of Wales's style when she visited Kobe after the event, crouching to chat to children and the infirm. When she actually hugged a woman who had lost everything in the disaster, she was accused of unimperial behaviour.

As Masa poured me another cup of green tea, he told me how he had finally made it to Kyoto, where Mr Ninagawa had given him a job at the guesthouse. Masa's plan had been to earn enough money to go back to his home in Otaru. But the legendary giant catfish lurking beneath Japan's rising and falling land was not on Masa's side: an earthquake hit Hokkaido, destroying his house and the rest of his paintings. He had no insurance. He was back to having nothing and became exhausted and deeply depressed.

'You know what I finally do?' Masa asked me. 'I think: I want no more depressive pill. No more sad time. I want to have laugh time. So I buy a laughing machine!'

'A what?' I asked.

'Please, one moment,' said Masa and disappeared next door. He returned with a small plastic contraption which, at the push of a button, emitted an infuriating burst of lengthy and demented voice-box cackling laughter. It was the sort of nerve-grating and irritating thing that made me feel like smashing it against a wall, which I'm sure was not the reaction its manufacturers had in mind. But Masa was made of less aggressive stuff and it worked for him.

'Ha ha! So great sound! Now whenever I am having sad feeling, I simply push button for instant happy time. Really, so fine medicine for sudden high spirit.'

I found the medicine for my 'high spirit' that morning when I opened a copy of the *Japan Times* (motto: 'ALL THE NEWS WITHOUT FEAR OR FAVOR') and was confronted with the headline:

MANY DADS WOULD LIKE TO BE BIRDS

I just had to read on:

> Many fathers wanted to be reincarnated as a bird, according to a survey released by a major clothing manufacturer. 155 [out of 2867] respondents said they want to be reborn as a bird, saying they could fly anywhere or they could reign supreme like a hawk or an eagle.
>
> Those wanting to be reborn as a woman ranked second, with 148 replies. The reason cited was that a housewife could enjoy a nap in the middle of the day with three meals a day guaranteed.

As Masa was back earlier than expected, I thought I would have to start looking for another place to stay, since the Toji-An was still *ippai*. But Mr Ninagawa, bless his rotten toes, made space for me to sleep in the futon storage and washing room that overlooked the car park, the flyover and the railway and I ensconced myself in the corner. I soon discovered that my futon-washing room doubled up as a thoroughfare for foot traffic gaining access to the washing lines strung over the flat-top roof, which could only be reached by clambering in and out of my window and on and off my bed, but I was still happy and grateful to have cheap place to stay in the middle of Kyoto.

Thanks to the loan of Masa's bicycle, I spent most of my short time in Kyoto riding all over the city, just seeing what came my way, which happened to be a myriad of temples and shrines. Kyoto was home to over 200 Shinto shrines and 1600 Buddhist temples, and some very impressive ones there were, too. Because Kyoto was one of the few Japanese cities to be spared from the 'carpet' bombings of the Second World War (thanks to some American scholars who persuaded their military to keep its hands off such a historical jewel), the vast assortment of temples and shrines were the real – mostly wooden – thing, in contrast to the numerous 1960s ferro-concrete reconstructions of so many of Japan's religious and historical sights.

There were exceptions, like Kinkakuji Otera, otherwise known as the

Golden Temple because its walls were entirely covered in extravagant gold leaf. Originally built in the late fourteenth century, the Temple of Gold seen today was in fact a 1950s counterfeit of itself built after the original temple was destroyed by fire – a fire caused not by some random Allied bomber slipping through the net, but by a fiery Zen monk who burnt the building down in protest against . . . well, against something. Even with its old-style newness, the golden three-storey pavilion was spectacular, hovering above its shimmering reflection in the lake upon which it floated ephemerally.

A few pedal revolutions down the road from the Golden Temple took me to Ryoanji, the Temple of the Peaceful Dragon (and of Screaming and Wailing School Parties), famed for its rock garden. Constructed around the beginning of the sixteenth century by the warrior Hosokawa Katsumoto, the garden, devoid of all greenery and with not a gnome in sight, comprised a stark collection of fifteen rocks, some of them edged in moss, apparently adrift in an ocean of perfectly raked sandy gravel and enclosed by a mellow earthen wall.

Over the centuries the garden, built as an area of contemplation, had been interpreted to represent a number of different things: mountain peaks rising through clouds; islands afloat in a cosmic sea; tigers tending their cubs; or a mandala of the great temples of Zen itself. Despite its *haiku*-like simplicity (or perhaps on account of it), I was overwhelmed by a desire to run across its meticulously raked gravel 'lawn' with the same sort of impulsive urge one has when faced with a field of virgin snow or a sea of unsullied wave-washed sand, or a stretch of green with a sign saying 'Keep Off The Grass'. Admirably, I managed to keep my destructive side in check and drank a can of Pocari Sweat instead.

More temples came and more temples went, ditto the shrines. Kyoto was a city in which it was all too easy to fall into hazy-headed historical hysteria and hit shrine-saturation point. Still, despite its superabundance of tourists, its monstrous concrete monoliths and its fume-belching traffic snarl-ups, the city was impressive.

Kyoto was home to some of the world's oldest and largest and most important and beautiful wooden structures. Of course it also contained a great many unimportant wooden constructions that looked just like the important ones, deceiving the incautious tourist (such as myself) into squandering some of their reverential awe on a mossy imitation built in 1962. But I did find the genuine articles, such as the far-from-fake Kiyomizu-Dera Temple, founded in 798 – non-fake, that is, since 1633, which was suitably ancient for me. Jutting magnificently out of Otowa-yam, the city's south-eastern foothills, the temple provided an extensive view over the sprawl of Kyoto from its massive veranda which, supported on hefty columns and pillars 139 metres high, projected out over the cliff.

'To jump from the balcony of Kiyomizu' was an expression the Japanese used when faced with a complex decision. The only complex decision facing me as I stood on its elevated deck concerned whether I should splash out on two, or maybe even three, *yatsuhashi* (dumplings filled with sweetbean paste). I found no inclination to 'jump from the balcony' and so I freewheeled back down the hill, pausing to sample the sticky dumplings in steep and narrow 'Teapot Lane'.

One of the most impressive wooden structures I saw in Japan was the pagoda of Toji – the one I had spotted peaking above Kyoto's rooftops just before I had been diverted into the Toji-An guesthouse. It was one of the two main temples of the Singon sect and the tallest in Japan, at nearly 55 metres. Toji Temple had been established in 794 by imperial decree to protect the city but the pagoda itself dated only from 1644. This made it no less impressive. Its soaring five storeys symbolised the five elements – fire, water, earth, wind and air – and the rings at the top of the pagoda represented the nine spheres of Heaven.

I had been fascinated by the way in which pagodas are constructed ever since climbing up into one outside Katmandu. It intrigued me that Japan's ancient pagodas had managed to withstand centuries of earthquakes and storms when more modern and seemingly solid buildings had collapased. What had the old builders known that the modern ones had forgotten? Fusakichi Omori, a seismologist, carried out tests in 1921 and claimed that 'no earthquake could be powerful enough to topple a Japanese five-storeyed pagoda'.

Professor Atsushi Ueda, giving a lecture in the late 1990s at the Japanese Embassy in London, explained that the answer to this mystery lay in the unique construction techniques used to build the five-storey pagodas. For instance, the fact that interlocking joints were used instead of nails created a flexible, loose-jointed structure which, during a tremor, moved in a 'snake-dance' rather than toppling over. The thick central pillar, or *shimbashira*, extending to the spire at the top of the pagoda provided a friction damper and was sometimes suspended from the second storey, where it acted as a pendulum that absorbed seismic energy. The pagoda's long, overhanging eaves also swayed and tipped in the event of an earthquake, creating the effect of a counterbalanced lever, which further enhanced the structure's stability.

Many of these features had been adapted by modern Japanese architects, so

that skyscrapers were able to withstand earthquakes in the same way that pagodas had been going for centuries. Hopefully.

Another good temple in Kyoto turned out to be Higashi-Hongan-ji, the
second largest wooden structure in all Japan (the world's largest is Todai-ji, in
Nara, south of Kyoto, which houses a giant gold and bronze statue of the
'Great Buddha', sixteen metres high). The temple was impressive not only for
its sheer size but also for its army of stocking-footed octogenarian, nonagen-
arian and even centenarian cleaners – all volunteers and all sporting sashes,
like a gathering of Miss Worlds – who were furiously polishing the magnificent
burnished black wooden floors of the temple's verandas.

The method they adopted for buffing up the boards was fascinating to
watch. Whereas my own floor-polishing approach would have been to crawl
around like an inebriated cockroach, polishing the boards in the same swirly
swabbing style that I employ for washing the kitchen floor, these energetic
grannies exhibited an entirely different technique. Working together in perfect
formation, they launched themselves into their respective polishing positions
as follows:

1. Sit on heels, hands in lap, clutching cloth.
2. With cloth still in hands, outstretch arms and raise in unison at an
   angle of forty-five degrees to floor.
3. Bend over until both cloth-clutching hands make contact with floor.
4. Push full body weight on to clutched-cloth hands and, emulating
   action adopted by cow for standing up, hoist hips skywards, keeping
   hands and feet on floor.
5. Accelerate in nose-diving position, pushing on cloth-clutching hands,
   and follow straight length of floorboard.
6. On reaching end of board, side-step to neighbouring board and execute neat U-turn.
7. Push off down new board, repeating identical bovine rear-raised polishing strategy.

Intrigued by this regimented and harmoniously synchronised floor-
polishing, I stood on the sidelines for some time, mesmerised by such an
effective operation carried out by an acrobatic troop of old-age pensioners.
Propping myself against an ancient pillar, I pondered that it was no wonder
that the Japanese could boast one of the highest life expectancies in the world.
Whereas in Britain the average ninety-five-year-old would have lost, if not their

marbles, then their muscles, the average ninety-five-year-old Japanese would still be as pliable as putty and found pushing heavily loaded wheelbarrows up vertical mountainsides, planting rice fields or nimbly impersonating a herd of nose-diving heifers as they efficiently polished huge temple floors.

Noticing my interest, a small faction of grinning cleaners broke away from the main pack to gather around me. After the usual inquisition in which they obtained my name, age, marital status, mother-country and purpose in Japan, I complimented them on their polishing technique. Before I knew it, I found a cloth in my hands and an ebullient sea of faces urging me on to have a go.

Having observed their floor-polishing skills in considerable detail, I should have taken to the whole elaborate process as smoothly as the proverbial duck to water rather than as a cow to slaughter. Instead, I was a disaster from the start, unceremoniously falling headfirst into the floor when my socked wheelspinning feet were unable to get a grip on the slippery boards. But to my antiquated audience I proved a big and seemingly hilarious hit, living up to the widely held notion that foreigners are stupid – that's part of their appeal.

In another part of the temple I came across a wall of sliding *shoji* (rice-paper panels) upon which had been painted a series of saying, proverbs, poems and thoughts, such as the 'Buddhist Hymn' by Shan-tao (613—681):

> Let us return in all haste,
> Tarry not in other lands
> But follow this Buddha alone,
> Who guides us to our original home.

Was Shan-tao trying to tell me something? I padded sideways a few paces (strictly no shoes of any description permitted in temple) and read an interesting idea by Kubutsu Shonin (1875–1943):

> Take it as proof of my ignorant status:
> that I begrudge the mosquito's
> partaking of this sin-ridden body of mine.

That night, as I lay awake, thrashing out wildly into the dark clammy air as a bombardment of mosquitoes laid siege on my 'sin-ridden' skin, I thought: to hell with my 'ignorant status' – I'm going to annihilate the lot.

181

The following morning I found myself walking along not far from Kyoto station, when a bald and small wiry man in big bifocals came up to me. He wore a pair of sloppy black slip-ons, a clingy and badly cut white office shirt complete with sweat patches, and a pair of tight, buttock-hugging, grey nylon trousers. I was taken aback the moment he opened his mouth – his word-perfect Oxford-English accent belied his oriental features.

'Do excuse me,' he said, 'but may I take the liberty of asking you where you are from?'

'I'm from England,' I said, with elevated eyebrow.

'England? How fascinating! A marvellous country indeed. May I take this opportunity of engaging you in a little conversation?'

Before I had a chance to reply, he continued, 'May I enquire as to what your purpose is of visiting Japan?'

'Are you doing a survey?' I asked, beginning to smell a rat.

'A survey? Goodness gracious me! Nothing of the kind. It is just that I have learnt all of my English thanks to your marvellous BBC and I simply wish to engage in a little conversation with a native English speaker. The World Service is a simply splendid service – would you not agree?'

'Yes, it's very good,' I said, keeping my cards tucked close to my chest.

'Now the fact that you are from England is really most interesting.'

'Is it?' I asked suspiciously. 'Wouldn't it have been more interesting if I had said I was from Outer Mongolia?'

'I beg your pardon?'

'Why is the fact that I'm from England so interesting?'

'Ahh, now this is because I like to keep abreast of the current affairs of your fine country. I find such matters to be of considerable interest. For instance, may I take this opportunity of asking your opinion on the possibility of ID cards being introduced in Britain?'

'ID cards?' I exclaimed, finding it hard to believe that I was being confronted by a complete stranger (a nerdy one at that) about the whys and wherefores of a British ID card while standing on a busy street in the middle of Kyoto.

'Please, do excuse me,' said the man. 'To keep you standing here in the heat is quite thoughtless of me. Perhaps you might care to join me for a light refreshment of some description? I know of a cosy little tea-room not far from here.'

Not being in the habit of disappearing into cosy little tea-rooms with dubious characters, I said, 'I'm sorry, but I'm afraid I've got a lot to do.'

The man's tone became a little harder. 'Could you modify your schedule for my requirements?'

With hackles rising, I said, 'No, I'm afraid I can't modify my schedule for your requirements, so goodbye.'

And with that I turned and walked away. Undeterred, the man, who was clearly not happy with his dismissal, took off after me.

'If I may,' he said when he pulled broadside, 'I will take it upon myself to ignore your refusal of my invitation and again ask you to join me for half-an-hour's English conversation in a cosy little tea-room.'

'No, I'm sorry, but like I said, I haven't got time.'

'Then I will ask you again to consider modifying your schedule to suit my requirements.' He was beginning to sound like a parrot repeating itself.

'Well, I'm sorry to disappoint you, but I don't feel like modifying my schedule as I've got a lot to do.'

I felt very tempted to say something a lot stronger, but I held my tongue. I'd become conditioned to being in a country of phenomenal politeness. But the nerdy pest became more pushy.

'I ask you to modify your schedule to suit my requirements,' he said, with a chin-thrusting and more threatening tone that made me feel he was about to hit me.

By now we had reached the corner of Karasuma-Dori and Shichijo-Dori, a busy junction opposite the station. I waited with the crowds at the lights for the signal to cross the road. Still the nerdy pest persisted.

'I ask you again to modify your schedule to join me for conversation in a cosy little tea-room!'

By now he was becoming visibly heated and he spat out his words in a most unbecoming fashion. In a mild state of disbelief, I looked at the squawking-parrot man and wondered if perhaps this loony was in fact some type of moronic wind-up automaton and that I had stumbled into a Japanese version of *Candid Camera*, out to catch gullible tourists on film. I decided that, if he couldn't accept 'no' for an answer, then the best thing to do was simply to ignore him. So I did, and stepped off the pavement with the surging crowds to cross the road.

Unfortunately, Parrot Man came too, still demanding that I modify my schedule to suit his requirements. Then he pushed me on the shoulder. I felt like throttling him but I didn't because . . . well, I was in polite, non-confrontational Japan, where it just didn't seem right to go around throttling people, or causing a scene, no matter how annoying they might be. It might have been very different had I been alone with this man at night on a dark, empty street, but here, in broad daylight, encapsulated in a crowd, I didn't feel worried about my safety – just angry.

When I spotted a policeman flowing towards us among the swirling tide of pedestrians, I didn't hesitate to stop him in his tracks.

'*Sumimasen* – excuse me,' I said – which was all it took to make Parrot Man turn tail and scarper off at speed the way we had come.

'Quick, he went that way!' I shouted, running after Parrot Man as he vanished into the mouth of the subway.

The policeman failed to give chase. Now, if I was a policeman and had been confronted by a ruffled foreigner urgently indicating that I should follow a suspicious-looking character beside her who had run off the moment she had approached me, my immediate reaction would be at least to make an attempt at catching the suspect, as something was plainly amiss. Instead, my Far Eastern, far-out-of-it Plod was reluctant even to quicken his pace. I found myself running back to goad him into action before manually steering him towards the subway.

Fortunately, an observant young *gaijin* had witnessed the whole sequence of events when he was crossing the road behind me and he had sprinted off after Parrot Man into the subway. Meanwhile my pursuit was much hampered by having to keep waiting for the slow-plodding Plod, who, despite a state of mild emergency, was dawdling like a window-shopper.

Feeling exasperated, I finally gave up on him and tore off alone down the subway steps, knowing there was precious little chance of catching Parrot Man but wanting at least to make an attempt at putting the wind up his nylon slacks. Scouring the densely crowded subterranean tubes was of course an impossible task and I soon retraced my steps back into the open, conscious that the window-shopping Plod was perhaps a lot wiser than I had given him credit for.

After all, chasing highly excitable foreigners on futile missions into the bowels of the netherworld was just not worth the sweat. The June humidity saw to that.

Wondering what might have happened to the gallantly pursuing *gaijin*, I resurfaced at the subway's entrance, where I was intercepted by an American who explained that he was the *gaijin*'s father.

'I was with him when we saw that real weird guy run off. My son told me to meet him here. Did you see him?'

'No,' I said. 'I hope he's all right.'

'Oh, I'm sure he'll be just fine – he's an aikido fighter!'

As I waited with the man for his son to return, I told him what had happened with Parrot Man.

'Jeez,' said the *gaijin*'s dad, 'sure doesn't sound like your average salaryman!'

He told me he was from Connecticut and had come to Japan to visit his son, who was living here while he trained as an aikido fighter.

'He's real tough,' said the father. 'He's made to do crazy things like thirty-kilometre runs with no shoes on and swimming in frozen lakes in the middle of January and sitting cross-legged for hours without moving.'

After a while the aikido fighter emerged at the rendezvous.

'Sorry,' he said, 'I lost him.'

I thanked him anyway for his hot-footed help and we all had a bit of a chortle about the tardy reaction of the dallying policeman before going our separate ways.

Later that afternoon, when I was crossing the junction where I had accosted the policeman, I spotted Parrot Man again. He was having what looked like a heated confrontation with a *gaijin* girl and I could well imagine the sort of 'modifying schedule' conversation they were having as I walked towards them. I was only a few paces away when Parrot Man caught sight of me and shot off into the safety of the subway. I asked the girl, an Aussie, whether he had been causing her trouble.

'Yeah sure,' she said, 'he kept fuckin' demanding I join him for tea!'

I told her I'd had the same experience that morning.

'Fuckin' slimy pansy!' she said, and we had a laugh.

Shortly after this encounter, I walked into the nearby TIC (Tourist Information Centre) to pick up some leaflets on Hokkaido. As I was rifling through a rack of pamphlets and brochures, I overheard a German woman talking to a man at the desk about how she had been pestered near the tourist office by a Japanese man who wouldn't leave her alone. She appeared quite upset. When I intervened, it turned out that the pest had of course been Mr

Modifying Schedule. The man at the desk was all too familiar with the story and told us that although the police had apprehended the man on several occasions, they were unable to detain him as he had not done anything serious enough for which to be charged. Yet.

That evening I met up with Mariko Inoue, the Japanese girlfriend of Jimmy Holmes – a friend of mine from Middlesborough who was living in Vietnam.

I had known Jimmy, a photographer who worked mostly for Oxfam, Christian Aid and Water Aid, for years. In the early days of my London-based cycle-trailer catering business, he was a frequent visitor to the kitchens I used, where he could always be relied on to hoover up any hob-top leftovers. One day he had turned up with Mariko, an intriguing character who fascinated me with her enigmatic ways. Although she spoke little English in those early days, she still managed (with Jimmy's help) to stir my interest about her homeland – a land for which, at that time, I held only a stereotypical image: too many people, too many cars, no room to move, no good for cycling.

Jimmy and Mariko both thought that Japan would be a great place for me to ride around and, after quizzing them further over several more platefuls of leftovers, I agreed. But then other destinations came along and Japan slipped on to the back burner, until one day in England I heard the spine-shuddering rhythms of the great Kodo, beating with primeval energy on their traditional *taiko* drums . . .

I met Mariko outside the Hotel New Kyoto, where we locked up our bikes before trotting across the road in the torrential June rain for something to eat in a little lantern-lit hideaway. Sitting up at the bar, we tucked into a tasty array of delicacies: *aburage* (fried tofu), lotus root, fried squid, tuna *sashimi*, raw egg, *misoshiru* (bean-paste soup), *onigiri*, *enokitake* mushrooms (which resembled clusters of bean sprouts), *umeboshi* (pickled plums), wild mountain vegetables and ginger-flavoured shrimps. As we chopstuck our way through our dizzying medley of dishes, Mariko told me she was back working at the university, where she did various administrative jobs for five and a half days a week. She said she couldn't wait to see Jimmy again – he was currently away for several months on a photographic mission in Laos and Africa.

When Jimmy had been doing some work for a guide book in Japan, he and Mariko had spent several months travelling together around the country. Knowing that the Japanese were one of the world's most homogeneous races, I asked Mariko how people reacted to her when they saw she had a *gaijin* for a boyfriend. She told me that it was generally fine in the big cities, where there were plenty of other foreigners.

'And the younger generation is usually okay everywhere,' she said, 'but sometime with older generation there is many problem.'

She described how sometimes these problems could be open hostility that she and Jimmy couldn't ignore, like the times when they were refused accommodation by one cheap hotel after another. But, more often than not, it was the subtle nuances of language and expression that people used to convey their disdain and disapproval – nuances to which Mariko was innately atuned, though they mostly passed by Jimmy undetected.

I discovered that some of their experiences were not dissimilar to some of those I had read about in John David Morley's book, *Pictures from the Water Trade,* an original and astutely told tale about the author's alter ego, an intriguing and immensely likeable character called Boon. Morley had immersed himself for several years in Japanese life and described from first-hand experience some of the 'deep sexual resentment of all Japanese men whenever they see a foreigner going with their women'. Boon acquired a Japanese girlfriend and soon found that 'when they appeared together in public the hostility towards himself was as unmistakable as the contempt for her'. In his relationship with Haruko – a relationship that Haruko kept secret from her own family – even cosmopolitan Tokyo showed it prejudices. Sometimes she would be openly abused, even by younger men.

> They called her *pansuke,* the slang for whore that had been current during the American occupation of Japan after the war. The use of period slang by older men who may have had unpleasant recollections at the sight of a Japanese girl walking out with a foreigner did not altogether surprise Boon, but coming from someone of his own generation it struck him almost as a betrayal.

Back in Maizuru I retrieved my rested and stabled steed from Keiko's house and galloped off through thundering rain to the port. Together with a cargo of cars, motorcyclists and half the Japanese army, I boarded the night ferry for the thirty-four-hour voyage to Hokkaido.

Unable to fulfil my customary desire of sleeping on deck, owing to the unremitting rain drumming down as loudly and as furiously as the Kodo, I made haste inside to stake out my territory in one of the two large communal cabins. These rooms consisted of the usual set-up found on most Japanese ferries: a flat expanse of carpeted no-shoes area upon which lay a rank of folded brown rugs (interwoven with the coarse black hairs of a thousand previous users) and a neck-cricking brown plastic 'brick-pillow'.

Most of the other passengers, not having to tether a bicycle in a car deck that was crammed with army trucks, had already established their positions by the time I ventured into the passenger-packed cabin. My first choices of position – against wall, beneath window and as far as possible from the dementedly blaring TV – had all been snapped up long ago. I had no alternative other than to launch myself into the midst of a sea of limbs and belongings and unfurled blankets until a sudden parting of the fleshy waves revealed a small mooring in which to anchor down for the night. Although horribly hot and stuffy and mixed with the noisome odour of vomit, noodles and sweaty feet, the air was not as bad as I'd feared. The mob of cigarette-addicted army recruits – all hooked on their Hopes and Seven Stars – had piled into the smoking quarters across the passageway.

My immediate neighbour on my port-side was a corpulent man who, despite the headachingly stuffy fug of the cabin, lay prostrate and unmoving with a blanket hoisted over his face. On my starboard side knelt a sprightly *obaasan* who gave me two pickled plum-filled riceballs and a can of *oolong-cha*. She was one of a group of elderly Christians travelling to Hokkaido to take part in some sort of missionary convention. I asked her where she lived.

'Kobe,' she said.

Kobe – a city which, because of its all too recent turbulent past, meant only one thing to me: the earthquake, 6000 dead, and Masa naked, but alive, with his watch.

'All the houses around us were destroyed,' said the *obaasan*, with one of those disorientating oriental smiles, 'while the house where I slept with my family remained perfectly untouched. None of my family was hurt. God protected us.' And she gave me a packet of fish-flavoured biscuits.

Bodies everywhere. Tightly packed and pickled together. Bodies of families and friends and loners and strangers. All thrown together, rubbing shoulders and elbows and buttocks. Some people picked at their packets or slurped on their noodles; others lay long lost behind fat doorstep-sized *manga* whose car-toon pages depicted the usual scenes of masochistic sex and maniacal flesh-slashing violence. Others simply lay with a vacuous expression, mesmerised by some riotously inane TV game show or, at one point, by a dubbed spaghetti western which offered the bizarre spectacle of John Wayne speaking fluent Japanese as he swaggered into town or ducked down behind big bullet-twanged boulders. There were cooking programmes, too – exquisitely elegant Japanese women looking quaintly abashed while doing something improbably delicate with dainty lotus leaves one moment, then wielding their samurai cleaver upon some wiggly-limbed and recalcitrant-eyed, suction-padded octopus the next. Two or three years later, some nine million Japanese viewers would be watching (with appalled fascination) the British *Two Fat Ladies* cookery programme. Apparently the Japanese looked on it as something of a horror show: the 'cringe appeal' arose from the sight of Jennifer Patterson and Clarissa Dickson Wright preparing their traditional meat and two veg, kneading the raw meat with big rings on their fingers. Mind you, some of the eccentricity of the two cooks was lost in translation: their normal hockey-pitch tones were replaced in the dubbed Japanese version by two high-pitched Japanese voices. The sight of the dumpy duo telling jokes and roaring with laughter was made all the more bizarre by the squeaky Japanese voices emanating from their very British throats.

On the ferry, I didn't have the pleasure of watching the two fat ladies. The TV wailed on, the lights blazed, and somehow most of the bodies that sur-rounded me slept – but not mine. It was too hot, too airless, too body-rammed, too claustrophobic. I tried ear-plugging, eye-shading and face-fanning, all to no avail. So, at 2.30 a.m., suffering from a severe bout of 'cabin fever', I pulled on my waterproofs and carefully picked my way across the bodies to head out on deck, where I stood battered and buffeted by the squalls while staring out over the immensity of a tempestuous black sea.

The stormy weather persisted and I spent all the next day lassoed to a sheltered nook on deck. Having rigged up a makeshift table out of my handlebar bag, I whiled away my time with diary-filling and letter-writing and making postcards by carving up cast-out cardboard food boxes I'd found outside the kitchens.

Whenever I returned inside to my basecamp and the scrum of flopped-upon-floor beings to pick up some more picnicking food from my panniered larder, the fusty waft of hot air-conditioned bodies hit me full-fug in the face. The TV continued to chatter away inanely while eyes either stared vacantly at its flitting screen or were sealed closed, asleep. It amazed me how much time everyone could spend asleep. Was this, I wondered, due to the lethargic elements of the stodgy airless atmosphere, or because of the frenzied and hectic manner in which most people appeared to lead their everyday lives? Or was it simply down to a surplus of soporific genes running rampant around their systems? Maybe people just had an affinity for lying in a state of dormancy. A survey in 1993 had found that well over half the population of Japan described sleeping as their favourite recreation.

When the Japanese were fighting the Russians in Manchuria during the 1904/5 war, the army's official leader, Prince Oyama (a famous hero of the Meiji Restoration that created modern Japan), spent much of his time asleep – leaving the actual strategy and tactics of battle to one General Kodama. Every afternoon Prince Oyama would stir from his slumbers, go to the camp and say, 'Are you still fighting the war?' And that was as it should be: he was a figure-head and his only role was to commit *seppuku* (self-disembowelling) if Japan lost the war. It was just like the system in Japanese big business: one man does the work, the other 'presides', taking the credit in the good times and the blame in bad ones.

That war must have been quite a relaxing one, if measured by the fact that a man's testicles hang low when he is relaxed. During a crucial naval battle with the Russians in 1905, the Japanese Chief of Staff apparently tested Admiral Togo's composure by putting out a hand to feel the position of his balls. The Chief was relieved to find them hanging down and passed this sign of confidence on to appreciative colleagues. The real danger sign would have been if he'd felt nothing, signifying that Togo had mastered the ancient Sumo trick of sucking the testicles into the body at will. I believe the kukri-wielding Gurkhas are capable of similar feats, keeping their vulnerable treasures tucked out of harm's way as they go into battle.

Towards early evening, when the rain finally decided to call it a day, enabling the saturated sun to send a spray of dying shafts of fire upon the glistening deck, I moved to a seat beside the tiny swimming pool (more pit than pool) where a sign on the nearby door of the ladies' outdoor changing-room said:

You are available to swimming. Please apply at reception.

The only other passengers to step outside and watch a watery sun sinking slowly over the horizon were a couple of elderly roly-poly women with wide, flat faces creased into smiles. The usual questions were lobbed my way: '*Hitori desu-ka?* – On your own, are you?', followed as always by, '*Sabishi-ku-nai?* – Aren't you lonely?'

No, I said, I wasn't lonely, I liked being on my own. And I could see they thought I was odd. It seemed that, in Japan, anyone who happened to be alone through choice was immediately classified as an oddball. George Mikes, in *The Land of the Rising Yen*, explained:

> Japan is a country of groups. It is an overcrowded island and groups form naturally, of necessity. Privacy as we know it is unattainable. . . . Privacy is equated with loneliness and loneliness is the utmost horror. . . . The group-mentality is as universal in Japan as the cult of the individual is in Britain.

Having delved briefly into the issue of loneliness before asking for my opinion on Japanese food, the two *obaasan* finished their brief inquisition by getting down to basics: had I yet (obviously in less solitary circumstances) produced any offspring? When I replied that I hadn't as I'd been a bit busy cycling, they immediately rummaged around in their identical Burberry bags and extracted several offerings: a packet of dried fish shavings, a disposable camera, a pack of 'Hello Kitty' tissues and a fountain pen. I batted them back with the customary confusion ('No, no.' 'Yes, yes.' 'No, no . . .') before I succumbed to their insistence, nodded gratefully and bowed, wondering whether their spontaneous generosity was on account of their inherent Japanese munificence or simply because they felt impelled to give anything they could to the lonely and childless individual before them.

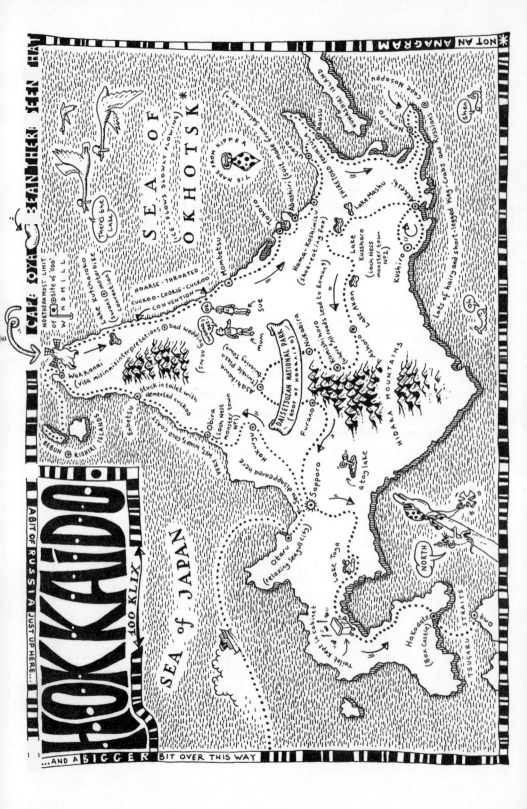

CHAPTER 9

Rainy Rainy-Free Land

As Hokkaido is at roughly the same latitude as southern France and is nationally known for its non-existent rainy season, I had expected to find a sunny, summery, mediterranean land. This huge island (huge by Japanese standards, that is – in reality it's a bonsai-bite smaller than Ireland) that formed Japan's northern frontier would, I believed, offer spacious dreams as well as untamed land, farms and forests, ranches and rivers, sheer cliffs and rolling pastures.

As the ferry sailed ever closer to the promised land, all I saw was a thick soupy sea of grey drizzly mist. It was cold, too – a cold that I had ardently longed for when gadding about in the wilting humidity of Japan's more southerly islands but which now, once experienced, felt disagreeably chilly, like the raw November bleakness of a wintry English day.

Climbing into more layers of clothing than I'd worn for months, I boarded my bike and rolled off through the unexciting port city of Otaru. At one point I pulled over to visit the tourist office and picked up a leaflet, which did an interesting job of extolling the virtues of Hokkaido. On a page entitled 'TAKING A STROLL IN THE AUTUMN SUNLIGHT', I read: '. . . seagulls come back to the seashore which was occupied by the people during the summer and they looked so relaxed'.

This struck me as an unusual concept – somehow I couldn't quite picture a relaxed-looking skreel of screeching gulls. I certainly didn't think that a 'relaxed seagull' was something that the wonderfully mad-capped and impossibly expansive-minded Tom Robbins had ever seen when he wrote that 'the trouble with seagulls is that they don't know whether they are cats or dogs. Their cry is exactly midway between a bark and a meow.'

My plan was to cycle clockwise around Hokkaido, thus keeping the sea on my left for the best views, as I am wont to do in left-hand-driving countries. The only trouble was that, thanks to an inordinate number of oil refineries, petro-chemical plants, a hard, grey coast of concrete and a mist so thick and wet that I might just as well have been cycling with my head in a bucket, I somehow managed to lose the sea. It vanished, just like that. One moment it was there on my port-side prow; the next, it had disappeared into misty oblivion.

So I found myself flowing inland, which was actually quite fortuitous as the temperature rose enough to peel off to shorts and the mist rose enough to see the landscape. And what a landscape it was, too: wide spaces, prairie skies, un-Japanese emptiness. Although Hokkaido represented nearly a quarter of the nation's total land area, it was home to only 5 per cent of the population. I had become so used to the space-at-a-premium and people-packed other islands that the wild rolling expanse of Hokkaido – with its seemingly unlimited open space, its pasturelands, its large white-fenced farms raising cattle and horses, its wooded terrain (forests cover 70 per cent of the island), its frontier towns, homesteaders' red barns, tractors, Harvestore silos and even 'cowboys' – appeared to be more American Midwest than cheek-by-jowl Japan.

The houses were a shock. They were no longer small and brown and crowded fifty to the dozen on top of each other, but two-storey affairs with vibrant red or blue roofs, lawns and fences and vast shoutable distances between each other – distances dotted with cows.

Due partly to the spaciousness, the people of Hokkaido have a reputation for being looser and franker than other Japanese, who tend to see the island as something of a last frontier, a primordial land, Japan as it once was. Today more and more Japanese escape the stresses and strains of the overcrowded, overpolluted towns and cities that clutter so much of the other major islands (Honshu, Kyushu and Shikoko) by setting up a new home in Hokkaido with a freer and more airy life for themselves.

For centuries, Hokkaido ('Road for the North Sea') was home to only a smattering of vanquished samurai, the rest of the population being the ethni-cally mysterious Ainu, the aboriginal tribesmen who lived mostly by hunting and fishing and gathering wild plants, and who were the north's oldest colony of non-Japanese. Until the eighth century the Ainu, who are thought to have occupied Tohoku, the northern part of Honshu, were relentlessly driven further and further northwards by the dominant Yamato, the forebears of today's ethnic Japanese. (Around 600 BC the main body of Japanese called their country Yamato – 'Great Peace' – and this later became Nihon, or Nippon, which means 'Source of the Sun', as seen from China. The modern word 'Japan' comes from the Chinese form of Nippon, 'Jih-pen'.)

The Yamato-led Japanese viewed the remote and mysterious island of Hokkaido, or Ezo ('Alien People Who Live in the North'), as it was once known, as a place running amok with wild barbarians. It was only after the Meiji Restoration of the late 1860s that mainstream Japanese began to consider it as a suitable place to live.

As a distinct people the Ainu existed now only in small communities in Hokkaido. No one knew exactly where this apparently Caucasian race had come from, though anthropologists (who called the Ainu the hairiest people in the world) thought they must be related to Siberian tribes. Over the centuries the simple, bear-worshipping Ainu had been persecuted by a series of 'barbarian subjugation' campaigns that had whittled away at their territory and their population numbers. In more recent times intermarriage had led to their survival as a separate race and culture being in severe doubt and there were now thought to be as few as perhaps 200 pure-blooded Ainu remaining.

In 1878, 117 years before I arrived in Hokkaido, the indomitable Victorian adventuress Isabella Bird, who relished hardship, was travelling in Japan and wrote in a letter to her devoted younger sister, Henrietta, that the Ainu had 'never seen a foreign woman, and only three foreign men, but there is neither crowding nor staring as among the Japanese, possibly in part from apathy and want of intelligence'.

During her journey into the interior of Japan, Isabella experienced the lives of the Ainu at first hand, living in their huts, sharing their food and drink and observing their ritual hunting of mountain bears. In another letter to her sister, she wondered about the past of the Ainu – or Aino (she used the old spelling):

They have no history, their traditions are scarcely worthy of the name, they claim descent from a dog, their houses and persons swarm with vermin, they are sunk in the grossest ignorance, they have no letters or any numbers above a thousand, they are clothed in the bark of trees and the untanned skins of beasts, they worship the bear, the sun, moon, fire, water, and I know not what, they are uncivilisable and altogether irreclaimable savages, yet they are attractive, and in some ways fascinating, and I hope I shall never forget the music of their low, sweet voices, the soft light of their mild, brown eyes, and the wonderful sweetness of their smile.

Isabella went on to compare the Ainu with the Japanese, her description of the latter being thoroughly disparaging – 'sunken chests', 'puny physique', 'the shaky walk of the men, the restricted totter of the women' and the 'general impression of degeneracy', for example. The Ainu, on the other hand, she found physically impressive:

All but two or three that I have seen are the most ferocious-looking of savages, with a physique vigorous enough for carrying out the most ferocious intentions, but as soon as they speak the countenance brightens into a smile as gentle as that of a woman, something which can never be forgotten.

She described the men as being of medium height, broad in chest and shoulder, thickset and very strongly built, with short, thick, muscular arms and legs and large hands and feet. And hirsute:

The bodies, and specially the limbs, of many are covered with short bristly hair. I have seen two boys whose backs are covered with fur as fine and soft as that of a cat.

She looked closely at their faces – the very high, broad and prominent foreheads that 'at first sight give one the impression of an unusual capacity for intellectual development', the small, low-set ears, the straight short broadnostrilled noses, the wide mouths, the lack of jowl, the full eyebrows forming 'a straight line nearly across the face', the large eyes ('very beautiful, the colour a rich liquid brown, the expression singularly soft, and the eyelashes long, silky, and abundant'), the small, regular white teeth . . . in general she found that their features were more European than Asiatic. But it was the hair that made them so extraordinary:

The 'ferocious savagery' of the appearance of the men is produced by a profusion of thick, soft, black hair, divided in the middle, and falling in heavy masses nearly to the shoulder. . . . The beards are equally profuse, quite magnificent, and generally wavy, and in the case of the old men they give a truly patriarchal and venerable aspect, in spite of the yellow tinge produced by smoke and want of cleanliness.

The great detail of Isabella's observations was astounding. Whipping out her tape measure, she checked the men's height (ranging from 5 feet 5 inches to 5 feet 6½ inches – about 1.65 to 1.69 metres), the circumference of their heads and even the weight of their brains. No, she didn't crack open their skulls – she estimated the brain weight by measuring the skull.

Isabella found the 'savagery' of the Ainu highly picturesque. She sat and watched a 'group of magnificent savages with the fitful firelight on their faces, . . . and the row of savage women in the background – eastern savagery and western civilisation met in this hut, savagery giving and civilisation receiving'.

As for the Ainu women, I would have felt quite at home with them myself because they were seldom as much as half an inch more than 5 feet tall (about 1.53 metres). She greatly admired their looks, describing them as:

beautifully formed, straight, lithe, and well-developed, with small feet and hands, well-arched insteps, rounded limbs, well-developed busts, and a firm elastic gait. . . . They have superb teeth, and display them liberally in smiling. Their mouths are somewhat wide, but well formed, and they have a ruddy comeliness about them which is pleasing.

The children were 'very pretty and attractive, and their faces give promise of an intelligence which is lacking in those of the adults'. They were also much loved, and many caresses were exchanged with them. Children were important ('a childless wife may be divorced') but they were kept well in order:

Implicit and prompt obedience is required from infancy; and from a very early age the children are utilised by being made to fetch and carry and go on messages. I have seen children apparently not more than two years old sent for wood; and even at this age they are so thoroughly trained in the observances of etiquette that babies just able to walk never toddle into or out of this house without formal salutations to each person within it, the mother alone excepted.

Isabella Bird was an extraordinary woman and a serious traveller, which came as something of a surprise to those who had known her in her younger days, when she suffered from crippling backache and tended to lounge about on a permanent rest cure until a doctor prescribed a long sea voyage. From then on there was no stopping her – galloping across the Rocky Mountains, going up the Yangtze in a sampan, travelling into Persia and Kurdistan and writing eight bestsellers about her journeys. Her Japanese adventures were recorded in the letters to her sister, now published in the book *Unbeaten Tracks in Japan,* which is a glittering mine of information about the very real people and situations she came across – no cherry-blossom prettiness for Isabella, but dirt, dilapidation, poverty, disease, vermin, mosquitoes, crazy horses, mildew and more.

A woman after my own heart – and stomach – she found 'the Food Question' to be an important one. She was amazed at the advice she had received from all and sundry when it was known that she intended to travel (alone) through the Japanese interior.

> If I accepted much of the advice given to me, as to taking tinned meats and soups, claret, and a Japanese maid, I should need a train of at least six pack-horses! . . . The fact is that, except at a few hotels in popular resorts which are got up for foreigners, bread, butter, milk, meat, poultry, coffee, wine, and beer, are unattainable, that fresh fish is rare, and that unless one can live on rice, tea, and eggs, with the addition now and then of some tasteless fresh vegtables, food must be taken, as the fishy and vegetable abominations known as 'Japanese Food' can only be swallowed and digested by a few, and that after long practice.

In the end, she suggested that travellers to 'the interior' should only take 'a small supply of Liebig's extract of meat, 4 lbs of raisins, some chocolate, both for eating and drinking, and some brandy in case of need'.

The weight that Isabella carried with her struck a chord with me. When cycling across the United States, I had stayed with a family who were curious to know the total weight of all my clobber (until then I hadn't really wanted to know myself, as I suspected the Rocky Mountains would appear a lot harder work if I did). They insisted that I climb on their industrial-size scales. As I stood there with arms trembling while holding my laden bike, they subtracted the weight of me. Bike plus equipment came to 118 pounds (53.5 kg) – and that was without my usually loaded-to-overflowing water supplies (as much as twelve litres in desert areas). Thus, in effect, I was cycling across America with the equivalent of more than forty bags of flour on board.

As for Isabella, her 'outfit' was of similar weight at 110 pounds (nearly fifty kilos), and this, plus the weight of her interpreter, Ito (90 pounds) proved to be 'as much as can be carried by an average Japanese horse'.

My two painted wicker boxes lined with paper and with waterproof covers are convenient for the two sides of a pack-horse. I have a folding chair – for in a Japanese house there is nothing but the floor to sit upon, and not even a solid wall to lean against – an air-pillow for *kuruma* travelling, an india-rubber bath, sheets, a blanket . . .

Kuruma was the Japanese version of the Chinese word *jin-ri-ki-sha*, or 'man-powered carriage', a conveyance that Isabella said had only been invented seven years before and already there were 23,000 in one Japanese city. Young men were flocking to the towns in their thousands 'to make draught animals of themselves' and apparently thereby reducing their lifespan drastically. They could 'trot forty miles a day, at a rate of about 4 miles an hour'.

The last in the list of Isabella's pack-horse load, but the most important of all, was 'a canvas stretcher on light poles, which can be put together in two minutes; and being 2½ feet high is supposed to be secure from fleas'. It seemed that lice proved a problem for her as well, making me wonder whether perhaps she should have taken a leaf out of the seventeenth-century Samurai handbook, *Hagakure*:

A Samurai's underwear should be made from the skin of a badger. This way he will not have lice. In a long campaign, lice are troublesome.

Wedged between the JR Sassho Line railway on one side and the wide Ishikari River on the other, I bowled along northwards across a flat valley floor towards . . . well, I didn't know quite where, except that I wanted to cross a snow-dusted ridge of low mountains to find my way back to the sea.

Featureless towns came and went. I couldn't get over the change in house-style. Plain flat boxes under those brightly coloured roofs. None of that fancy tiling stuff with the ornate ornamental fish flicking their fanciful sculptured tails to the sky that I'd seen elsewhere in Japan. And everything so big. Having become so used to the compact, compressed and crowded life of the other islands, this sudden expansiveness came as a shock to my system. I didn't know what to do with it all. It felt a little too draughty, a little too strange – as if a wall of protective familiarity had suddenly come tumbling down. How odd, I thought, because it wasn't as if I was cycling anywhere *that* big.

When she eventually arrived there, Isabella had been much taken with Hokkaido – the 'real' Japan. 'It is a lonely and a silent land, fitter for the hiding place than the dwelling place of men,' she wrote. And later, after being knocked from her horse, badly injuring her ankle, while crossing a mountain pass, she completed her story of the mishap with a flourish: 'Ah, but it was glorious! The views are most magnificent. This is really Paradise.'

Although people were a lot thinner on the ground in Hokkaido, I found that gifts of generosity and invitations of accommodation still came flooding my way. While I did an admirable job (if I may say so myself) in accepting so many presents, I never – save for once – took anyone up on their offer to sleep in their home. The reason for this is not because I didn't want to but because I didn't want to enough. Having reached a land where, suddenly, there was enough space to swing not only a cat but a whole string of swings without sending a single feline flying, I wanted to be out in it, out in all that space – day in, day out; night in, night out.

Although four walls and a bath are nice, camping is better. I like the fresh and free feeling of roving around with a home in my bag – a home that unravels itself from a compact package the size and weight of just one bag of flour. A home I can set up wherever I so choose: on a mountain ledge, a sunset beach, beside a racing river, in a grassy nook or a sheltered glade. I love the easy simplicity, the unceasing versatility, the gratifying practicality, the portable and flexible freedom.

I had discovered that when the Japanese get a taste for something, be it animal, vegetable, mineral or plain horrible, they tend to go a bit overboard – for Burberries, brollies, Minis, baths, concrete, slippers, Beatrix Potter, the Brontës, Shakeys Pizza or mobile phones for pets, to name but a few. The craze for one Hokkaido town through which I passed, Hokuryu-cho, appeared to be for sunflowers – imitation sunflowers, with not a real one in sight. Their big sunny faces were moulded on and into everything: streetlamps, building façades, railings, signposts, rubbish bins, shop windows, doors and gates. There was even a monstrous sunflower hotel which, judging from the influx of tour buses, was doing hot business with the throngs of flag-waving tourists. Odd.

Things were to get even odder. Entering the seaside town of Obira, I happened upon a colossal roadside sculpture of the Loch Ness Monster overshadowing a sign that said: 'WELCOME ROMANTIC SEASIDE TOWN'.

The coast road stretched northwards ahead of me, long and flat, and into a strong, wet and decidedly Siberian wind. So where was this season of sun to which I had run to escape Honshu's season of rain? Seemingly nowhere to be found. Since landing on Hokkaido I had experienced almost nothing other than blustery cold, grey, mist and rain and an all-pervading lurid gloom. 'Never known a summer like it! It's usually hot and fine by now!' said the shivering locals, cocooned in muffling scarves and hats and gloves and thick winter coats – a combination of clothing and comments that did little to boost my chilled-to-the-bone wind-blasted spirits.

Yet even when the stiff arctic wind rattled my kneecaps and goose-bumped my thighs, I remained steadfastly clad in my cycling shorts, conscious of the edifying study conducted in Japan which had ascertained that women who wore skirts during the autumn months were more able to tolerate winter cold. I presume the same goes for Scotsmen. Anyway, what with my luck so far in attracting a glacial summer, I felt it was only judicious to try to toughen myself up for the undoubtedly worse weather in store.

Slowly I pressed onward, upward, into the gales that sheeted in freezing swathes off huge swollen seas, thundering upon the wave-lashed coast with sullen force. It was evident that this part of Hokkaido was not unused to being battered to pieces by the elements: the steep ridge of wind-washed hills that followed the north-west coast rose like an enormous crest of waves petrified on the cusp of breaking. Nestled at their foot, paint-peeled blue and green wooden houses hunkered down out of the wind behind elaborate barricades of weathered boards that, during the less stormy months, could be removed, leaving

201

a latticework of rough wooden scaffolding through which the locals surveyed the sea.

I took a breather by sheltering out of the wind behind a small shrine set back from the road. It must have been festivity time as the shrine was decked out in a magnificent array of bright, flapping banners. When I poked my nose around the front, I found a pedestal of plates surrounding a small altar containing a selection of bananas, *daikon*, carrots, oranges, apples and sweetmeats. Over on one side sat a big aluminium tea pot and two small china cups. Old sepia-tinted photographs, of the shrine and rows of women in kimonos and men clad in dark robes, hung skew-whiff on the wood-beamed walls. Up at the front, beside the prayer box (a large chest with a wooden grille into which coins could be thrown), the floor was carpeted with bouquets of flowers surrounding a vast bottle of *sake*.

When I returned to my alfresco rest spot in the lee of the shrine, I found that two cans of Georgia coffee and three hot riceballs wrapped in foil had been placed on my mat. I looked around to see if I could see the giver but, other than the whining wind sharpening itself on the corner of the shrine, all was quiet.

I was halfway through consuming my second ball of rice when a toothless old man appeared from behind a wall and shuffled over to tell me that the offering of sustenance had come from his wife.

'We live over there,' he said in Japanese, pointing to a small hut of a house ravaged by a cold, salty wind. 'We've never seen a foreigner in this shrine before.'

After a few more words about the state of the weather ('It's usually hot and fine by now!'), he performed a fetching little bow and shuffled away behind the wall.

That night I camped on the outskirts of Tomamae-cho in a sheltered nook overlooking the Kotanbetsu River. Swaddled in my sleeping-bag, I tuned in to the World Service and was surprised to hear headlines featuring a piece of local-to-where-I-was-lying news. One of Japan's domestic flights had been hijacked at Hokkaido's Hakodate airport by a fifty-three-year-old former bank employee from Tokyo who was armed with . . . a screwdriver.

The next day proved memorable for its abundance of cuckoos, rather than sunflowers. They were everywhere – on signs, in trees, in flight, on telephone lines. Even in toilets. When I pulled up for a pit-stop at Enbetsu-cho's shiny new information area on the outskirts of town, I entered the ladies to the calls of a cuckoo. At first I thought a cuckoo must have got caught short in a cubicle, but then I realised that the call was emanating from a few discreet speakers embedded in the walls. The previous year I had come to grips with Japan's affinity for pre-recorded sounds of flushing to cover up any embarrassed woman's unsavoury tinkles, but piped Cu-zac . . .?

I pushed onwards past fieldfuls of Friesian cows – a sight that kept on surprising me, despite the fact that roughly 90 per cent of Japan's pastureland is found in Hokkaido, and nearly as much of its dairy produce comes from there.

At Teshio-cho, Route 232 (which I had been following northwards up the coast) veered inland before merging with the fat and fast-sounding Route 40. Reluctant to leave the sea, I sought out a minor road that for some sixty-five or seventy kilometres waved *sayonara* to all forms of civilisation (except for a couple of eateries) as it hugged the coast, cutting a long straight swathe through a scenic slice of the Rishiri-Rebun Sarobetsu National Park which, on this mainland side, contained the Sarobetsu and Bakkai Wildflower Garden and the Sarobetsu Marsh.

There was a teeth-chattering headwind and a thundering cavalcade of gravel trucks swooshed past, sending a sharp shower of their stony loads stinging into my face, but the Sarobetsu route was a wild and wonderful ride through marshland and through meadows containing a chaotic profusion of brilliant flowers. Actually the scene was only special as long as I kept my sights set seaward, to port, because the starboard view was less enticing: gravel pit after gravel pit after gravel pit. Evidently Japan's National Parks are not solely a pleasing shade of green.

With frozen extremities, I finally arrived in Wakkanai, a windswept port city that sits out on a limb on Hokkaido's northernmost fringes. I had planned to give arctic camping a miss for that night and instead try to locate a so-called Rider House, which I had read about in a book called *Cycling Japan* that contained a collection of specifically recommended routes for . . . well, cycling in Japan. Its editor, Bryan Harrell, was also the editor of *Oikaze*, a non-profit-making cycling information newsletter based in Tokyo.

The book explained that rider houses were 'a phenomenon seemingly found only in Hokkaido, [which] offer extremely inexpensive and fun lodging for riders, whether they be of the motor- or pedal-bike variety'. Harrell said that the best way to track down a rider house was to look out for makeshift signs along the road as new houses seemed to 'pop up' on a regular basis.

Apparently, two-wheeling it around Hokkaido was a popular pastime for summer-holidaying students, though I had seen precious little signs of such an activity apart from some trailbikes on the ferry. Surely the season of non-sun wasn't acting as a deterrent?

With a raw, wet wind howling viciously around my weary flanks, I was buffeted along the quasi-urban squalor of Wakkanai's coast road in search of a bikers' lodging called 'Rider House Friend'. But thanks to its elusiveness (which I felt had something to do with the low level of murky cloud impeding all visibility), Wakkanai's Rider House was no Friend of mine. I asked two schoolgirls dressed in the standard blue-and-white sailor suits if they knew the way, but they just galloped off in a fit of giggles.

Isabella Bird had encountered similar reactions:

Usually when one makes an enquiry a Japanese puts on a stupid look, giggles, tucks his thumbs into his girdle, hitches up his garments, and either professes perfect ignorance or gives one some vague second-hand information, though it is quite possible that he may have been over every foot of the ground himself more than once. Whether suspicion of your motives in asking is at the bottom of this I don't know, but it is most exasperating to a traveller.

In the end I aborted the Rider House Friend mission and headed back into the centre of town. Too cold and wet to do anything sensible like get warm and dry, I eventually camped near the port on a postage-stamp patch of park beside a block of toilets, which was not quite the sort of end to the day that I had envisaged. And I'm sure that neither was it quite the sort of end to the day envisaged by a tourist couple from Hiroshima who stumbled across me when they were taking a quick ten-minute walkabout away from their coach-party. They decided I was such a rare species that the husband, a Japanese-language high-school teacher, asked me to sign his special sightseeing notebook (issued as standard fare to all of his tour group) in which he had been noting his observations of the tour. He then gave my hand a hearty shake before he and his wife disappeared back into the all-enveloping mist.

The following morning I woke up early – not because of the bone-chilling cold or the tent-flapping wind, but alerted by the sound of someone calling my name outside my door. Bleary of eye and numb of extremities, I unzipped the door to find the Hiroshima schoolteacher squatting down with his wife.

'Harrow, Jodie-*san*,' he said. 'Excuse me to disturbing sleeping time but in short moment we have leaving Wakkanai and we think last night in so warm hotel for you in sleeping cold and we have conclusion really you are fine strong bone person! Please we like to give you extended invitation – no expiring date! – to our home in Hiroshima. Any time fine – this year, next year, or maybe many year after – all very fine! Any time happy to see!'

Then his wife leant forward to hand me their bag of offerings: one box of cognac-flavoured chocolates, two cans of Georgia coffee and a packet of sweet-corn-flavoured crisps inside which I discovered (only after they had gone) a hidden 1000-yen note.

The teacher had also given me his business card, on the back of which he had written:

> Have a nice trabell!
> I am glad to see you yesterday.

It amazed me that all I had to do to elicit such spontaneous and good-humoured generosity was to travel (or even 'trabell') alone on a bike, look a bit odd, camp in a park and look very cold. But then, such was the story all over Japan.

After the meteorological miseries that Hokkaido had thrown at me so far, dawn in Wakkanai broke sparkling and clear. With my soul-dampened mood rising with the mists, I rolled off with elated spirits a few kilometres down the road to Noshappu lighthouse, which stood bright and bold on a tip of the cape just north of Wakkanai that juts out into the Soya Straits.

Looking north, I could just make out Russia's Sakhalin Island and wondered how they were coping in the aftermath of the recent devastating earthquake, which had claimed thousands of lives. It was bewildering to stand on a large, far-flung lump of Far Eastern rock on the edge of the world and be able to gaze upon a segment of Russia – a vast land that stretched westwards to Europe across ten time zones.

Setting eyes on Sakhalin reminded me of another terrible disaster that took place in the skies over the area, hitting the headlines one summer just after I'd left school. On 1st September 1983, radio monitors were working routinely at the secret listening post at Wakkanai. They were tuned in to the frequencies used by Soviet fighter pilots and before dawn on that day they picked up a highly unusual exchange: Soviet fighter planes were scrambled from a base on Sakhalin Island to intercept a plane flying over it from the east. The intruding aircraft was headed directly for Vladivostok, headquarters of the Soviet Union's Pacific Fleet. One of the Soviet pilots attempted to challenge the pilot of the mystery plane but received no response. His orders were to shoot, so he flew close, fired two heat-seeking missiles into the side of the plane and reported back that 'the target has been destroyed'. At Wakkanai, the larger, westward-flying plane suddenly dropped off the radar screen.

Within hours it became inescapably clear that the Soviet pilot had shot down a Boeing 747 airliner of Korean Air Lines carrying 269 passengers and crew, including an American Congressman. The news of the disaster reached me down the wires of my Walkman radio while I was sunning myself on a beach in Greece, euphoric with the feeling of being fresh out of school with O-levels over and free at last to venture off on my bike across exotic and distant lands.

The sun rose higher into a gloriously cloudless sky. Looking westwards I could see the offshore islands of Rebun and volcanic Rishiri, both of them National Park beauty spots (hopefully without gravel pits). Spotting a ferry rippling out that way across the choppy Straits, I decided to linger no longer and to head out to the islands as soon as I could.

Three hours later I was ensconced upon the sunny decks of the *Queen Soya* ferry as she skimmed past Cape Noshappu and out to Rebun, Japan's most northerly island. When I rode down the ramp into Kafuka, Rebun's main town, the sun felt back-glowingly warm.

I knew I was going to love the place as soon as I discovered that the island had only one set of traffic lights. Although hotels were springing up and various roads were being widened, Kafuka was still just a small hotchpotch of higgledy-piggledy shops and homes where foot-power and cycle-power happily ruled the ways over that of the motor.

Spinning south a short way along the narrow, car-free coast road, I arrived in the small salt-sprayed village of Shiretoko on Rebun's southernmost tip. Here life seemed to revolve around fishing and seaweed. Men sat beside walls of vibrantly coloured floats, bent over nets – unravelling and mending them, or spreading them out to dry. Village women in industrial purple rubber gloves crawled around on their hands and knees over open expanses of gravel, fastidiously removing weeds one at a time with sharp-bladed penknives to prepare the area as a drying bed for *kombu*, a large-leaved, succulent brownish-green type of kelp that was harvested from the deep cold waters off Hokkaido and was an essential ingredient in the Japanese basic stock, *dashi*.

Later I passed two rusty bicycles propped on their stands at the roadside, their black wire baskets overflowing with big, glistening sheets of rubbery seaweed that cascaded over the sides. The *obaasan* bicycle owners, heads covered in large, flowery, visor-peaked kerchiefs, stood at the water's edge in their short white rubber boots, dredging the sea shore of kelp with long hooked poles.

Oblong blue-netted baskets swung vertically in the sun, hanging from walls or corners of the weather-beaten homes. The baskets had several shelves, each layered with an assortment of filleted fish and weird sea creatures. Suspended from the eaves of some of the houses, whole sides of fish were left hanging to dry like old brown socks.

The air, bright and pearly clear, smelt freshly potent and salty from the fish and the shiny wet weeds of the sea. I watched an old, thin-as-a-fin fisherman in a narrow wooden boat as he rowed with one foot on an aft-operated oar. At the same time he was leaning over the side to peer into a glass-bottomed box (which he used like a diver's mask) and scooping up his catch of seaweed with a hooked pole.

Rebun may have been a world away from mainstream Japan, but nowhere was far enough to escape the monolithic concrete sea-wall eyesores. Here the massive moulded polygrams came in the shape of giant perforated golf balls. It was hardly surprising that Japan was endeavouring to make a fortress of its coastline, especially with the recent Sakhalin earthquake and the continual threat of *tsunami* (*tsu*, port; *nami*, wave). For some people, though, living behind a vast wall of concrete was not enough assurance that 'port-waves' could be kept at bay. The *Japan Times* reported the story of a Tokyo commuter called Katsuo Katagaru, who

caused havoc on a crowded tube train when his underpants suddenly inflated. The rubber underwear was made by Katsuo himself and designed to inflate to thirty times their original size in the event of a tidal wave.

'I am terrified of water, and death by drowning is my greatest fear,' said Katsuo, aged 48. 'Unfortunately I set them off accidentally while looking for a boiled sweet. They were crushing everybody in the carriage until a passenger stabbed them with a pencil.'

Down at the cape I spread myself on a large and sunny table-top rock to picnic on my second breakfast as the waves surged around the pedestal of my dining-room. The wind blew fresh and strong so I bundled myself up in my overused waterproofs, through which the sun penetrated a gentle warmth. It reminded me of the glowing feeling that comes with experiencing the first tentative, heat-stirring, back-warming rays of a milky English sun waking from winter.

With stomach filled to the brim, I stretched out on the rock-top and gazed up beyond the towering cliffs into the clear aqua-blue, where seabirds dipped and soared and spun in the flow of the thermals. Out to sea, hovering close to the horizon, the majestic volcanic mound of Mount Rishiri rose from the waves, an ethereal halo of wispy white clouds crowning the peak of its conical slopes. It looked for all the world as if the much venerated Fuji had slipped her terrestrial moorings and sailed away with the southerly breeze to drop anchor in the chill, blue depths of the great northern Sea of Japan.

As Rebun was a mere twenty-three kilometres long, it took me no time to nip north through a smattering of fishing villages along the flat and scenic sea-lapping coast road to the small town of Funadomari, where I stocked up on food supplies before cycling down the road to Lake Kushu-ko. Here I discovered an 'official' campground situated in a long, grassy field containing four pit-toilets and a communal open-sided shelter with a couple of long, narrow sinks like metal ditches. I also discovered where all of Hokkaido's two-wheeled movers and shakers seemed to congregate: the field was abuzz with a rally of hip young motorcyclists lolling around in beer-swilling clusters among a jazzy array of nifty tents.

There was only one other cyclist – a small, compact and impressively fit and muscular man in his late sixties with a wild weathered face as dark and brown as a Brazil nut. He immediately latched on to me, wanting to know exactly what species of strange foreigner I was, and the ins and outs of where I had been and where I was going and so on. He spoke with such incomprehensible speed that I ascertained little information from him other than that he was cycling around the periphery of the four main islands of Japan.

Having accepted an invitation to a barbecue with a raucous mob of tight leather-bummed bikers, I gathered (over a feast of fat, fresh salmon) that a popular hiking trail ran the entire length of Rebun's west coast. It was called the Hachi-ji-kan Haiking Kursu (Eight-Hour Hiking Course) for no other reason than it was supposed to take the average pair of legs eight hours to complete. I decided that, weather permitting, I would attempt to tackle the route the following morning.

With the dawn dawning as good as the day before, I filled my flimsy foldable rucksack with food, water, map and waterproofs and, leaving my trusty steed tethered to my tent, set out on the six-kilometre walk to Cape Sucoton-Misaki on Rebun's north-west tip, from where I could launch myself to hike the trail's twenty-five kilometres along the coast.

After humping along the shore past a lung-clogging cement works, a flotilla of fishing boats and a couple of villages, I climbed up a hill and arrived at the Cape just before 7 a.m., feeling as if I had hiked at least half of the course already. In fact I felt so well exercised (which is just another way of saying I felt extremely tired and hungry) that the prospect of eating my entire day's food supplies in one fell swoop before stretching out in the sun on the cliff-top, lulled by the sound of the surf crashing on the rocks far below, struck me as so appealing that I decided to do just that.

The next I knew, I was being rudely aroused from a delightful doze by the high-voltage babble of excitable voices. Evidently some things never change: a century ago Isabella Bird had remarked that, in Japan, 'A low voice is not regarded as "a most excellent thing". The people speak at the top of their

209

voices and, though most words and syllables end in vowels, the general effect of a conversation is like the discordant gabble of a farm-yard.'

Groggily, I opened my eyes and looked up into a sea of grinning faces and flashing cameras. During my surf-soothed stupor of dreamy weariness, a couple of tour buses had arrived on the scene and their contents now surveyed me with an exceedingly animated air of intrigued curiosity. '*Chiizu! Chiizu!*' they chorused, cameras firing away as fast as machine-guns at the confused prostrate form spread out in the sun before them. Once again, the cycling sightseer had become the sight seen.

The promising outcome of this encounter was that, by regarding me as some sort of half-starved vagabond, they showered me with gifts, most of which were fortuitously edible. Thus I was able to consume the equivalent of about four breakfasts on the trot and still have enough surplus food to continue – or, rather, begin – the Eight-Hour Haiking Kursu.

With energy levels replenished, I set off with a buoyant spring in my step and climbed up into the spectacular cliff-carved hills that lay ablaze with a carpet of exotic wildflowers. Not for nothing was Rebun known as the Floating Island of Flowers. Alpine plants, which in other areas could only be seen on mountains more than a thousand metres above sea level, bloomed all over the island even at sea level. In ancient times, Rebun had been connected to the Asian continent but had been separated by a rise in sea level caused by global warming some seventy million years ago. One result had been that the island escaped from invasion by southern plants and became home to around 300 kinds of alpine plants, including a number of varieties that can only survive on Rebun, due to its unique climate and geological features.

One of the most celebrated local flowers was the Rebun Atsumoriso (*Cypripedium macranthum* to blooming botanists), which belonged to the orchid family. Because the flower's shape resembled a particular bag worn by eleventh-century sergeants in order to fend off arrows, the plant had been named after a famous young aristocrat, Atsumori, who had died in battle (obviously his flower-bag hadn't come up roses). Other varieties of this plant growing in areas outside Rebun had red or purple flowers but Rebun Atsumoriso, which could only bloom on the island, had creamy-coloured ones which, judging from the ones that popped up along my way, were no less spectacular than their gaudier cousins. But, glorious floral things that they were, I wouldn't go so far as to describe them in the far-fetched lyricism of the local tourist leaflet, which said:

These flowers seem as if they speak the words of the living earth directly to our minds through their figures. At the end of a day of flower visiting, a divinely solemn afterglow colors the sky, but after a while the night comes with silence and the whole sky is filled with stars.

I rambled onward over green and tussled cliff-tops for several kilometres until I dropped down to the small fishing village of Nishiuedomari, the only coastal area of Rebun that is not choked by seaweed. A path led up to a wooden observation point overlooking the crystal-clear water of the weed-free harbour. It was on this lookout deck that I bumped into Koji, one of the biking boys I'd met at the barbecue the previous night. He was a little agitated, because he was looking for his Rolex – he'd left it there the day before. The viewing deck was a popular spot with tourists and locals alike, so I felt it was highly unlikely that his watch would still be in the same place as he had left it.

Of course, I was forgetting that this was Japan, a country of conscientiously upright people whose attitudes to petty pilfering left those of other industrialised nations stuck shamefully in the shade. Despite all the comings and goings of people who, I'm sure, would have loved a gravitas-giving Rolex on their wrist, Koji's 40,000 yen watch was still there. Someone had carefully placed it in a small cellophane bag and attached it to a beam in the corner, with a scrap of paper noting the time and date that they'd found it – such remarkable honesty in the face of temptation!

Down in the village a housewife, espying me walking past with my pack, called me into her kitchen a step up from the track to give me six fried potatoes on sticks, which she was making to sell in a stall down by the harbour. Before I left, she gave me a bowl of *fuki* (a wild vegetable not unlike rhubarb), two packs of dried *ika* (cuttlefish) and a can of chilled green tea.

From Nishiuedomari, the Hachi-ji-kan Haiking Kursu headed inland, following tractor tracks across open rolling hills that vaguely reminded me of England's South Downs. Everywhere fields of wildflowers dazzled the eye, their sweet, heady scent a-spin on the wind.

Before long the trail narrowed as it cut its way through a forest of conifers and jungly woods, complete with weird whooping birds. Every few kilometres the terrain became something dramatically different: shaly slopes, wild burnt-orange cliff-tops, expanses of dwarf bamboo, empty coves, waterfalls, streams, stretches of long rocky beaches. A sprinkling of tiny, and mostly seasonal, villages were no more than collections of weather-battered shacks, huddled together in the shelter of coves, where bent-back folk sat in clusters picking away at ravels of fishing nets or hanging bucketloads of seaweed to sun-dry from lattices of rough wooden racks.

One old sea dog, wearing an oily vest, torn black tracksuit bottoms rolled up to the knobbles of his knees and a pair of biblical sandals, beckoned me over to share a flask of *oolong-cha*. As I drank my tea, he chatted and tinkered with an old outboard engine, riddled with rust, that he said he'd been trying to mend for months and wouldn't give up until he'd succeeded.

Even though it was the height of summer, Rebun's famed wildflower-laced Haiking Kursu was virtually devoid of fellow hikers. The only people I met were a steel-maker salaryman from Nagoya who was so in love with Rebun and Rishiri that he returned without fail every year, a group of boisterous knapsacked geriatrics picnicking with much merriment in a cove, and a young and frighteningly fit eighteen-year-old who was treating the Hachi-ji-kan Haiking Kursu as a trial of endurance by running its entire length in order to attain some sort of survival certificate.

As for me, I preferred to take life at a somewhat more leisurely pace – snacking little and often on the copious edible booty I bore on my back, or stretching out in the oh-so-rare sun on a hot grassy knoll with the perfect petalled blooms of edelweiss and other such fine flora, their delicate scents drifting across my face.

After a mid-afternoon lull because I'd been washed by a wave of limb-pounded weariness, I set off with second wind to tackle the remaining few kilometres that led me along a melodramatic coastline of natural rock sculptures – one of which was Jizo Iwa, a mighty stone spire forty-four metres tall that rose up magnificently from the sea. I arrived at the southern tip of the island just as the sun plunged behind a rocky outcrop that perfectly resembled the silhouette of a cat.

From the tip of the island's tail, I humped along on leaden legs back along the east coast and the fishy seaweed communities through which I had ridden the previous day until I reached Kafuka, where Koji (Rolex restored) spotted me admiring the island's only traffic lights and gave me a lift back to the campsite on the back of his bike.

That night the birds sang all night long, punctuated by a coarse and hoarse-throated cuckoo. Unable to sleep, I drowsily reached for my trannie and tuned in to Radio Netherlands (motto: 'We get the whole world talking'). They were doing a piece on the history of famous department stores. Just before falling into a cuckoo-reverberating slumber, I learnt how Harrods was nearly dragged into a murder case in 1909 when a customer was accidentally shampooed to death in the Hair and Beauty Salon.

The next morning the weather had flipped on its head again and blew cold, windy and wet. After packing a dripping tent into my panniers, I rode around the wave-sprayed cape of Kaneda-no-misaki before heading south through the village of Horodomari, whose seafront was lined with ranks of low, long-handled wheelbarrows overflowing with slimy mountains of kelp. As I rode through the village I peered into the steamy windows of houses built right on the road and was amazed at the number of men I spotted lolling on the *tatami* in front of the television while their aproned womenfolk were left to grapple with the elements as they trawled the shoreline for seaweed or crawled around on the ground to pick through the stones of the sea-vegetable drying-beds.

The sun bored a welcome hole in the clouds as I caught the mid-morning ferry to the imposing island of Rishiri, lying some ten kilometres south-east of Rebun across the the Rebun Straits. The cone of Mount Rishiri, erupting from the sea, was crowned by a circle of cloud. From the wind-scoured decks of the inter-island ferry, I gazed out towards the elevated wonders of the venerated mount (1719 metres high) and felt an intense urge to scale its perfectly coni-cal slopes. By the time the boat was entering the mouth of Kutsugata harbour, I had made up my mind: I was going to climb to the top of Rishiri-*san*.

Arising at 4 a.m. to embark upon the ascent, I initially felt a bit dubious because clambering up fairly substantial mountains was not a pastime with which I was well acquainted. Also my footwear – a pair of threadbare trainers – left a lot to be desired for a potentially perilous climb. For the first few hours I slid around hopelessly in the glutinous mud of the narrow-rutted trail on the lower slopes. The trail wove its way upwards through woods before opening out into dense shrubbery so thick it swallowed my legs.

Rumour had it that climbing Mount Rishiri was 'the' thing to do when visiting the island and, judging from the number of specialised trekking groups in no-nonsense breeches and stout walking boots I had seen accumulating down at the port, I had imagined that climbing the volcano would involve simply following a steady procession of tourist pilgrims as they tramped their determined way to the top. As it turned out, save for a small straggle of lung-puffing bikers who were making heavy work of the mountain in their mud-clogging, clod-hopping beefy great motorcycle boots, happily I saw not a soul.

That is, until the final hour of the climb, when the western approach trail from Kutsugata that I was following merged with the northern approach trail from Oshidomari, which resembled a motorway of pedestrianised mountain mayhem. Vociferous tour group after vociferous tour group clambered past, hell-bent on touching the top for the compulsory *chiizu* peace-pose photo session and a quick chopstick of lunch before rushing back down to the bottom again.

That evening, down in Kutsugata campground, I asked one of the bikers whom I had passed on the trail why the Oshidomari route was so popular.

'Ahh,' he said, 'because our way have five time more difficulty and majority of person I am believing have preferring for more easy time walk.'

That made me feel so good that I ate another seaweed riceball to celebrate. Then the biker, noticing that my bike was pink (albeit a bashed-up, seen-better-days kind of pink), told me with a come-hither grin that in Japan, as the colour pink was directly associated with sex, I was in effect riding around on a sex machine. Ah so, *desu-ka*? I later learnt that the word *iroppoi*, which literally means 'colourful', used to mean 'sexy' – the *iro* (colour) referred to is pink.

The ride around Rishiri's circumference road (about sixty-five kilometres) took me through a couple of towns and a sprinkling of villages, past temples and shrines and a spate of low and ugly company workers' homes like blocks of concrete flats tipped on their sides. Fortunately there still remained plenty of traditional houses nestled into the foot of the mountain – mostly wooden cabins rooted among hearty plots of vegetables. In many cases the cabin windows were covered by removable wooden struts to prevent the furious winds that ravaged the island from smashing the glass. I had only seen this feature before at the opposite end of Japan, in the tropical, typhoon-raked archipelago of Okinawa.

Along a straight, breezy stretch of road, I came across a small festival of floats that were sailing along in a drum-beating procession. Surprised to see a cycling *gaijin*, the entire flotilla of small white trucks stopped in their tracks.

'You are America?' asked a jovial round man.

'No, I am not America.'

'You are one person?'

'Yes, I am one person.'

And the next thing I knew, a floatful of drunken merrymakers had heaved me on board, bike and all, to have a go at beating their drums. Considered as something of a novel find, I was unfortunately called upon to sing a rousing and patriotic song from my country of birth.

'Yes please for hearing fine tuning America song!' said the jovial round man.

'But I am not American, I am English!' I reminded him.

'Ahh so, *desu-ka?*'

'Yes, *desu-ne* – that is so.'

'Please you are very fine King of English song!'

'Or maybe even Queen?'

'Excuse me?'

'Do you mean the Queen of England song – the National Anthem?'

The round man looked confused. 'Excuse me but I speak not so fine King's English.'

Before our communication breakdown could break even further, I took a deep breath and quickly mumbled the tuneless but topical ditty:

> I know the King
> I know the Queen
> I know the Prince of Wales
> But I don't not know no one who
> Don't want no nine-inch nails.

The drum-beating floaters can't have been too impressed, because I was soon released back into the wind of the open road and continued on my way with two dried fish, a jar of *sake* and a kamikaze-style bandanna emblazoned with a non-combat 'Hello Kitty' motif.

215

That night, collapsing in my tent as a combination of rain and wind threatened to tear me from my moorings, I tuned in to a reception-wavering World Service and heard how around 115 people had been killed in Seoul when a department store had suddenly collapsed. Shoddy construction was blamed.

CHAPTER 10

Flower of Tomcat: Fine

Back in windy Wakkanai, I had one major mission in mind: to renew my visa. In most countries this task was guaranteed to test all powers of patience and, after the misunderstandings and misinterpretations of my visa-extending experience in Kagoshima the previous year, I wondered what joys awaited me in Wakkanai.

In the Japanese embassy in London I had picked up a list of the cities in Japan that had immigration centres. Wakkanai was one of those cities, listed with a telephone number but not an address. As it was a port city, I felt the most obvious place to locate Immigration would be either the ferry terminal or one of the solid nondescript buildings that fronted the docks.

I asked a man behind the desk at the ferry terminal where I might find the immigration office as I wanted to extend my visa. He didn't seem to understand, so I pulled out my passport, thumbed through the pages until I found the one with my entry stamp into Japan and demonstrated to him what I was after. He looked at me with a bemused grin before indicating that I would find what I was looking for on a nearby stand of postcards. A postcard of Wakkanai's terminal building was a nice idea but not quite what I had in mind.

'No, not postcards,' I said. 'I'm looking for Immigration to extend my visa.'

That is not precisely what I said, as I couldn't find the all-important words 'extend' and 'Immigration' in my Japanese dictionary. So instead I substituted 'Customs' for the latter and 'expand' for the former and emphasised the point by thudding my fist down on the applicable page in my passport to indicate an authoritative stamp.

The man's face changed from one of bemusement to one of unrestrained brightness and I felt he had finally twigged. Jumping down off his seat, he trotted round the end of the desk and led me over to a table in the hall where three hefty souvenir stamps and ink pads lay. Picking up the stamps, I peered at the indented prints on their bases. My hopes sank. I tested all three stamps on some pages in my diary. One was a picture of a ferry sailing off Hokkaido's northern cape and encircled with the *kanji* for 'Welcome to Wakkanai'. Another depicted a steam train trundling down the tracks in . . . India? . . . Cumbria? . . . British Columbia? . . . who knows? I certainly hadn't seen any steam trains in Wakkanai. The third picture showed a fetching scene of mountains and flowers topped with the words: 'DREAM ISLAND RISHIRI'. All very pleasant but not the sort of thing that would pass in my passport at Passport Control.

By this stage, a small circle of the ferry terminal man's colleagues had gathered around to see what sort of a stir the cycling *gaijin* was causing. So, hoping that someone must, if not speak English, then at least grasp the gist of my 'expanding Customs' Japanese, I reiterated just what it was I was seeking. I was in luck. One young man latched on to my language and charade of gesticulations and declared, 'Sorry, there is no Immigration in Wakkanai!'

This was not the news that I either wanted to hear or felt like accepting, especially as Wakkanai appeared to be a haven for Russian immigrants. So I showed the young man my list of Japanese immigration centres and circled Wakkanai. The man beamed but looked blank. Then, not before time, it dawned on me that I should try ringing the listed Wakkanai telephone number. I did so, but unfortunately the voice that answered spoke in a language which, if not Russian, was something not too far removed from it.

Returning to the young ferry man, I asked him if he would be so good as to lend an ear to the number I dialled in the hope that the indecipherable language emitting from the phone made some sense to him. Happily it did, and an extended (or even 'expanded') conversation ensued, based mainly around a fast fusillade of *hai, hai, hai*'s.

So many yes, yes, yeses didn't give me many clues, because 'yes' doesn't mean 'yes' in Japan. It simply indicates that the person has understood what the other party has said, or at least acknowledges that they've asked a question. It doesn't for a moment imply that the *hai, hai, hai*-er agrees with them. If I asked, 'Is this the road to Tokyo?' the answer was likely to be 'yes'. I was also likely to receive a 'yes' if I asked, 'Where is Tokyo?' Heads stuck in swings and roundabouts is what that's all about.

At last the young man replaced the receiver and said, 'Mmmm, Immigration two block away.'

'Ahh so, *desu-ka?*' I replied brightly, feeling I might be getting somewhere.

The man insisted on showing me where the Immigration building was, even though he had never been there, so I ended up following his car on a meandering wild-goose chase around the port. Finally we pulled up outside a large, white building. After walking up the steps to check that we were at the right place, the young ferry man turned to me and said something like, 'Well, bless me! In all my years working in the port, I never knew Wakkanai had such a thing as an immigration centre!' Then, after a lot of bowing and shakings of hand, he clambered back into his car and drove away.

I entered the building, climbed the stairs and walked into the small, stuffy immigration office, where a sumo-shaped man was expecting me. I told him that I would like to extend my visa. He looked at the entry stamp in my passport and said, 'You are applying too early for extending visa,' which was precisely what I'd feared he might say.

'This is because I won't be able to cycle in time to any other immigration point before it expires,' I said, 'so I thought it was better to apply too early than too late.'

'Excuse me?'

I repeated exactly the same thing in exactly the same tone of voice all over again. The sumo man smiled the smile of the confused and asked me to 'please, wait a moment'.

I waited.

The man picked up the phone and a lengthy discussion followed, entailing a rapid staccato of sounds shooting into the mouthpiece. Finally the man passed the receiver to me and said, 'Please for speaking explanation.'

I took the phone and, a trifle tentatively, said, '*Moshi-moshi.*'

'*Moshi-moshi*,' came the reply and I launched headfirst, as best I could, into a coherent explanation. Once finished, the voice on the other end said something very fast and totally unintelligible in Japanese, which I calmly answered with the standard fail-safe Japanese reply: 'Ahh so, *desu-ka?*'

With a large smile, I then handed the phone back to the sumo man, trying to convey to him that the whole baffling conversation had gone swimmingly. After firing another round of vocal ammunition into the receiver, he put down the phone and asked to see my plane ticket, which was a guarantee of my leaving Japan. Oh dear. I'd been here before in the not-too-distant past.

'I haven't got a ticket,' I said, 'as I'm planning on taking the ferry to Korea and I can't get a ferry ticket yet because I don't know how long it will take me to cycle back down through Honshu to Shimonoseki.'

'Excuse me?'

I repeated the same sort of thing in the same sort of way, only I made it sound even more complicated – believing that complicated words in this case might make for an easier life.

My ploy worked. Bypassing the ticket issue, the sumo man asked me how much money I had. By slipping a decimal point sideways a peg or two (accidentally, of course), I managed to convince him that I had sufficient funds to continue my travels in his country and to leave it. As easy as that. Then, instead of being sent to the office canteen in the bowels of the building in order to attain the necessary 4000 yen *syunyu inshi* (extension stamp), as had happened in Kagoshima, I was directed to Wakkanai's main post-office, where I took the opportunity of picking up my poste restante at the same time.

Back at the immigration office I handed over my stamps, filled out a few forms, received a few stamps in return, performed a few bows and then cycled away.

Several hours later, lying in my tent in a noisy but sheltered nook behind the kitchens of a big harbour-front hotel, I opened a letter from home to discover that my brother had most inconveniently decided to marry his Hungarian girlfriend in a few weeks' time. I was not amused. I mean, honestly, how inconsiderate can you be? Fancy choosing to get married just when your hedonistic sister was happily swanning around on the opposite side of the planet! What's more, this was not the first time such an ill-planned occasion had arisen. Only six years before, my eldest brother had equally inconveniently announced his forthcoming marriage just when I was in the throes of cycling (or bumming around) in India on my way to Australia.

The only cheerful thing to come out of this latest putting-a-spanner-in-my-bicycle-workings news that I could think of was that at least I didn't have any other brothers waiting in the wings to become wedded when I was gallivanting around the world. Two brothers who exhibited such traits was quite enough.

But the facts had to be faced. As much as I wanted to wriggle my way out of any matrimonial festivities in order to continue spinning down the spine of Honshu before sallying into Korea and beyond, I would have to pay heed to parental urgings to return home. Hailing, as I do, from a paltry-sized family (no grandparents, no aunts, no uncles, no cousins, no steps, no halves and no semi-quavers – just two brand-new nephews and a doddery smattering of moth-eaten cats), all kith and kin – especially ones who were potential wedding-cake makers – were in much demand to boost a negligible showing of our 6.2 family members. Of course, I didn't *have* to go to the wedding; I *could* save my oriental wanderings from being thrown well off the rails – but did I really want to fall out of flavour with the remains of my family, who, when all is said and done, are really quite amiable souls to be among (for short periods)?

So, without further parsimonious thoughts (such as the 4000 yen I had just wasted – not to mention the time! – on extending my expanding visa for nothing), I booked myself on to a flight that would deposit me home with a whole day to spare to bake the cake.

With a long way yet to go and time tight on my heels if I wanted (which I did) to finish riding around Hokkaido before rolling down half of Honshu to make it back to Tokyo, I had to push my legs into gear and get a move on.

Early one wet misty morning I took off out of Wakkanai and rode into a raw coastal wind past an endless straggle of second-hand car dealerships run by big, shifty-eyed Russians, until I reached Cape Soya – the northernmost limit of Japan. As I stood at the top of the country, I thought what a long, thinnish rising land it was, the archipelago stretching north to south for 3200 kilometres – which was as far as from the Shetland Islands to Casablanca.

Here at Cape Soya, among the ranks of tour buses, I took a momentary break for the obligatory snapshot of the trig point before climbing up the hill behind the car park where, oddly, there stood a windmill. Just what was Japan coming to? First it was potatoes, then cows, and now windmills.

On the windmill hill there also stood a multi-fingered signpost of the sort that many countries position on the end of their extremities, listing the crow-flying distances to certain destinations. Scanning this Cape Soya sign, I read:

SAKHALIN USSR	43 km
ISHIGAKI	2,849 km
BAGUIO (PHILIPPINES)	3,820 km
TOKYO	1,106 km
ANCHORAGE USA	4,845 km
GRENOBLE (FRANCE)	10,639 km

Ishigaki was Japan's southernmost island. But Grenoble? Why land-locked Grenoble?

Even more curious than finding Grenoble on a Japanese finger-post was the sudden appearance of two students travelling around Hokkaido by scooter. On learning that I was riding around Japan by bicycle, the lads exclaimed, 'Ahh, *sugoi*! – That's great!' Then they gave me a map, a pair of gloves and a Pocari Sweat.

I found these boys curious not so much for what they were doing (plenty of other students were by now busily scootering too), nor for their spontaneous generosity (months before, it had become clear to me that Japan was a nation of phenomenal givers), but more for the strange words that lay emblazoned upon the backs of their jackets. The boy who gave me the gloves wore the statement:

PINK IS MY FAVOURITE COOL OK

while the one who gave me the map and the Pocari Sweat had a jacket stating:

FLOWER OF TOMCAT: FINE

I said to the boys, 'I like your jackets.'
'Thanks!' they replied, clearly chuffed.
'Do you understand what they mean?' I asked.
'Excuse me?'
'Do you understand what the English says on the back of your jackets?'
'English?'
'Yes. The phrases "pink is my favourite cool ok" and "flower of tomcat: fine".'
'Ahhhh sor, English word – please explain.'
'Sorry, I'm afraid I can't,' I said, 'as I've no idea myself.'
'Excuse me?'

'I don't understand your jackets' English messages.'

'But you are England person?' said glove-giver boy.

'I know,' I said, 'but I'm afraid I'm totally flummoxed by the English on your jackets.'

'Excuse me?'

Thinking perhaps I shouldn't have embarked upon this confusing line of enquiry, I decided to give it one last bash: 'The English on your jackets makes no sense to me. I was just wondering whether it means anything to you.'

'English on jacket?' said the Pocari Sweat boy. 'Ahhhh, sure, so cool.'

So that was that. As I rode away into the cold dripping mist, I ruminated on the rather idiosyncratic Japanese use of English and reflected on my reaction to my interpretation of it. After all, surely it was only natural for a native English speaker to look at English as English and to expect it to make sense? But it was slowly dawning on me that this was one of the first and most common mistakes that foreigners made in cross-cultural communications with the Japanese.

I once read somewhere that, in Japan, English was not used as just English. It was also used to create mood, as an exotic ingredient, to exude sophistication, to help the Japanese feel less provincial and more cosmopolitan, more international. When used in this manner, English didn't have to remain true to its original English-language meaning and it could do away with all grammar and syntax.

Take Pocari Sweat. Pocari meant nothing to the foreign visitor, but 'sweat' wasn't something any English-speaker would associate with a refreshing, energy-giving drink. Actually, 'Pocari' didn't mean anything in Japanese either – it had simply been chosen as a brand name because it 'sounded good' to the Japanese ear.

Nonsensical Japlish phrases permeated everything and were particularly used to sell products. It was the foreignness of the words that made them attractive – like the Japanese bottle which bore the slogan 'Pass My Morning Water', or like the popular brand of toilet paper called 'My Fanny', or like Daihatsu Motor deciding that the ideal name for its new 'minica' was the 'Naked'. Another car manufacturer's researchers decided to seek inspiration among the names of medieval English heroes and called their car Cedric, after a Camelot knight. Other Japanese vehicles, according to Tony Thorne in an article in the magazine *HOTAIR*, had suffered under names like Starion (which might or might not have been the Japanese pronunciation of 'stallion'), Guppy, Gorilla, Dumbo, Mum and D-Bag.

Heading south along Cape Soya on a low, flat coastline that was jagged with rocky promontories and pounded by a fresh surging surf, I again felt the invigorating sense of emancipation that came from Hokkaido's unrestrained elbow-room. Apart from the occasional vehicle, I had the road to myself and bowled along with a damp but frolicking wind.

On my right the Soya Hills, bald and rolling, tumbled towards the sea. Fishing villages lay few and far between, acting mostly as supply stations to the mighty fishing fleet that trawled the Sea of Okhotsk – a body of water hemmed in by the east end of the Asian continent and numerous islands, including Hokkaido. In the northern hemisphere, the Okhotsk was the southernmost sea to become ice-locked in winter, when 80 per cent of its surface could be covered with ice floes. The Amur River, running between Russia and China, poured fresh water into the sea, diluting the salt water. Icy Siberian winds could then freeze the water, creating the floes. In the Ewen (Lamut) language, the name Okhotsk originally meant 'broad river'; in winter, 'ice river' was more apt.

Although it felt cold enough for floes, seaweed rather than ice ruled the waves now. Everywhere I looked those curious, iodine-rich vegetables of the sea lay carefully weighted down, stretched across beds of cleaned rock and covered with enormous webs of blue or green nets.

One afternoon the sun made a rare appearance and the scene around me was of cows and barns and haymaking. Before long I reached Lake Kutcharoko, which the tourist leaflet claimed was the 'northernmost lake in Japan', even though a quick glance at my map clearly revealed (unless I was holding my map upside-down, which was quite possible) that there were at least two more northerly lakes: Poro and Onuma.

Whatever its position, Kutcharoko's lake was a fine one. Designated a national recreation area by the Environment Agency, the lakeside also included Hakucho Swan Park where, in late autumn or early spring, more than 10,000 migrating black swans would stop over to rest their wings.

Camped on the green grassy shore of the lake was a bastion of bikers, who readily wooed me into their group by giving me prize position at their night-long barbecue. There was a strong solidarity among bikers – not just in Hokkaido but throughout Japan. On the road they invariably acknowledged each other (even motorless me) with a raised hand, or a nod of the head, or even a feisty punch of the air with a raised 'united' comradely fist. At rest stops they would all park facing in the same direction, sitting around with cans of Georgia coffee or Pocari Sweat, admiring each other's machines, studying maps and talking about where they had been, what they had seen, or where they were going. Those riding anything more powerful than a scooter made a point of being dressed for the part in chaotically colourful body-hugging leathers and fancily painted full-face helmets.

Riders in their late teens or early twenties tended to favour either tractor-tyred trailbikes or low-slung domestic-made racing machines with high-pitched whining engines and psychedelically painted fairings. There was also a strong prestige market (especially among the slightly more 'mature' generation) for foreign bikes, mostly Harley Davidsons. These Harley riders tended to be of two very different types: those who acted respectably, travelling the highways with friends in solemn, well-disciplined processions of twenty or more machines; and the others – oriental Hell's Angels, greasy, long-haired and even bearded (rare for Japan), with bandannas, earrings, oily bash-you-in-the-head boots, studded jean jackets and tassled leathers marked with the Harley or 'gang' insignia.

Whatever the category of rider, their bikes would unfailingly present a polished showpiece of perfection with dazzling chrome, high wide handle-bars jutting upwards like metal antlers, and gleaming paintwork emblazoned with decals and badges. Like modern Angels the world over, these Japanese Harley riders portrayed themselves as the last truly free spirits, only at peace by shattering it when speeding down the highway on their Harleys. It was odd to think that the original Hell's Angels were US pilots who, returning home from the Second World War and taking their name from a notorious wartime bomber squadron, began riding bikes and raising hell on the West Coast.

Bigger than any Hell's Angel was Mr Soichiro Honda, a keen motorcycle boffin, who went to Britain in the 1950s. When he was refused permission to take a look around a British carburettor plant, he returned to Japan with suitcases full of engine parts that he had bought in English shops. His entrepreneurial plan was not just to make copies of his 'souvenirs' but to improve on them, which is precisely what he did, in a venture that made him one of the most famous manufacturers of cars and motorcycles in the world. Western critics might profess to scorn the Japanese for being cheap copyists, but even they have to admit that it is quite nice to drive something that doesn't keep breaking down and that actually works.

Talking to Hiro, a university student riding a souped-up super-shiny Yamaha Virago, I learnt (over a bowlful of barbecued squid rings) that in order to attain your motorcycle licence in Japan you had to be both mechanically inclined and endowed with biceps. This was because the test for machines of 400 cc or over began with the applicant laying the bike carefully on its side on the ground and then picking it up again – which, judging from my own hernia-inducing experience of righting my non-cycling sister-in-law Mel's Moto Morini 400 when someone reversed into it, was not something to be undertaken gladly.

To make just one mistake in the written test (which had two separate sections: one for mechanical knowledge and one for the Highway Code) was to invite certain failure. This was a far cry from the British motorcycling test (which I had recently tucked under my Sam Browne belt) in which you mostly needed luck, not nous or a doctorate in motorcycle maintenance. To prove the point, my examiner – a surprisingly jocular and garrulous fellow (for some obscure reason I had always imagined that examiners of every description were stupendously dull and humourless) – told me, just before I was about to execute my Emergency Skid (I mean, 'Stop'), how his friend had crashed into the back of a bus while taking his test and yet still managed to pass. I hasten to add that this had been in the not-so-distant past when British examiners used to loll around on street corners while examinees went buzzing off to do their thing (like crashing into buses) round the block, rather than being hotly followed by their radio-connected and eagle-eyed examiner on a monster machine, as they now do.

Hiro, a dedicated smoker, who was puffing away on a pack of Parliaments, used his open-face crash helmet as a seat as we sat around the barbecue. I remarked that bike helmets were like cycle helmets – they made better chairs than hats. Hiro agreed.

'I do not like,' he said. 'They have much uncomfortable and in hot sunshine day I have many problem with head smell!'

'Ahh so, *desu-ka?*' I sympathised, and suggested that to combat the problem he should perhaps take a tip from his predecessors, the ever-savvy samurai warriors. Before going into battle, they were reputed to burn incense in their helmets so that any enemy whipping off their heads would at least be offered a pleasant fragrance, if not sight. Such thoughtful chaps, those sword-wielding, flesh-slicing samurai!

My stay at Lake Kutcharoko coincided with a day-long festival which comprised lots of music and dancing, children's running races and drumming competitions and stalls selling bowls of mountainous tangles of noodles, skewers of grilled squid, sticks of chocolate-dipped bananas and salmon the size of surfboards. More than 250 children, togged up in their traditional kimono kit, danced with burning torches around a great big bonfire. The music, although appropriate, was not so traditional: the melancholy melodies of *Swan Lake* were amplified so loudly from the tannoy system that the music was distorted almost beyond recognition. The day culminated in a spectacular firework display over the lake.

Back at the all-night barbecue, one of the bikers – a pony-tailed student in a well-worn red jacket, on the back of which he had painted the slogan 'BORN TO BE FREE – ON THE ROAD AGAIN' – invited me to join in a game they were playing. Before I could think up a suitable excuse to spare myself certain embarrassment, I was blindfolded and positioned in front of a huge watermelon with a plastic bottle in my hand. Born-to-be-free Boy grabbed hold of my shoulders and spun me round and round on the spot until I thought I was going to be sick. Removing his hands, he stepped back and told me to try to bash the watermelon with the bottle. Lashing out wildly with the bottle after the frenzied and disorientating twirl of spins, I was surprised to score a direct hit on the melon. This produced a high-spirited cheer from my drunken audience and earned me the prize of the bashed fruit plus two jars of *sake* – not bad going for someone whose navigational skills had landed her in Japan instead of New Zealand the previous year.

The rain continued to throw itself at me as I sprinted down the coast, the air resounding with the sound of those repetitive, gravel-throated cuckoos, reminding me of Basho's *haiku*:

> Cuckoo –
> sing, fly, sing
> then start again.

Riding through a tedious suburb of garages and car showrooms and yards of scrap metal and second-hand cars, I finally arrived in Mombetsu, the largest fishing port on the Okhotsk coast. Mombetsu was also the location for what the tourist leaflet described as the 'unique Garinko Go' – a sightseeing vessel adapted for viewing the ice floes. Sailing across a sea of pack ice sounded interesting but, seeing as it was cuckoo season and not ice-floe season, I couldn't, so I didn't.

Being a port city, Mombetsu was crawling with sailors and fishermen. There were plenty of Russians among them – big burly fellers built like supertankers, with horny hands, wild beards and huge shoulders as wide as the Japanese were high. Avoiding the downtown area (known for its abundance of sleazy nightlife), I continued along the coast for about thirty kilometres in torrential rain until I splashed into a campsite on the shores of Lake Komukeko. Near the entrance a sign read:

> Komuke International Campsite we would like
> to refer to for your attention is a calm,
> sunshiny campfield situated beside the Lake
> Komuke. We are sure that you will be satisfied
> with the human relationship and natural blessing.

The place resembled more a lake itself than a 'sunshiny campfield' (it was raining so hard now that there were floods) but I did receive a sort of 'natural blessing': my first hot shower for seventeen days. Until then, my 'showers' had been by way of sluicing myself with mugfuls of cold water drawn from any conveniently located outdoor tap that I happened to happen upon along my way.

Once a raucous army of schoolchildren clad in identical blue tracksuits had given up on the rain and departed down the road in a fleet of buses, the only people left to anchor down on their moorings and watch the lake-site water levels rising were myself and a pair of cold, wet, miserable-looking bikers.

The campsite was run by an elderly couple, who received the news that I was travelling alone with wide-eyed amazement and much sucking of teeth and sunshiny smiles. Having been brought up in a country that tended to view solitude as abhorrent, they found it impossible to believe that my solitude was freely and gladly chosen and relished.

Whether it was on account of my 'lonesome' status or because I was simply a *gaijin*, or both, Mr and Mrs Sunshiny were as effusive and generous as ever with their Japanese hospitality. When the rain showed no signs of easing, Mrs Sunshiny gave me an umbrella to prevent me from getting soaked every time I sprinted from my tent to the toilets. When I declined their invitation to sleep in a large *tatami*-matted room in the modern reception building, saying I was fine camping (which I was – I had luckily pitched my tent on a slight mound which, so far, had spared the need for any bailing out), Mr Sunshiny insisted on erecting an elaborate extra tent of blue tarpaulin over my existing tent, aided with poles, ropes and rocks, to act as a sturdy buffer zone against further torrential onslaughts – a tent-within-tent.

Later that evening, when they invited me indoors to take tea and sweetmeats presented on lacquer trays, Mr and Mrs Sunshiny again expressed amazement that I was travelling alone. Was I not frightened? It must be so dangerous, they said.

Dangerous? Isabella Bird found Japan just as safe as I did. After she had travelled 1200 miles in the interior, she wrote: 'I believe that there is no country in the world in which a lady can travel with such absolute security from danger and rudeness as Japan.' It was still true more than a century later. Of the many countries in which I've cycled, I rate Japan and Iceland as being the safest of all – which is quite strange: Iceland has a population of a quarter of a million, compared with Japan's 128 million (Japan's land area is just over three times that of Iceland) and yet I felt equally safe in both.

Nor am I the only one to link Japan with Iceland. Film-maker Fridrik Thor Fridriksson, who put Icelandic cinema on the map when his 1991 drama *Children of Nature* won an Oscar nomination as 'Best Foreign Film', also made a road-movie, *Cold Fever*, about a young Japanese who travelled to Iceland to pay tribute to his parents by performing a long-delayed proper burial ceremony at the isolated spot where they had died years previously. When the movie was released in 1995, Fridriksson said in an interview for *Time Out*:

It may sound strange, but the Icelandic people and the Japanese are actually quite alike. Both these islands have been isolated in the past, both peoples had to travel a lot, and both are firm believers that if you eat a lot of fish oil, you'll be okay with your brain.

That night, after jettisoning a brazenly foraging red fox from the door of my tent, I tuned in to the World Service. The latest news on the collapsed department store in Seoul was that a nineteen-year-old shop assistant had been rescued alive from the rubble after sixteen days. He had survived by chewing on cardboard boxes.

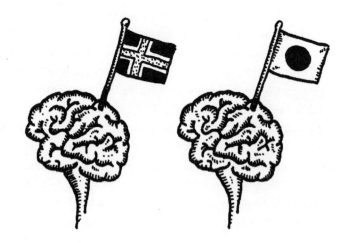

CHAPTER 11

Wet Side of the Sun

With no let-up from the rain, cold and mist, I had to aquaplane on as the days left until my flight were fast disappearing. I set off on the road to Abashiri in hurricane winds, rampant rains, bone-chilling cold and deeply flooded roads. So this was Hokkaido, Japan's only rainy-season-free island? Huh! This was some sunshiny land!

A local fisherman did nothing for my sodden morale when he told me how this area of Hokkaido characteristically enjoyed a high percentage of clear days with sunshine and had less rain and snowfall throughout the year, because of its oceanic climate. In fact, to cap it all, he told me that the nearby inland city of Kitami was famous for taking advantage of the total amount of sunshine it received – one of the highest levels in Japan – by staging solar-car races. Solar-car races? Polar-car, maybe, I thought disbelievingly, as the arctic rain hammered down on my head.

I skirted the top of Saroma Lagoon, a huge body of water nearly 100 kilometres in circumference separated from the Sea of Okhotsk by a long, narrow sandbar and no doubt a pleasant sight, but I missed it in the mist.

Just outside Tokoro-cho, I came across a very exciting discovery: a cycle track. No ordinary cycle track was this. It was a spanking new surface-perfect stretch of two-laned asphalt running well away from the road, sometimes on elevated sections, sometimes on elaborate bicycle-only miniature Firth-of-Forth bridges. For nearly thirty kilometres I sailed along this mother of all cycle tracks in sheer two-wheeling heaven. Unlike cycle tracks in other parts of the

231

world (the one on London's Waterloo Bridge springs to mind), there were no parked cars, no diesel-belching buses erratically stopping in my path, no bits of broken glass, no shoddy and ruptured surfaces with hub-deep ruts, no sudden spoke-snapping back-breaking kerbs to drop off, no 'CYCLISTS DISMOUNT' signs, no tangles of stiles or chicanes or bollards to negotiate – there was nothing at all that necessitated a slackening of pace. There were no shared areas, no dogs, no horses, no skateboards, no micro-scooters, no rollerblades, no dawdlers, no hazards. In fact, there were no pedestrians and no other cyclists at all. The road was all mine! I was free to roam as I pleased, free to wheel with ease. The whole ride proved so much fun that I even forgot to miss the sun.

Waterlogged, but happy, I arrived in Abashiri, the name of which is said to translate as 'Wearing the Red Kimono', referring to the gowns worn by local convicts in bygone days. Here, to gain a short respite from the wet, I paid a visit to the Prefectural Museum (memorable for an Ainu suit made entirely from salmon skin), the Okhotsk Drift Ice Museum (memorable for its . . . well, iciness – visitors were handed a down-filled jacket on arrival) and the Abashiri Prison Museum, memorable not only for the fact that its prison guards carried swords a mere thirty or so years ago but also for Yoshie Shiratori, a Houdini-like prisoner who managed to escape four times – once by ingeniously spitting his evening ration of *miso* soup on to the screws holding the metal bars in place on the wooden doors until eventually the liquid weakened the wood, enabling him to free himself from the jail after six months of spitting.

I spent the night camping on the sodden and swollen shores of Lake Abashiri with yet another clutch of miserably cold and wet motorcyclists. When a young Harley rider turned up – dressed in matt-black open-face crash helmet and flying goggles, with a matching black dog in helmet and goggles riding pillion – and started wooing potential customers to the local rider house down the road, everyone eagerly packed up, attracted by the prospect of sleeping in the warm and dry, leaving me alone at the lakeside.

This suited me fine. Despite the rain, it was nice being outside with the dripping trees and the quiet, misty lake. Anyway, what was a little more wet when I had been wet for weeks? After a while, I was sinking quite happily into the whole sodden swing of things, hardly noticing the musty sleeping-bag, the mouldy shoes, the soaked socks. Even my decidedly webbish feet looked normal to me.

Later that night, radio pinned to ear (batteries on the wane), I heard a discussion about guns on VOA: those who liked them, those who didn't. The gun lobby lot talked like shooters the world over, protesting that it was not guns that killed people but those who pulled the trigger. The US National Rifle Association was campaigning to lift Clinton's ban on specified semi-automatic weapons. The anti-gun person said how much the American citizen's constitutional right to bear arms was costing lives. For example, the US rate of homicide was sixty-three per million population; in Japan, where it was nearly impossible to get a gun licence, the rate was just one-third of one person in a million.

Keen gunman replied that, in America, gun ownership caused a small increase in domestic shootings (particularly at the end of winter, when cabin fever set in) but it deterred a huge amount of other crime. It was an acceptable trade-off, he said. Then someone retold a true story. A few years back, in Vermont, a Wisconsin man had broken into a pharmacy. As he was escaping across the field with his drugs, the old lady who owned the place opened her bedroom window and blasted her shotgun into the raider's right buttock. 'I hope you remembered to steal some painkillers,' she yelled and then blew off his left buttock as well.

The wind and the rain swept me onwards past the Koshimizu Gensei Kaen (Natural Flower Garden), which had twelve kilometres of dunes blooming with over fifty species of wildflowers, producing a dazzling electric effect that lit up an otherwise dull grey day. There was also a food stall in the tourist shop that sold baked potatoes cut in half and served on sticks – sort of lolly-pots.

That evening I had a bit of trouble looking for a suitable spot in which to camp, as the land was too waterlogged. Finally, just outside the small town of Hama-Koshimizu, I spotted a school set back from the road. Within the school grounds and close to its entrance, I saw an open-sided bicycle shelter with a corrugated roof which looked as if it could be a promising bedroom for the night. I cycled up the drive and entered the school building to see whether anyone would mind if I camped beneath the bike shelter once the children had cycled off home.

Of course, none of the teachers I asked minded at all – they just found it an odd request. But, they said, it is cold! It is wet! It is windy! And the ground of the shelter is concrete! Gaa!

Being a species of human who can sleep like a sloth with multiple sharp-edged rocks sticking into my spine, a cold bed of concrete was of no concern to me – at least, not with my whip-it-up-anywhere free-standing tent on board. The teachers, unable to believe (in spite of my protestations) that I could possibly be comfortable sleeping among the bicycle racks, invited me to spend the night in the classroom instead. To sleep in the dry and the warm was tempting but, for one of those reasons that baffle the better parts of my judgement, I still preferred the idea of sleeping outside in the biting, wind-driven rain with flimsy nylon walls, a corrugated-iron ceiling and a concrete mattress for comfort.

Just as I was settling down for the night in my draughty tent-flapping quarters, I heard a man's voice at my door.

'Jodie-*san* – you have hungry?'

Poking my head outside, I found Seiya Terashima – one of the more senior teachers I'd met earlier – smiling enquiringly.

'Hungry?' I said, having already consumed over half a pannierful of food while I was ensconced in my sleeping-bag. 'Umm . . . well, yes.'

One of the many infinitely nice things about cycling is that you can stuff yourself senseless without suffering from the slightest inkling of remorse. Instead of replying with a restrained 'I'd better not' to tantalising offers ('Would you like any more?'; 'Why not finish it off?'; 'Another piece?'; 'One more spoonful?'; 'Why not lick the bowl?'), you can unashamedly revel in the pure unrestrained calorie non-counting gluttony of it all and gleefully answer: I'd love some more; I'll gladly finish it off; I can eat ten more pieces or spoonfuls (and will!); I'll lick the lot. Thank you, very nice. Can't wait for breakfast. What? All right, let's have it now.

'Ahh, fine news!' replied Seiya. 'You are my special guest invitation into my house for eating occasion. But first we go to *supaa* with Yoko because for eating experience we must first make visit for shopping food.'

Yoko Ookohi was a young, newly graduated teacher who spoke no English other than 'Ahh, sorr-great!'. ('Yoko,' I would say, 'could I use your toilet?' 'Ahh, sorr-great!' she would reply.) The three of us bundled into Seiya's car and off to the *supaa* we went – a *supaa* that turned out to be an old wooden store run by an ancient couple with a chaotic collection of boxes, piled all over the floor, containing anything from seaweed and chickens to noodles, rice or lively eel-like creatures with very large fangs.

'Now,' said Seiya, turning to me as we levered ourselves over the boxes, 'please explain what food variety has best suitable tasting to your Western tongue.'

'Well, Seiya,' I replied, 'my Western tongue likes Japanese food very much.'

'Excuse me?'

'I like Japanese food very much,' I said, quickly adding after glancing at the fanged eel-snakes, 'as long as it's dead!'

'Ahh so, *desu-ka*? With Japanese food you really have agreeable liking?'

exclaimed Seiya, with considerable amazement. He then translated what I had said to Yoko, who looked momentarily shocked before responding, 'Ahh, sorr-great!'

'You like *sakana?*' asked Seiya, to which I replied that, yes, I liked fish very much indeed.

'Fine news! So we will have Japanese eating experience of c*han-chan yaki.*'

And without further dietary consultations, Seiya slapped a fat slab of fresh salmon down on the counter. Along with the fish went a cabbage, a couple of handfuls of onions, mushrooms and tomatoes, and four huge, rosy-red apples. My offers to pay were swept aside swiftly.

The cooking took place in Seiya's home, a tiny two-roomed apartment owned by the school. The apartment was part of a long, low, featureless block that housed all the teachers, crammed close together.

Along with Seiya and Yoko, another teacher – a shy young man called Akira Kikuchi – joined us for supper. As it turned out, he took full command of the cooking: the *chan-chan yaki* happened to be his speciality and he set about preparing it in front of our eyes. Upon the low table at which we all sat cross-legged, Akira placed a griddle on which he stir-fried slices of onion, cabbage and mushroom before slapping on a few fat fillets of salmon. After turning the salmon he poured over a sauce made from *miso* and *sake*. Once the sauce was bubbling, Akira declared it was ready. Rice from a pink-flowered rice cooker that sat on a mat beside the table was loaded into my bowl. Then, with chopsticks, we lifted chunks of sizzling *chan-chan yaki* into our bowls. Every time there was a gap on the griddle, Akira would whack on another slice of salmon and fry up more vegetables.

Halfway through our very fine 'eating experience', we were joined by another friend of Seiya's – a local farmer called Takaaki Takemoto. He was a small, stout man with a jovial face and the strong, horny hands of someone who spends most of their working life outdoors in all weathers. At first Takaaki conversed with me only in Japanese, as he spoke no English other than 'Have a nice day!' – or so he said. But the more beers he put away, the more his English improved, until I discovered that he could actually speak English (laced with an American twang) very well.

He told me that on his farm he grew corn, wheat, potatoes and beet. 'But, paahh! – this summer is upside-down summer – all it make is raining for every day. My crop are not so happy with living every day in bath!'

I gathered that Takaaki farmed several acres, which by Japanese standards was a large area. The average size of a Japanese farm was a mere three acres (not much more than a hectare), one-fiftieth the size of the average British farm and less than one-hundredth the size of the average American farm. What's more, over 80 per cent of all Japanese farms were tiny one-family businesses with less than two-and-a-half acres – a far cry from Australia, where farmers tended to measure their land in kilometres.

Japanese agriculture was in a bad way. Less than a century ago, the majority of the population still worked on the land, as their ancestors had done for hundreds of years. Either everyone worked together when planting and harvesting crops, or everyone starved. But whereas immediately after the Second World War young men as a matter of course still followed in their fathers' footsteps and became farmers, now the farmers themselves urged their own sons to desert the land and head for the cities, to go to university, to become high-flying salarymen.

The daughters went too – very few Japanese girls wanted to raise their families in the country and instead they went to find careers and husbands in the cities (husband material was defined by *sanko* – the 'three highs': a high income, a graduate of a highly reputable college, and a height of at least 1.78 metres, which was only an inch or two short of six feet tall by my reckoning). Fewer than 2000 young people a year now chose agriculture as a career and the remaining farmwork was falling increasingly on the shoulders of women, children and the elderly.

Like any other industrialised nation, Japanese farming had become much less labour intensive with the huge change to machinery, though there were still plenty of stooped bent-backs in the landscape, slopping through the rice paddies, deftly twisting their arms under the muddy water, up to their elbows in chilled silt, weeding the crop or transplanting seedlings, just as their forefathers had been doing when Isabella Bird observed them grubbing around in the slush to 'puddle' up the mud round the roots of the rice plants.

After supper, Yoko invited me into her apartment for a cup of 'Sixteen Leaf Tea'. Because she was a junior teacher, her flat was nowhere near as well maintained as Seiya's. The whole place smelt musty, which was hardly surprising as the roof leaked and a large plastic receptacle sat in the middle of the floor catching the steady drips. The toilet was of the malodorous non-flushing pit variety and demanded much care in use if you wanted to avoid losing a foot down one of the many rotten holes in the floor around its base.

Just before 11 p.m., after chatting away over our multi-leafed tea for an hour, I made a move back to my mist-shrouded tent, leaving Yoko to go to bed. Or so I thought. Instead, she told me that she still had at least a couple more hours of work to do. I apologised for keeping her up, but she insisted it had been 'Ahh, sorr-great!' and anyway, she said, every night she worked until at least 1 a.m. and then caught four hours' sleep before beginning work again at 5 a.m.

Suddenly I felt very lazy. When any of my office-bound friends quipped that my life was just one big holiday, my defence mechanisms would spring to alert and I'd insist that my onerously demanding easy-come, easy-go saddle-bound lifestyle was really (yes, *really*) immensely taxing on one's stress levels. I mean, worrying over whether you would make it to the next town in time to replenish dwindling food supplies before the shop shut, or fretting about whether the sun would ever show its tent-drying face again – it could cause no end of anxiety. Then things like discovering that that shop, the only one for a hundred kilometres (which you've just broken all land speed records to reach with thirty seconds to spare before OPEN flipped to CLOSED), had just sold its last packet of Quaker Oats and run out of bananas – well, it's enough to make you grow old before your time! The unrelenting trauma of it all could burden you down, making it feel as if it was you and not your steel steed that was carrying the full weight – all thirty-eight flourbags' worth – of your (semi-edible) panniers upon your own drained and drooping shoulders.

This time around, though, I graciously admitted that perhaps Yoko did work a smidgen harder than me. But only a smidgen, mind.

The following morning I awoke at six. The god-forsaken heavens were emptying their buckets again. My stress levels rose another notch. Another hard, wet day with not a glimmer of blue.

An even worse waking discovery was that during the night one of my shoes had been mauled by a fox. I found its remains (the shoe's, not the fox's) submerged in the middle of the flooded school playground. Putting the saturated trainer back on felt like tying a water butt to my foot. Never mind Reservoir Dogs (or Foxes) – I had Reservoir Feet. Oh, woe was me – the *stress* of it all! But a cheering thought, as they do say (or as a small clutch of free-wheeling vagabonds might say), was that a hard day on the road is better than a good day in the office. Not that I've ever had an office . . .

The next day, the rain stopped. The sun came out. Suddenly, it was hot. I stripped off. Summer, at last! And summer it stayed for two short weeks – a summer that couldn't have appeared in any better place than the remote National Park of Shiretoko Peninsula.

This spectacular, barely civilised finger of volcanic rock, jutting out sixty-three kilometres into the Sea of Okhotsk from the north-east of Hokkaido, felt close to fulfilling the Ainu translation of its name: Shiretoko – 'End of the Earth'.

Thanks to a complete lack of roads leading to its interior, Shiretoko Peninsula was still a decidedly wild and untamed slither of land where brown bears roamed. I spent the fortnight based in a wooded campground halfway up the mountain road that crossed the lower end of the peninsula between the small fishing towns of Utoro and Rausu. Over the road from the campground, across a mountain river, lay Kumanoyu ('Bear Hot Springs'), a free *rotenburo* where every evening I wallowed beneath the stars with the local fishermen's wives in the fiery and sulphurous waters.

The free National Park campground, tiered up the hillside and frequented mostly by bikers and backpackers and the odd cyclist and family of four for good measure, was in a valley between two alluring peaks – Mount Onnebetsu (1331 metres) and the more enticing Mount Rausu (1661 metres) which, weather permitting, I planned on climbing.

Some unwelcome visitors had also taken up residence at Bear Hot Springs campground: not bears, not bums, not sunbed-bagging Germans, but crows – the common Japanese carrion crow, to be precise. These raspy, cawing birds, which pecked out the eyeballs and ripped at the viscera of splattered road-kills, were not appealing at the best of times and the winged black beasts of Shiretoko did nothing to ameliorate their species' notorious reputation.

In the early quiet of my first morning, I was sauntering across the campground towards the toilets when I was suddenly set upon by a vicious mob of dive-bombing crows – huge, demonic apparitions aggressively attacking me about the head like something from a Hitchcock nightmare. Out of breath and feeling shaky, I made it to the safety of the toilet block with eyeballs still intact. From there, I watched the ranks of demolition-crew crows growing alarmingly as nearby recruits flocked in for an eager peck of the action, stationing themselves in the branches of the surrounding trees.

The evident anger of the birds was scary. They weren't just angry, they were talon-hopping mad, pugnaciously tearing into the branches on which they capered and clawed, stabbing at the bark and sawing off small branches with their Black and Decker bills. It was as if they were saying: 'Hey, you down there – see this branch? Well, it could just as soon be your neck!' Yes, these birds were not to be messed with.

Elsewhere in Japan the crows were less aggressive. The wily crows of the northern Honshu city of Sendai were famous for having reinvented the wheel, albeit it as a nutcracker, by enlisting unwitting Sendai motorists to help them prepare their dinner. These city-slicker crows, who by all accounts were far from bird-brained, had discovered that if they dropped walnuts from above the cars, the cars would drive over the nuts and crack them open. The traffic was slow-moving enough for the birds to fly down after their nuts and pick up the pieces. (It was slow because these were learner drivers, who were not allowed out on the roads until they had passed their driving test and so they practised in sort of grown-up dodgem cars.)

In another part of Sendai, the crows displayed even more cunning. They perched on traffic lights beside pelican crossings, waiting for the traffic to stop when the lights turned red. Then they flew down and deliberately placed their nuts right in front of the tyres. The nuts were conveniently crushed when the lights turned green, but the crows, with an advanced road sense, fathomed that it wasn't safe to collect the nut pieces from among moving traffic. So they would wait until an obliging pedestrian pressed the 'Walk' button. When the lights turned red again, the crows had plenty of time to collect their spoils while the pedestrians crossed the road. It was only a matter of time before the crows would learn to press the 'Walk' button themselves.

One morning a strange face appeared in the Bear Hot Springs campground. A foreign face. I hadn't seen one of those for a long time – at least two months – so I felt justified in having a good stare. It was a man's face. As I lay on my stomach, propped up on my elbows in the mouth of my tent, I peered down the tiered slope to the spot where the *gaijin* was setting up his domed home below, and tried to guess from which country he hailed.

Not easy. With some travelling types, you need only to glance at them to discover their nationality. Take the average overseaing American, for example, who tends to take after their national dish – the Big Mac – and who has the peace-shattering vocal power of a troupe of howler monkeys on heat. Then there is the sun-bleached Antipodean, who has either the flat, six-pack, washboard stomach of a surfboard or the world-weary body-battered build of a camper van that has been on the road for years.

Closer to home, the average German Boris is (not that I like to stereotype, of course) a loud, large and gangly-limbed frankfurter; the standard Scandinavian resembles a smorgasbord of several titillating courses; and the standard Mediterranean is an open-shirted and hairy-chested amphitheatre of hot, bullfighting bravado. As for spotting those born in my own motherland – well, that's easy: we tend to bear an uncanny resemblance to white sandwiches in sandals and socks.

But trying to guess the homeland of the tent-erecting *gaijin* was not proving so easy. I was fairly certain he was a European who, on account of his somewhat swarthy appearance, hailed from some sleepy, sun-baked, olive-growing land. This conjecture was confounded when I caught a few words of the chatter he shared with his Japanese companion (a voluptuous, raven-haired beauty) as it sounded to my non-linguistic ear to be the lingo of the land of the doughty *babushka*. I was right in a way, though the man was not himself a Russian, as I discovered when we met.

Hovagim ('call me Hovar') Bakardjian was Bulgarian by nationality and Armenian by blood. He was a biomedical engineer who had won a scholarship to study in Hokkaido at Sapporo University. It was here that he had met his girlfriend, Hiroko Suda, who was studying the heady subject of Russian literature.

Because Hiroko's English was not as good as her fluent Russian, and because Hovar's Japanese was not as good as the incredible assortment of other languages he spoke (Bulgarian, Armenian and Russian, of course, and also German, French and English), they communicated together in fluent Russian, which was something to behold. The windy-stepped tongue of the post-Soviet superpower is not what one expects to hear bursting from the cherry-blossom lips of a mystical, moon-faced Oriental.

Hovar and Hiroko invited me, in English, to join them outside their tent for a spot of lunch. Over a bowl of Hovar's speciality – pasta with cheese and olives – he told me how he was not much taken by Japanese food, especially not beancurd.

'I find tofu cruel food,' he said. 'It looks just like a delicious Bulgarian cheese but tastes of water. Very disappointing!'

Intrigued by Hovar's background, I asked him about his Armenian ancestry and how he came to be born in Bulgaria.

'My father's parents came from a large and wealthy family in Armenia which owned an olive plantation,' he said. 'Not long after my grandparents married – my grandmother was fourteen, my grandfather a year older – Turkey invaded Armenia and massacred one-and-a-quarter million Christians. My grandparents managed to escape together to the coast, where they were rescued by an Egyptian ship that took them to Alexandria. They lived there for three years but my grandmother was a very frail woman and could not take the North African heat. She nearly died. Fortunately she had a distant relation living in Bulgaria, whom they finally found in Sofia – which back then was little bigger than a town.

'My grandfather was a metallic craftsman and he set up a business making saucepans and things like that, which were much sought after by Bulgarians because craftsmen of this nature were few. Armenians are traditionally hard-working people. They don't give up. My grandfather made good money and he and his wife lived well.'

I asked Hovar if he knew what had happened to the rest of his grandparents' relations during the Turkish invasion.

'Apart from one of my grandmother's sisters, who was living in Istanbul at the time of the massacre, they all perished,' he said.

As for Hovar's immediate family, his father was also a biomedical engineer and lived in Bulgaria with Hovar's mother and brother in Russe, on the Romanian border. His brother, following in the family footsteps, had studied biomedical engineering for several years at university but abandoned it when Bulgaria opened up to the West.

'Suddenly there were very few professional jobs available in Bulgaria and my brother saw no point in continuing with his studies. So together we built a shop on to my parents' house, where he set up a business selling flowers and crystal.'

Hovar asked me if I had ever been to Eastern Europe. I told him that I'd cycled across Poland and Czechoslovakia in the mid-1980s, and a few years later through Hungary, Romania and Bulgaria – six months after Ceauçescu had been shot.

'In fact,' I said, 'I might even have cycled past you, as I rode right through Russe – where I remember buying some rancid sheep's cheese – before sleeping in a cornfield on the outskirts of the city listening to the 1990 World Cup final on the World Service.'

Hovar laughed. 'So you have fine memories of my country!'

'Errr . . . not bad,' I lied, remembering how I had been attacked and held captive by a mad-drunk Bulgarian man who had seemed intent on putting an end to me.

Talking about the differences and changes that had occurred in his country since the early 1990s, Hovar explained that life for Bulgarians was better in many ways but not in others.

'For instance,' he said, 'there are very few jobs available now. In a communist society everyone has a job but life is hard – there is little food and always there are shortages of this, shortages of that. I seemed to spend half my life waiting in line for our rations. Like the East Germans, everyone in Bulgaria wanted the ways of the West but then, when it happened, we all wanted to go back to how it was before.'

Hovar paused for a moment and, with his thick, dark eyebrows furrowed, looked thoughfully and a trifle wistfully at his last few mouthfuls of pasta.

'But of course it is better. It had to happen before the ones at the top took everything. People were fed up. They were desperate for change.'

He took a gulp of the strong black coffee he had brewed up on his camping stove before continuing.

'You know, Eastern Europe opened up not because Eastern Europeans are weak people like the West makes out – we didn't give in to Western pressure and propaganda – but because of the few at the top who became too rich and too greedy for power. In theory, communism can work well, but not when it becomes so divided by a selfish few. The West makes out they're the strong ones, the ones with power, but really they were just afraid of the East. And they still associate the East with being a dangerous place. Attitudes have changed little towards accepting Eastern Europeans as hard-working and intelligent people. We chose to open up to the West, otherwise there would have been a war. We were very wise.'

We sat silently for a while. Hovar spoke so fervently that it was enough just to sit and listen, to hear a first-hand account – not polluted by Western diatribe and messy Western politics. To hear it from the heart, from someone who really knew.

'Of course, life would be so much better now in Bulgaria if it wasn't for the war in Bosnia and Croatia. Now there is no trade between Bulgaria and the former Yugoslavia, so we're back to times of terrible shortages. Every day people are getting poorer. And now there is much more crime, too.

Apart from when I went off on walks or cycling excursions around Shiretoko, I spent most of the rest of my time with Hovar and Hiroko. After months of struggling and straining with Japanese and answering the daily barrage of standard questions ('One person?' 'Yes, I'm one person.' 'Is that so?' 'Yes, that is so.' 'On a bicycle?' 'Yes, on a bicycle.' 'From America?' 'No, from England.' 'England?' 'Yes, England.' 'Where are you sleeping?' 'I sleep in a tent.' 'In a tent?' 'Yes, in a tent.' 'As one person?' 'Yes, as one person.' 'Ahh so brave!' 'No, not so brave.' 'Are you not lonely?' 'No, I'm not lonely.' 'But it is so dangerous!' 'I don't think it's so dangerous.' 'Really so brave!' 'No, really, I'm not so brave.' 'You have husband – children?' 'No, I have no husband or children.' 'Mmm, you are not lonely?' 'No, I'm not lonely.' 'Is that so?' 'Yes, that is so,' . . . and so on and so on), it was wonderful to have a lengthy conversation again. Much as I love travelling as 'one person' with no need to string together coherent sentences, instead just swimming along in an unproductive swirl of thought, I do miss regular bouts of elongated discussion. Of course, there is one simple solution to that: learn the lingo of the land through which you are travelling. But, for a tongue-tied type such as me, that is not as easy as opening your mouth to eat that piece of cake.

Hiroko hailed from the city of Nigata, an industrial hub and main transportation centre along northern Honshu's Sea of Japan coast. She had two younger brothers, one of whom still lived with her mother in Nigata. She hardly knew her father, a construction engineer, as for most of her life he had lived in Tokyo on account of his work.

Hiroko spoke English a lot better than she had initially made out and only occasionally would she turn to Hovar when an English word escaped her. Then she, a Japanese, would ask him, a Bulgarian, in Russian for an English word.

She told me how she had won a scholarship to Sapporo University and was currently trying for a second scholarship to study in Russia. Knowing that the Japanese were not that fond of Russians, I asked her what it was that had drawn her to their language and literature.

'Japan and Russia does not have so good relationship together,' she said. 'I became interested in the country because, really, Japan is not so far from Russia and I wanted very much to understanting our neighbour. For making better relationship. To not understand, to always turn your back, I think make for many problem between many country.'

So in September she was off to study Russian for ten weeks in Vladivostok – a mere sumo-throw across the water from her family home in Nigata.

Depending on whether or not she succeeded in obtaining a scholarship, she hoped to go on to study in Moscow.

Although Hovar and Hiroko had studied English at school for about the same amount of time, the difference in their confidence and ability to speak the language was huge. Hiroko spoke it well, but Hovar spoke it outstandingly well, often using words that were way beyond my capacity even as a native English speaker. Whereas Hovar understood everything I said when I spoke at my normal speed, Hiroko had much difficulty. Hovar was older than Hiroko (he in his early thirties, she in her early twenties) and had also had a lot more opportunity to engage in English conversation – and anyway Europeans, apart from us white-socked-and-sandalled Brits, are highly impressive linguists. But I was still interested to know whether or not the differences in the way they had been taught English at school played a major part in their ability to speak it.

With Hovar's help, Hiroko explained that she'd had no conversation whatsoever during her English lessons at school. Instead, pupils were fed information by their Japanese teacher. They learnt by rote. Questions or discussions were non-existent. Pupils were expected to keep their mouths shut and ears open and, being of a conformist society, they complied.

'What was, was what went,' translated Hovar, who'd had a very different learning experience.

'My English teacher was, I think, from Brighton. He was young and much fun and I remember he walked around in the rain with a very large transparent umbrella that went down to his waist. None of us had ever seen such an umbrella and we thought it a big joke – an umbrella you could almost wear!

'Along with studying a lot of literature – Shakespeare and Chaucer in particular – we were always encouraged to speak, to give opinions and ideas on different authors, to diverge and discuss different aspects and angles and views on a huge variety of issues. We never had any inhibition to speak – in fact we would say virtually anything that came into our heads. Our teacher actively encouraged it. We were always laughing and joking. He was like our friend.'

As for Hiroko, even at university she could neither offer any ideas nor question anything.

'Japan tries to give impression it's changing,' she said, 'that it is more open, but underneath everything stay the same. Like socialist society, Japanese people cannot say what we are thinking, only what is acceptable for saying. Always we must do what we are told. No individualism, no questioning the way, no questioning rule too. In Japan we have many . . . mmmm . . .'

Hiroko paused for a moment in thought, before asking Hovar something in Russian.

'Nuance,' he said.

'Nuance,' repeated Hiroko, a little uncertainly. 'In Japan we have many nuance. For foreigner these are very hard – actually most impossible for detection. But really tiny difference and action can mean very a lot for Japanese people.'

'All this is very true,' agreed Hovar. 'In Japan, school and university are similar in that the students never ask questions about the way things are done. They must just accept whatever their teacher or professor tells them is fact. They do not question him. They simply comply and do the same as everyone else.'

'How easy is it for you as a foreigner studying in a Japanese system?' I asked Hovar.

'It is not easy at all! I find life at the university hard. My colleagues in the lab don't accept me, because I do things very differently from everyone else. For instance, I work very, very hard, very, very conscientiously, all the time. I'm always working on new experiments. It is important for me to learn as much as I can – to never waste any time – as I feel privileged to have a scholarship. But for my colleagues, after their stressful school years of intensive work, university for them is like a vacation. Really, it's very easy. They are not interested in work. They sit around relaxing and laughing loudly – messing around and joking like young teenagers. When the professor enters, they adopt a studious role – they pretend to work. They do only what is told of them, nothing more.'

He paused, thoughtful for a moment.

'I had always imagined,' he continued, 'that by coming to Japan to study, I would be working in a group – that we would all be benefiting from each other's ideas, bouncing ideas off each other. But the reality is very hard. Not only am I not accepted, but I get no help from my professor whatsoever. Had I known it would be like this, I would never have come to Japan.'

'But I am very happy you come to Japan, even if you have problem time,' said Hiroko softly, twanging on the heart strings.

Hovar smiled at her but he wasn't going to let any starry-eyed stuff get in the way of what he wanted to say.

'You know,' he continued, 'we foreigners have this fixed idea of Japan – a nation of people who work impossibly hard, all leading incredibly stressful lives – but this is just a fallacy. Japan has only achieved its ballooning progress because everyone is complying, everyone flows in the same direction. They all follow along on a sort of conveyor belt. They are stiflingly conformist. There is little difference of opinion. Of course, it is true that there are many people who do work feverishly hard – the top men in companies, for example – but the majority do little work.'

He exchanged glances with Hiroko but hardly paused for breath.

'I've seen it myself – and Hiroko too – that most people just sit around smoking and laughing and chatting and reading *manga*. They may work long hours, but this is not so hard because a lot of their work is just repetitive: they do the same thing all day, every day – day in, day out – but under no particular pressure. If most Japanese were to work as intensely as I do in the lab, they couldn't survive on such little vacation. I work so intensely that had I not taken this week off – a week that my professor was very loth to give – I believe my health would have been seriously affected. This week will probably be just long enough to control it, but not long enough to relax properly.'

Hiroko was listening sympathetically and Hovar still had a lot to tell me.

'You know,' he went on, 'it's been proved that after intensive work, three weeks is the minimum time necessary to really unwind. My professor just could not understand why I needed a vacation. It was very hard to be granted permission. I had to write many letters and have many meetings with the head of department. As a result I have been totally ostracised and will be treated very coldly on my return next week.'

Hovar looked down for a moment and then added, 'Yes, Japan is so very different from everything I ever imagined.'

CHAPTER 12

Bear Spring Sprung

After my previous enjoyable escapades of scrambling to the top of appealing peaks elsewhere in Japan, I had been hoping for weeks that the weather gods would shine on me enough in Shiretoko for an attempted ascent of Mount Rausu, the summit of which was snow-covered from October to June.

Down the road in Rausu, I visited the National Park offices of the Shiretoko 'Nature Center' opposite a factory. A sign outside said 'WELCOME TO THE NATURE ZONE'. Inside the Nature Center I gathered that two trails led to the top of Mount Rausu – the easier and more popular starting from Iwaobetsu Onsen on the north side of the mountain, and the longer and reputedly more arduous one beginning from the Bear Hot Springs campground. This was the route I fancied. There should be fewer people on it and also starting from my tent was very handy – I wouldn't have to cycle back over the Shiretoko Pass before I even started walking.

Concerned about my inappropriate footwear (the same old trusty pair of dog-eared, fox-chewed trainers), I asked the man at the Park office what state the trail was in and whether he thought my shoes would be up to the job of ferrying me to the top of Mount Rausu and back. He looked at the grips of my trainers (such as they weren't), sucked air through his teeth and tilted his head before delivering a grinning green light. As for the trail, he implied it was a piece of cake: just follow the route marked by pink ribbons.

The news of a route lined with pretty pink ribbons came as a bit of a blow, knocking flat on its head any notion of 'intrepid exploring' that I might have had. Did the likes of Livingstone battle their paths across alien territory way-marked by fetching little ribbons? Somehow I thought not.

Actually, to be honest, I was quite relieved about the ribbons because, when all is said and done, who in their right minds really wants to end up on a mountain (major or minor) tired, cold, lost, hungry and half dead? Not me, thanks. I'd prefer the safe and dainty ribboned route any day. What goes up I'd like to get down – alive.

Back at the campground, Hovar told me that he and Hiroko were also thinking of climbing Mount Rausu, but only if the sun was shining. I told him that the man in the Park office had said that the weather forecast was supposed to be good for the next few days.

'Do you know how long it might take us?' asked Hovar.

'Well, he said that it was a straightforward seven or eight hour climb to the top, along a trail marked by pink ribbons.'

'Pink ribbons? That's nice! When are you thinking of going?'

'The day after tomorrow,' I said, 'but the one thing that puts me off is the state of my shoes – they've hardly got any grip left on them. The man thought they'd be fine, but I'm not so sure. I'm planning on going on a trial run along some of the trail tomorrow to see what it's like and whether my feet will hurt from feeling the rocks through the soles.'

Hovar told me that he, too, only had a pair of trainers in which to climb the mountain. But his were in good nick, with a hefty ridged grip that in my eyes certainly looked sturdy enough to tackle a ribbon-lined trail.

All this mountain and trainer talk put Hovar in mind to tell me about his near-death experience several years before, when he'd attempted to climb a snow-covered mountain alone in Czechoslovakia in a pair of cheap plimsolls. At one point he had slipped and tumbled down a steep escarpment, but he managed to stop his fall by grabbing hold of a rock.

'Otherwise I would have fallen to certain death,' said Hovar, very certainly. 'To climb back I had to carefully dig holes in the snow for my hands and feet and move very slowly to avoid falling off the side of the mountain'

Well, if people go climbing mountains in their shoddy old trainers, what do they expect? I mean, honestly!

That evening a curly-haired Englishman in white socks and sandals (yes, really!) turned up at the campground. After I had recovered from my initial shock at setting eyes upon such a foreign oddity again, I fell into conversation with the sandalled white sandwich as I wandered past his tent on my way to do my washing-up. His name was Andy Jones; he hailed from Lancashire, had gone to Hull University and was currently living just outside Tokyo in Chiba, teaching English for two years.

'It took me a while to get used to my students,' he said. 'Whenever I asked them questions they wouldn't say anything. There was just silence. At first I panicked, but I soon realised that this was the Japanese way – that there's always a big silence before they say something.'

I asked him if he had taught English in any other country and he replied that he had, once in Spain and another time in a cement factory in Poland.

'That was a big shock,' he said. 'The whole place was cold, grey and depressing.'

Andy lived in what he called a 'shoebox' – a minute *tatami* room in an old and decrepit building, paying 50,000 yen (£350) a month for the privilege. For someone who had spent a lot of time hill-walking in the Lake District, he said the best thing about being in Japan was making the most of his days off by escaping into the Japanese Alps. He had been wanting to get to the relative wilds of Shiretoko for a while and, now that he had, he was planning on climbing Mount Rausu before following the mountain range to the end of the peninsula. I asked him when he was intending to set off.

'Tomorrow morning,' he said, 'about five.'

Hovar, who had joined us, said that he had just heard on the weather forecast that a typhoon (which had left fifteen people dead in South Korea) was supposed to be blowing our way.

'A typhoon?' I said. 'I thought Hokkaido was supposed to be the only island in Japan that's typhoon free.'

I could just about put up with the rainy-season-free maxim being broken, but typhoons . . . ? This was getting silly.

'Never mind the forecast,' said Andy, unperturbed. 'I'm going to go anyway. I haven't got much time before I have to be back in Chiba. Can't let a spot of wind and rain put me off, you know.'

'Well, if not the weather, watch out for the bears!' I said.

'Oh, there are supposed to be bears, are there?' he said, as nonchalantly as if he had just been told to beware of a runaway hamster. 'That could be interesting.'

That night it rained so hard that several tents came adrift from their moorings, the high blustery winds sending the ditched domed homes bowling across the campground like big boisterous beach-balls. Morning dawned wet, windy and shrouded in thick, tree-wrapping mist. Definitely not the sort of weather for charging up mountains. Or so I thought. Although Andy didn't embark upon his multi-peaked mission as early as planned, he did go. We neither saw nor heard of him again.

By early afternoon the weather had cleared enough to enable a test-run of my flimsy, foolhardy footwear along the lower slopes of the trail. Needless to say, they proved more than inadequate – their well-worn soles caused me to slip around in the sludge, wheel-spinning hopelessly out of control before ending up splayed splat in the mire like some junior Turkish mud-wrestler.

At one point I was overtaken by a bemused troop of hikers, all kitted out in identical mountain-clambering attire with telescopic Leki hiking poles and hefty no-messing-with-mud boots. Around their necks on lanyards swung bells of the sort that are more commonly found adorning the dewlaps of Alpine cows. Perplexed by the walkers' bizarre propensity for emulating a herd of high Heidi-pastured bovines, it wasn't until they had long disappeared from sight (but not from sound) that it dawned on me that the bell necklaces were bear-scarers.

Slipping and sliding back to base in my mud-clogged and ineffective mountain-scaling footwear, I decided that as I had no boots to hand I would, if I wanted to live (which I did), have to abort any ideas I had of scaling Mount Rausu. Later, still kicking myself that I hadn't embarked on my excursion around Japan better kitted out, I was in the process of throwing away a bag of rubbish into one of the campground's big metal dumpsters when what should I find nestling among the refuse but a pair of stout walking boots! Apart from a broken lace and a scuff on the toe, they were perfectly foot-worthy. What's more, they fitted me like a glove.

With weather forecasted to be fine, I arose at 4 a.m. the following morning. After eating a mountainous breakfast, I pulled on my freshly laundered boots and entwined myself into the chaotic straps of my collapsible knapsack. Hovar and Hiroko had planned to join me, but when I went to rouse them from their sleeping-bags they told me they were so tired that they would sleep a bit longer and maybe catch me up when I stopped for my second breakfast (they had by now become acquainted with my big-for-a-small-person appetite). So I set out alone, which actually I was very glad to do. Being an unsociable sort at heart, I hadn't been too keen on the prospect of climbing along with a clatter of chatter.

For the first few kilometres the trail led me through airy woodlands of conifers and silver birch. Every so often my olfactory senses would be assailed by the heady aroma of some sort of deliciously sweet-smelling flora.

Having seen no one since I left the campground, I was a trifle startled when a man suddenly lurched out from behind a thicket of foliage wielding an extremely large fishing net. It turned out that he was a butterfly-catcher, in hot pursuit of a number of the brightly-winged marvels that were to be found flitting among these green and pleasant hills. After scowling at the catcher to convey my displeasure over his undesirable butterfly-pinning pastime, I continued on my way over a stretch of loose rocks until I hit a small but spirited river.

By now it was about 9 a.m. and already gloriously hot. Feeling this was a suitably scenic spot for putting away a second breakfast, I settled myself on a sun-warmed rock beside the river and chomped my way through two bananas and four riceballs while giving Hovar and Hiroko a chance to catch up. With still no sign of them after an hour, I decided to forge ahead lest I risk not making it back down from the top before dark.

After nearly burning off my recycled boots when springing from rock to rock across a thermally heated sulphur-stained stream, I continued up the mountain, following the dainty small knots of pink ribbon and the occasional pink-painted arrows on rocks that marked the route. Before long, I came across a chubby little man resting on a rock, his puffed and ruddy face soaked in sweat. Round his neck hung a bear-scaring cowbell. More intriguingly, he was clad in full lederhosen and his sweaty dome was topped with a khaki felt hat adorned with a feather. Had it not been for his oriental physiognomy, he would have looked quite at home yodelling and dancing a thigh-slapping jig high up in the Bavarian Alps.

He told me he had started out on the trail at 3.30 a.m. and had found the going a lot harder than he had imagined. Dabbing his brow with a folded handkerchief, he said he thought he would probably turn back as he was 'velly tired'.

I carried on a little way until I hit a snowbank the size of a house. Suddenly there were no more signs of any well-trodden trails or reassuring painted rocks or route-marking ribbon. Hmph! Negotiating a hulking great wall of snow was not something I had expected. To a shiny new novice, it all looked a bit too much like serious ice-picking stuff. After all, I had embarked on this pink-ribboned hike for the view and not for some heroic, glacier-scaling, life-threatening feat. I didn't want crevasse-laced obstacles that could swallow you whole; I wanted an easy ride.

As I stood pondering the problem, feeling neither happy nor quite sure what to do next, the wheezing lederhosen man stumbled on to the scene. He took one look at the daunting snowbank barring our path and collapsed on the ground in a mild state of despair. I told him not to fret because at least we knew which way was down. Then I offered him a banana and he offered me something that looked suspiciously like a pickled fish-eye (not a pleasing swop) before extracting from his rucksack a super-tech GPS navigational aid. Never mind global positioning satellites, I thought, I want my pretty pink ribbons.

Following a lot of digital beeping and button-pressing, Mr Lederhosen consulted his map before declaring that Mount Rausu lay over the snowbank. Ahh so, *desu-ka*? Not good news. Wondering whether there was a way around the snow, I told him to sit tight on his hosen of leder while I went to investigate a possible alternative route.

After fighting my way through a tangle of undergrowth for half an hour and getting thoroughly disorientated and distressed without my comforting ribbons to guide me, I gave up and returned to Mr Lederhosen, who was slumped snoring on a rock in the shade. The sound of approaching cowbells signalled a party of advancing bear-scaring climbers and I decided to bide time to see whether they might have any bright ideas about tackling the snowbank that barred our route.

Finally the bell-ringers appeared. They turned out to be a super-fit couple from Osaka with their two equally energetic young teenage offspring. The husband, an English-teacher, had no doubt about the route.

'Certainly it is into the snow!' he proclaimed and immediately set about scaling the overawing snow-packed obstacle by digging holes for his hands and feet (he'd obviously taken a page out of Hovar's book). Without so much as a quiver of hesitation, his buoyant family of cowbells followed eagerly in his wake.

Mr Lederhosen, who had by now stirred from his sweaty slumber, took one look at the snow-scaling family, decided he didn't like what he saw, quickly picked himself up and declared, 'Excuse me, velly tired. Bye bye.' Turning tail, he set off down the mountain at a cracking pace, the cowbell busily donging round his neck.

The question was: which bells did I follow – the ups or the down? With the day still young and my energy levels feeling nowhere near depleted yet, the decision was not a difficult one. Up I would go, but not by the snow. Scaling a wall of snow was new ground to me and I didn't like the idea of putting my trust in a slippery substance of unknown density through which I could fall. It may have been tough enough to hold a family of four, but sometimes it only takes one more banana to rock the boat.

Instead, I opted to rip my limbs to pieces by hauling myself through an area of sharp-wooded shrubbery that clung to a steep escarpment bordering the snowbank. When I at last emerged at the top, battle-scarred but victorious, I discovered that the snowbank was but a mere morsel of a magnificent, intimidatingly massive tongue of ice and snow that spilled off the mountain into a vast ravine.

The gentle donging of cowbells drew my attention to the distant specks of the feisty family of four, who were traversing this giant ridge of frozen snow as if it was nothing more than a small snowy hiccup. It was then that I noticed a rope suspended widthways high above the icy ravine. Tied to the rope fluttered several knots of pink ribbons. Hallelujah! I was back on track. Back into familiar path-finding territory. So I ate a banana to celebrate. But once my moment of mild euphoria had dissipated, I was still left with the decidedly worrisome matter of crossing the snow which, pink ribbons or not, I still didn't trust. Pondering, I sat on a rock, ate a riceball and took a few snapshots because, even if this ice-tongue was about to eat me alive, it did look rather splendid.

I was still hovering in a state of indecision when, popping up over the snowbank I had just skirted, appeared six strapping lads attached to six strapping rucksacks, with climbing helmets and ice-picks swinging off their backs. These boys meant business, of that there was no doubt.

They were, they told me when they curbed their stride for long enough to exchange a few words, at the beginning of a ten-day trekking expedition of the whole mountain-peaked peninsula, each trekker carrying with him fourteen days' supply of food. Clearly, they knew what they were doing. After they had assured me that the glacier-like obstacle was perfectly safe to walk on, I set off without further delay, trailing behind them confident in the knowledge that if the ice was strong enough to take six brawny men and their ten-ton loads, then it should be strong enough for a relative lightweight like me with a bag of bananas.

Once over the glacier, I was back to good old terra firma – rocks and carpets of heather, leading to an open plateau stretched between the two peaks of Mount Rausu and Mount Io. With the top of my chosen mountain now in sight, I steamed ahead with second wind until I hit the well-trodden and shorter trail that led up from Iwaobetsu Onsen. Gazing down from the plateau upon this alternative route, I was filled with a great sense of relief that I had chosen the way I had, as I watched an army of cowbelling ants, resembling walking raisins, crawling in line up the mountain.

I hit the summit at precisely 1.05 p.m. – nearly seven-and-a-half hours after setting out – and was rewarded for my efforts by a spectacularly sweeping view of the mountainous peninsula which, from where I perched, plunged down to the fishing town of Otoro and the Sea of Okhotsk on one side, and Rausu harbour and the Pacific on the other. Beyond Rausu lay the long, narrow, mountainous island of Kunashiri, which belonged to the group of islands off Hokkaido's north-east coast known as the Kurils. When the Russians joined the war against Japan for the few days between Hiroshima and VJ Day, they seized the opportunity to occupy the four small islands of Shikotan, Habomai, Etorofu and Kunashiri, all of which had been under Japanese control. The tiny population of Japanese fishermen was shipped to Hokkaido and, despite repeated protests that the islands and offshore shipping rights were Japanese, the Russians still ruled these roosts as I looked down upon them.

Although the Kurils didn't add up to more than 3000 square kilometres (no larger than the Balearic Islands off Spain), they controlled vital seaways into the Pacific Ocean. They were only a tiny portion of the many territories that Japan lost control of at the end of the Pacific War – territories that had been claimed as part of the pre-war Japanese empire and that included southern Sakhalin and the Ryuku Islands along with a number of other Pacific islands, Taiwan and Korea. But it was the Kurils that had remained such a major source of friction between Russia and Japan.

The one foreigner I met on the top of Mount Rausu was an Aussie called Lionel whose long wavy red locks were semi-retained within a tightly tied Agassi-style bandanna printed with unseasonable Santa Clauses. He wore cut-off jeans for shorts and a pair of dated Chelsea boots. He told me that he was studying at Sendai University (some sort of marine research to do with the chemical reactions of algae) and apparently he hated every minute of it.

'The only good thing about Japan,' he said, 'is escaping into the bush.'

I have to admit I hadn't realised that Japan had a bush. I could feel the 'surely not cows and potatoes in Japan' syndrome stirring within me again.

When Lionel discovered that I had plans to cycle round his Antipodean land in the not-too-distant future, he said, 'Bikin' in Oz is a great idea, mate, but just watch out for those real cranky and deadly poisonous tiger snakes – they can chase you at awesome rip-shit speeds.'

Thanking him for this nugget of travel advice, I left Lionel shaking a stone out of his Chelsea boot and embarked upon my descent. I had made it to the top but I still had a long way to go and, despite having packed my head-torch, I was anxious to make it back to base before dark.

Apart from stopping every so often to eat a handful of food, cram in a mouthful of squashed banana and swig several mouthfuls of water, I moved fast. The only people I saw on the descent were the agile family of four from Osaka – I caught up with them on the glacier. I was glad to meet them on this dicy stretch, because I had been a bit concerned about crossing it alone. But now, should I fall through a crevasse, it was reassuring to have someone around to watch me go (unless they fell in too).

When we reached the mighty snowbank, which had so nearly been my mismatch, I still chose to fight my way back down through the thicket of sharp, skin-tearing overgrowth that skirted the wall of pack ice, despite the father declaring, 'But Jodie-*san* – snow really fine safety surface!'

These proved to be fateful words. No sooner had he launched himself into his snow-ploughing descent than he lost his balance and plummeted out of control on to the rocks below. For a few horrific moments he lay crumpled and ominously still – time enough to make me feel certain he was nothing other than very dead. Then he suddenly sprang to his feet, shook off the snow and proclaimed, 'Ha ha! Very lucky man indeed!'

Once over the snow I was over the worst. With the prospect of supper spurring me forth, I left the Osaka family in my wake as I sped down the mountain, making it back to my tent just before sunset at 17.52 hours. The nineteen-kilometre clamber, which included my misguided navigational wanderings off the pink-ribboned route, had taken exactly eleven hours and twenty-two minutes.

My feet, though thankful for the boots, were in a sorry state of worn skin and blisters. But more troublesome than the state of my feet was the thought of what could have become of Hovar and Hiroko. They were nowhere to be seen. As I hadn't met them on the mountain, I presumed that they had chosen to abort the idea of a climb and had spent a day out somewhere else instead. At their domed base, all remained quiet.

After a supper of tinned tuna and rice, I limped across to Bear Hot Springs and had my back scrubbed by a pneumatic fisherman's wife before lowering myself into the fiery, skin-disintegrating waters to ease away the efforts of a very long day on the unaccustomed hoof. I was in mid-soak when Hiroko appeared, looking utterly exhausted. After washing herself on the stones, where my fisherman's wife was now massaging the back of an equally well-padded *obaasan* in energetic flesh-slapping style, Hiroko joined me in the steaming *onsen*.

She told me that she and Hovar had set out to climb Mount Rausu only fifty minutes or so after me but had become so lost that they never made it to the top. The snowbank had sent them way off track, following an alternative route through thick woodland until they had climbed above the tree line and reached what they thought was the top but which proved not to be.

'Anyway,' said Hiroko, 'today was fine adventure, but tomorrow I think I am preferring for reading book!'

I, too, spent the next day taking it easy – catching up on all my washing, mending, bike tinkering, toenail-cutting, diarying and letter-writing in preparation for continuing my rocky ride around Hokkaido. In between my tasks I spent my time chatting with Hovar and Hiroko, who were now my new neighbours, having uprooted their dome-of-a-home from the lower levels of the campground to be in the more scenic position up beside me.

For a few days we had this quiet and secluded upper eyrie to ourselves. On our final afternoon a group of bikers appeared and, with the choice of pitching their tents virtually anywhere else on the campsite, they had no qualms about plonking themselves right on top of Hovar and Hiroko, leaving little more than a foot between their surrounding tents.

For the rest of the day and all of the night, they sat around shouting and shrieking with ludicrous laughter as they threw back (and up) their canned beer. When they finally ran out of beer, they played nocturnal football with the empty cans and stumbled drunkenly over Hovar and Hiroko's tent. Although clearly upset by the boys' behaviour, the couple made no complaint to them about the obstreperous noise they were creating. They simply resigned themselves to the sort of behaviour that was only to be expected from a bunch of fashion-following youngsters away from home and it would just have to be tolerated, whether they liked it or not. I expressed my surprise that the boys could be so unashamedly brash for such a considerate and conformist society.

'This is typical Japanese youth vacation behaviour,' Hiroko told me. 'Away from work place and colleague and friend and family – away from conformity of their everyday life – these people act very much differently, very undisciplined. Really they don't have any care, they have and do as they are pleasing.'

Hovar remarked that this younger generation of Japanese might try to rebel against the system by claiming that they had no interest in or knowledge of Japanese tradition, history and culture, but they all tended to fall back into the Japanese way in the long run.

'This is true,' said Hiroko, 'and when Japanese take job in foreign country, they still do everything Japanese way. This only way they are knowing and for them this give very much security and better feeling of acceptable in foreign culture.'

The proverb 'A man far from home knows no shame' sprang to my mind, as did the unappealing spectacle of English lager louts.

The following morning I met Hovar and Hiroko down in Rausu to see them off on the bus back to Sapporo. When we bid farewell, Hiroko gave me a very public un-Japanese hug. Hovar gave me a very un-European bow (hello, I thought, what's going on here?) before he reached for my hand and, raising it to his lips, kissed the back of it as if we were in *Pride and Prejudice.* I was getting very confused.

Climbing into the bus, they both told me to make sure I came and stayed with them in their university digs when (and if) I made it to Sapporo. Then Hovar, knowing that my brother was about to marry a girl from Budapest, said, 'And remember to warn your brother that Hungarian wives make dangerous women!'

I smiled knowingly, though I had no idea what he was going on about. I just put it down to some sort of Eastern European thing.

The rain rained. Heavily. But I didn't mind. I had scaled my peak on a perfect day, so I was happy. Before heading south, I turned left at Rausu to cycle as far as I could up the eastern coast of Shiretoko before the road ran out.

The coast was a coast of seaweed and just about every octogenarian I passed was busily engaged, one way or another, in the process of preparing the weeds of the sea for sale. Tiny weather-battered *obaasan*, togged up in yellow oilskins, black gumboots and purple rubber gloves, dragged bucketloads of the stuff from waterlogged wooden boats; others fastidiously laid it out to 'dry' on scrupulously scrubbed beds of rock. More vegetables of the deep hung from eaves or covered any spare space of ground in front of the local houses. Lawns of seaweed. Land of seaweed. Sea of seaweed.

Carrying on up the coast road I came across Seseki *onsen*, a small open rockpool surrounded on three sides by the sea. I clumped down the steps to the beach, crunched my way over the stones to the open-air, public-view *onsen* and plunged a thermometer finger into its waters. It was octopus hot. It was also raining. And windy. And wavy. The prospect of submerging myself in a steaming rockpool on the beach in the rain, in the wind, with the waves, was too good to miss. As the pool was a free-for-all, I was on the point of trotting back to my bike to get my swimming costume before searching for a secluded nook in which to change when I thought that, as there was no one around, I would be daring and go in starkers.

Turning my face to the sea, I whipped off my clothes, rolled them inside my jacket to keep them dry, and then sank into the piping-hot waters of this wondrously wind-blown rocky sea-embraced *onsen*. The rain poured, the sea roared, my skin sizzled. My body melted. Ecstasy.

Time wallowed by. I kept trying to tell myself to get out before someone came along, but I couldn't bring myself to do it. To step back into the cold. To step back into the grey. To step back on my bike. To get back on the road. To ride and ride before being sucked back into a plane. I shouldn't linger so long, I thought; I've got to get to a wedding. But what was a wedding when I could sink slowly to heaven here?

The sound of heavy boots crunching over the stones of the beach brought me back to my senses. Turning to look over my shoulder, I saw a motorcyclist approaching. Uh oh, I thought – caught in my altogether. With no time for me to know what to do, or even to get too embarrassed, the leather-clad rider was upon me. I sank a little deeper.

'*Konnichiwa!*' he said.

'*Konnichiwa!*' I replied.

Then, without standing on ceremony, he peeled off his leathers, pulled off his underwear and lowered his tightly toned frame into the hot waters beside me.

'AAAcheeeEE! – HOT!' he sighed. Closing his eyes, he rested his head back on the rocks and stewed.

How nice, I thought. How nice to make no song and dance or suggestive quip about coming across a rare species of foreigner, dressed in what Isabella Bird called 'nature's costume', submerged in a water hole on the beach. And despite bobbing beside a totally naked and virile young man, I felt completely at ease. How nice. How rare. How odd.

Apart from '*konnichiwa*', we said nothing else to each other. We just enjoyed the time and the place for what it was, for what it was worth. Finally I dragged myself out, tugged on my clothes, walked back to my bike and cycled away.

Further up the road towards Aidomari, I passed old people as thin as nails living in corrugated shanty homes on the beach. The flat, flimsy roofs were prevented from blowing off in the wind by being weighted down with random planks and beams of driftwood and bundles of rocks wrapped in chicken wire. I was surprised by the poverty. The warm, rosy-red rays of the industrial sun of this rich rising land evidently had not reached these old people.

Before long, the road ran out. There was nowhere left to go except to turn round and ride back down the peninsula the way I had come. But first, I filled up my water bottles in a small, dark wooden restaurant whose house specialities were *todo yaki* (fried sealion) and *kuma ramen* (noodle and bear-meat soup) – definitely the sort of place to turn a Greenpeace person green.

Over the road, I sat on a coil of thick ropes on the quayside of a small, messy harbour reeking of putrid fish and snapped open a can of Pocari Sweat. It wasn't long before I found myself under attack from an angry pack of rapacious crows. Although I was by the sea, there were no seagulls – just crows. Had I been a few months earlier, I could have seen some much more desirable birds: the regal and mighty sea eagles which cruise these icy northern skies from January through to March. But for now, all I had to contend with were these berserk and vicious crows – which, incidentally, do not (as popular opinion has it) take the shortest route 'as the crow flies'. Instead, that's the rook. And it's the rook, not the crow, that is the target of the scarecrow. The question is: how do you tell crows from rooks? If you see a lone rook, it's a crow. If you see a flock of crows, they are rooks. Easy. Well, my parliament of rooks was several squadrons of crows, for sure. At least, I think they were.

As I rode back down the peninsula towards Rausu, a Yamaha Virago pulled alongside. Prised within the leathers was the biker with whom I had stewed in the seaside *onsen*. Without stopping or saying anything other than a luck-wishing '*Ganbatte!*', he passed me a can of Asahi beer and revved on his way.

Back in Rausu, I diverted course to visit the harbour. It was a stunning sight. The fishing fleet, back from nocturnal netting missions and now moored side by side in perfect formation, resembled more a force of frigates than a small town's flotilla of fishing vessels. They were all huge, all dazzlingly white, and all adorned with millions of yen-worth of advanced technology. The fishing grounds they patrolled were some of the richest in the world. When Japan had owned all the thirty or so Kurils (which formed a volcanic arc stretching 1200 kilometres from the Kamchatka peninsula of the Russian Far East to the Japanese archipelago), it had taken 40 per cent of the country's salmon catch from these waters. No wonder the Japanese were so anxious to get them back.

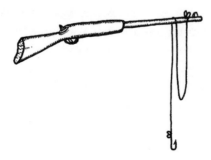

'GIVE US BACK THE OCCUPIED ISLANDS' was the non-messing message of the hoardings that sprouted at intervals from the verges on the road to Nemuro – a city and area famed for its large variety of crabs, including the king, the short-legged king and the hairy crab. Nemuro itself was on a clawed peninsula at the end of which lay Cape Noshappu, the easternmost point of Japan. From here I spotted Kaigara, one of the much squabbled-over islands of the Kuril chain, which sits only 3.7 kilometres off the coast. Looking through the Noshappu lighthouse telescope, it was possible to espy Russian soldiers at their monitoring posts.

Strangely, most Japanese up here didn't appear at all worked up about all the nearby territorial issues. Wandering through Nemuro, I was surprised by the profusion of signs in Russian, and at how easily the local residents rubbed shoulders with the influx of Russians – Russians who, as in Wakkanai, seemed to be dab dealers in second-hand cars.

It was bitterly cold at Cape Nosappu. It was also very noisy, thanks to a profusion of tannoys around the crab stalls and the tourist centre, blaring out an incessant supply of slushy, sugar-sick Japanese boy-loves-girl pop songs. A short distance away stood a spectacularly ugly eternal-flame memorial, its vast arch of dirty rust-coloured concrete ruining an otherwise pleasantly wild and scenic spot.

By the time I'd had a mosey around the cape, my fingertips were numb with cold. I rode back along the north coast of Nemuro's claw, past the odd fishing hamlet and occasional old wooden farm, one of which had a rusty sign swinging at the end of its lane announcing that within its land lay 'REGISTERED HOLSTEINS'. Holsteins? In Japan? I felt another Friesian fit of non-oriental potatoes and windmills coming on.

The skies may have been grey but the verges and pastures were crowded with a blazing array of wildflowers; one field was carpeted with purple irises. Elsewhere it was swampy land with a desolate scenery of decayed pinetrees. And there were lakes, their banks lined with herons, their surfaces with swans. Everywhere there were hungry mosquitoes, in search of blood. My blood.

These little beasties had also made a habit of spiking their nasty little probiscises into the tender nineteenth-century flesh of Isabella Bird. 'Freedom from fleas and mosquitoes one can never hope for,' she wrote. 'Last night the mosquitoes were awful. If the widow and her handsome girls had not fanned me perseveringly for an hour, I should not have been able to write a line.'

Unfortunately I had neither handsome girls nor boys to fan me. My nights within tent were passed in a continuous nagging, nerve-jangling quest to annihilate every single one of the whining, gore-swollen winged enemies that had jumped or flown across no-man's-land into my nylon dwelling. But again, I did not fare as badly as Isabella. It was not just mosquitoes and fleas: she also had to contend with rats that 'gnawed my boots and ran away with my cucumbers' and rat snakes that lived in the rafters and, when 'much gorged', occasionally tumbled down on top of her mosquito net. Then she was badly stung on one hand in a two-pronged attack by a hornet and a gadfly, combined with inflamed bites from 'horse ants'. Suffering too much pain and fever from all these stings, she consulted Dr Nosoki, an 'old-fashioned practitioner' who held out against European medical practices.

A strong prejudice against surgical operations, specially amputations, exists throughout Japan. With regard to the latter, people think that, as they came into the world complete, so they are bound to go out of it, and in many places a surgeon would hardly be able to buy at any price the privilege of cutting off an arm.

Dr Nosoki did not offer to cut off her insect-inflamed arm, but Isabella found among his cures a choice of ginseng, rhinoceros horn, powdered tiger liver and, most interesting of all, unicorn horn. The latter, in a lotion, was applied to her wounds, which improved to the degree that she felt 'bound to give him the credit of the cure'.

I spent a couple of nights on a hillside campsite outside Nemuro overlooking the cold, grey, mist-wreathed sea. It rained so hard that the campsite owner, an old man, invited me into his cabin to warm up and dry out. I asked to see the weather forecast on his television and discovered that the whole of Japan – apart from Hokkaido – lay broiling under sunshine. Tokyo was a sizzling 37°C – about thirty degrees hotter than here in Nemuro. Every bit of the big blob of an island on which I was shivering was covered by near-freezing temperatures and black rain clouds. Never mind sun: there wasn't even a glimmer of hope that the heavy rain might just consider petering out from time to time.

I longed to hear the baton-wielding, bespectacled Japanese weatherman adopt that uniquely British Met Office-speak and talk about 'showers interspersed with longer periods of rain'. At least then I would know that, although I was going to be constantly wet, I wouldn't get wet in quite such a continuously wet way. The old campsite man said he had never known a summer so wet or so cold. I said I could believe him.

The morning I left it was no better – in fact, it was even worse. The mist that had rolled in overnight was so thick that I could scarcely see my own feet, let alone the patch of road in front of my wheel. It was as bad as an English November and I found the words of that curmudgeonly wag, Thomas Hood, circulating round my brain:

> No shade, no shine, no butterflies, no bees;
> No fruits, no flowers, no leaves, no birds – November!

Was it winter? Was it summer? No, it was Hokkaido – a land with a season unto its own.

After stopping to warm up at a small roadside café called the Coffee Cottage, where the *mama-san* gave me a hot bowl of noodles on the cottage (which, being Japan, was nothing like a cottage), and after crossing a bridge over what a sign said was the Salmon Culture River, I turned off the busy Route 44 and followed a small network of country roads that proved so enjoyably quiet that they made up for all the cold and the wet and perpetual fog.

For a while I saw nothing but trees as I cycled for miles and miles through forests of conifers – could have been Sweden or Canada, or anywhere but Japan. Occasionally I passed a patch of rogue trees, all draped in a gossamer of beards just like in those forests of huge tortured limbs that soar into the American West Coast skies of Oregon and Washington.

I rode on. Saw no one. No houses, no cars, no animals, no people – no one. All human life seemed to have dissolved into the face of the earth. Needing a pee, I leant my bike against a roadsign and decided to save myself the bother of clambering up the long grassy bank and fighting through the dripping foliage just to conceal myself from no one. I simply set to on the roadside.

I was in mid-mission when a van came bouncing out of the mist, full of very surprised workmen. Great timing! Fast rush of blood to face. Tried to turn invisible, but sadly didn't work. Caught at half-mast. Very embarrassing. Very bad luck. Should have known better. Should have known that the moment you think you're safe, you've entered the danger zone. Should have known that someone, somewhere, always appears out of nowhere. Stop in the middle of the Gobi and you'll get caught. Stop in the middle of Mars and something with eyes will pop out of the planetary woodwork for sure.

Then, round the corner and over a creek, what should suddenly emerge from the mist but a very modern, very plush, very out-of-place block of public conveniences. Too late but, never being one to pass a toilet by (even though I had just been), I dismounted and paid it a visit.

Japanese toilets never fail to surprise, no matter how often you might stop to use them. For instance, by simply crossing the threshold of this one, I set off an automatic rendition of a jazzed-up Japanese version of 'Yesterday' that played to me, and me alone, throughout my short sojourn. The moment I stepped back outside, the oriental Beatle was cut off in his prime.

A car drew up, two men in the front and two women behind. The woman on my side rubbed a porthole in the steamed-up window, saw me and waved. I waved back. The driver stepped out of the car, stretched, sighed with an 'isssh-hheeer' noise through his teeth, and nodded in my direction. I nodded back. What happened next surprised me. Although he was a mere ten paces away from a 'Yesterday' serenading public toilet, the man instead chose to relieve himself a step away from his car. His companions seemed neither shocked nor embarrassed by his actions.

Then the man in the passenger seat stepped out and followed in the driver's stream of flow, so to speak. Both men were apparently oblivious not only to the toilet block but also to the *gaijin* who stood astride her mount, paralysed into a mild state of surprise.

Maybe they just thought that using the toilets was a waste of time when they could water the tarmac instead. Or maybe they'd had a previous experience

263

with these musical conveniences and wisely wanted to spare their ears from a jazzy rendition of 'Yesterday'. But then maybe I was just getting my knickers in an unnecessary twist in a country where urination fails to shock. When a certain politician – a hot candidate for becoming prime minister – was caught on camera having a whaz against a gingko tree in the gardens of the Diet, it did him no noticeable harm in the eyes of the public at all.

For the next couple of days I carried on along the coast, carving my way through a fog so thick that I might just as well have been cycling with two dirty wet wads of cotton wool pulled over my eyes. The rain fell steadily while a razor-sharp wind cut me to the core, throwing itself relentlessly into my frozen face. Summer in Hokkaido: what a hoot!

I was heading for Kushiro, a city that the tourist leaflet succinctly described thus:

The 'Big World/Get-in-Touch-with-Nature Resort Vision' encompasses international resorts and recreation, and the development of tourism incorporating dairy and fishing environments. Its aim, focused around the three national parks of Kushiro Marsh, Akan, and Shiretoko, is to create places where people can explore the wonders of nature, and recreate outdoors. Establishment of a Tourist Information Center, expansion of Kushiro Airport, and development of a road network are included. 'On a heading toward the world!' is a phrase that best captures the spirit of modern Kushiro. Yet classic gaslights shine here, too . . . warm, romantic, piercing the fog. Theirs is a nostalgic glow, a sign, a symbol, a welcoming embrace. Welcome, all, to Kushiro – this new, old city by the sea.'

As well as classic romantic gaslights, Kushiro was famed for its swampy area north of the city inhabited by numbers of endangered *tancho-zuru* (red-crested white cranes). But I saw neither bird nor 'new-old' city as, attempting an escape from the cold and unromantic 'piercing fog', I veered off course at Akkeshi and headed inland towards the mountains.

Actually I got a bit lost in Akkeshi. I was looking for a minor road that would lead me into the hills to the small town of Shibecha. Drawing up outside a supermarket, I asked a woman with a young son if she could point me to the right road. Obligingly, she launched into some elaborate directions to reach Route 44 where she indicated, sketching a little map, that I should turn right. After following this road for four kilometres, I was then to turn left on the Shibecha road.

Dutifully, I wiggled through the backstreets until I joined the truck-rushing Route 44 where, as instructed, I turned right. But turning right felt wrong so, after about a kilometre, I turned round and rode back past the junction where I had first joined Route 44 and went on a little further until I found what I was looking for – a side road heading north to Shibecha. The fact that the woman had given me wrong directions bothered me not in the least and I thought no more about it, getting on instead with enjoying a wonderfully quiet country road that led me out of the fog through lush rolling hills full of wildflowers and birdsong.

After I had been riding for an hour and a half towards the ever-closer allure of the distant mountains, a car overtook me and then stopped a little further up the road. A woman stepped out and gestured for me to stop. As I drew alongside, she looked very sheepish and embarked upon a perplexing series of apologetic bows. Then I recognised her as the woman who had given me navigational help in Akkeshi.

It turned out that, realising she had sent me in the wrong direction, she had spent the past two hours searching for me to offer her most sincere apologies and also give me a bag of groceries (containing a chunk of melon, a bunch of seedless black grapes, two grapefruit-sized apples, a jar of pickled cucumber, a container of sweet red beans, two cans of Georgia coffee and a *bento* of *sushi*) to make up for her 'so terrible mistake'. Her son also had an offering for me: an energy drink called 'WILSON energy assist PRO GEAR'.

By that stage, laden with armfuls of booty, I was even more embarrassed than they were. For the next few moments we stood in the road beneath stormy skies bowing and nodding insanely to each other in a state of confused awkwardness.

During this exchange, the only traffic to come along was a centenarian on a slow, back-firing scooter holding a long-handled hoe. He was so taken aback by the unexpected sight of this odd, semi-foreign nodding scene that, with his head corkscrewing in our direction, he swerved clean off the road and into a bush. Happily, neither he nor his hoe suffered any detrimental effects and, without further stir, we all went on our separate ways.

After a night of 'camping' in a bus shelter to take cover from a ferocious storm, I arrived the next day amid the splendours of Akan National Park – an area dominated by volcanoes, caldera lakes and vast swathes of virgin forests.

And tourists. And tour buses. And the distorted wailing and screeching of over-amplified loudspeakers that seemed to bother no one else but me. Were all these people, I wondered, simply suffering the noise in polite silence, or had years of being reared on such obnoxiously intrusive noise dulled their senses? Then I remembered what Hiroko had told me when I'd asked her how the Japanese managed to put up with the nationwide practice of broadcasting such brain-rattling rackets on public PA systems with loudspeakers strung along streets so that the noise ricocheted from city to town to village to mountain top. At first Hiroko hadn't understood what I meant.

'You know,' I said, 'all those loudspeakers attached to shops, to lamp-posts, to telephone poles, to cars, to trucks, to motorbikes, blaring out their announcements, their adverts, their messages, their sirens, their martial music, their on-the-hour ditties all over the towns and cities and countryside.'

Hiroko looked momentarily puzzled. 'Ahhh,' she said, understanding what I was on about, 'Japanese people do not consider this noise. Public announcement is very normal. We do not notice it.'

When I told her that I found the incessant and omnipresent wails outrageous and at times felt angered enough to sabotage the speakers and disconnect the wires, Hiroko looked at me in horror.

'But it is very terrible crime to make damage with system!' she said. 'Japanese people do not notice such many noise because . . . mmmm . . . we know there is nothing we can do. *Shikato ga nai* – it has to be.'

And so a land committed to world peace continued to make a peace-shattering din.

CHAPTER 13

Twinkle Plaza Twinning

I had just cycled up a sizeable mount to the asphalted 'scenic over-look' of Lake Mashu. Lots of tourists. Lots of buses. Lots of noise. Lots of *aisu-kuriimu* and souvenirs, too: improbably priced souvenirs like dead mink, fake stuffed seals, loads of geodes (some a mere snip at £3000) and graceless wood carvings of bears holding disproportionately huge ears of corn between their teeth. Outside, real live corncobs were boiling away in big bubbling caul-drons for an astonishing 350 yen per ear – £2.50 each. Daylight robbery!

I bought a cob – couldn't resist it. Couldn't resist the tantalising taste-bud bouncing allure of the fat, juicy golden kernels. Aware that I was eating away money, I chewed each mouthful at least fifty-seven times to savour the flavour and make the most of my yen. I didn't eat the whole ear – I only ate half, saving the rest to relish for supper. I know corncobs are best eaten fresh but it's not always possible to follow Mark Twain's advice to cook them over a fire you've just built in a field.

With kernels of gold lodged in my teeth, I left my bike against the car-park wall and walked away from the throngs of people and hubbub of noise until I stood on my own in relative peace, overlooking Lake Mashu, which the Ainu called 'Lake of the Devil'. This devilish pond was a big caldera lake and one of the deepest in Japan. With no water flowing either in or out, it was also a lake of great mystery. On sunny days you could look into it deeply (almost forty metres), as this Devil of a Lake ranked as one of the clearest on earth – or, as the tourist bumf put it, 'the second highest transparent depth in the world'.

267

So I looked deeply. With the sun being so shy of late, I found myself gazing down upon a grey and murky mist-swirling soup, ringed by rock walls 200 metres high. But I could see the tiny island of Kamuishu, floating in the mist in the middle of the lake. The island was the tip of a volcano that had formed inside the caldera.

For a few hours I wandered alone among the hills surrounding the lake. Although the mist had lopped the tops off the nearby mountains, it was still possible to see that the whole area was thickly covered in dense forest. The density of trees was actually not unusual for Japan which, contrary to my original beliefs, was a country covered not so much with crowds and cars and concrete and neon, but trees. Green, green trees.

Such a high proportion of natural forest and plantations might have suggested a huge logging industry but that was not the case, for a number of reasons. First of all, the trees themselves (from subarctic conifers in Hokkaido to deciduous and evergreen temperate broad-leafed species throughout the other three main islands) looked healthy enough and often smothered the landscape, but apparently they were too small by logging-industry standards (though they looked pretty big to me).

Then there was the land itself. Typically the trees grew on steep slopes, making it incredibly difficult to haul out the timber once it had been felled. Although there was a soaring demand for timber for the construction and paper-making industries, domestic production had actually been falling in recent years and the future of local timberyards was under serious threat.

Yet in Abashiri on the Okhotsk coast I had been amazed by the mountains of logs and seas of logs passing through the port. I had presumed, having seen so many forests throughout Japan, that the logs must be Japanese ones for exportation. It turned out that the opposite was true: Abashiri was a 'designated' port for the importation of timber. The volume of cargo handled annually was more than a million tons and was set to increase.

It seemed that Japan liked its forests sitting prettily on the mountains and preferred to buy in the forests of other lands – where the cutting down was a lot cheaper and the quality much better than in Japan. American pines were deemed the bee's knees for building timber (imported in vast quantities by big, fat-cat building companies) and western hemlock was good for posts. From the southern half of the American continent, Japan was importing large amounts of native hardwoods from Chile for making high-grade paper and vast amounts of other rainforest trees from Brazil in particular.

Japan's local timber businesses claimed that importations could be slashed if only the country's own forests were properly managed. Japan, they said, should be capable of being self-sufficient in timber. But nobody was listening; nobody seemed to be able to see the trees for the wood.

Leaving lofty Lake Mashu to the mountain devils, I plummeted down a ten-kilometre descent during which I clocked up my all-time top speed: a hilariously hair-raising 54 mph (87 kph) on a long, steep, straight stretch that just sort of fell away. With adrenalin pumping and wheel rims smoking, I screeched to a halt at the bottom of the sulphur-stinking mountain of Io-San.

Standing at a mere 510 metres, Mount Io makes up for its lack of size with its pure volcanic force. Gingerly stepping among the profusion of loudly hissing vents and holding my breath through the denser clouds of billowing rotten-egg steam, I felt as if I was wandering over a gigantic pressure cooker about to blow its top.

Where the air was ripe with the eggy whiff of sulphur, the ground was thick with *chiizu* peace-snapping tourists and with little clusters of *obaasan* doing a keen trade in selling small bags of hard-boiled eggs that they had cooked in the steam. One *obaasan* tried to tempt me into parting with 400 yen for a pack of five, but when I told her I couldn't eat that many as I was on my own, she gave me two for free. What with my half-mauled corn on the cob, supper was looking good.

It was also looking a whole lot cheaper than some of the inedible offerings for sale over in the tourist centre, like carved totem-pole bears which were going for 3.6 million yen – a multi-mind-boggling £24,000! I thought about loitering around to see whether there really was anyone with a fat cheque book and a slim brain prepared to part with enough money to buy at least twenty top-of-the-range custom-built bicycles (or 10,285 Hokkaido-reared boiled ears of golden corn) for the sake of walking away with an astronomically expensive wooden dust-collector. But the rumble of distant thunder put me out of my musings and swiftly back in the saddle again, as I had the more important pursuit of finding a place to camp.

Riding through the small spa town of Kawayu proved to be a hot and steamy experience. The town sat on top of a whole series of hot springs, and steady streams of steam spurted from the street's manhole covers – it felt like riding over the blocked spouts of a thousand buried boiling giant kettles.

Through the plumes of swirling steam I could just make out the gaudy souvenir and trinket shops lining the street, outside some of which sat bearded old Ainu busily carving miniature totem poles and bears with mouthfuls of fish.

Down the road I came upon a large and tawdry dinosaur. This was 'Kusshi', Japan's plastic-moulded equivalent of the Loch Ness Monster. More monsters? They were obviously reproducing fast – I'd already sighted one in the 'WELCOME ROMANTIC SEASIDE TOWN' of Obira.

The presence of Nessie's relation signalled my arrival at Kussharo Beach, a tacky, touristy and tarmacked area on the shores of Kussharo Lake, which, judging from the rash of tents, was evidently a camping hot-spot.

As dusk was already upon me, I decided to join the fray and wheeled my bike around a scrum of big family tents, all rubbing guylined shoulders with each other. I pushed my bike past a number of tent-proud housewives – one was fastidiously sweeping the tight unpeopled spot of ground directly outside her front door, another armed with dustpan and brush was clearly intent on removing every single sandy grain of grit from her marquee-sized, insect-netted eating area. Another woman was in the process of single-handedly erecting a tent around her snoozing husband as he lay snoring away on a mat inside.

Having a small compact tent, I was able to find a relatively secluded space at the far end of the campground among a tight tangle of trees on the banks of the lake. My nearest and only neighbours were a family consisting of several generations, all sleeping together on a huge inflatable mat that filled the entire floor-space of their tent.

Being a volcanic area, hot springs sprang up all along the shores of the lake. My neighbours had built their own en suite *onsen* by digging a deep hole on the 'beach'. Over this hole they had built a wooden box. Then they had lined this box-bath with plastic sheeting in which they rigged up an ingenious device that enabled the whole thing to fill with piping-hot thermally heated water.

The box-bath family turned out to be generous as well as ingenious. After treating me to a feast of barbecued fresh fish, they invited me to have free use of their beach-based *onsen*. Later that evening, I sank into the hot spring of the box-bath and wallowed happily as I watched sporadic forks of lightning splintering the purple-black skies over far-away mountains.

A short distance down the road from Japan's Loch Nessie, I stopped to have a look round a small Ainu museum. Outside the museum stood a row of

slightly ramshackle souvenir shops. As I pushed my bike past, a mad-eyed woman beckoned me into her shop for a cup of tea. She plonked me down on a chair that was draped with a grubby fur rug and then she erupted into a burst of witch-like cackles. Her face, half hidden by a black mane of long, tangled hair, looked not at one with the world. Enrobed in a creased and faded kaftan-like gown, and with a beaded bandanna wound tightly round her head, she was like some sort of far-out, Far-East hippy. When she spoke, I understood nothing. It was not a Japanese I recognised. Was it Ainu? I didn't know.

Her small, dingy shop was a chaotic scene of dusty souvenirs. A dog-eared mutt slept in a heap beneath a dark shelf. A motorbike was parked near the counter which, judging from its flat tyres and thick coat of dust, had not gone very far very fast for a long time. An old T-shirt of Bob Marley was pinned, crucified, to the wall alongside a curly-edged poster of the Rolling Stones. A youthful Mick Jagger pouting his rubber lips over a shelf full of Ainu-carved trinkets – odd combination.

Outside in the sun (*hai*! *hai*! – the sun! – hello, oh distant memory!), three sightseeing girls from Honshu stood fancy-dressing themselves in traditional Ainu clothing, complete with the not so traditionally velcro-fixed beards that the gift shop offered for hire. Once enrobed in this colourful and brightly embroidered garb, the girls burst into giggles and peace-posed for their holiday snaps.

Oh dear, I thought, what a sorry state of affairs! Where were the real Ainu, the real people of this land – the people the Japanese considered to be a strange, hairy and unsophisticated race who were best trodden out of society, apart from the odd handful who could be plonked in museums or 'reserves' for the tourist to ogle and giggle at and, in effect, to deprive of both their culture and their dignity?

In the purlieus of Mashu Spa, I stopped at a crab-selling tourist park to use the toilets. The curtains in the spick-and-span washroom section bore the fabric-printed missive:

> LET'S SKIP ABOUT
> Hurry up and go to the woods,
> and run around together.

Bewildered, I read these words again. And again. And again . . . until my mind fuzzed over in an advanced state of perplexity. Where, I wondered, was this country coming from? Where was it going? Maybe it was best not to give such matters too much thought. Maybe it was better to let the whole of jolly Japan skip about in the woods together, because surely, if more people and more nations were simply left to skip around the trees together, the world would be a skippier and happier place.

After picking up a convenient bag of convenient edibles in a convenient store that answered to the conveniently succinct, albeit curious, name of 'We Me', I cycled off in a skippy frame of mind to consume my purchases (packed-rice triangles, *tempura*, peanuts, bananas and *oolong-cha*) beside the swiftly sweeping Kushiro River that bisected the small town of Teshikaga.

As I was sitting on a bench in the sun (yes, the sun still shone, but I was holding my breath) while gazing at the river with a mouthful of rice, a canoe suddenly swept by with a paddling person. This canoe was swiftly followed by another and another and another, until it amounted to a whole shoal of canoeists who, judging from their expressions, were just as surprised to see me as I was to see them.

My surprise sprang not so much from the sight of the canoes on the water (I'd have been a lot more surprised to see a train or a plane or a Great Dane floating past) as from the positions the canoeists adopted to sit in their craft.

They didn't sit – they knelt, on knee pads, and paddled. Perhaps I shouldn't have been surprised: after all, I was in Japan, a nation of kneelers rather than sitters.

Next stop: Lake Akan, and the Ainu-degrading, souvenir-selling, waterside tourist-trap town of Akankohan Spa. This garish and overtly demeaning place (which claims to be part of a 'traditional Ainu village') came as a bitter disappointment after riding through the mountains along the spectacular forty-two kilometres of Akan Transverse, where my spirits had soared along with the terrain.

Rolling down Akankohan's main street, I passed a lacklustre fox chained to the pavement outside the door of a speaker-blaring souvenir shop that sold (along with a menagerie of carved bears and totem poles) stuffed foxes and mink pelts. Every shop was the same: tacky Ainu-belittling junk.

I wandered down to the lakeside, from where a flotilla of tourist-laden excursion vessels left to ply the silky blue waters of the lake. Most of them were off to view the *marimo*, or 'God's Fairies' – the strange round clumps of green algae that took 200 years to grow to the size of a tennis ball and which had the capacity to pop up to the surface or sink to the bottom of the lake, depending on the weather.

The town's public-address system announced the fact that it was noon-on-the-nose by launching into a screechingly distorted and mountain-reverberating rendition of 'Edelweiss'. Edelweiss? Pur-lease, I thought. As I blocked my ears, feeling as far away from understanding even an infinitesimal fragment of Japan as ever, I looked at the *chiizu* faces around me gaily posing for album-sticking snaps, all apparently and inexplicably oblivious to the out-of-place and out-of-time Edelweiss-clashing clamour that ricocheted around us. If you don't like it, I thought, leave. So I did. And a good thing too. Time was marching on, with many a mountain and miles left to go.

Another good road, the Ashoro-Kokudo, led me out of Akan territory, past the impressive might of volcanic Mount Me-Akan (Mr Akan – I had earlier skirted its spouse, O-Akan, or Mrs Akan) and down along a joyfully undulating valley floored in a sunny array of corn and potato and wheat fields dotted with farm buildings. Every so often I passed roadside stalls selling boiled corn for 200 yen (£1.30 – cheap!) and melons that were a snip at a mere £30 for two. At one point an army jeep pulled over on to the verge in front of me and a young lad in cargo pants jumped out to give me a can of Aquarius sugar-pop fizz. He told me he was on a two-year jaunt, jeeping it around Japan. A fellow vagrant – a Japanese one at that. A rare species, for sure.

The kilometres clicked by. In the small town of Ashoro I rode down the main street as a Japanese version of 'Eleanor Rigby' wailed out over the PA system. In Kamishihoro a fat little man approached me as I stood drinking a can of Pocari Sweat outside 7-Eleven and said, 'I show you biggest lunch in Japan.'

'Pardon?'

'I show you biggest lunch in Japan.'

'Biggest lunch?'

'Yes, biggest lunch.'

'Thank you,' I said, 'but I've already had lunch.' Although I could have eaten another one, something told me I didn't want to eat it with this man.

'Excuse me?'

'I've already eaten, thank you.'

'Mmmm . . . yes . . . excuse me?'

Uh-oh – communication breakdown. Both parties faltering and flailing, grappling at the strings. If in doubt, I thought, don't bail out, just try a fresh approach.

'Can you speak in Japanese, please,' I said.

'Speaking Japanese?'

'Yes, Japanese.'

'You are having understanding in Japanese?'

'A little.'

'Ahh so, *desu-ka?*' said the man, in utter amazement.

A long pause accompanied his look of bewilderment before he said something very fast in Japanese.

'Slower, please,' I said.

'Excuse me?'

'Please speak more slowly. My Japanese is not that good.'

The man repeated the sentence just as fast.

'Slower, please,' I said again, but it had no effect. A rapid barrage of words was fired my way. I asked him to repeat it again, and again, and then, except for one word, I began to get the gist. The stumbling word was *bokujo*.

'*Chotto matte kudasai,*' I said, and obligingly he waited a moment as I rummaged in my handlebar bag for my dictionary.

Looking up *bokujo*, I found it meant 'ranch'. Not before time, I realised I had tripped up again on that old pronunciation chestnut of Japanese confusion between the letters R and L. All the man had offered was to show me Japan's biggest ranch but I, making a meal out of a mountain, had mistaken it for lunch.

Anyway, the upshot of this long shot was that I declined the man's ranch-viewing invitation as I wanted to reach Nukabirako Lake before nightfall. So I carried on, cycling north out of Kamishihoro past a curious balloon-shaped billboard telling me that 'ALL ROADS LEAD TO ROMAN'.

After an hour or so of riding in hard rain (again), I found a rolled-up camping mat lying on the roadside which I surmised might have flown off the back of a camper's motorbike. However it may have got there, it looked worthy of investigation, so I dismounted. Shaking it open, I discovered it was a double mat with an insulating layer of bodyheat-reflecting foil on one side. Very useful, thought my scavenger's mind. All it required was a quick wash-off. Despite the fact that I already had my faithful been-through-thick-and-thin ten-year-old yellow Karrimat on board, I wasn't going to pass by the opportunity of gaining another mattress to filter out the rocks and so I lassoed it to my mountain of ever-growing bags on the back rack.

A little further along, after topping up my water supplies at a strange wood cabin called 'TEEPEE COFFEE AND LUNCH', I was in the midst of lumbering up a quiet mountain road when I came across another camping mat lodged halfway down a bank. This time it was a long roll of insulated blue foam. Hello, I thought, what's going on round here? Was comfy sleep no longer a necessity for camping? Was there maybe some sort of campers' ritual that, on passing this way, required appeasement of the possible stormy wrath of the mountain gods by offering them a peaceful night's rest upon one's mat? Or was there someone who was simply not very good at securing mats to the back of their pack?

Whatever the reason, I felt it incumbent upon me not to say no to a gratis piece of roadside booty (a comfy one at that). Telling myself I was doing my bit for clearing up the landscape by divesting it of unsightly highway detritus, I dutifully strapped the mat to the rear of my buckling and bucking mount.

With well-worn panniers already bursting at the seams with what I like to term 'essential equipment' but which in truth is probably no more than a lot of excess fodder, and what with the overflow spilling over into a medley of carrier bags tethered to the pannier's webbing along with a motley assortment of laundry trying to dry, I felt more than ever like a roving vagabond – or perhaps a migrant salesman who could offer a very nice line in sleeping mats. 'Yes, madam, is it a double-insulated or a single-cell model you're after?' 'Well, to you, sir, I could do the three-quarter-length Silverback for a very reasonable 10,000 yen.'

When, I wondered, would I learn to say no to roadside rubbish along with all the other litter and clutter that seemed to infiltrate my panniers by a phenomenal form of osmosis, and travel around with a sensible weight instead? Indeed, when would I finally latch on to the philosophy of Freya Stark, who advised: 'Most of your luggage is a hindrance . . . discard all this, and sally forth with a leisurely and blank mind.'

At least I could take pride in having got the bit about sallying forth with a 'leisurely and blank mind' down to a fine art. It's not that I don't start my leisurely and blank-minded trips with high hopes for feather-weight travel. I spend hours, days, even weeks before I set out on a long-range cycling jaunt reading up on the pros and cons of the latest top-notch high-fangled travelling equipment, and schlepping around outdoor stores picking up and feeling all manner of weird and eclectic textiles, before returning home simply to weigh the world-weary things that I've been using for years, but just cutting a bit more off them each time.

If I was a backpacker, then my views on weight would indubitably be very different, making me a prize minimalist. But I'm not a backpacker – I'm a bikepacker. And that's the joy of bicycles: they do all the hard work for you. They make it possible to lug around all manner of unnecessary and hefty paraphernalia on board and yet you scarcely notice the difference in weight. Got any room for a couple of maps, three paperbacks, five spare tent pegs and ten packs of porridge? Why, certainly, just stuff it down the sides or strap it on top. How about an *obaasan*'s offering of a watermelon and two giant cabbages? Please, be my guest, there's plenty of room on my rear. Squeeze on half a ton of roadside flotsam and jetsam, including this here kitchen sink? But of course – the pleasure would be mine!

Bicycles are like pack-horses, only better, as they don't produce flatulence or hoof you in the hips or steal your oats. What's more, they are your freewheeling, flexible friend capable of sallying forth into territory where any four-legged beast would fear to tread. And when your own legs are feeling weary and wobbly of knee, you can simply dissect your trusty steed and transport it by cramming it in the back of a passing friendly boot. Try doing that with a horse and you'd have nothing but dead meat on your hands.

Tunnels. Lots of tunnels. Didn't look good. Looked very bleak. Very black. But what was this – an alternative to being buried alive beneath the tunnelling wheels of a truck? A saving-grace cycle path sent from heaven led me over a dam and round a lake until I fetched up in the strange one-street town of Nukabira, which resembled an odd mix between some deserted Wild West cowboy haunt and a concrete bunker.

For a town sitting just within the boundaries of Daisetsuzan National Park (the largest in Japan), the place was weirdly quiet. The only people I saw were a man in the post-office who said that it was going to rain tomorrow, an old woman in a grocery store who said it was going to be sunny, and a boy on a motorbike from Kyoto who said it was going to be a mixture of sun and cloud.

In the event, it poured without pause. On and on, strong, hard, stinging rain. Not great weather for cycling over mountain passes but if I waited for the sun I'd be waiting till the crows came home. So over I went. Couldn't see a thing. I rode through a world of all-enveloping mist and wintery wind. In fact, it was so cold that I was forced to fashion a fetching hat from a towel. Socks sufficed as mittens.

Rain turned to hail. It was head-hurtingly hard. It was head-hurtlingly cold. Summer in Hokkaido? What a bunch of roses!

Known as the Roof of Hokkaido, thanks to its 2000-metre high range of mountains, Daisetsuzan National Park was renowned for its impressive landscape of volcanic peaks, steep highlands, precipitous gorges and multi-coloured swathes of wildflowers. One of the park's many highlights was supposed to be Sounkyo Gorge ('Gorge Reaching to the Clouds'), a twenty-four-kilometre ice-sculptured marvel of chiselled perpendicular cliffs 150 metres high on massive columnar joints, punctuated with feathery threads of spectacular waterfalls with fancy celestial (and chocolatey) names like Shooting Star, Milky Way and Galaxy.

Owing to weather conditions beyond all control and belief, the waterfalls might just as well have been called Stormy Star, Foggy Way and Gloopy Soup for all I could see on the evening that I arrived beneath the cloud-engulfed cliffs. Ever hopeful that the weather would improve (though heaven knows where such hopes came from), I camped in a nearby wood, where a very drunk man asked me to marry him.

'Not now, thanks,' I answered, 'I've got to wash my socks.'

The next morning I was rewarded with 1.75 minutes to view the gorge before it started raining again.

I raced onward, downward, through a valley of terraced rice fields (known as *dandanbatake* – 'step-step fields') until I entered the stupendously unpleasant urban sprawl of Asahikawa, Hokkaido's second largest city, through which flows the fine Ishikari River. When I beached in a violent storm at the railway station to pick up a map of the city from the tourist office situated inside 'Twinkle Plaza', I noticed that I was in Asahigawa station, as opposed to Asahikawa. I later discovered that this was not so much a spelling mistake or mispronunciation as a trifling example of the way that the Yamato Japanese like to think they have the upper hand over the native Ainu.

In the Ainu language, the original translation of Asahigawa meant 'River Where The Waves Are Raging' which, when spoken in Ainu, sounds almost identical to 'River Where The Sun Rises'. The encroaching Japanese, having a hot-spot for their emblematic Rising Sun, opted to name the city Asahikawa but the Ainu, determined not to lose track of the original meaning, managed to keep their Waves-Are-Raging name alive by making sure that Asahikawa's station remained as Asahigawa on the map. Or something like that. Simple, really.

While wading through the wodge of tourist leaflets I'd picked up at the Raging River station, I was amazed to discover that the city of Asahikawa was twinned with Normal, Illinois. Now, I could bet my bottom dollar that most tourists who read this city-twinning fact would have found it of no interest whatsoever, but to me – why, it was a stunning revelation: it just so happens that I have five generations of dead relatives lying in a cemetery in Normal. And how many tourists to Asahikawa-gawa could claim *that?*

Not only had I heard of Normal – I was also familiar with the place because, when cycling across America exactly three years before, I had spent a couple of weeks there with my mother, who had flown out to show me where she had grown up during the war as well as to sort out death duties and suchlike following my grandmother's death. My mum's old sepia-tinted photographs of Normal showed a quaint American Midwest small town full of charming clapboard houses, complete with rocking-chairs on verandas and swinging mesh-covered porch doors. One picture, which I had on my wall at home, showed Hammett M. Senseney, my great-great-grandfather, standing in his braces at the counter of his coal dealer's office at 304 North Main Street on 12th August 1913. Seventy-nine years later the once tidy wood-boarded shop, with its sun awning and Stars and Stripes flapping illustriously outside the window, stood boarded up and derelict, graffiti slashed across its front.

Modern-day Normal, known for little more than being home to the nation's first Steak 'n' Shake restaurant, was sprawled out over rich Illinois farmland around the old Route 66 and was distinguishable only by its featurelesssness. It did, though, have a tidily pressed Ku Klux Klan robe hanging in a glass case in the Old Courthouse Museum in Bloomington (its slap-bang neighbouring city, with which it blends into one) – a reminder that the South didn't have a monopoly on racial hatred.

Oh, and more recently Normal had been able to boast the dubious claim of becoming the centre of what turned out to be the largest sexual harassment suit in American history. Many of the 700 women out of the workforce of 4000 at Mitsubishi Motor Manufacturing of America, whose auto plant lay on the edge of Normal, claimed to have been systematically tormented by male co-workers. As part of their campaign, they paraded with placards that read:

REAL MEN
DON'T PINCH
THEIR CO-WORKERS!

Apart from a possible Mitsubishi link, the only reason I could suggest why Asahikawa and Normal had been lumped together as twins was because of their unimaginably humdrum shopping malls. Asahikawa's central mall, which stretched north from the confusingly named station, was even heralded by

JNTO (Japan's National Tourist Organisation) as being the country's 'first vehicle-free promenade'. Well, I suppose that the old adage 'if you've got it, flaunt it' can apply to the most mundane of things.

I spent a stormy night in Asahikawa, camping with a homeless man who was well sozzled on *sake* in a park beside the city's River Where The Waves Are Raging. And they were, too – it was that windy and that wet. Before going to sleep, I heard a bit on the radio about the history of the portable transistor.

In 1953 Dr Ibuka, head of a small Japanese electronics company, visited America to observe work being done on transistor radios at Texas Instruments, who were manufacturing transistors under licence from Bell Laboratories. Within a couple of years Dr Ibuka's firm, renamed Sony Corporation, had made its first transistor radios. By 1958 the company had made the first shipment of its new product to the US. Although the Americans had invented the transistor radio, it was Japanese physicists and engineers who did pioneering work in miniaturising the parts and introducing an age of mass-produced electronic goods.

Sony mounted an effective advertising campaign in America for a portable radio that would fit into a shirt pocket. In fact, the radio turned out to be slightly too big for the average shirt pocket, and so, with typical Japanese cunning, Sony enlarged their salesmen's pockets so that the radio would fit.

At five o'clock the following morning, I was woken from my slumber by a series of shockingly loud grunts and moans and sighs coming from close by. Poking my head out of my tent, I was surprised to set eyes upon a mountainous mass of colliding flesh. Four sumo wrestlers, all naked except for a scanty knot of thong, were practising their peculiar body-grappling art. In particular, they were working at their *shiko* – the fine spectacle of the wrestlers raising their tree-trunk legs high before stamping them down on the ring to crush any evil spirits that might be lurking underfoot.

With a stormy tailwind, I swept swiftly southwards. At the foot of the Tokachi mountain range the fertile plain of the Furano Basin was a riot of blooming lavender, with vast expanses of purple hillsides. Elsewhere grew potatoes, beans, beets, asparagus and the strange sight of vines (Furano wine was a local speciality).

Furano, Japan's most famous ski resort, was lyrically described in typical Japanese tourist-leaflet style as:

> The city, you feel the
> various four season,
> Overflow with poetical
> sentiment and roman.

When I arrived in Sapporo – Hokkaido's cultural, economic, administrative and political centre – the tourist-leaflet writers were in even more fantastical form, describing summer in this big, busy, neon-blipping city as an environment where:

Forest leaves express their ripening by the darkness of green. Sweet scents of clover and day-lilies beckon from the field, where the grass has already grown high enough to conceal children at play. Even behind the clouds, the sun draws nature to its fullest tide of fecundity, delighting the eye with multiplying beauty. We wonder, will the glorious sunshine of midsummer fully satisfy our longing? Like sunflowers, we turn to the sun to store jealously its blessing of light.

Even the most alert weather man cannot predict how many midsummer days we will be able to enjoy this year, but that does not matter. Resort places are already full of people. Around August 20th, the air whispers the end of summer. In roadside heges ripening fruits of wild roses grow, a poignant reminder of the fleeting season.

What on earth were they on about? What sun? What glorious sunshine? What midsummer days to enjoy? End of a fleeting summer – before it had even begun?

Sapporo, which ranked fifth in size behind Tokyo, Yokohama, Osaka and Nagoya, was closer to Vladivostok than it was to Tokyo. That said, it actually felt a lot closer to America, in the way that its straight, wide streets criss-crossed the city like a checkerboard. This was because Sapporo's history officially dated from 1867, when the name of the island had been changed from Ezo to Hokkaido and the Kaitakushi (or Colonisation Commission) had been established here, involving US advisers in helping to design the city on the Chinese/American grid system. Prior to that, the population of what would become Sapporo had stood at around ten people (today it was 1.7 million) in two families – one in a tiny Ainu village on one side of the Toyohira River and the other in a tiny village on the opposite bank.

The name 'Sapporo' was derived from a combination of Ainu words meaning 'long, dry river' – a blatant misnomer, as the Toyohira River was in fact a very long wet one. The weird and mysterious logic of the indigenous Ainu vocabulary was far beyond the comprehension of a take-it-as-you-see-it bicycling *gaijin*.

Owing to the Western influence on the design of the city, Sapporo had some interesting buildings constructed from materials other than concrete – such as the grand red-brick neo-baroque Old Hokkaido Government Building and the 110-year-old wooden clock tower whose chimes (evocative of a Far Western world) still marked the hour. It was also astoundingly leafy and blessed with an abundance of magnificent parks, compared with the virtually green-free cities I'd seen throughout the rest of Japan.

While Sapporo was constantly adding to the 160,000 trees that currently lined its streets, it seemed that, if the dream of a certain Mr Ishimizu came true, there would soon be another olde-worlde non-concrete slab of a building to be found sitting pretty in the midst of the city. I had first read about the plans of Mr Ishimizu, the millionaire president of the Ishiya chocolate company (which made the premium 'Snow-Lover' brand), in Christy Campbell's article in the *Sunday Telegraph*, the remains of which I had picked up off a seat on the 16.24 train from Waterloo to Portsmouth.

Isao Ishimizu, a fifty-one-year-old former boxing champion, planned to re-create 'the heart of medieval Chester' in the middle of Sapporo, where he was building an enormous leisure complex and museum dedicated to the history of chocolate. He had succeeded in buying the demolished remains of a magnificent Merseyside mansion – the neo-Palladian Underlea House (originally built in 1859 and lying in forlorn chunks in a farmyard for the past twenty years) – and was planning to ship it, stone by stone (250 tons in all), in thirty containers to Japan to be rebuilt by English stonemasons as a VIP guesthouse.

The museum would have the added attraction of a huge indoor curling rink ('Scottish things, like golf, are very popular in Hokkaido'), built in half-timbered Tudor style to imitate the old buildings of Chester and looking like 'a cross between Liberty's, the galleon-like London department store, and the fashionable end of Ladbroke Grove' – which didn't seem very Scottish but in Hokkaido they thought it did.

When Mr Ishimizu had visited Chester, he thought it was 'fantastic'. He said that there were ancient towns in Japan but that Sapporo was a new industrial city and 'we are very open to different styles'. He was more than happy to spend a possible £100 million on his dream. As he said:

> Most people in Japan think I am pretty strange. But I have to achieve something unique for myself, for my city and for chocolate. You know chocolate was introduced to Japan by the English a century ago? It is appropriate we have made our museum using British things.

Ahh so, *desu-ka?*

In Sapporo, I stayed in Hovar's dingy ground-floor university apartment, where there was just room for a bed but little else. It was so minute that, unless very intimate, it was impossible for two people to be in the cell-like bedsit at the same time. Ignoring my protestations that I would be fine camping in the city park, Hovar gallantly gave me full use of his room while he moved out to stay with Hiroko.

Having returned to the hectic, hurly-burly life of studying (happily an unknown experience for me), both Hovar and Hiroko were so busy that we saw very little of each other. However, from those few brief moments that they managed to snatch together with me when I would meet them at the station for something to eat in the nearby and inexpensive White Cozy, snippets of conversation stood out.

Hiroko told me that the fact that many schoolchildren fell asleep during their classes was seen as quite acceptable by their teachers, who felt that if a pupil did not want to learn (or was too tired to learn after being force-fed with interminable tedious facts) then that was their look-out.

'Sleeping in school lesson is the Japanese way,' said Hiroko.

Another time, Hiroko asked me how I managed to find a *minshuku* not only in cities but also in out-of-the-way towns and villages.

'Well, I either recognise the *kanji* for *minshuku*,' I said, 'or I just ask someone for directions.'

'You ask?' exclaimed Hiroko, genuinely amazed. 'And Japanese people are giving you helpful?'

'Yes,' I said, 'everyone's always very helpful. Some even go to considerable trouble by drawing me elaborate maps while others go out of their way to lead me to the door.'

Hiroko looked flabbergasted, so I asked her what was wrong.

'But it is not Japanese way to ask or give direction.'

'Not the Japanese way?' I said. 'But if you're lost or looking for a hotel or *minshuku*, how do you go about finding it?'

'We go to Japanese Travel Information Centre for asking with helpful.'

'Yes, but they're only in cities,' I said, 'and anyway, what do you do if they're closed, or for that matter, what do you do if you're lost and can't even find the TIC offices?'

'Excuse me?'

'If you're already lost before you've even found the Tourist Information Centre where you want to get directions, then how do you go about finding it when you can't go about asking someone for directions to help you find it?' I asked, rather wishing I hadn't, as I was obviously beginning to get a bit lost myself.

'Mmmm . . .' said Hiroko.

So we left it at that. Hovar told me that he had learnt early on in his stay in Japan not to ask the Japanese for directions because they either ignored him or became angry.

'I believe there is a big difference between the way Japanese people react to foreign boys and foreign girls,' he said.

And I thought: how odd.

Apart from its size, the most interesting thing about Hovar's tiny bedsit was the small selection of books that he had stacked on a shelf, the subjects of which bore testimony to the saying that you can tell a person through their books. To be honest, I don't know if there is such an adage, but there should be one, as it's plainly true. Hovar's reading material included:

> *Complete Sonnets*
> *The World's Wisdom*
> *Armenian Wisdom*

The Mathematical Universe
Computers, Patterns, Chaos, and Beauty
Strange Attractions – Creating Patterns in Chaos
IKEBANA – Japanese Flower Arrangement

Hovar was made of heady stuff – certainly a soul with whom it would be worth spending a good deal of time in the hope that a nugget of his complex and extensive knowledge might infiltrate into one's own creaking cranial matter. Unfortunately I couldn't linger for long enough to test this theory as, with a wedding to get to, time was not on my side.

Riding out of Sapporo along a cycle path that followed the Toyohira River southward, I met an Aussie called Laith who wheeled broadside on a bit of a bashed-up bicycle.

'You a pommy?' he asked.

I admitted that I was.

'You don't see too many pommies round here,' he said, as he crunched his way through the gears. 'Jesus,' he said, 'this is a real gummy bike, mate.'

It appeared that Laith was 'bumming about' in Sapporo for several months, working when he felt like it as a surfing wet-suit salesman.

'But I'm thinking of giving it up to concentrate on juggling. That's where you can make good money. Two mates of mine – both street artists – can make 350,000 yen [£2300] a month by working as professional jugglers.'

Back home in Oz, Laith had turned his hand to an assortment of professions in the past, like working as a panel-beater – which involved punching out crumpled bits of cars to make them operable again.

'After chauffeuring limos,' he said, 'I worked a while on a 'gator farm. They're great guys, 'gators – gentle as babies; you can sleep with them. It's the crocs that eat you.'

I asked Laith if he had made many Japanese friends in Sapporo.

'You know, mate,' he said, 'I've learnt to keep my friends on a string. The trouble with the Japs is that one moment they love you and the next they don't want to know you. Like my ex-girlfriend – one moment she was salivating all over me, and the next thing I knew she'd turned to ice. Weird, man.'

By this stage I'd had enough of Laith so, spotting a nearby public convenience, I took the opportunity of shaking him off my tail by saying I was diverting course to the toilet. When he said he would wait for me, I put him off the notion by giving him the Captain Oates line that 'I may be some time'. It did the job nicely.

Leaving Sapporo sprawled across the low Ishikari Plain (the neck of land that stretches for 300 kilometres from the coast of the Sea of Japan on the west to the Pacific Ocean in the south-east), I climbed steadily upwards into the mountains of Shikotsu-Toya National Park – Hokkaido's most popular hot-spring hot-spot for tourists.

Approaching the top of one mountain, I was overtaken by a van that pulled off the road just in front of me. The man in the van was a toothless workman who had a white budgerigar perched parrot-fashion on his shoulder and wore a T-shirt with the slogan:

WHERE COMMUNISM WORKS
THE WORLDS WISDOM

The man said something to me which, on account of his toothlessness, I didn't understand. Then he reached into his van and gave me two cans of Pocari Sweat. For some inexplicable reason, instead of saying *arigato* (thank you) as I'd intended, I said, '*Obrigado!*'

Budgie Man gave me a strange look, as well he might do because I had suddenly thanked him in Portuguese – which struck me as not only worrying but most perplexing, especially as I didn't even speak that language. I must have said *arigato* at least 50,000 times during the past few months, but the word had curiously gone clean out of my head.

Maybe the budgie had put me off. Or maybe I'd had one Pocari Sweat too many. Or maybe I was just tired (which I was). Or maybe my brain was simply becoming submerged by all the rain, diluting its powers of sense and sensibility.

Shikotsu-Toya National Park is a park of frisky volcanoes, virgin forests, caldera lakes and body-boiling hot springs. But apart from 17.5 minutes of surprising sunshine, the weather was so appalling that the area remained in my memory only for my inability to see anything other than a remarkably unremarkable low blanket of cloud. Wet cloud. Very wet cloud.

That said, there were in fact three memorable moments. The first was finding my third camping mat at the side of the road which, needless to say, I snaffled away on top of my heaving pack. The second was being most enjoyably vibrated in the stimulating volcano-simulating 'Experience Room' of doughnut-shaped Lake Toya's Volcanic Science Museum, where a film entitled 'Japanese Islands of Fire – A Record of the Mount Usu Eruption' was shown on a screen big enough for a drive-in movie while the shudderingly loud sound effects of an eruption at the centre of an earthquake rumbled and roared through sixteen ear-clearing woofer speakers.

The last memorable moment was camping in the small but neatly tended roadside park of a mountain hamlet, where I slept beside three saplings: one each of hemlock, fir and yellow cedar, which had been 'donated by the people of Lake Cowichan, Canada 28 July 1995', as a nearby plaque informed me. Quite why the fine folk of Lake Cowichan should donate these three budding young trees to a nondescript Japanese village situated halfway across the world was one of those mysteries that had to remain a mystery, as I found not a soul around to enlighten me on the arboreal wherefores and whyfores. And frankly, I didn't really care – not when I was trying to dry all of my two pairs of socks overnight in a wet tent.

Every time I studied my map, I kept breaking out into a mild state of rising panic. With just under four weeks until my brother's wedding, I still had more than 2400 kilometres to go – exceedingly mountainous ones at that, like Honshu's Rikuchu Kaigan National Park, which borders the Pacific and is known as the Alps of the Sea.

I could have made life easy for myself by spending a leisurely time finishing off my ride around Hokkaido and then either catching the train down through Tohoku to Tokyo or taking the boat, but the irrational stubborn side of me didn't fancy that idea. It was doggone determined at least to attempt to cycle all the way.

Onward I raced, following the truly terrible truck-laden National Route 5, which hugged the heel of Hokkaido's narrow kink of land that hung like a boot off the south-westernmost part of the island. A hell's-teeth headwind battered me all the way, so viciously strong that it turned me into a seething and cursing devil. Its strength was such that it was impossible to let my mind wander even for a second: every time a great swaying articulated lorry ripped past, I had to use every miniscule molecule of concentration and wind-waning strength to prevent being sucked beneath its slewing underbelly.

A National Route it might have been but the road was narrow. It was just wide enough to allow a couple of trucks to pass each other with a slip of wind to spare, and certainly not wide enough for them to negotiate past a cyclist at the same time – a cyclist four camping-mats wide at that. So, to avoid a premature death, I had to keep a constant check on the trucks bearing down on me from both fore and aft and then, when I gauged they were about to meet with tyre-squashing force, I would brace myself and veer off on to the verge with a bang.

Apart from too many close shaves with the Route-ripping trucks, my ride to the port of Hakodate was interesting for only two things. One was meeting a mountain mushrooom seller, who told me he used satellites to help him search for *shiitake*. The other was pausing to use a roadside WC housed in a vivid pink block painted with the words 'CABINET DE TOILET'. Excuse me? *A cabinet de toilet?* What were the Japanese playing at? Why this sudden *soupçon* of *français*? Moreover, how did they intend it to be pronounced: 'ka-bee-nay', or 'cab-net' as in your plain-speak, bog-standard, user-friendly kitchen or bathroom cabinet? And why 'cabinet' anyway? Toilets aren't kept in cabinets. Cabinets are for things like tins of baked beans and cat food, towers of Tupperware or packets of disposable razors, or a disarray of long-out-of-date pills and potions that tampering toddlers half kill themselves with when they mistake them for Smarties or fruit squash. Cabinets are most definitely *not* where you keep spare toilets. Whatever next?

Well, what came next was 'Box Castle', otherwise known as Hakodate, which, apart from being one of the first three ports (along with Yokohama and Nagasaki) in Japan to open to foreign trade in 1859 after the country's 200-year isolation, was the place from where I stepped off Hokkaido on to the HNF ferry for the short voyage across the Tsugara Straits to Oma-cho, a remote coastal town sitting on the northern tip of Honshu's Shimokita Peninsula.

The narrow strip of Tsugara Straits separated the big island of Hokkaido from the bigger island of Honshu and also served as a rough ecological boundary between the fauna and flora of middle and northern Asia. This in some ways made Hokkaido more similar to Siberia – a fact to which my over-active summer goose bumps could testify.

CHAPTER 14

The Bike Beat

The axe-shaped Shimokita Peninsula was part of Aomori, one of the six prefectures that made up the most northern district of Honshu, known as Tohoku. Long ago the area, known for its vastness, mysteriousness and inaccessibility, had been called Michinoku, meaning 'interior' or 'narrow road', and had been the very region in which Basho, Japan's great seventeenth-century *haiku* poet, had travelled and written his much acclaimed *Narrow Road to the Deep North*. In 1689, on the eve of his departure, he had said: 'I might as well be going to the ends of the earth.'

In many Japanese minds, these were still as apt words now as they had been then, for it was in Tohoku that tradition clung most tenaciously. As a result, the area was often considered backward by the more 'progressively' minded. 'Sophisticated' Tokyoites tended to regard the place as a remote and strange hinterland of unconquered nature, a place where the people were slow and uncivilised and lived in an impenetrable land of 'snow country'. (In fact the 'Snow Country' was only a melancholy part of the western coast where freezing winds from Siberia battered everyone and everything that lay in their path.)

Although only eighteen kilometres of water separated Hokkaido from Honshu, I still felt certain that I would be crossing a magical meteorological line and would be passing from a cold northern island battered by wind and shrouded in rain to one of searing sun – just like the one I had seen on the television weather map. But when I rolled off the ferry in Oma-cho I was soaked to the bone within seconds, thanks to my mysterious yet dramatic ability to arrive in a supposedly typhoon-free area just in time to catch the tail end of a typhoon.

I succeeded in aquaplaning down the road as far as a hospital, where I tidal-waved through the doors to take shelter in the foyer. After a while, a friendly old man with one leg, a glass eye and a glass of *sake* offered me a banana and the use of his bed. Accepting the former but declining the latter, I sat with the patient as he puffed his way through a pack of Mildo Sevens and watched the sort of daft and intensely aggravating television games show that makes you want to sling a sledgehammer into the skull of every dementedly screaming contestant.

With the storm still flicking its tail outside the window, I accepted the semi-legless man's invitation to take tea (which tasted of *sake*) with him while the television yabbered on. When he fell asleep – obviously I was riveting company – I took the opportunity of switching channels and watched an intriguing programme about a Japanese construction company that was hoping to offer holidays in space between 2015 and 2025. The plan was to build a sixty-four-room hotel in a space-station orbiting the earth. But being bound for a Black Hole would not be quite as cheap as your average trip to the Costa Blanca on a chartered airbus out of Luton. The first tickets for the interstellar tour, there and back and a week or so in orbit, would set space travellers back about £2 million return.

The celestial package trip would offer a variety of entertainment such as space walks, space sports, and a stint of artificial gravity – essential for those wanting a shower in space. No doubt one of the highlights, yet to be trumpeted, would be the novel thrill of weightless sex. Looking out of the window post-coition, it would be no exaggeration to say, 'This time, the earth really did move.'

Aware that the day of my flight was getting closer and closer, I finally decided it was high time to make a move – even with the rain still thundering down. Leaving the legless man to his *sake*-flavoured snores, I braced myself against the raging onslaught of the unsympathetic elements, zipped up my jacket and hit the flooded road.

The ride down the wild and rugged sea-lashed coast was truly splendid. The vehement, tempestuous and raging conditions only added to the dramatic flavour of the whole experience as I sped through the spray and streamed along, with the surge of exuberance that comes from being battered and buffeted by the ravages of nature as I rode the terrestial waves steadily southwards.

The road, narrow and twisting and happily devoid of traffic, clung to a rocky and mountainous coast. Every now and then I sailed through fishing villages consisting of low clumps of mostly wooden houses huddled around small harbours lively with fishermen and their ever-busy wives sorting through tangles of nets. Cycling around the axe-head of Shimokita-hanto felt so far removed from so much of frenetic Japan that, despite my lack of time, I veered off course to spend a few more days in the area.

In Kazamaura-mura, a friendly fishing village on the Metaki River, I met an elderly couple who invited me into their home to have a rest from the rain. They fed me, washed me, dried me, and gave me a tiny *tatami* sea-view room. That night, as the wind and rain clawed against the rattling window, I could just make out the distant beams of the oscillating squid boats out to sea, burning brilliant lamps to attract the ink-blooded *ika.*

A string of shellfish farms laced this northern coast but they had almost petered out by the time I crossed over to the western handle of Shimokita's axe. Suddenly the road lay flat and straight and hectic with traffic.

Just south of Yokohama-machi, before rejoining the main road, I had my first encounter with a Japanese flasher. He was a slow-moving motorist (and an apparently acrobatic one) who managed to raise his rear off the seat and reach a sort of position of levitation before thrusting his unimpressive area of elevation (so to speak) halfway out of the window – without, sadly, crashing into a lamp-post.

I continued along Route 279, the flat, fast road that hugged the coast of Mutsu Bay on one side and the Ominato Line railway on the other. On the east coast of the peninsula, a mere ten or so kilometres away as the rook flies, lay Rokkasho, a place described in Bryan Harrell's *Cycling Japan* as 'the town made famous for its storage facility capable of storing three million drums of nuclear waste'.

As the only country in the world to be the victim of atomic attack, you'd have thought that Japan would want to keep a wary distance from all things nuclear. In the early 1990s, Japan had momentarily signed the Pacific Nuclear Free Zone Treaty, which stated that Japan would not manufacture or possess or allow nuclear weapons to be brought into its territories. But then the government nullified the treaty in a secret agreement that allowed the US to bring nuclear weapons into Japanese territorial waters aboard American ships.

You might also have thought that such a densely populated country as Japan, sitting at the centre of the 'ring of fire' earthquake zone and suffering more earthquakes than any other country in the world, would realise that it was a bit dicy to rely on lots of nuclear power stations (fifty or so) to provide the country with over a quarter of its electricity. According to the Atomic Energy Commission, all of the nuclear power facilities were 'earthquake-proof'. Well, if they say so, then that's all right – or is it? Although the power stations were said to be of 'seismic approved designs', what would happen when a 'big one' came to town, even if they were built to the design of a five-storeyed pagoda? Any seismic engineer knows that nothing can be guaranteed earthquake-proof. Kobe's elevated highway system was said to be able to withstand the shakes of any 'quake, as was San Francisco's Bay Bridge, but they both came tumbling down.

Just north of Noheji, I spent a Friday night camping on the beach along with a pack of weekending US servicemen and their families out from Misawa Air Force Base. Lots of beer, lots of noise, lots of very-strange-to-hear-again English. The weather had been bad all day – the usual mixture of drumming rain, wild winds and head-level mists – but my neighbours, a six-foot-four triangular-torsoed, crop-topped GI (who gave me Andy McNab's *Bravo Two Zero* to read) married to a diminutive Korean woman, told me the forecast was for a fine weekend.

I found this hard to believe when our tents spent most of the night being pummelled by a ferocious storm that blew with whipped-wave fury off the bay but, amazingly, the morning dawned blue and clear and hot. As the day fired itself forwards, the heat only got hotter. And clammier. Hello humidity, I thought, I'd forgotten just what fun you could be: constant rivulets cascading from temples; sticky tacky skin acting like a magnet for grime; sweat-soaked shirt stuck to back; tent like a sauna; sleep as in fever; a constant and unquenchable thirst.

In Misawa I got caught up in a carnival – mad masks, mad music, mad noise. Eager arms hoisted me up on to their chaotic-drumming garish-dragon float and gave me a beer, a bandanna, a fan and some food. A drunken man, wearing a spiral of towel round his head and a garland of plastic flowers round his neck, planted a kiss on my bare shoulder – a brazen move for Japan. But then, this was not Japan; it was festival time – hot, sticky, heated-fun festival time – when the Japanese climbed momentarily out of their harmonious and undemonstrative shells and shook themselves free.

Riding out of Misawa, I found myself sucked on to the thirteen-kilometre Misawa to Momoishi-machi toll road which, rather than car-clogged, was crowded with nose-to-tail dragonflies – sun-blotting clouds of them in the air, torpid swathes of them stuck to the wide black ribbon of heated bitumen. In fact there weren't any cars at all, apart from an official toll vehicle that waved me down. Its uniformed driver informed me with an apologetic smile that the toll road 'no allowing bicycle'.

By this stage I had almost reached Momoishi-machi and had heroically fought through swarms of several thousand dragonflies helicoptering into my face and flapping horribly down my shirt. The man now wanted me to turn round and ride more than twelve kilometres back to where I had joined the toll road, rather than simply continue for another half a kilometre to exit at Momoishi-machi. As I didn't fancy retracing my tracks fruitlessly into a hale and hearty headwind heavy with face-flapping, bra-bombing dragonflies, I opted to play dozy *gaijin* and continued rolling south.

The smiling official became more and more agitated until he finally stopped his car in front of me, jumped out of the vehicle, bowed and, still smiling, beseeched me to comply. Although the exit to Momoishi-machi was virtually under my nose, I felt almost contrite about my intention to continue along the toll road come what may. And although it appeared senseless to leave an empty road on which I could see I was doing no harm (apart from giving a lot of dragonflies some pretty bad headaches) when I was within striking distance of my exit, I thought: why am I ignoring this man's wishes when it's his job, his road, his country? I was the alien invader.

So, with a mind that was obviously sun-befuddled and dragonfly-drunk, I turned round into a fiercesome, skin-grilling wind to cycle north for an hour (along a road that had just taken me only twenty minutes to ride) until I exited back in Misawa.

I then spent the rest of the fruitless afternoon getting thoroughly lost amid a totally confusing tangle of narrow back roads that were all very pleasant but appeared to lead me absolutely no closer to Hachinohe, which I had been hoping to reach for the night. At one point I thought, hell, if in doubt simply head for the sea, and I surfaced closed to Sabishiro Beach, which was the spot where in 1931 the American pilots Pangborn and Herndon had taken off in their bumpy monoplane, the capricious *Miss Veedol*, to complete in just over forty-one hours the first non-stop trans-Pacific flight. Had I been here a month later, I could have joined in the fun and frivolities of the *Miss Veedol* festival held on the beach every September.

While I was cycling in the environs of Misawa Air Force Base, my eardrums suffered a battering from the stratosphere-shattering noise of fighter jets bulleting across the skies. The local Japanese residents were becoming increasingly distressed and exasperated by the presence of the airbase and had even staged protests demanding the withdrawal of the Americans from the base. Not long after riding past its gates, I heard how a Japanese woman had won 6.9 million yen (£46,000) after being thrown from a horse startled by a US fighter flying overhead.

I finally made it to Hachinohe but I almost wished I hadn't – it looked just like any one of the country's many concreted, car-clogged industrial cities. The only faintly enjoyable moment was when I stopped to buy a can of *oolong-cha* from a vending machine that was situated in front of a shop called:

MAGIC! 50
Orderemade FormaleBisiness
suits. Fashionwardrobes.

As I sat on a crate in the shade, drinking my chilled Chinese tea, I spotted a boy, casually smoking a Hope as he sat astride his stationary scooter, who wore a T-shirt covered with the words:

'POWER 1000'
'Mountain bike sports' riding across big
mountain, go across a river, a steep hill.
Let's go our goal! Every one knows how
to ride a bike. the battle of oneself 'The Bike
Beat' get out of hard way off road. reach
the climax, the limit of one's abilities.
Cheer up! Dream of success 'Bike Sports'.
Let's go right on! Let's chance it! We're mover.

And reading that made getting lost all worthwhile. Yes, I thought, I'll go right on! I'll chance it! I'm mover.

After losing myself again among a maze of petrochemical plants down at the port, I emerged on the scenically rocky and winding coast road and made it to the tourist town of Tanesashi by early evening. The beach was a scrum of crew-cut GIs camping with their Japanese girlfriends – lots of beer, lots of barbies, lots of fireworks, lots of litter, lots of get-a-headache ghetto-blasters, lots of steamy bodies, lots of sex.

Filling up my water bottles in a wash block humming with hopelessly beautiful Japanese girls in tight, skimpy skirts and contour-hugging tops and high, dagger-sharp heels, I felt like a right ragamuffin – which is exactly what I was in my sweaty, sun-faded shirt, threadbare oil-stained shorts and scuffed, fox-chewed trainers. Gazing dazedly through bloodshot, sun-blasted eyes at my grimy, burnt-out, sweat-drenched reflection in the mirror, I thought: oh dear, what a sorry sight! While the seductive, beach-doll sexpots around me polished and painted their cherry-lipped faces, and adjusted minimalistic hems, I stayed just long enough to sluice off some sweat and pick remnants of some airborne insects out of my eyes before heading off to find a place to sleep.

Feeling marginally refreshed, albeit still exhausted, I mustered enough energy to thread a path across the littered beach through knots of cavorting couples until I found a relatively secluded spot on a concrete block beside the upturned hull of a small wooden fishing-boat. Unfurling my luxurious, multi-mattressed bed (four mats high, offering elevated beach viewing!), I took up my well-padded position upon the concrete block with a pannier full of food. As I grazed my way through my bag-load of cyclist's fodder, I contemplated the scene spread out before me.

The beach was all bodies. Beautiful bodies. Big, broad, bronzed Americans with their lithe and luscious raven-haired beauties. There were hardly any Japanese men, but those that I did see – playing plastic-batted, foam-ball tennis in ankle-deep sea – looked half the size and stature of the giant GIs.

Isabella Bird had not been impressed with the shapes of the men that she saw – men she called 'mannikins'. 'The skin is very yellow,' she wrote and went on to describe them as 'small, ugly, kindly-looking, shrivelled, bandy-legged, round-shouldered, concave-chested, poor-looking beings'. She noted 'the miserable physique' but added that 'they look far broader in the national costume, which also conceals the defects of their figures. So lean, so yellow, so ugly, yet so pleasant-looking, so wanting in colour and effectiveness.'

Funny the way she reeled off a barrage of belittling insults ('ugly, ugly, ugly') and yet threw in a sprinkling of 'kindly-looking', 'pleasant-looking' and 'really quite nice-looking' to soften the blow.

She wasn't too taken with their hairstyles, either, saying that most of the men (at least those from the 'lower classes')

> wear their hair in a very ugly fashion, – the front and top of the head being shaved, the long hair from the back and sides being drawn up and tied, then waxed, tied again, and cut short off, the stiff queue being brought forward and laid, pointing forwards, along the back part of the top of the head. This top-knot is shaped much like a short clay pipe. . . . Formerly the hair was worn in this way by the *samurai*, in order that the helmet might fit comfortably, but it is now the style of the lower classes mostly and by no means invariably.

More succinct, though no more complimentary, was Paul Theroux's description of the Japanese as 'little bow-legged people who can't see without glasses'. But then Theroux, famous as much for his entertaining travel books as for being a difficult and prickly character who makes acerbic and discourteous comments about all and sundry, did once describe Queen Elizabeth II as 'muffin-faced' and 'slightly haemorrhoidal'.

Before I knew it, Obon (the Festival of the Dead) was upon me – the time when the spirits of departed ancestors were deemed to return to their native place. With both religious and secular Japanese respecting this ceremony, which involved people returning to their *furusato* (home town) for a mid-August three or four days of feasting and dancing, the roads became a nightmare of bumper-to-bumper traffic.

In Buddhism, Obon is called Urabon – 'Ura' meaning pain from starvation (in Sanskrit) and 'bon' meaning food container, or salvation from the pain (in Chinese). By the seventh century, these foreign ideas had combined with Japan's indigenous faith to make Obon rituals: it is believed that descendants can save ancestors from pain in the 'other world' by offering them food during Obon.

The presence of the spirits carries no suggestion of fear or dread – far from it. One of a family's first acts is to visit the local cemetery to light lanterns and burn incense beside the family grave and maybe even light a small fire in the ritual of *mukae-bi* (welcoming fires for the spirits). The rising smoke provides a route by which the spirits can descend to earth and enables the family to chat with their ancestors about what both sides have been doing. At the end of Obon the spirits travel back the same way via *okuri-bi* (sending-off fires), or by river lanterns that are floated to symbolise the spirits' departure. Escorted by fire, the spirits can move from one world to another.

The Japanese believe that they live in the same spiritual world as the dead – it's just that they live on one side of the universe, while the dead live on the other. By talking to them and offering the dead person's favourite food or books or musical instruments, the family can cross the so-called 'river' and everyone, living and dead, can meet up for a good time. There are colourful parades and night-time lantern-lit dancing, usually in an open space in front of the local village temple, with drummers drumming and big circles of clapping, swaying dancers.

That's the way it should be: fun and joviality. No weepy, morbid, black-clad stuff. Just colour, music, excitement and laughter.

As the time zipped by and I forced myself to race onwards to ride distances that clearly didn't please my lacklustre legs, my life melted into a hugely sweaty and overheated blur of head-throbbing exhaustion. Every day the sun fried me further to a frazzle. Perversely, I longed for cloud, cold, rain, shivers – Hokkaido! I hated the sun. The heat was absurd. The humidity was absurd. The mountains were absurd. The amount of baggage I was hauling over the mountains was absurd. The sweat that poured in gallons from my pores was absurd. My head hurt, my legs ached, my skin fried and died. Hundreds and hundreds of kilometres of head-hot hell. All a bit nonsensical, really – I was supposed to be on holiday, was I not?

The heat, the gradients, the leg-quaking trauma of the countless long and filthy tunnels aside, it was the feeling of having to rush, to force myself on, my ridiculous inability to accept defeat and take the train, that made it so bad. And, illogically, I resented having to race, deeply and utterly. I reached the stage of such exhaustion that in a mad-eyed state I began to resent everything within my dissipated, sweaty-minded world. I even went so far as to resent the fact that my brother was getting married, if for no other reason than I was having to rush, having to catch a plane, having to go home, when all I wanted was just to keep on riding.

Over the months I had become moulded into a routine of travelling in this alien land where, although it was almost as strange as it had ever been, I felt more at home than at home. Life was simple. Life was easy. Life was noncommittal. Everything I wanted, everything I needed, was on my bike. I looked, I listened, I lived outside. My major concerns were what would I eat, where would I sleep, would I be safe? Every day I watched the weather, packed and unpacked and moved on. It felt normal, natural.

In the land of the rising yen I lived cheaply, a lot more so than I did back home. Often I would spend no money for days – not because I didn't try to but because people wouldn't let me. People gave and gave. Look, I'd say, I have money. But it was no good; the gifts kept on flowing.

My body felt finely tuned and, apart from the last few days of utter exhaustion, strong. I felt happy, explodingly, almost shamefully, guiltily happy. Sometimes I'd be riding along in one of those rosy-glowing moments when everything was in tip-top form – wind, weather, road, view, bike, people, energy – and I would be hit by a sudden bolt of sheer body-rippling joy, shooting me up to the lofty heights of an endorphin-bursting peak. The sort of moment that sends a turbo-boosted sense of wellbeing rocketing through your system, making you want (rather ludicrously, and almost embarrassingly) to thank anything and anyone that comes your way.

And then suddenly, before you know it, the wind shifts to whack you in the face, or a devil-fanged hound gives chase, or a tyre bursts, and the bubble bursts and you bash your shin on a flesh-eating sharp-toothed chainwheel and the real world brings you crashing back down to earth with a curse and a bang.

At night I would crawl into my tunnel of tent and be almost too hot, too wrecked, too exhausted to eat. The most I could do was to rip off all my sweat-soaked clothes and lie flat on my back on top of my sheet sleeping-bag. But with inner-tent temperatures hitting the fiery forties and humidity levels at a hundred per cent, causing my head to throb, sleep was virtually impossible. Instead I lay as if in a state of fever, wearily fanning my body with one limp hand and squirting water over it from my bottle with the other, in a fruitless attempt to cool down. All around me was the prehistoric chorus of thick, bean-green cicadas that clung hidden among the trees, invading any chance of sleep with their chirpings and trillings and raspings – a mystically tropical sound, filling the feverish night.

The last few weeks of straining from dawn to dusk over a relentless hurdle of vertiginous mountains, in a heat so searing it was producing record-breaking temperatures in this part of Honshu, took a big toll on both body and mind. My levels of patience evaporated with my energy. Everything made me short-tempered and bristly and thoroughly unpleasant. I swore at the sun, at the wind, at the endless mountains, the endless tunnels, the endless noise and shrieking of the omnipresent tannoys, the endless traffic, the endless questions. 'Are you alone?' 'Yes, I'm alone.' 'Really alone?' 'Yes, really alone.' 'As one person?' 'Yes, as one person.' 'By bicycle?' 'Yes, by bicycle.' 'Are you not scared?' 'No, I'm not scared.' 'You are America?' 'No, I am England.' 'Is that so?' 'Yes, that is so.' Aaaarghhhh!

I became angry too because travelling with zero tolerance was not the way to travel. Above all, it was not fair on the locals. I was sure I was rude, but I had no energy, no patience to behave any better. I felt angry with myself for behaving like this, for letting myself get this way. Why couldn't I be sensible and, instead of half-killing myself, let the train take the strain? Why? Because I couldn't. Because unfortunately I seemed to get these irrational theories that it was good to experience (or if not experience, get a taster of) physically strenuous times; to push yourself to the limit because, so I told myself, you never knew when you might need to call on or at least have some knowledge of your resources in times of need or disaster – like finding yourself lost in the middle of a jungle after surviving a plane crash or marooned on a mountain. Or something like that. Maybe my *Lord of the Flies* mind was running away with me, but I always believe it is best to be prepared for the worst as best you can.

I also believe that it's good to scratch the surface of what it feels like to be in pain or discomfort. Not the sort that comes from standing wedged in among undesirable bodies on a commuter train at the height of the rush hour, but the physically demanding out-in-all-elements sort that only the poor, the homeless, the abandoned or victims of a war-torn nation can feel.

As I put this theory (of sorts) to the test, wreaking havoc upon my body while forcing it to get me places (like Tokyo) that it really didn't want to go, I told myself that to experience the exhausted state, as I did, would be beneficial in the long run for giving me more empathy towards those who had no choice other than exhaustion. In hindsight, a more likely theory is that maybe I was just losing my cranial screws.

One thing I was losing for sure was weight. Fat was fast falling off me. Flaked out in my tent at night, I could feel my hip bones sharp and hard, piercing the skin. My collarbone protruded like a cliff ledge, while my ribs felt like a twiggy xylophone. No matter that I drank more than a litre of water an hour, most of my weight was simply being sweated away along with my energy – a strange, blurry-headed sensation of evaporating completely away.

Things momentarily improved when, for the first time in weeks (or was it months?), I spent a night sleeping indoors in air-conditioned bliss. I usually hated air-conditioning with a vengeance. I hated the sealed-in, ozone-destructing artificiality of it all. But not now. Now I loved it to death. Turning it down to shivering levels, I luxuriated in the novel experience of snuggling beneath my futon's quilt and slept a deep and sumptuous sleep.

My air-conditioned heaven came courtesy of Hotel Boyo. This was a fairly siezable hotel, situated on a slight hill that overlooked the major fishing port of

Kesennuma – the 'World Tuna Capital' which, so said the tourist leaflet, boasted more tuna boats than anywhere else in Japan.

My stay in Hotel Boyo had been totally unplanned. On arriving in the city, I had been looking for a temple or shrine in which to camp when a ferocious thunderstorm struck out of the blue. Diving into the nearest shelter that came to hand, I found myself in the lobby of Hotel Boyo, where I met Eiichi Kato, the hotel's young and very charming senior managing director. Mr Kato, on account of his travels in America and brief stint at university in Oregon sixteen years before, spoke good English, albeit beguilingly idiosyncratically. He told me proudly that Hotel Boyo, which was owned by his father, was the oldest hotel in the whole of Kesennuma, having been built in the 1960s. An ancient three decades ago! I did my best to look suitably impressed, then I asked him how long he had been working in the hotel.

'For two year now,' he said.

'Where were you working before?'

'Before hotel I was making selling of diesel engine for tuna ship. But because fishing has very much declining trade, I change to hotel business.'

'Is the hotel business doing well?' I asked.

'Ahh yes, very fine indeed. Fishing trade is maybe dying slowly death, but tourist trade is next for very big boom trade!'

With the rain still pummelling down and the streets now flooded, Mr Kato was taken aback to learn that I was planning to find a place to camp once the storm had passed.

'Please,' he said, 'I have you with a no-charging Hotel Boyo room as my bicycle speciality guest!'

Not quite sure how to take that one, I followed him upstairs. Sure enough, he offered me a large and very splendid 'no-charging' *tatami* room that over-looked the scenically stormy bay. What's more, I had my very own, tiny tea-serving maid in a kimono to tend to my every need.

Before I'd even had a chance to wash, Mr Kato had invited me to join him downstairs for a beer. During our drink together, I told him that I was now on my way to Tokyo, having cycled around Japan.

'This is so fine example of foreign woman strength,' he exclaimed. 'Certainly this will be making for Number One newspaper news!'

Before I knew it, he was telephoning Shimada Hisateru, a journalist friend of his who worked for the local paper, the *Sanriku Shimpoh Sha.* There was obviously not much hot news about, because twenty minutes later I was being instructed to *chiizu* into the camera lens of the paper's photographer as I sat astride my loaded mount outside the doors of the hotel (the downpour had stopped). Once the snapshot shoot was over, Mr Hisateru launched into a lengthy interview as we took tea together.

Mr Kato offered to spend the following day giving me a guided tour of Kesennuma – an offer I had to refuse as I had no time left for dilly-dallying. But by springing out of futon early, I did momentarily diverge off course to look around Kesennuma's vast fish market, where I found the catch spread out on the floor beneath arc lights waiting for the wholesale auction to begin.

Huge tuna, the size of submarines, lay berthed in neat, regimented ranks. They were not the endangered blue-fin (the sleek swimming machines that earned the nickname 'Porsches of the sea' and which, thanks to a flourishing air-freight industry, turned up at Tokyo's Sashimi market where a single fish could fetch $80,000 or more at auction – the fisherman's equivalent of winning the lottery) but they were still magnificent streamlined creatures. As I stood gawping at them, I eco-thought: I wonder how many dolphins lost their lives in tangled nets for this lot?

Outside, on the water, the enormous fleet of dazzling white, battleship-sized tuna boats sat gleaming in the fierce morning sun.

Mr Kato had asked for my address so that he could send me the cutting from the *Sanriku Shimpoh Sha*. True to his word, by the time I arrived home a brown envelope lay waiting for me, containing my *chiizu*-grinning form surrounded by an impressive but meaningless swirl of aesthetically pleasing *kanji*. There was also a typed letter:

Dear Ms Josie Dew,
How are you? It was nice to knowing you when you stoped by our place. I was impressed by your energetic action. How was rest of your trip? I hope everything was fine with you. I had an experience for spending one year and six months in USA about sixteen year ago. I traveled around the States by car during my stay. I could learn a lot through that travel and stay. I don't have a chance to go abroad recently but I do like travel other countries. I like travel by myself like you do, so there are so many things came up in my mind when I talked with you last time. Unfortunately, I didn't have enough time to talk with you and show around my city maybe next time. I'm chaseing the time everyday as a typical Japanese busines

man now, so I had feel envy for your free lifestyle I know there are many difficultiness to be free but you are doing it. It is wonderful. Please write me.

    Take care,

    Eiichi Kato

PS I enclsed an aricle about you on the local news paper which reported by my friend as you remember.

Following another leg-pounding, head-pounding day of gruelling mountains and sizzling heat, I arrived a sweat-soaked wreck in Matsushima – a bay within a bay brimming with hundreds of rocky pine-topped islands, long regarded as one of Japan's three most scenic landscapes. Yes, there they are: those three most famous, most snapped sights have popped up again. I had of course long since ticked off the other two on my been-there-done-that list – the great crimson *torii* gate of Miyajima's 'floating' shrine, and the upside-down through-your-legs view of the Bridge of Heaven sand-spit at Amanohashidate.

Three hundred years before my arrival, poetical Basho had turned up at Matsushima and had been so bewitched (and evidently lost for words) by the beauty of the place that, lyrical soul that he was, the best wordly offering he could bestow upon the wonder spread out before him was:

> Matsushima, Ah!
> Matsushima!
> Matsushima!

Matsushima, which is the name given to the whole area surrounding Matsushima Bay, was first referred to as one of Japan's three most beautiful scenic spots in a book written by Hayashi Shunsai, a Confucian philosopher of the Edo government, about 280 years ago. No doubt in those days the bay was definitely something to 'Matsushima, Ah!' about, but in today's Japan it looked no great shakes to me.

I tried to see beauty, I honestly did. I spent a day (a day I could ill afford), from sunrise to sunset, floating among the islands and visiting the many temples and shrines, but I just couldn't seem to get into the swing of things and wax lyrical about the much-famed sight that I saw. Maybe I was Famous-Sight

Weary (which I was), or maybe there was just too much tourist-trap clap-trap and concrete and tour-group whistle-blowing and *chiizu* peace-poses (which there were), or maybe I had just seen much better unexpected sights elsewhere in Japan (which I had). Whatever the reason, I gave it as good as I could in the circumstances, before I kicked my flagging pistons into action for the final 400-kilometre assault to Tokyo.

CHAPTER 15

Pachinko Prey

The closer I was sucked towards the urban insanity of Tokyo's sprawling concrete and car-swollen, swallow-you-whole conurbations, the worse everything became: the heat, the humidity, the traffic, the pollution, the noise, the concrete, the state of my bike, the state of my bones, the state of my mind. Hell-bent on getting to my flight on time, I switched myself to auto-pilot and, like a clonked-out zombie, just rode and rode.

During those last few death-defying hundreds of kill-me-off kilometres, I experienced only four noteworthy events. The first was somehow finding myself caught up in a game of street football with a bunch of rumbustious schoolboys in Prussian uniforms who called me 'Harrow-Gally-Rineker!'. Despite the persistent injuries that had made Gary Lineker a disastrous investment for his Japanese club, Nagoya Grampus 8, who had paid a £3 million transfer contract for him, he was still widely acknowledged as a triumph in Anglo-Japanese relationships. To add to that, Gary could boast improving his golf swing in Japan, notably with the son of his next-door neighbour, the President of Toyota.

My second 'event' was realising too late that I had cycled clean past the small town of Hiraizumi, where I could have visited Chusonji Golden Hall, an ancient mausoleum for three Fujiwara lords, paved and walled with gold. I later read in a copy of Lonely Planet's guide to Japan that the Hall was 'one of the few cultural sights in Tohoku that should not be missed'.

The third thing I remember was cycling through the traffic-choked city of Hitachi, bidding the place an Ohio good morning by chanting:

Ohayo Hitachi
Oh high-tech city,
Ohayo Hitachi
Oh high-tech city,
Ohayo . . .

for no other reason than I felt like it – such was the sorry state of my overheated head.

The fourth event took place somewhere among the chaotic web of roads that ensnared me and dragged me ever deeper into the great manic vortex of neon-dizzy Tokyo. People-crammed compact concrete houses stretched endlessly along streets lined with hoardings, shadowed by a sky tangled with telegraph wires and cables. And I was lost, again. An easy state to be in, map or no map, in Japan. I had a map but I needed a better, bigger, ten times more detailed one.

When lost in countless other Japanese cities, my technique had been to enter the nearest convenience store, find a local street atlas and copy down or make mental notes of the relevant roads and streets to lead me out of the fix. So that's what I did here: I utilised a street map in a 7-Eleven. Then I went back outside to my bike, which I'd left leaning against the front window.

As I was in the process of repositioning my map on top of my handlebar bag for ease of mid-flight navigation, I suddenly became aware of a man mumbling in Japanese very close behind me. Turning round, I was surprised to find a small, red-shirted man, mid-forties, with two gold incisors, standing practically on top of me. Even more surprising was that he was in the process of indecently exposing himself to me. In broad daylight! With people around! With the door to 7-Eleven a mere penis-length away!

I couldn't believe it. I couldn't believe the brazen impudence of the man. Although I seem to have had more than my fair handful of flashers in my time, I have fortunately never been in such close proximity to one as I was to this cocky chap milking his miserable little Wormwood Scrub for all it was worth.

I don't like my personal space being invaded at the best of times, but this was ridiculous – Incisor Man was standing close enough to be almost wearing my shorts. Such audaciously impertinent behaviour for a Japanese man so shocked and incensed me that my immediate reaction was to grab him by the collar and shake him silly – a simple enough act, seeing as he was as short as I am tall.

Whatever reaction the man had been anticipating from me when he embarked upon his indelicate mission, I could bet my bottom dollar that he hadn't been banking on being shaken like a terrier-trapped rat. He looked terrified. As soon as I had finished telling him what I thought of him in my uncharitable native tongue and as soon as his feet had touched the ground, he bolted off down the street like a whippet with a bee up his bum, fumbling for his flies.

Without a moment's hesitation I took off after him, scattering a plethora of perplexed pedestrians as I went. With the intimidator now the intimidated, the tables had suddenly been turned. I was tasting domination – and it felt wonderful! All my cycling exhaustion had suddenly evaporated. As I ran, I was charged with an adrenalin-rushing high. Now that it was me who had the power, I wasn't going to let him go. The chase was on.

As I ran, the thought suddenly struck me that maybe the man was a decoy. Japan may be a largely crime-free society compared with most other nations, but there's always a bad spring onion in every bunch. What's more, I was in no small-time backwater – the Aum Shinrikyo deathly subway nerve-gas attack Tokyo lay just around the corner. I had left my money, my passport, my air ticket, my diary, my camera and every Tom, Dick and Harry of my personal effects on my unlocked, unfettered steed back at 7-Eleven. Maybe Incisor Man's partner-in-pants was at this very moment helping himself to my worldly, worn-torn possessions – small and humble though they were, but one does tend to get a trifle attached to one's Katmandu-purchased flip-flops and mosquito-corpse-stained tent, don't you know? And was it really worth losing one's valuables and not-so-valuables for the temptingly irresistible sake of scaring the flies off a flasher?

Well, yes and no. 'No' won the day and I made a hasty retreat back to my bike . . . but not before I noted that Incisor Man had darted across the street and down an alley alongside a *pachinko* parlour.

Happily, my bike and belongings were just as I had left them (draping one's baggage with a motley assortment of dank cyclist's laundry obviously acted as a simple yet effective deterrent to thieves) and, remounting, I took off down the street.

As I rode past the *pachinko* parlour, I was amazed to catch a glimpse of Incisor Man cowering just back from the entrance of the alley. I carried on as if I hadn't seen him and then, once out of sight, I nipped through the traffic to turn right, and right, and right again, hoping to make a loop round into the back of the *pachinko* parlour. Riding up on to the pavement, I followed a path through a wall and found myself in the parlour's car park. Yee-haa! I was back on the storming warpath again.

Within moments I was entering the back end of the alley, not really expecting that Incisor Man would still be there. But there he was indeed – crouched down with his back to me, peering anxiously out towards the street, which just went to prove that some men really do keep their brains in their balls.

The moment intensified as my moment of revenge drew to a head and, with the runway clear to take him unawares from behind (so to speak), I gave my pumped-up adrenal gland free rein to shoot its load. Grabbing my bicycle pump, I wielded it over my head as I charged my steed down the alley, emitting a blood-curdling battle-cry as I bore down on my pitiful prey.

Terrified, he spun round, his eyes on stalks. Before I had a chance to give him a good bicycle pumping, he had fled through a side door into the dazzling *pachinko* palace.

Hurling my mount aside, I went crashing through the door after him and, within seconds, had entered the inanely flashing, blipping, blurping pinball world of noise, neon, steel, money and men. Lots of men. Line after line, row after row. Hypnotic-eyed, blank-faced, glued to their stools. All the same, looking the same, playing the same. Everywhere balls – steel balls, glittering and crashing and rattling through vertical labyrinths of shiny nails. Only a handful of heads turned to stare at me momentarily as I strode purposefully along the tops of the aisles, searching for my *pachinko* prey.

I found him halfway down the fifth aisle, skulking on his seat as he pretended to fire ball-bearings on a machine that he so plainly just wanted to swallow him whole. As I swaggered up to him like a hip-holstered Lone Ranger striding through a dusty saloon-door-creaking town, he looked a broken man. In fact, he looked so helpless, so hopeless, that now it had come to the crunch I found I didn't have the heart to humiliate him in front of his fellow countrymen. After all, it wasn't as if wapping out his wanger was anything *that* bad. It was more his problem than mine.

Anyway, just because I thought I could handle him (as it were) all on my own, was it really fair to vent on him all my feelings of anger, frustration and powerlessness (if that was what I was doing) generated by the many and far bigger untrousered males who had tried to threaten and intimidate me in the past? Probably not. And now that I had him, what was I going to do – gouge out his eyes and cut off his balls to add to the collection bouncing around in the pinball machine? Hardly.

So, without making a show, I simply bent down and said to him quietly, in no uncertain terms, '*YA-ME-TE*! – LEAVE ME ALONE!'

If I'd known the Japanese put-down for 'What you showed me looked exactly like a penis, only smaller', I would have said it. But I didn't, so I couldn't. Whatever, I felt that Incisor Man had been warned. Quietly jubilant, I left the flashing world of the ball-crashing *pachinko* palace and cycled off up the road with rejuvenated vigour.

That evening I was still in such a good mood that when I was interrupted while packing my stash of supper provisions into my panniers outside A-COOP supermarket by a man clutching a cigarette who said, 'America?', I simply smiled sweetly at him before replying, 'No, *Igirisu* – England,' in a calm and gentle manner that was quite different from my prickliness of past weeks. Some good, as well as steam, had obviously been released by my conquest over the Pinball Flasher.

The man, tossing the butt of his Lucky Strike into the gutter, launched into the standard interrogation of a lone *gaijin* on a bicycle.

'You are one person?'

'Yes, I am one person.'

'Really one person?'

'Yes, really one person.'

'Ahh, that is great! You are one person from America?'

'No, England.'

'Ahh so, *desu-ka*? You are indeed two person?'

'No, I am one person. I am alone. One person from England.'

'Ah, is that so?'

'Yes, that is so.'

'Where please for you sleeping?'

'In my tent.'

'*Tento* – you have *tento*?'

'Yes, I have a tent, here, in my pannier.'

'Ah, so small tent for two person only. That is great!'

'Thank you, but I'm the only person in it. I am alone.'

'Ahh so. But so danger.'

'No, it's not dangerous.'

'Really, no danger?'

'No, it's really not dangerous. Japan feels very safe.'

'Ahh so, *desu-ka?*'

There then followed much sucking in of the man's breath – a sign that, as well as inferring difficulty, can be interpreted as good breeding and politeness in this oriental world full of etiquette landmines.

'Yes, so you have lonely?'

'Lonely? No, I'm not lonely.'

'*Hai, hai!* I am believing you say you have lonely.'

'No, not lonely. Alone. I'm alone. I don't get lonely at all.'

'*Hai, hai!* You have tall. All Japanese so small!'

'Excuse me?'

'*Hai, hai!* So tall!'

'Who's tall?'

'Mmmm, yes – you very tall person I am believing.' The man shuffled closer to me. '*Hai, hai!* See please, we have height similarity!'

This man, with his friendly, flat shiny face and raked, black, perfectly parted hair, was beginning to lose me. Tall – why tall? Why veer off the customary questioneering script and suddenly speak about being tall? And anyway, I wasn't tall, I was small. Like him. What had I said that made him think tall? I thought back. America. England. Tent. Danger? Not danger. Alone. Lonely? Not lonely – not lonely at all. At all!

'Oh, *sumimasen* – sorry, I didn't say "tall", I said "at all".'

'Yes, ha ha! So tall!'

Oh dear, there was no going back now. The man was stuck on tall. So, feeling it was better and easier just to go with the flow of the moment rather than reverse back up the long winding road of congested confusion, I said, 'Yes, yes, so tall. In fact you're as tall as I am small!'

After all, what's a confusing conversation for if it's not for getting lost somewhere in the gyratory-system world of speech?

Strangely, amid all the cross-party misinterpretations and misunderstandings, I spent a most enjoyably garrulous night with the tall-small man and his tall-small family in their small-small home. I got fed, I got watered, I got my bike oiled, I got gifts given, I got clothes washed, I got body washed – in fact I got body scrubbed by the small-tall daughter in a small-deep bath. And I got futon-flat happy. Just the sort of perfect pampering I needed to pep me up and spur me forth on my final spin of a fling to my flight.

So the following morning, feeling as simultaneously tall as I was small, I flung an enthusiastic leg over my big-small bike to rejoin the long, circuitous road that would suck me into the chaotic, concrete, car-infested world of Japan's prodigiuos neon-blipping capital.

A GAIJIN'S GLOSSARY

Some Japanese translators use a phonetic system of vowels with a bar over to indicate pronunciation or stress. In this book such vowels have been doubled in the case of a and i (e.g. *chiizu*).

[Note: 'lit.' = 'literally']

aikido: martial art that puts equal emphasis on the spiritual and the physical self and borrows from the disciplines of judo, karate and *kendo* (the Japanese art of fencing)

Ainu: the original inhabitants of Japan, said to be of Caucasian stock because of their rounded eyes, hirsute appearance and naturally wavy hair

aisu-kuriimu: ice-cream

anago: conger eel

arigato: thank you

atsui desu-ne?: (lit. 'are you hot?') it's hot, isn't it?

Basho: Japan's greatest *haiku* poet (1644–1694)

benjo: (older word for) lavatory, toilet (room), water-closet

bento: lunchbox, usually containing rice and fish, often sold at railway stations

bisuketto: biscuit

bokujo: ranch, stock farm, pasture

bonsai: the art of growing dwarfed ornamental varieties of trees or shrubs in small shallow pots by selective pruning (*bon*, basin, bowl; *sai*, to plant)

cha: tea

champon: noodle soup

chan-chan yaki: fried dish made with salmon, vegetables, *miso* and *sake*

chigen-sai: a spinach-like vegetable

chiizu: cheese

chotto matte kudasai: just a moment, please

daikon: giant white radish (up to 40 cm long with circumference of 25 cm or more), usually grated and served with many dishes, or sliced and pickled

daimyo: feudal lords during Tokugawa shogunate who had virtually complete control over their domains

dandanbatake: (lit. 'step-step fields') terraced rice fields

dashi: a basic Japanese stock, based on shavings of dried bonito fillets (*katsuobushi*), seaweed (*kombu*) and water

desu-ka?: is that so?; really? (usually preceded by 'ah so', circumstances of conversation dictating how long the 'ah' is)

desu-ne: that is so; yes it is

domo arigato gozaimasu: thank you very much

dozo: please (when offering something); go ahead; be my guest

eki: railway station

fugu: pufferfish, globefish

fuki: a wild vegetable, looking similar to rhubarb

futon: thick padded quilt-like mattress, easily rolled up and stowed during the day (the stuffing ranges from rice hulls to foam rubber); eiderdown

futsu: a slow train (stopping at all stations)

gaijin: (lit. 'outside person') foreigner

ganbatte!: do your best!; have strength!; good luck!

gatta-ballo: gate-ball (Japanese-style croquet)

genkan: (lit. 'hidden barrier') entrance hall or foyer where shoes are removed or replaced when entering or leaving a building

geta: traditional raised wooden clog-like sandals with toe-thong

gwaeilo: (Cantonese slang) white people; foreigners

habu: poisonous snake found in Okinawa area

habuzake urume: snake wine

hai!: yes!; okay!; understood!; fight! (Literally 'yes', but actually, in certain contexts, it can mean only passive acknowledgement that the addressee is paying attention. Note that *hai* is not equivalent to 'yes' in the English sense, which can sometimes – often in my case – lead to misunderstanding and misinterpretation.)

haiku: seventeen-syllable poem containing a *kigo* or season-word

heiwa: peace

hi: day

hitori: alone, one person

Igirisu: England; Britain

Igirisu-jin: English person

ika: cuttlefish

ippai(no): full

irasshimase: welcome (as a greeting), heard when entering homes, shops, restaurants and even lifts – there is no need to respond

iroppoi: lit. 'colourful', but used to mean sexy. The *iro* (colour) referred to is pink, which is directly associated with sex.

Izanagi and Izanami: brother and sister deities and lovers who created the islands of Japan when they descended to earth at Amanohashidate

jigoku: hell, or hot springs

jikatabi: traditional split-toed boots worn mostly by builders, carpenters and workmen

jinja: Sinto shrine, easily spotted by the *torii* gate at its entrance

jitensha: bicycle

joshi kosei: trend-setting schoolgirls who consider it fashionable to be seen in their drastically customised school uniforms (*joshi*, woman, girl; *kosei*, individual character)

kamikaze: (lit. 'divine wind') name given to the typhoon that sank Kublai Khan's invading armada in the thirteenth century; also name adopted by suicide pilots in Second World War in their effort to duplicate this fortuitous storm

kanji: Chinese calligraphic characters (ideograms) used in Japanese script (used along with *kana* to write Japanese)

Kannon: Buddhist goddess of mercy – comes in many renditions throughout Japan

kasutera: Castilla (region of Spain)

Kirishitan: Christian

kohii: coffee

kokin guzzu: antibacterial substance used to create germ-free goods

kombu: kelp

konbanwa: good evening

konnichiwa: (lit. 'this is the day') good afternoon, hello

kudasai: (lit. 'to give') please (added to the end of a request)

kuma ramen: noodle and bear-meat soup

kuruma: long-handled man-powered rickshaw

kyaria wuman: career woman

kyuku: express train service

mama-san: owner or manageress of a *mizu-shobai* establishment; also of guest-house, etc

manga: a comic (contents often include soft porn)

marimo: round clumps of green algae, peculiar to lake in Hokkaido

Meiji: (lit. 'enlightened government') the throne name of Mitsuhito, Emperor of Japan, who ushered in the Meiji Restoration of the 1860s whereby Japan was roused from its long dormancy and feudalism and entered into the modern age. The Meiji Era was the period of the Emperor's reign (1868–1912).

minshuku: authentic Japanese-style guesthouse – good family-run budget accommodation

miso: thick brown paste made from fermented, mashed, salted soybeans and used like bouillon; can also be made from barley or rice. Basic to many dishes.

misoshiru: soup made from *miso* – forms part of traditional Japanese breakfast and often contains **wakame** (large flat seaweed) and tofu. A wide range of differing types of *miso* is used, from *shiro miso* (light, sweet, and lightly salted) to *hatch miso* (pure unadulterated bean paste).

mizu: water

mizu-shobai: 'water trade', colloquial name given to one of Japan's largest and most conspicuous entertainment trades encompassing cabarets, night-clubs, bars, assignation inns, 'love hotels' (specialising in short-time room rentals), 'soaplands'(bath and massage parlours) and geisha houses. The primary ingredients of the *mizu-shobai* are alcoholic drinks and attractive women.

mompe: traditional baggy work trousers worn by women in rural areas

moshi-moshi: hello (on the phone)

Nihon or **Nippon**: (lit. 'Land of the Rising Sun' or 'Source of the Sun') Japan

nihon-cha: Japanese tea

nori: Japan's most popular edible seaweed, dried in paper-thin sheets and used to wrap around *sushi* and riceballs. *Nori* has been cultivated in Japan's gentle bays and narrow inlets for over 300 years. Harvested during the cold winter months, it is carefully washed and then slowly and evenly dried in square forms, much like the traditional method of paper-making.

notte kudasai: please hop in

o-: prefix used in polite speech as indicator of respect for the thing or person in question (see *-san*)

obaasan: affectionate name for an old woman; grandmother; sometimes used with a hint of condescension

ohayo: morning

ohayo gozaimasu: (lit. 'it's early') good morning

ojama shimasu: I'm going to be a nuisance

ojama shimashita: the nuisance is over

onigiri: round or triangular riceball sprinkled with sesame seeds or wrapped with dried seaweed, usually filled with fish or spicy vegetables – very popular for picnics and snacks

onsen: hot springs; spa. Usually surrounded by various guest accommodations.

oolong-cha: Chinese tea

oyasumi-nasai: (lit. 'please take a rest') goodnight

owabi: apologise

pachinko: pinball played on vertical machines

pan: bread

pansuke: whore

ramen: white Chinese noodles adapted to Japanese palate, served in big bowls in a chicken stock with vegetables and/or meat; can be eaten hot or cold

rotenburo: open-air bath, naturally occurring hot springs

ruusu: loose

ryokan: traditional Japanese inn

sabishi: lonely

sakana: fish

sake: potent rice wine with 15–16 per cent alcoholic content, usually served warm in *ochoku* (thimble-sized cups). Although it can be made anywhere in Japan, famous *sake* are produced in regions that have a supply of good water, or good quality rice. One of the many sayings about *sake* is that it has ten merits: it is the best medicine, a prolonger of life, a meal for the traveller, a friend to those who live alone, a convenient excuse to visit without invitation, a disperser of sorrow, a social leveller, a relief from work, a harmoniser of all men, and an overcoat against the cold. Another saying is that one should drink *sake*, not be drunk by it.

sakyu: sand dunes

samurai: warrior aristocrat in feudal Japan – a privileged class permitted to wear two swords as a sign of their caste. Below them were the common people: farmers, artisans and merchants. The samurai were abolished after the Meiji Restoration.

san: mountain (also *yama*, *zan*)

-san: suffix used in polite speech as an indicator of respect for the person to whom it is attached

sashimi: bite-sized pieces of very thin slices of fresh raw fish (sometimes beef, poultry or horse meat) served with soy sauce, *wasabi* and thinly shredded ginger

sayonara: goodbye

seppuku: suicide by disembowelment (less vulgar term than *hara-kiri*). In feudal times this ritual was the exclusive privilege of nobles and samurai.

seremame: type of bean

shikata ga nai: what can be done?; it can't be helped; it has to be

shima: island

shimbashira: thick central pillar of a five-storeyed pagoda

shinjinrui: species of human – refers to younger generation who are fast changing from the traditions of older society

Shinto: the polytheistic indigenous religion of Japan, which propounds that all living and even inanimate objects have souls. Ancestor worship and purity are two basic tenets. State Shinto, prevalent from the Meiji era to the end of the Second World War, was a bastardised form that made the Emperor an omnipotent living god. Shinto in Japan is called *Kami-no-Michi* (The Way of the Gods).

shogun: warlord, military ruler of old Japan to whom all *daimyo* and *samurai* owed allegiance. In pre-Meiji times the Shogun was the actual ruler of Japan; succession was hereditary as long as a family could remain in power. The Shogun was always invested by the Emperor.

shoji: sliding room-divider panels made of thin translucent sheets of rice paper pasted on lightweight wooden frames. The traditional purpose of *shoji* was a screen to block the view rather than a door to bar entrance. Modern *shoji* may have panels of frosted glass rather than rice paper.

soba: long noodles made from buckwheat, with squared corners, and colours that vary from grey to brown. They are served with a sprinkling of shredded pork, beef, chicken or egg with leeks and mushrooms in a bowl of fish stock. They may also be served cold with an accompaniment of soy sauce, freshly chopped onions, ginger and minced horseradish.

sokkusu: socks

sugoi: wonderful; amazing; great

suido: straits

sumimasen: excuse me, I'm sorry, I apologise; thank you, I'm grateful

sumo: Japanese wrestling

sushi: lightly vinegared rice, seasoned with salt, sugar and *mirin* (sweet rice wine) and moulded into bite-sized mouthfuls, overlaid or mixed with raw fish, shellfish, seaweed, vegetables or omelette.

syunyu inshi: extension stamp

takenoko: bamboo shoots

tancho-zuru: red-crested crane

tatami: floorcovering on which shoes are never worn, made of plaited rush cover on top of a straw pallet reinforced with yarn, and sunk into the floor. *Tatami* mats are used as a unit of room measurement.

tempura: fritter-like dish consisting of various kinds of fresh seafood, meat and vegetables (green pepper, carrots, aubergines, mushrooms, lotus root) coated in a batter of egg and flour (*koromo*) and quickly deep-fried in sesame or pure vegetable oil until they turn translucently glazed. These morsels are dipped into *ten-tsuyn* – a sauce of *mirin* (sweet *sake*), fish broth and soy sauce to which grated *daikon* with pimento powder and/or fresh grated ginger is added to taste. *Tempura* is served with a bowl of rice and a small dish of pickled vegetables.

tento: tent

todo yaki: fried sealion

toki doki: sometimes

tokkyu: type of train service

torakku: truck

torii: entrance gate to a Shinto shrine

tsunami: (lit. 'port wave') tidal wave, usually following sea-centred earthquake

udon: long white and slightly thick type of noodle made from wheat and served with a sprinkling of shredded pork, beef, chicken or egg with leeks and mushrooms in a bowl of fish stock

uoiciba: morning fish market

ura dori: backstreets

yaku-sugi: cedar trees

yamabuki: type of flower

yamete!: stop it!; leave me alone!

yatsuhashi: dumplings filled with sweetbean paste

yusu hosuteru: youth hostel

zaru soba: cold noodles

zoki: rubber sandals

APPENDIX

Equipment Department

Bicycle

Frame	Custom-made 18″ ROBERTS bronze-brazed, touring angles, pink. Built in 1988 by Chas Roberts, traversed several continents and still going strong.
Wheels	Saturae 26″ H × 22 rims, DT stainless steel spokes. Hand-built by James Shaw to last and have never caved in on me.
Hubs	Campagnolo Nuovo Record 36-hole large flange
Tyres	Avocet Cross 26 × 1.5
Headset	Campagnolo Nuovo Record
Handlebars & stem	Cinelli
Brakes	Shimano Deore XT Cantilever
Brake levers	Campagnolo Super Record
Cranks	TA 150 mm
Chainrings	Chris Bell's precision-made and virtually inde-structible round 'EGGS': 24/36/40
Chain	Sedisport
Freewheel	Suntour 13–32
Derailleur (front and rear)	Shimano Deore XT
Gear levers	Campagnolo Nuovo Record
Pedals	Campagnolo Gran Sport
Bottom bracket	Specialised S1
Seat post	Strong

Saddle	Terry
Racks (front and rear)	Blackburn
water bottle cages	Blackburn
Mudguards	Milremo
Brake blocks	Scott Matthauser
Brake hoods	Modolo
Handlebar covering	Titus, padded leather
Toe clips	Cateye, nylon
Toe straps	Christophe
Computer	Cateye ATB
Bike light (rear)	Vistalite LED (Light Emitting Diode), attached to rear rack
Bicycle bell	Make unknown – found at the side of the road on Vancouver Island, BC
Panniers	Ortlieb – which proved totally rainy-season waterproof
Front	Front-Roller Classic (old style)
Rear	Bike-Packer Classic (old style) with additional outer pockets
Handlebar bag	Tika CT30 Delux (plus shoulder strap)
Rack pack	Ortlieb Roll 'N' Snap, size medium – useful for cramming extra food supplies on board.

Sleeping Arrangements

Tent	The North Face Tadpole 1.85 kg (4 lb 1 oz), with no-see-um insect netting side walls and door – a lightweight, capacious and fast-to-erect, pitch-it-anywhere, free-standing tent
Pegs	8 × The North Face Super Tent Peg (virtually indestructible) 2 × Chouinard T-stakes (indestructible) 1 × small spare aluminium inner sleeve in case of breakage
Groundsheet	The North Face, made-to-measure for Tadpole tent – super-lightweight, fast-drying (picked up in a sale bin in REI, the camper's seventh-heaven outdoor store, in Los Angeles) 1 × cheap plastic sheet cut to size to fit door storage area
Sleeping-bag	1 × The North Face Kazoo 1 kg (2 lb 2 oz), three-season goose-down bag – works a treat

1 × home-made cotton sheet sleeping-bag, 140 g (5 oz). Easy to wash and good for keeping the very not-easy-to-wash Kazoo clean. Also adds a little extra warmth, if needed. Converseley, it's vital in hot conditions when the last thing you want to go to bed with is a blood-boiling down-feather bag.

Sleeping-mat 1 × Karrimoor Karrimat Expedition, ¾-length, yellow, 10 oz (285 g). I used to take a Therm-a-Rest Ultralite ¾-length self-inflatable mat, but the Karrimat, being a 'closed-cell' foam pad, is lighter and puncture-proof (important when flinging it down on thorny ground for food stops, etc).

Kitchen Department

Stove – none. I went stoveless to Japan because I felt like being clobber-free on the cooking front. I'm quite happy gnawing on raw food day in, day out, and rustling up inedible-looking mixtures with any unlikely ingredients I can lay my oily hands on.

1 × plastic food container – doubles up as a 'bowl' for mixing the above mish-mash, while the lid acts as a chopping board

1 × big plastic mug – also gets used as a bowl and, at a push, a bath

2 × plastic screw-top containers into which I decant jars of honey, etc

1 × small and serrated Kitchen Devil sharp knife with home-made reinforced protective blade sheath

1 × Swiss-made Kuhn Rikon vegetable peeler. Lightweight, strong and sharp. Without a doubt, best peeler I've ever peeled with (and, being a cook by trade, I've peeled with a few in my time). It's so good it even makes peeling 45 kilos of potatoes a pleasurable experience. In some countries (i.e. ones in which crops are treated with heavy doses of 'night soil'), I peel everything that can be peeled in the hope of preventing some mysterious and potentially lethal disease-causing bacterium from running amok in my gut.

1 × lightweight stainless steel spoon

1 × lightweight stainless steel knife

1 × Permaware durable plastic teaspoon

1 × pot scourer, cut in half

1 × 7 cm tea towel

1 × lighter – used mostly for burning toilet paper

3 × water bottles (to fit my bicycle frame-mounted bottle cages)

1 × Ortlieb 4-litre waterbag – lightweight and collapsible and easy to store (also works well as a pillow and cushion)

Plastic bags – all conceivable (and inconceivable) shapes and sizes and amounts. Without at least a dozen bags full of plastic bags I'm lost. I like to rustle.

Rubber bands – most of which I make from old pairs of rubber gloves that have sprung a leak (a prepared-before-the-programme top-tip I picked up from *Blue Peter* circa 1974) and used for sealing my plastic bags full of all and sundry.

Clothing

1 × Rohan fully waterproof jacket with hood

1 × pair Rohan waterproof trousers – no specific model as these were prototype one-offs

1 × Rohan Polartec Fleece top – lightweight and warm and is almost dry as soon as it's washed and wrung out

1 × Bell cycling helmet, white (which, because of the heat, did not see a lot of contact with my head). I now use a Specialised King Cobra.

1 × sun visor (bought for $2 in a hippy shop in Hawaii in 1992) – saves my nose from multiple peelings

1 × pair Nike trainers

1 × pair flip-flops (bought in Katmandu in 1988 for about ½p) – essential for use in showers to avoid picking up all sorts of undesirable foot infections, etc

1 × pair Rohan lightweight ¾-length baggy trousers – pack down to nothing

1 × pair black cotton-lycra leggings

2 × pairs stripy cotton-lycra home-made cycling shorts (material bought cheaply from a stall in Berwick Market, London W1)

1 × pair baggy cotton shorts (bought in a kite shop on the island of Molokai, Hawaii)

2 × cotton vests (sleeveless T-shirts)

1 × cotton T-shirt

2 × bras (excellent insect traps during downhill descents)

3 × pairs M&S knickers (wear one, wash one, keep one spare)

3 × pairs white ankle socks (ditto the above)

1 × pair long blue walking-boot socks

1 × swimming costume

1 × pair swimming goggles

1 × bandanna

1 × woolly (fleece) hat

1 × pair lightweight thermal gloves

1 × big cotton scarf – good not only for blocking out neck draughts but also for makeshift slings, bikini tops, blindfold (when trying to sleep in brightly lit places), emergency towel and shopping bag

1 × pair lycra-backed, leather-palmed and padded cycling mitts (though most of the time it was too hot to wear them)

1 × mini towel. One of the few advantages of having a mini body is that you only need a mini towel.

Washbag/First Aid and Other Paraphernalia

Washbag – small, lightweight stuff-sack filled with toothbrush, toothpaste, shampoo, soap, etc

Dental floss – not only for teeth, but for making washing lines, tying up parcels, mending panniers, strong thread, makeshift guy ropes, making trip-wires around tent to forewarn of any unsavoury characters prowling around at night

Lip-salve stick with sunblock

Sun-block cream – gave up on this after a while as Japan was just too humid and the cream refused to be absorbed into such sweaty skin

Insect repellent – or, judging from the number of mosquitoes I attracted, was this simply mislabelled insect fodder?

Tiger Balm – good for headaches, pulled muscles and making your eyes water

1 × face flannel

1 × 10 ml bottle Hypercal tincture (Ainsworths Homoeopathic Pharmacy) – heals cuts in a jiffy

1 × small phial each of Arnica tablets (for injuries, shock, etc) and Arsen Alb (for food poisoning)

Face moisturiser cream – decanted into small plastic bottle

1 × small container of multi-vitamins and minerals – to reach (hopefully) the parts that a diet of seaweed and octopus tentacles didn't reach

1 × 10 ml bottle Tea Tree essential oil (good antiseptic)

1 × 10 ml bottle Lavender essential oil (good for everything from burns to insect bites to soporific pillow aromas)

1 × packet Puritabs (in case I found myself faced with suspect water supplies)

1 × hefty supply of the all-essential toilet paper (collected in small doses from various sources en route)

1 × pair Boots Travel bands – worn on wrist acupressure points to help control 'motion sickness' (though to have any effect on a plane I should perhaps try wearing some on my ankles and neck as well)

1 × pair washable foam earplugs – essential when bedding down en masse with several hundred ferry passengers, all of whom seem intent on doing anything but sleep

Small selection of plasters and bandages

Assortment of safety pins, needles, extra strong 100 per cent polyester thread

Mini nail-clippers and file; ultra lightweight plastic clothes pegs

Waterproof card clearly stating blood group

Cut-off pencil; half a rubber; airmail paper and envelopes; permanent black marker pen; biro; stamps; 'business' cards; mini Pritt Stick and Sellotape

1 × small black notebook (usually an Alwych from Waverley with an 'All-Weather' cover) that acts as my never-far-from-reach diary

Calculator – credit-card sized, solar-powered (good for currency calculations and for those all too frequent moments when the simplest of calculations goes clean out of head)

Oxford Minidictionary (good for those all too frequent moments when the simplist – whoops, I mean simplest – of spellings goes clean out of head; also never fails to prove an intriguing read)

Mini Japanese dictionary

Lonely Planet Japanese and Mandarin Chinese phrasebooks

Photocopied sheets of selected Cantonese phrases

Books – vital in order to enter another world (preferably fictitious) at least twice a day. In Japan, where books in English were non-existent outside of the cities, I carted around a weighty library on board my bike for fear of running out of the all-essential reading material.

Maps – even if you don't know where you are, it's nice to think you do

Mini compass – if in doubt, head north (or should that be south?)

Mini thermometer – for dangling off handlebar bag (even if it's not very pleasant to know it's 46°C inside your tent, it's still quite an interesting fact to log in the diary and to bore friends with on postcards)

1 × mini folding hand-fan

1 × mini mirror (50p-sized) – indispensable for hoiking airborne insects out of eyes

1 × Swiss Army knife with scissors – vital for making postcards out of cardboard boxes

1 × mini address book – crammed full of mini words and mini names and mini numbers

1 × money pouch – with traveller's cheques, cash (dollars and yen), Visa card (in Japan far more places take Visa than Mastercard), BT Chargecard (a boon for phoning home), insurance, driving licence, international driving permit, plane/ferry tickets, YHA membership card, passport, spare passport pictures (photocopied details of passport, traveller's cheques, credit card theft information etc are stored elsewhere in my baggage along with supply of emergency money)

1 × Dog Dazer – battery-operated ultrasonic dog deterrent (helps to spare a shin or two from ending up as a bicycle-chasing dog's dinner)

1 × Petzl Micro head-torch – not only suffices as bicycle light but also v. useful for sparing the hands for inner (or outer) tent activities

1 × Mini-Maglite Solitaire torch

1 × collapsible rucksack – useful for a jaunt in the hills and for cramming last-minute food supplies on board overladen mount before setting up camp

Oakley sunglasses (and case) – to protect eyes from sun, wind, rain, grit, dust and winged insects

Sony Walkman Sports personal stereo plus four cassettes of custom-made compilations

Sony mini shortwave radio – can't leave home without it

Cheap digital Casio watch – with alarm

Cannon Sureshot camera – for quick, easy, no-messing snaps. Highly recommended as it's still going strong after fourteen years despite being full of Saharan sand, doused in several rainy seasons, frozen and boiled, dropped on multiple occasions and involved in various bicycle head-on collisions.

Cannon AE1 Programme with Tamron 70–210 lens – also standing the test of time miraculously well after spending nineteen years bouncing around on my bike

Padded bicycle-crashproof camera case

20 × Fujichrome Sensia 100 film (36 exposures) – good all-rounder

1 × mini Minox tripod (essential for taking self-timered, self-posing snaps)

Spare batteries for camera, torch, radio, bike light and Walkman (which handily all take the same size of battery)

Leica 8 × 20 BCA mini binoculars. Immensely useful for spying on all sorts of things. Also a boon for homing in on distant out-of-eyesight signposts (especially ones at bottom of hills) to prevent having to cycle all the way up to it and then all the way back again when you discover you've gone the wrong way.

Bicycle Tools and Bicycle Bits

1 × spare tyre: Michelin Hi-Lite Express 26 × 1.50 (folds in three for easy storage)
1 × spare inner tube
3 × plastic tyre levers plus puncture repair kit, including talcum powder to prevent tube sticking to tyre
Spare spokes, brake, gear and straddle cables
1 × mini cross-head screwdriver
1 × mini flat-head screwdriver
Allen keys – to fit all allen bolts on bike
1 × Park cone spanner (for removing pedals)
1 × mini adjustable spanner
1 × 8/9 mm open spanner
1 × 10/11 mm open spanner
1 × 15 mm TA crank spanner
1 × TA crank remover
1 × chainlink tool (plus few spare links in case chain breaks)
1 × block remover
1 × spoke key
Few spare nuts and bolts, mini oil container, camera film cannister of good quality bike grease, piece of picture wire, spare pannier clip and Fastex clip, spare pieces of big and small webbing, curtain rings, rag, rubber gloves, gaffer tape, insulating tape, short length of 4 mm rock-climbing cord
2 × karabiners
6 × plastic cable ties – indispensable for the fix-it department
1 × mini Leatherman knife with pliers (pliers prove very useful for making things out of roadside rubbish)
1 × bicycle pump
1 × mini bicycle pump (as emergency back-up)

1 × cable lock and padlock

1 × Ortlieb waterproof map case (only fault with this was that the manufacturers placed the Ortlieb logo in the middle of the case, which inevitably
was just in the position I wanted to be on the map)

3 × bungie cords – essential for lassoing ten tons of superfluous kit and several
hundred kilos of Japanese grandmothers' home-grown giant radishes and
cabbages on to rear rack.

INDEX

For the latest news about Josie's travels and information on all her books, please visit her website at:

www.josiedew.co.uk